AF572456

Hannah Wilke

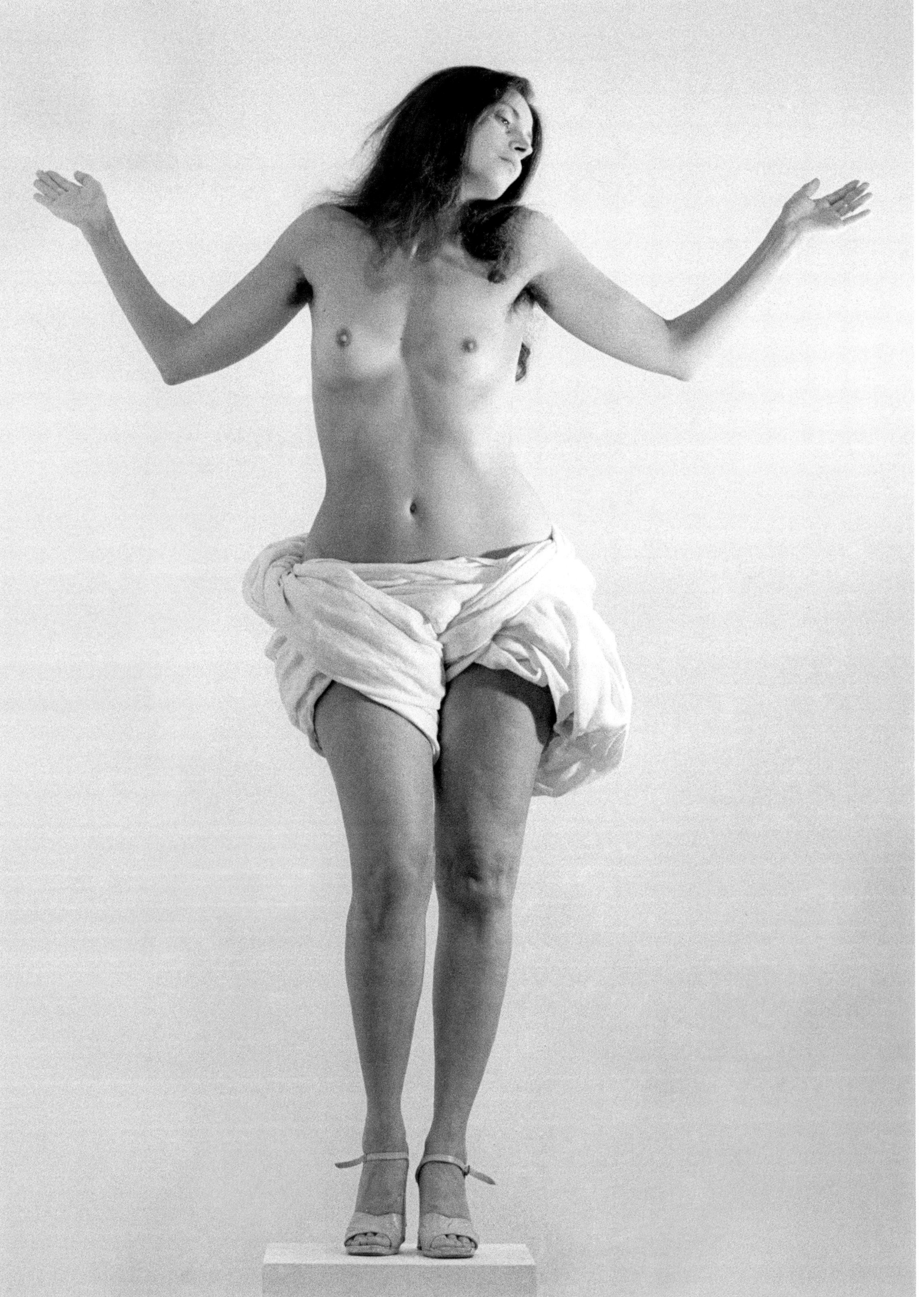

Hannah Wilke

NANCY PRINCENTHAL

PRESTEL MUNICH • BERLIN • LONDON • NEW YORK

front cover: Hannah Wilke, *S.O.S. Starification Object Series (Curlers)*, 1974 (detail). Black-and-white photograph, 40 x 27 in.

frontispiece: Hannah Wilke, *Hannah Wilke Super-t-Art*, 1974 (detail). Twenty black-and-white photographs, 6½ x 4½ in. each, 40¾ x 33in. framed

back cover: Hannah Wilke, *Intra-Venus Series #4, July 26 and February 19, 1992* (detail). Two chromogenic supergloss prints, 71½ x 47½ in. each

Prestel, a member of Verlagsgruppe Random House GmbH

PRESTEL VERLAG
Königinstrasse 9, 80539 Munich
Tel. +49 (0)89 24 29 08-300 · Fax +49 (0)89 24 29 08-335

PRESTEL PUBLISHING LTD.
4 Bloomsbury Place, London WC1A 2QA
Tel. +44 (0)20 7323-5004 · Fax +44(0)20 7636-8004

PRESTEL PUBLISHING
900 Broadway, Ste. 603, New York, NY 10003
Tel. +1 (212) 995-2720 · Fax +1 (212) 995-2733

www.prestel.com

Prestel books are available worldwide. Please contact your local bookseller or one of the above addresses for information concerning your local distributor.

Library of Congress Control Number: 2009943147

British Library Cataloguing-in-Publication Data: a catalogue record for this book is available from the British Library.

The Deutsche Bibliothek holds a record of this publication in the Deutsche Nationalbibliografie; detailed bibliographical data can be found under: http//dnd.ddb.de

Editorial direction by Christopher Lyon
Edited by Sarah Valdez
Editorial assistance by Ryan Newbanks

Design and layout by Katy Homans
Origination by Embassy Graphics, Winnipeg · Manitoba
Production by The Production Department
Printed and bound in China through Asia Pacific Offset

Verlagsgruppe Random House FSC-DEU-0100

ISBN 978-3-7913-3972-6

Contents

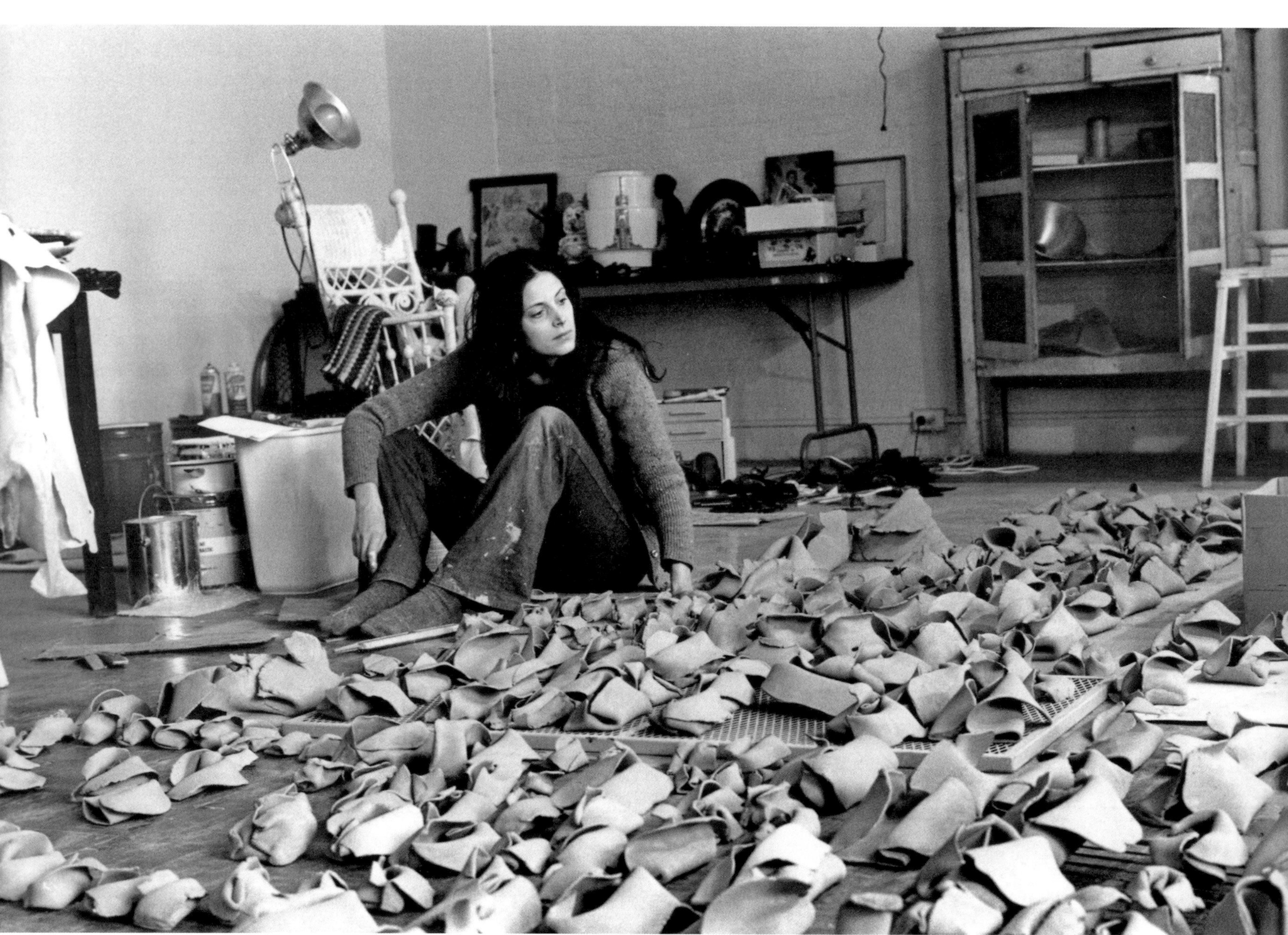

INTRODUCTION

Affirmative Actions

"My work is more optimistic than I am," Hannah Wilke said in a 1985 interview.[1] Coming from an artist who maintained the weakest of boundaries between her work and her life, it is a strikingly paradoxical statement. But it expresses a fundamental condition of every project she undertook, from abstractly sensual ceramic sculptures to the most explicit of photographs and videos. Perhaps more than her sexual candor, the quality that distinguished Wilke among her peers—and that forms the most illuminating comparison with artists of succeeding generations—was her spirit of affirmation. When she was extravagantly beautiful and when she was not; when her personal life and professional career were flourishing and when they were balked; and whether the cultural and political circumstances called for celebration or gloom, she used her art to broadcast her strengths and vulnerabilities, to insist on their importance, and to model the positions that must be struck for women to have a fair share of the world's manifest bounty.

That is not to say that Wilke's was an art of straight-ahead activism, on behalf of either sexual freedom or women's rights. She was not much of a team player (though she could be an inspiring leader). But she was an unremitting supporter of women's liberation. A term that has long since fallen out of favor, it captures both the spirit of the times in which Wilke's work emerged, and her particular character as an artist. She was dedicated to unburdening women, herself first and foremost, of the cultural constraints that had inhibited their pursuit of pleasure and of power. In the late 1960s and early '70s, that insistence—and that appetite—were enraging provocations to many, women as well as men, in and out of the more elevated precincts of the arts. And, to a surprising extent, they are demands that remain unwelcome. It would be a gross generalization, but not wrong, to say that the postwar

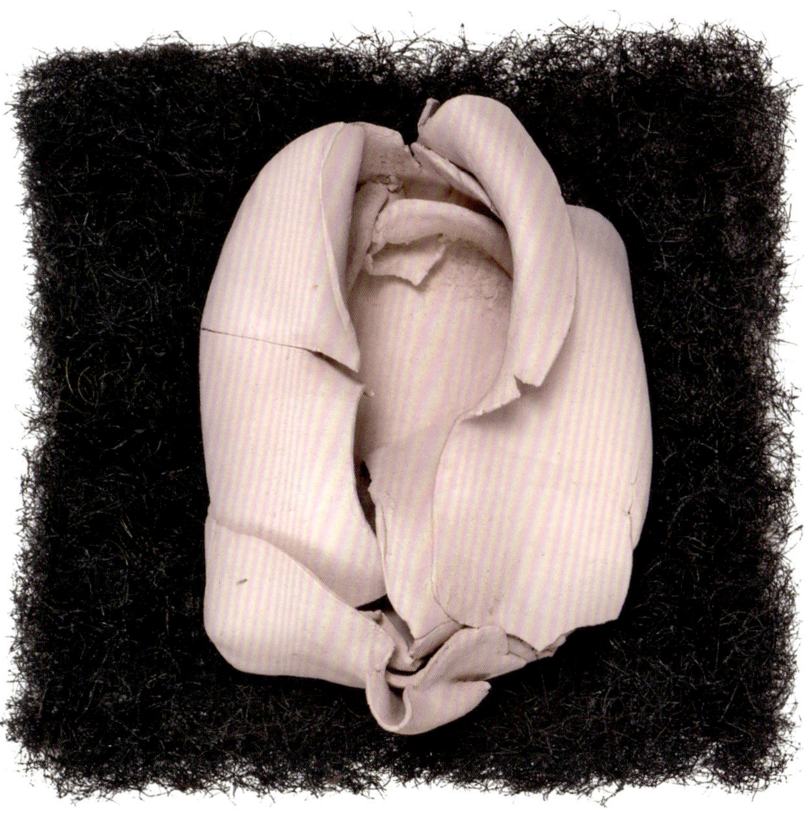

opposite:
Hannah Wilke in her Broome Street studio, New York, 1973

Teasel Cushion, 1967. Terra cotta, Liquitex, and Astroturf, 9¾ x 7 in.

avant-garde impulse can be recognized in its successive incarnations by repudiation of fixed, aspirational goals in favor of strategies of disruption and expressions of discontent. The inclination has only grown stronger; skepticism (or its darker siblings: abjection, false innocence) remains the hallmark of progressive twenty-first-century art. There was no inclination that Wilke resisted more vigorously, in her life as in her work.

If challenging the distinction between the personal and the public was a defining aspect of Wilke's pursuits, it is a choice that can be described in conceptual, strategic, and psychological terms. Not only did she make her private life available as subject matter to an exceptional degree, she also considered character to be less destiny than project: an entity that could be shaped, like clay, or video footage. Among her favorite novels were Goethe's *Elective Affinities* and Thackeray's *Vanity Fair*, both studies of the relations among love, money, and power. The first is a Romantic tragedy, the second a comedy of manners, though those labels obscure their many shared features, including extramarital unions and, for the noblest characters, thwarted love. And both feature orphaned young women who, of necessity, kicked over the traces. In Goethe's *Elective Affinities*, which preceded Thackeray's novel by roughly a generation, Ottilie, the book's heroine, turns away from her married lover in saintly renunciation. *Vanity Fair*'s Becky Sharp applies the gifts with which she is generously endowed toward a heartily enjoyable exercise in vertiginous social climbing. Neither woman comes to a happy end. But both have a good run while their luck lasts, in full possession of pleasures that defied conventional morality. And both novels, as it happens, feature the staging of tableaux vivants as crucial plot points—live enactments of famous paintings that were popular society entertainments through the nineteenth century and into the Gilded Age (they also feature in Edith Wharton's *House of Mirth*). In *Elective Affinities* and *Vanity Fair*, female characters who are less pure and good, though perhaps not less compelling, than their respective novel's nominal heroines take a star turn in such tableaux, posing, in costume, as various famous female subjects. It is impossible to refrain from finding parallels in Wilke's personal and professional trajectories, both of which revolved around ongoing processes of self-creation.

That's not to say she was at all dishonest or circumspect about who she was, or where she came from. On the contrary, her background became an increasingly integral element of her work. Wilke was born Arlene Hannah Butter on March 7, 1940, in New York, where her family lived on the Lower East Side. Her mother's parents were Hungarian, and, though Jewish, not as Orthodox as her father's parents, who were Russian-Polish. Yiddish as well as English was spoken in Wilke's extended family. Being Jewish was, Wilke believed, fundamental to her outlook, even if it was seldom an explicit theme in her work. "My consciousness came from being a Jew in World War II. I was born in 1940, and I was a Jew. I realized what it would be to be annihilated just for a word,"[2] Wilke said in a 1989 interview. Her sister, Marsie

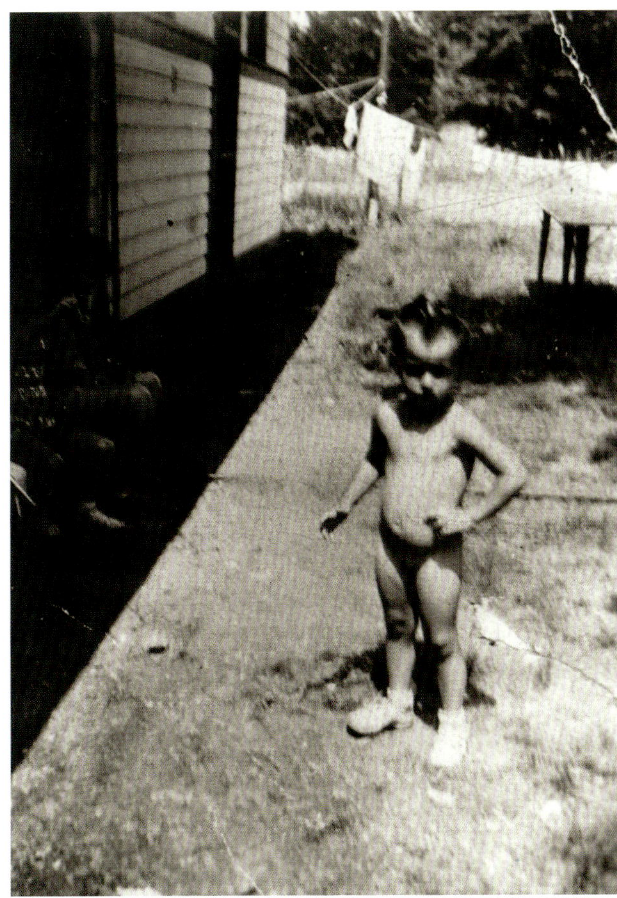

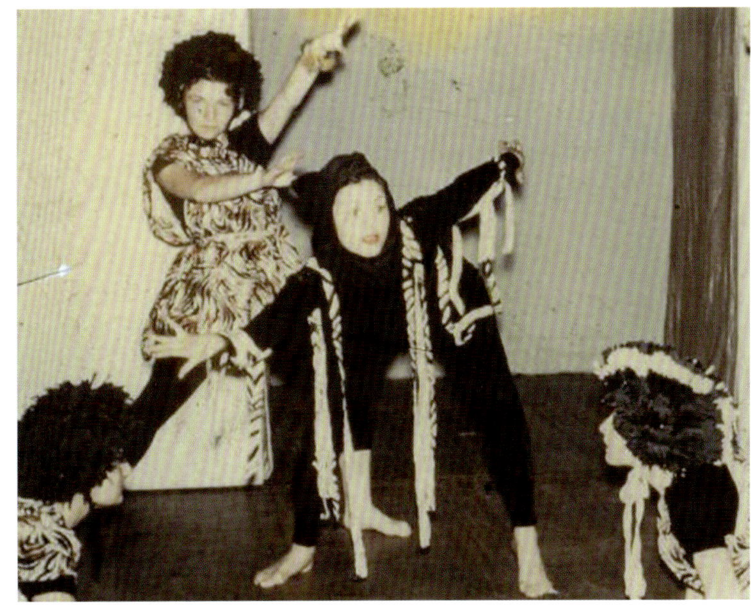

First Performalist Self-Portrait, 1942–79 (detail). Image used for two of three black-and-white photographs in triptych, 19¼ x 35 in. overall

Hannah Wilke (Arlene Butter) in high school dance performance, Great Neck, N.Y., ca. 1955

Scharlatt, notes that there were relatives on their mother's side who died during the Holocaust, though they did not know them personally. In New York, the family's commitment to Judaism followed a typical New World pattern: the girls went to Hebrew school at a Reform temple; the family celebrated the major holidays but attended religious services only sporadically, at a Conservative synagogue; they did not maintain a Kosher kitchen. In a word, they assimilated.[3]

Wilke's father, Emanuel Butter, was an attorney. Scharlatt remembers him as a shutterbug (he was an early fan of Polaroid cameras), and the earliest photograph of Hannah that found its way into her art shows her as a two-year-old toddler, wearing nothing but white shoes and anklet socks, one hand to a pudgy hip; it was taken at a bungalow colony in a rural upstate New York area still known as the Borscht Belt, where the family spent time during the summer. Also following a postwar norm, the Butters soon moved away from the old immigrant urban neighborhood in Manhattan, initially to Queens. In her sixth-grade autograph book, Wilke announced her intention to be an artist. In 1952, the family moved again, to Great Neck, a suburb where Wilke attended high school, graduating in 1957.

Wilke was also seriously interested in dance, and, like most teenagers but perhaps to a different degree, in her own image. "By the time I was 14 or so," she later recalled, "I had started posing nude, before *Playboy* existed." (She was roughly right; it was founded in 1953.) "I had my sister help me take the photographs, and I posed in my mother's mink stole with little high heels on."[4] The photograph to which she refers, an image taken in 1954, shows Wilke in nothing but the fur wrap and

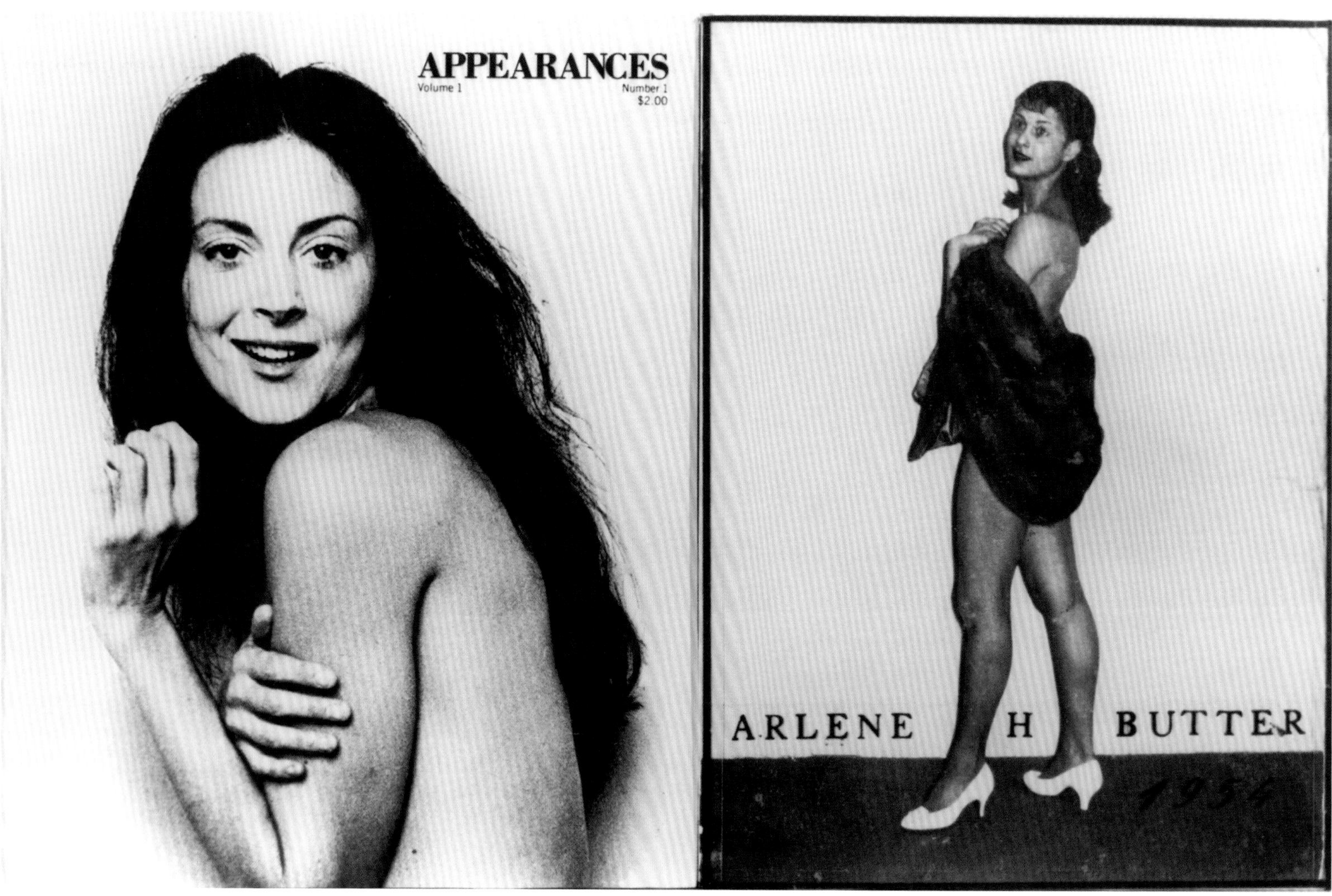

Cover of Appearances and Arlene Hannah Butter, 1954–77. Diptych of two black-and-white photographs on board, overall dimensions, 24 x 36¾ in.

white pumps, staring upward with an expression that is a little grand and a little silly. In 1977, she paired it with a photograph of her beaming, dazzling, unquestionably adult self that appeared on the cover of the first issue of *Appearances* magazine. Even the early photo alone, though, demonstrates her keen sense of self-presentation, and her uninhibited ambition to be a star. Auspicious, too, is her uncannily astute choice of friends. "My first boyfriend was always saying to me, Hannah, movies are the new art—not 'art.' And his name was Francis Coppola. That was when we were 15, in high school, but of course he was right."[5] (And of course he wouldn't have called her Hannah; she went by Arlene until her mid-twenties; they remained friends in adulthood.) Yet for all her precocious self-possession, Wilke sustained, throughout her life, an enormously appealing innocence. Next to her radiant photo in her high school's yearbook for 1956, the year she was a junior, one female classmate wrote, "to the only genuine naïve siren I know."

If it seems, in retrospect, that Wilke was well launched as a performer by the time she graduated from high school, it is also true that she had already demonstrated both talent in and commitment to the visual arts, devoting considerable time to drawing. On the advice of an art teacher, she enrolled at the Stella Elkins Tyler School of Art in Philadelphia (now Tyler College of Art), from which she earned a B.F.A. and a B.S. in education in 1962. (She later took art history classes at New

York University, including one taught by Irving Sandler, who clearly recalls her ambition and audacity.[6]) One period of student drawing in particular stayed with her in memory, though the work did not survive. "I drew myself when I was sick with mononucleosis, and I didn't have a subject, so I became my own subject," she recalled.[7] Joanna Frueh, who has written extensively about Wilke, reports that during this illness, "she painted both the shadows of her body movements on Masonite and a realistic series, in pink and blue, of herself nude."[8] In another interview, Wilke remembers the work as being quite sexually explicit: "I started doing nude drawings of myself . . . when I got mononucleosis when I was 17 years old, and my husband-to-be, after I had made a pink and blue self-portrait and handed it in, . . . he made me throw it out, he was so embarrassed by it . . . it was very 'dirty stuff.'"[9] But if her future husband—Barry Wilke, an industrial designer whom she met in college—took offense, it seems that Wilke was somehow able, then as later, to take liberties without apology or regret.

In 1961, seven months after her 1960 marriage, Wilke's father died. From 1962 through '65, she taught art at Plymouth-Whitemarsh High School in Plymouth Meeting, Pennsylvania. After moving with her husband to Riverdale, New York, a middle-class neighborhood in the Bronx, Wilke taught at White Plains High School for five years starting in 1965, the year she divorced. (Wilke remained an active and dedicated teacher throughout her life; from 1972 until 1991, she taught at the School of Visual Arts, in New York.) By the mid-'60s, while still teaching teenagers at her day job, she had already begun making the abstractions with vaginal imagery, in drawings and in sculptures of various mediums, that she would continue to create throughout her career. Scharlatt wonders if Wilke would have taken the step from sexualized abstraction to nude performances and photographs of herself had their father lived, though Wilke had already set out on a path of sexual disinhibition before his death. For her part, Wilke told an interviewer in 1978 that while women always have "a closeness with a mother, you're working for your love for your father, 'cause you're never really sure of it; you're always sure of women's love."[10]

In any case, it is her mother whose presence is felt most strongly in Wilke's work. Frueh notes that "Wilke began performing and having herself photographed nude in 1970, after her mother's mastectomy," when she "wore her mother's wounds,"[11] though there was a four- or five-year lag before the photographs Wilke made of herself nude first appeared. When Mrs. Butter's cancer returned, in 1978, Wilke embarked on a series of photographs documenting the toll it took, forswearing (with mixed results) her own career for the four years until her mother died. Unquestionably, Wilke put her relationships with everyone who mattered to her—her family, her romantic partners, their children, her beloved pet birds—at the center of her work, just beside her own image, never less than commanding.

Many who were close to Wilke, including Donald Goddard, her longtime companion (they lived together from 1982, marrying shortly before her death) and Ronald Feldman, whose gallery has represented her since 1972, have noted her lifelong quality of childishness, which competed until the end with a quite evident sophistication.

Just as important was a deep-seated impatience, remarked by her sister, with sadness in herself and others, and an inclination when frustrated toward anger rather than despair. In an undated notebook entry, the adult Wilke wrote, "alienation is an alibi." It was an alibi she resoundingly declined.

Along with other women artists of her generation, Wilke's work has lately attracted renewed interest and acclaim. But her particular spirit of self-affirmation has not been emphasized in this reevaluation. Instead, the most recent criticism written in support of Wilke's work has praised it for portraying sexuality as a condition marked by alienation and fragmentation. She has been extolled as a pioneer in revealing feminine identity to be a cultural construction; her picture of the female body has been hailed for revealing its irresolvable complexity and manifold inner contradictions. Amelia Jones, for instance, writes, "Hannah Wilke explores her body/self as always already not her own and enacts femininity as, by its very definition in patriarchy, inexorably performed . . . doubly alienated, removed from the lure of potential transcendence."[12] Wilke's work, according to Jones, exemplifies a "post-1960" tendency toward the "postmodern articulation of subjectivity as fundamentally decentered and contingent."[13] Of a project in which Wilke used the voices of friends and family—and, ultimately, her own naked body—Jones writes, it "involves an enactment of herself as always already implicated in these voices, open to them, *constituted through them*."[14] In short, "We can only 'fix' Wilke as an open-ended and unfixable performance of femininity."[15]

The framework within which Jones's essay is situated includes the writing of such theorists as Judith Butler, who herself builds on the work of Simone de Beauvoir, Luce Irigaray, Jacqueline Rose, and others to argue that "If sexuality is culturally constructed within existing power relations, then the postulation of a normative sexuality that is 'before,' 'outside,' or 'beyond' power is a cultural impossibility and a politically impracticable dream, one that postpones the concrete and contemporary task of rethinking subversive possibilities for sexuality and identity within the terms of power itself."[16] At the basis of Butler's writing is an attack on the conventional binary understanding of gender. "As Rose points out," Butler writes, "the construction of a coherent sexual identity along the disjunctive axis of the feminine/masculine is bound to fail."[17] In Butler's view, "Gender is a complexity whose totality is permanently deferred, never fully what it is at any given juncture in time."[18]

The force of this argument is considerable, and Jones's application of it to Wilke's work is careful and sympathetic. But it misrepresents Wilke's intentions. While Jones cites writers at the time, such as Arlene Raven, who wanted to reclaim the female body "from its patriarchal construction as a passive object,"[19] what Raven wrote, approvingly, of Wilke is that she "insists on Eve and beginning at the beginning,"[20] which certainly seems to cast her as an essentialist if not a biological determinist. Peggy Phelan believes that given the misogynist culture of academia in the early 1980s, "it behooves us to consider carefully the vehemence of the denunciation" of essentialist, body-centered work, "if only as a symptomatic repression of something threatening." And while she finds Jones's writing on Wilke "especially inspired," Phelan cautions that Jones "sometimes misses the drama between the complexity of verbal language and a still-not-interpreted language of the body. I am not suggesting that there is some deep occult somatic language that we can somehow translate and employ. Rather, I am trying to frame the space that slips away."[21]

But even Phelan recommends an oblique perspective, and draws a veil of language over sexual parts and acts whose exposure was understood to be considerably less complicated when Wilke developed her work than it became subsequently. To put it simply, that exposure was inseparably tied to agency, to individual self-expression and personal freedom. True, the late '60s and early '70s were years of cultural and social complexity that defy all generalization, especially concerning sexual freedom. But for all the women in Wilke's cohort, an immense act of courage was required to present their nude bodies and to broadcast their desires, whether physical, emotional, or professional. As Laura Cottingham puts it, "Art, like 'the personal,' was accepted by seventies feminist practitioners to be political; that is, to exist within historical space that had been produced and was therefore potentially transformable through human action."[22] The force of will required to take such action is obscured by the shift to a postructuralist critical position—a shift undertaken, ironically, largely under the aegis of feminism. Wilke wasn't committed to exploring desire as an elusive cultural construction. It was her successors who put their clothes back on and entered into the series of masquerades with which we're still engaged. Though Jones says there is no important difference between Wilke and Cindy Sherman, in many ways they are fundamentally opposed. Sherman has always disappeared into the characters she enacts for her photographs; Wilke invited us to enter her life in its every particular—and, equally, to find our own lives reflected there.

In the mid-1960s, "difference" had not yet been introduced as a rubric for positive self-identification. To explore the experiences that accrue to all women because of the specific nature of female bodies was the likeliest way to establish a sense of shared purpose. The language of the time as expressed in the titles of some of its key publications—*From the Center* (curator and critic Lucy Lippard's essays from the early '70s); *Through the Flower: My Struggle as a Woman Artist* (the autobiography of Judy Chicago, who more than any other artist is associated with the essentialist impulse); *Our Bodies, Ourselves* (the pioneering women's health guide, first published 1973)— states the impulse clearly. To be centered, to be open, to know oneself inside out, to put a mirror between one's legs, to find the universal in the individual, were motivating goals. The shift in critical fashion represented by Jones's analysis of Wilke, and reflected in the art of the present as well as its criticism, reflects anxiety about the integrity of our bodies and the scope of self-determination in a corporatized, globalized and, especially, technologized world. But to attribute these concerns to Wilke is ahistorical. By the standards of candor and self-determination for which Wilke was such an ardent spokeswoman, we look weak and self-indulgent, unwilling to stand out and speak up. We accept being labeled "spoken subjects," "always already" (to use a favorite Derridean phrase meant to indicate how we are caught up in language) constrained, distracted, dispersed. However accurately these terms represent the emotional texture and philosophical assumptions of our own moment, they don't ring true for the period in which her work emerged.

Wilke's career wasn't wholly and permanently determined by the sexual politics of the '60s and early '70s—she worked until she died, in 1993, and her art evolved in keeping with its context. Nor was she ever really bound by "second-wave" feminism's dominant preferences. Moving freely among generations in her choices of mentors and associates, she admired, and was admired by, Duchamp and de Kooning as well as artists of her own generation, both men and women, and including Pop artists, Minimalists, and Conceptualists; her romantic involvement with Claes Oldenburg, from 1969 through 1977, was crucial artistically as well as personally. As tied to her family of birth as to her professional community, she was, like all interesting artists, essentially anomalous. Yet much about her work and her outlook was shaped by the cultural politics of the era in which the possibilities for women in the arts changed radically.

As it evolved within the art world, feminism grew out of not only the civil rights activism of the time, but also patterns of exclusion specific to cultural institutions. This was partly a matter of museums and galleries failing to exhibit the work of women. But feminist art also responded to the macho posturing of the hard-drinking, hard-living Abstract Expressionist generation, which was followed by the equally masculine ethos of Minimalism and Post-Minimalism, with their emphasis on industrial processes and materials. That the simple, overt repression of women in the 1950s was not significantly lifted in the '60s but instead gave way to different patterns of misogyny, in which strenuously innocent female flower children and earth mothers too often undertook compliance as a better alternative to being deemed uptight, was an equally important condition for the formation of activist gender politics. Though popular fashion at the time introduced gender-bending styles, from Rudi Gernreich's unisex clothing to waist-length hair for men who wore granny glasses, beads, and bells, these sartorial provocations, like other aspects of the period's cultural "revolution," had debatable impact on real male/female relations. The first issue of *Ms. Magazine* appeared in 1972, as did the first edition of *The Joy of Sex*. These two new manuals detailing the possibilities and protocols of behavior in an era of widely touted sexual freedom confirmed the robust divisions still in place between the sexes: the first celebrated women's achievements and opportunities; the second, while it had the merit of popularizing the idea that sex could be talked about and should be enjoyed, was decidedly less focused on female than male experience. When *New York Magazine* ran a cover story in February 1975 on "The New Sexual Frankness," its author wondered how, "with female sexuality so much in the open," a single provocative act—an "ad" that had recently run in *Artforum* by Lynda Benglis in which she appeared nude; Wilke had also used her body in a magazine advertisement—could "churn up such a storm." Art historian Linda Nochlin, whose 1971 essay "Why Have There Been No Great Women Artists?" was a resounding shot across the bow, answered, "Women are still caught up in their old role of bearers of virtue."[23]

Ms. was a mainstream sequel to such pioneering undertakings as the 1966 founding of NOW (National Organization for Women), established by Betty Freidan in response to the federal government's reluctance to enforce Title VII of the Civil Rights Act, which prohibited gender-based discrimination. More specific to the art world, there was, in New York, a burst of activity protesting the underrepresentation of women in museums. It was also a response to discrimination within the activist groups themselves. For instance, in 1966, two women who encouraged the leading dissident group SDS (Students for a Democratic Society) to insert women's rights into the organization's resolution for change were attacked with tomatoes and thrown out of the convention.[24] In 1969, W.A.R. (Women Artists in Revolution) was formed to demand change from New York's Museum of Modern Art (it was a splinter group of the Art Workers' Coalition, more broadly aimed at inequities and political laxity in museum policy, including the reluctance of major museums to take stands against U.S. involvement in Southeast Asia); the Ad Hoc Committee of Women Artists was founded in 1970 by Lucy Lippard, Poppy Johnson, Brenda Miller, and Faith Ringgold to protest the paltry representation of women in that year's Whitney Museum of American Art Biennial (it was 5 percent). The conditions at the time for women in the art world, as outlined in a numbered list by Lucy Lippard in 1971, included "4. treating women artists as sex objects and using this as an excuse not to visit their studios or not to show their work. ('Sure, her work looked terrific, but she's such a good looking chick if I went to her studio I wouldn't know if I liked the work or her,' one male dealer told me earnestly. 'So I never went'); 5. using fear of social or professional rejection to turn successful women against unsuccessful women or vice versa; 6. ripping off women if they participate in the unfortunately influential social life of the art world (if she comes to the bar with a man she's a sexual appendage and is ignored as such; if she comes with a woman, she's gay; if she comes alone, she's on the make); 7. identifying women artists with their men ('that's so-and-so's wife; I think she paints too')."[25] Concluded Elizabeth Baker, in a passage also written in 1971 and quoted by Wilke in an installation seven years later, "It is obvious that good art has no sex. Women artists themselves are the first to assert this. Even so, dealers are rarely impartial about the sex of their artists. Many major galleries tend consciously to hold down the number of women artists they represent." In a footnote to this statement, Baker substantiates the claim: "A winter 1970–71 spot-check by telephone of ten galleries turned up 190 men and 18 women." The galleries she called included Castelli, Paula Cooper, Marlborough, and Dwan.[26] Baker also noted that while "the burdens inherent to surviving in a lonely, demanding, and capricious profession"—making art—"fall with particularly destructive weight on women," the situation can be especially "painful . . . when two artists marry, and the world assumes that the husband is the only serious one of the pair. Career conflicts are not infrequent."[27]

Both Lippard and Baker were writing from New York, and describing conditions that would have been all too familiar to Wilke; indeed the points quoted above apply to her with particular force. But Los Angeles is where feminist art took most cohesive form. The Los Angeles Council of Women Artists (LACWA) was formed in 1970, with an emphasis on education and on independent institutions for women. In the fall of that year, Judy Chicago founded the Feminist Artist Program at Fresno State College (now California State University, Fresno). The next year (1971), the program moved to the brand new California Institute of the Arts, where, under the direction of Chicago and Miriam Schapiro, the students, all female, created "Womanhouse" in the fall of 1972, taking over a deserted Hollywood mansion. They cleaned and repaired it, and each created an installation in one of its rooms. Thematic concerns focused on bodies, their functions, and the domestic duties traditionally fulfilled by women: breasts, menstruation, childbirth; cooking and cleaning. Womanspace, a community art gallery with 700 members, followed a year later, as did, in short order, a host of other feminist organizations. That the Feminist Art Program took root at CalArts at just the same time that John Baldessari launched a "post-studio" course of instruction there whose graduates have been credited with forming the core of the Pictures Generation—early students included David Salle, Jack Goldstein, Matt Mullican, and James Welling—suggests how sexually polarized the era was; to judge by its record, Baldessari's now-legendary program produced almost no women artists (one exception is Barbara Bloom).

Wilke had been living in New York since the early '60s, but in 1970 she spent five months with Oldenburg in Los Angeles, where he was working on prints at Gemini G.E.L., and where Wilke's sister had moved after her divorce. Wilke's first solo show in L.A. was at Margo Leavin in 1972 (her first exhibition at the Ronald Feldman gallery in New York appeared the same year), and she continued to return often to California throughout her life. Her relationship with the burgeoning feminist scene was, however, uneasy. Donald Goddard told Wilke scholar Saundra Goldman, "Wilke claimed that [Judy] Chicago had visited her studio in 1969 while she was living in Los Angeles, and that Chicago saw her early vaginal work and encouraged her to give it up."[28] According to Scharlatt, Wilke believed that Chicago had dismissed her work and then appropriated it as "core imagery," for which Chicago was credited. If Wilke was not associated with the CalArts group and its leaders—or with any other feminist collective—she did not refuse political action; for instance, she joined Anita Steckel's Fight Censorship group at its founding in 1973, along with Judith Bernstein, Louise Bourgeois, Martha Edelheit, Joan Semmel, and others.

Of course, many women were wary of collaborative programs (including, as a documentary[29] made for public television shows, most of the participants in Womanhouse; with touching reluctance, nearly all admitted to the difficulty they experienced in assuming the yoke of communal responsibilities and linked identities). Many, too, were leery of the deeper notions of collectivity that motivated some feminist artwork of this time. Easiest to label, and dismiss, as essentialist is work that promoted

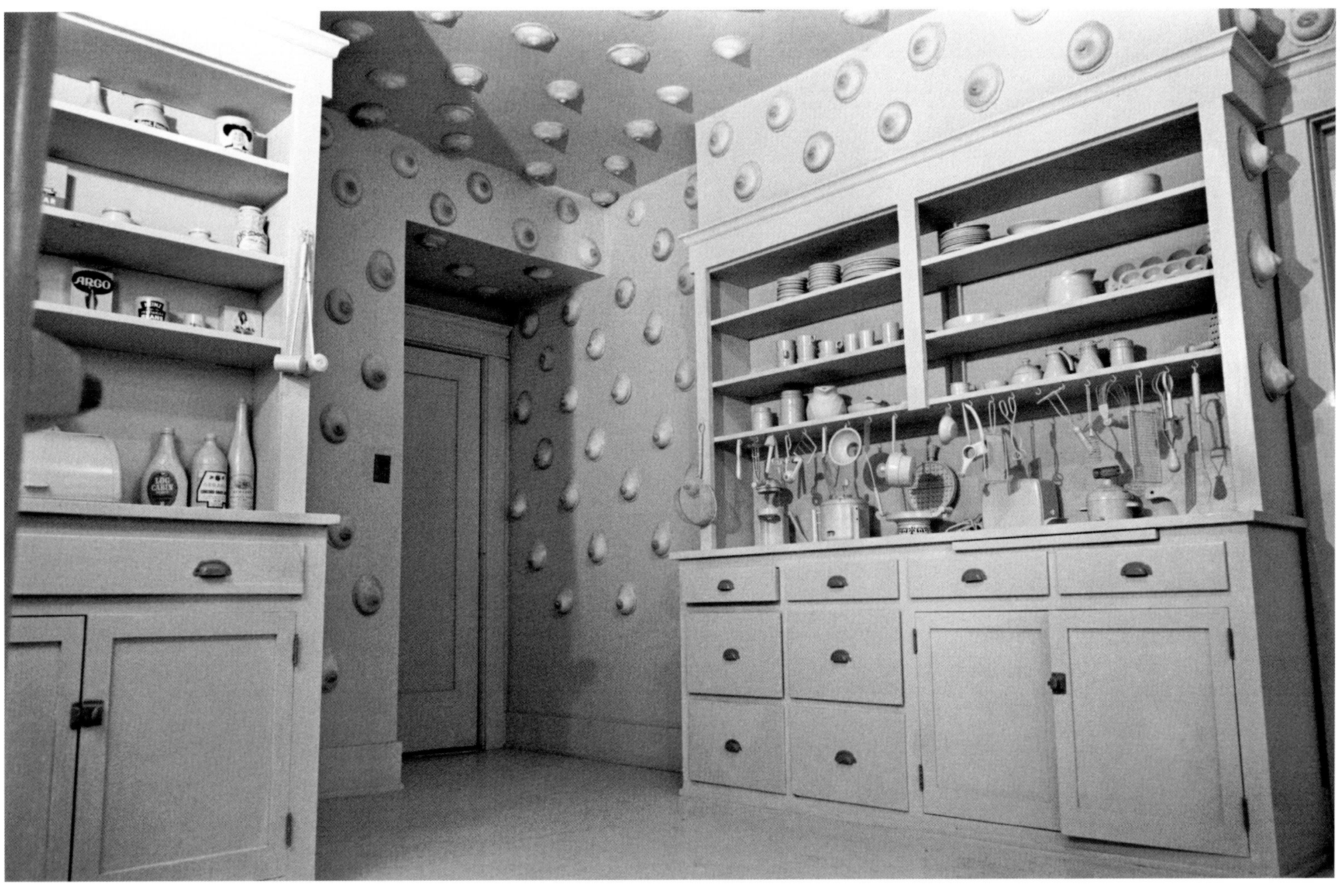

Susan Frazier, Vicki Hodgetts, and Robin Weltsh, **Nurturant Kitchen** from **Womanhouse**, 1972. Mixed medium installation.

mythic notions of women's power and identity, and embraced a deterministic view of gender that helped fuel the poststructuralist reaction. For instance, Marybeth Edelson rhapsodized, in 1974, "The ascending archetypal symbols of the feminine unfold today in the psyche of modern Everywoman. They encompass the multiple forms of the Great Goddess. Reaching across the centuries we take the hands of our Ancient Sisters. The Great Goddess, alive and well, is rising to announce to the patriarchs that their 5,000 years are up—Hallelujah! Here we come!"[30] It is worth noting, in relation to such celebrations of a mythic, collective female consciousness, that interest in the collective unconscious, especially as formulated by Carl Jung, had been widespread among the Abstract Expressionist generation and some of their heirs, and retained more cultural currency, in 1974, than the various Lacanian formulations that so vigorously resisted its heroicizing tendencies. Embracing a collective consciousness was a considerable part of the antiestablishment inclination of the time; universalism was after all a premise of the worldwide socialist revolution to come, as well of the ostensibly benevolent, preindustrial societies whose patterns of equality women hoped to reinstate. Supported also by other local anthropologists and historians, Judy Chicago too believed in a pre-patriarchal, utopian culture, and hoped to model it in both the form and (with less success) the production of her best-known work, the monumental project of ceramic plates and embroidered table linen titled *The Dinner Party* (completed 1979; p. 18).

At the same time, many women artists of the '60s generation favored a more nuanced model of feminist art. As early as 1973, Arlene Raven, who didn't conclusively exonerate Wilke from charges of essentialism, wrote, "Female forms are not stationary . . . biological determinism [is] an idea to which feminism is opposed." Raven's remark is quoted by Amelia Jones[31] in an essay about Chicago's defining work, in which Jones goes on to say that "ultimately it is . . . the impossibility of ensuring an empowering rather than objectifying reading of centralized imagery that explains the mixed reception of *The Dinner Party.*"[32] This tension, between enlarging the sphere of expressive possibilities—and of professional opportunities—for women by promoting recognition of gender-specific experience, and avoiding the reduction of women artists to a circumscribed and generalized set of characteristics, was at the heart of feminist cultural debates at the time, and continues to color the critical reception of the artwork produced in those years. Working toward empowerment and in the face of inevitable objectification, Wilke negotiated this balance throughout her career, speaking for, and about, her own experience as a woman.

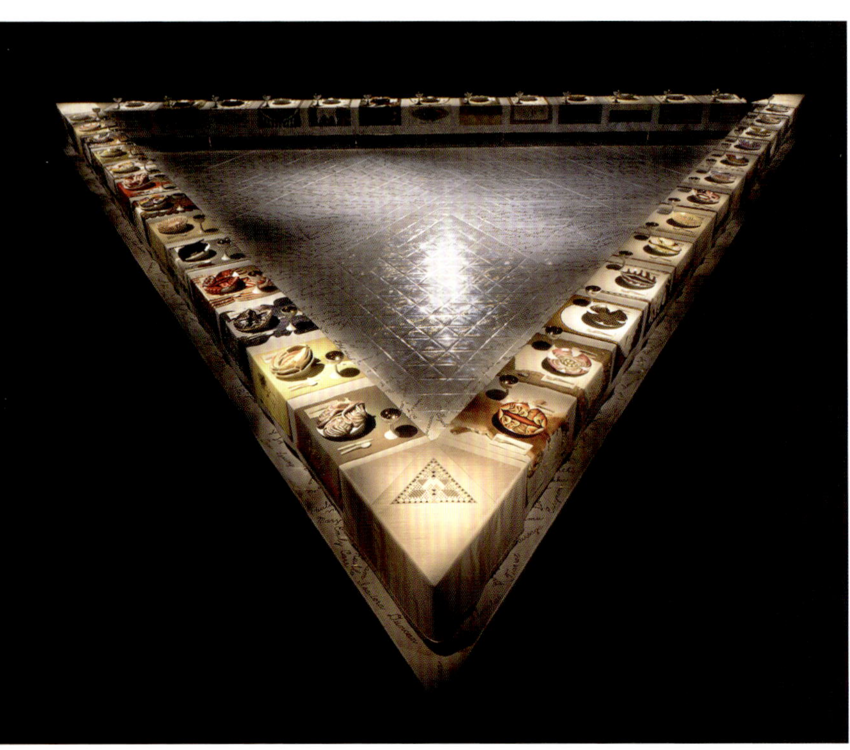

Judy Chicago, **The Dinner Party**, 1974–79. Mixed mediums, 48 x 42 x 3 ft.

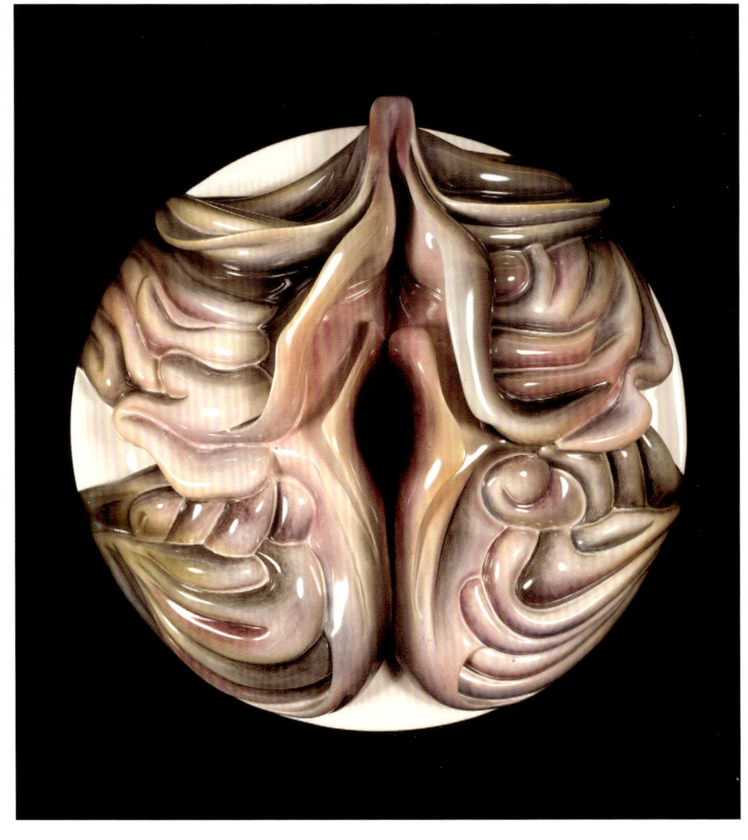

Detail of the Georgia O'Keeffe plate from **The Dinner Party**

CHAPTER ONE

In Part

On the occasion of a 1966 exhibition that included her sexually suggestive ceramic boxes, Wilke said to Lillian Roxen, "When you're beautiful, and I'm resigned to the fact that I am, no one ever looks *inside* you."[1] As was so often the case, she was inviting a double reading. The first and more obvious was a plea to see her inner life in all its emotional and intellectual richness. The second, more immediately relevant, and humorously provocative in a way Wilke relished, was to look inside her body, starting between her legs. By 1966, she had already been making explicitly sexual ceramic sculptures for at least half a dozen years, most suggesting vulvas and many also including phalluses. In one scale, format, and medium or another, she continued to produce vaginal, labial, or uterine sculptures for the rest of her career.

It is these sculptural works, more than the photographic and performance-based work which followed, that submit Wilke to the debate about essentialism. Judith Barry and Sandy Flitterman-Lewis, for instance, looked back a short distance to write, in a 1980 article establishing a typology of feminist art, "One type of women's art can be seen as the glorification of an essential female power. . . . This is an essentialist position because it is based on the belief in a female essence residing somewhere in the body of women. It can be found in the emphasis on 'vagina' forms in painting and sculpture; it is sometimes associated with mysticism, ritual and the idea of a female mythology." Of two "essentialist artists" they chose to name, one was Wilke. Their judgment of the impulse was summary. "Feminist essentialism in art simply reverses the terms of dominance and subordination. Instead of the male supremacy of patriarchal culture, the female (the essential feminine) is elevated to primary status."[2]

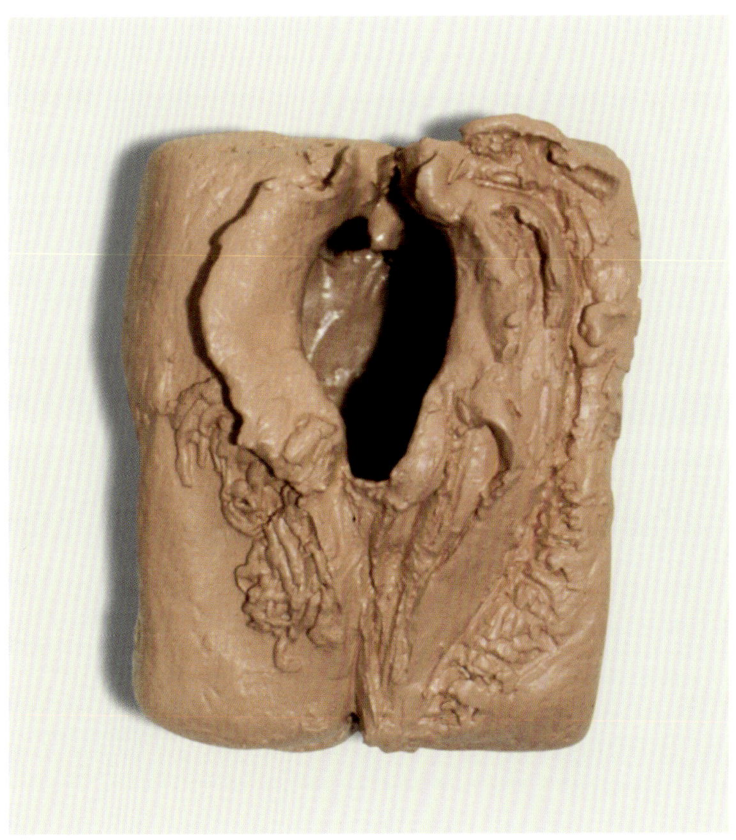

It Was a Lovely Day, 1964. Terra cotta with Liquitex, 3¼ x 3¼ x 4½ in.

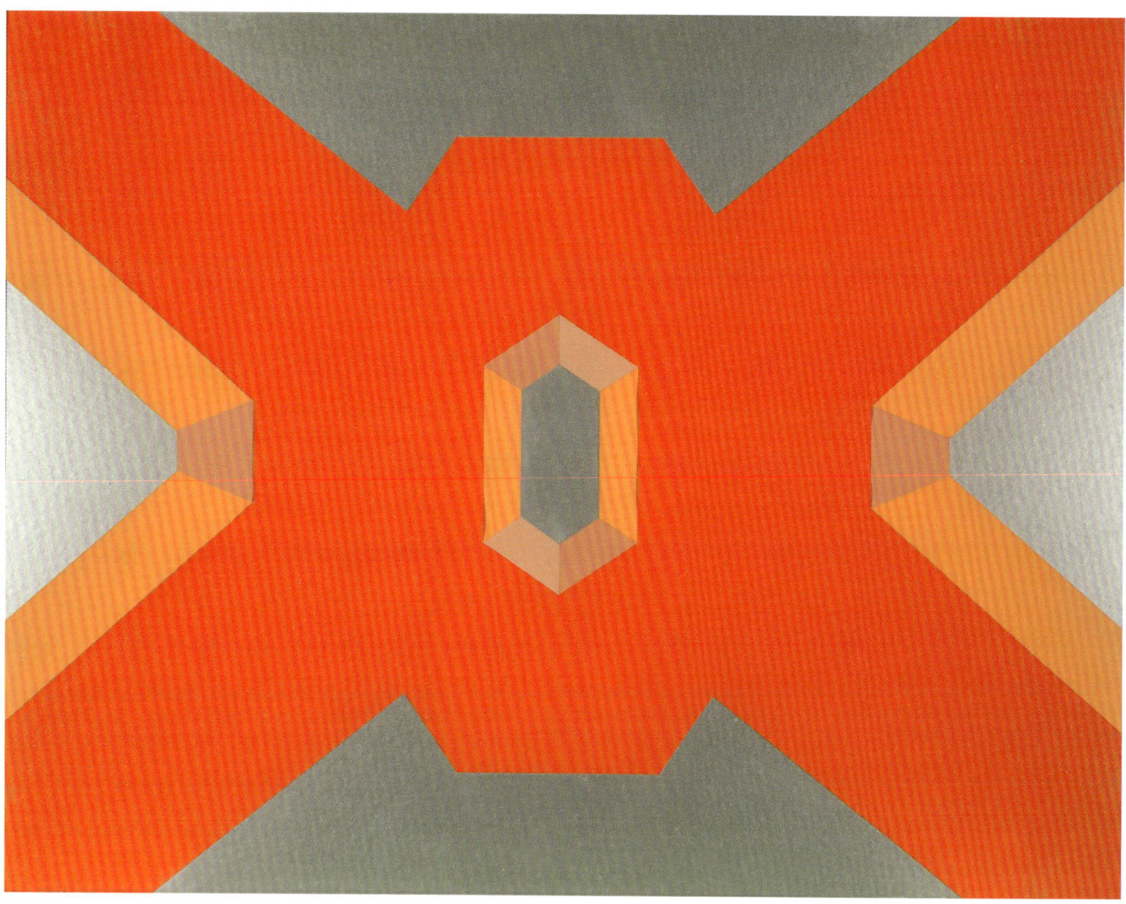

Miriam Schapiro, Ox, 1969. Acrylic and paper collage on board, 17½ x 22 in.

In 1973, Judy Chicago and Miriam Schapiro had asked, in an essay called "Female Imagery," "What does it feel like to be a woman? To be formed around a central core and have a secret place which can be entered and which is also a passageway from which life emerges? What kind of imagery does this state of feeling engender? There is now evidence that many women artists have defined a central orifice whose formal organization is often a metaphor for a woman's body."[3] That they answered their own questions with the assertion of "evidence" suggests how much they wanted to be seen as identifying a principle that was transhistorical and international, rather than as simply prescribing a formula for their contemporaries. Their primary example was Georgia O'Keeffe, a dubious flag-bearer. (In the essay "O'Keeffe's Femininity," Anne Wagner writes, "Her consistent public claim that she painted 'what she felt' was in her view not exactly the same as the public's claim that she 'painted as a woman.'")[4] But they also referred to their own work, citing Schapiro's precise, geometric painting *Ox* (1969) as "an insignia for the assertion of self that all female artists search for, a female counterpart to Vetruvial Man."[5]

Even for women determined to hold the higher ground of gender-blindness, the existence of traits reliably associated with women's self-understanding and self-expression proved hard to deny. Thus Lucy Lippard wrote in 1973, about her landmark 1966 show "Eccentric Abstraction": "When I first heard Judy Chicago's and Miriam Schapiro's theories about the high incidence of central-core imagery, of boxes, ovals, spheres, and 'empty' centers in women's art, I vehemently resisted them. I was still resisting them when we visited the women's show I organized for the Aldrich Museum, and they ran from work to work shouting 'there it is!' There it was. I was astounded." While allowing for the reader's, and viewer's, similar resistance, Lippard felt compelled to make note of what she'd seen, writing, "Here, in any case, for your own consideration, are some of these elements that recur: a uniform density, or overall texture, often sensuously tactile and repetitive or detailed to the point of obsession; the preponderance of circular forms, central focus, inner space (sometimes contradicting the first aspect); a ubiquitous linear 'bag' or parabolic form that turns in on itself; layers, or strata, or veils; an indefinable looseness of flexibility of handling; windows; autobiographical content; animals; flowers; a certain kind of fragmentation; a new fondness for the pinks and pastels and ephemeral cloud colors that used to be tabu unless a woman wanted to be accused of making 'feminine' art."[6] As it happens, Wilke's work would include almost all these features in turn.

But it was the women artists in Los Angeles connected to Judy Chicago's Feminist Art Program who insisted most vigorously on the importance of forging a language of body-centered womanhood. For instance Faith Wilding, a student in the program, announced in 1971, "[We are] not indiscriminately interested in just any art made by women, for a lot of women have emotionally and psychically internalized the male world. . . . We are interested in a level of sensation and sensitivity directly related to cunt sensation. I'm not talking about sex or orgasm as much as I am about the experience of cunt as a living, seeking, pulsating organism.'"[7] Looking back, she recalled, "Inspired by the idea of doing images of 'cunts'—defiantly recuperating a term that traditionally had been used derogatorily . . . we vied with each other to come up with images of female sexual organs."[8] On the occasion of a 2007 exhibition reappraising the women's art of that era, Richard Meyer wrote, "Beyond asserting a shared female experience at the level of the body, the feminist use of the word 'cunt' in the early 1970s constituted a reverse discourse whereby the language of sexual degradation was claimed and rerouted by those it was meant to belittle. 'Cunt art,' according to Schapiro and Wilding, was a transgressive spark that flashed across the arid field of female representation, signaling new possibilities and provoking laughter, embarrassment, secret glee—and strong disapproval."[9]

Not coincidentally, this was also the moment that Germaine Greer's *The Female Eunuch* (1970) was released; the spirited and immensely popular book was often cited in art criticism of the time. Greer's chapter on "Sex" begins, "Women's sexual organs are shrouded in mystery . . . Part of the modesty about the female genitalia stems from actual distaste. The worst name anyone can be called is a *cunt*. The best thing a cunt can be is small and unobtrusive: the anxiety about the bigness of the penis is only equaled by anxiety about the smallness of the cunt. No woman wants to find out that she has a twat like a horse-collar."[10] Compare her rousing campaign of disinhibition with a statement by Wilke: "My interest in developing a specifically female iconography for both sexes in the early '60s was in direct conflict with a society that prohibited its citizens from and sometimes arrested them for using the words 'fuck,' 'cock,' and 'prick.' In the United States the state of nudity is still a

Early box and six phallic and excremental sculptures, 1960–63. Clockwise from top left: terra cotta, 7 x 4½ x 4¾ in.; terra cotta, 2 x 4¼ x 3¼ in.; brown plaster of Paris, 1¾ x 3 x 2¾ in.; brown plaster of Paris, 2½ x 2¼ x 2 in.; terra cotta, 4½ x 5 x 5½ in.; white plaster of Paris in two parts, 6 x 5 x 6 in.; terra cotta, 7 x 5 x 5 in.

problem. My concern is with the word translated into form, with creating a positive image to wipe out the prejudices, aggression and fear associated with the negative connotations of pussy, cunt, box."[11] (And note that the difference between Greer as a guide and Butler, or Irigaray, or Lacan, is not just one of orientation but also of readability; the academicization of feminism and the premium it placed on difficulty in all its implications was not yet in place in 1970.)

Of course, there were dissenters, even among soi-disant feminists. One of the epigraphs that Andrea Dworkin chose for a 1979 diatribe against pornography is this quote from Kate Millet's 1973 book *The Prostitution Papers*: "Somehow every indignity the female suffers ultimately comes to be symbolized in a sexuality that is held to be her responsibility, her shame. . . . It can be summarized in one four-letter word. And the word is not *fuck*, it's *cunt*. Our self-contempt originates in this: in knowing we are cunt. This is what we are supposed to be about—our essence, our offense."[12] But the balance of opinion among feminists was in favor of freeing previously embargoed language and imagery. In her irrepressible impulse to use every means at hand, visual or verbal, to liberate women's bodies from such constraints, Wilke was exceptional in her courage, inventiveness and unflagging commitment.

Wilke began making sculptures with sexual references almost as soon as she began making art. "I started making fiberglass pieces in my senior year in college, because its plasticity allowed me to create curvilinear and architectonic form simultaneously,"[13] she told Ruth Iskin. "I painted them black in the tradition of metal sculpture. Fiberglass at that time was a brand new material (this was 1959/60, I graduated in 1961). Those sculptures were abstracted arm- and leg-like structures reaching up with big separate centers connecting them, and they were definitely vaginal. I named them with erotic titles (*Embouchure*, *Nymphaea*, *Candida*, *Oncos*—for oncoming, etc.). I was aware by the time I was 20 that they were vaginas and we talked about it in college at the time." Strikingly, she adopts the same tone as Chicago and Schapiro in noting her evolving awareness of what she was doing, as if the sculptures themselves were a form of objective evidence, a kind of independent corroboration of an expressive urgency that didn't yet have a descriptive or critical vocabulary. Similarly, in a 1989 interview, Wilke said, "from about 1959 or '60 I did what could be considered erotic landscapes and fountains. Then from '60 to '63 I worked in ceramics, creating layered vaginal forms in natural browns and terracotta. I added color in around '63, pink ceramics, and that's when the vulvic forms evolved."[14]

Whatever the combination of honest surprise and disingenuousness there was in Wilke's recollections about her work's development, the earliest terra-cotta and ceramic sculptures are indeed gnarly, polymorphously funky objects of conflicting expressive purposes. Among the early unglazed and unpainted ceramic and terra-cotta works is a small untitled box of 1960–63, combined with half a dozen phallic and excremental shapes, and with an overall form that is both a generic receptacle and a vulva. Another dark untitled box from the '60s (many are not dated more precisely) is

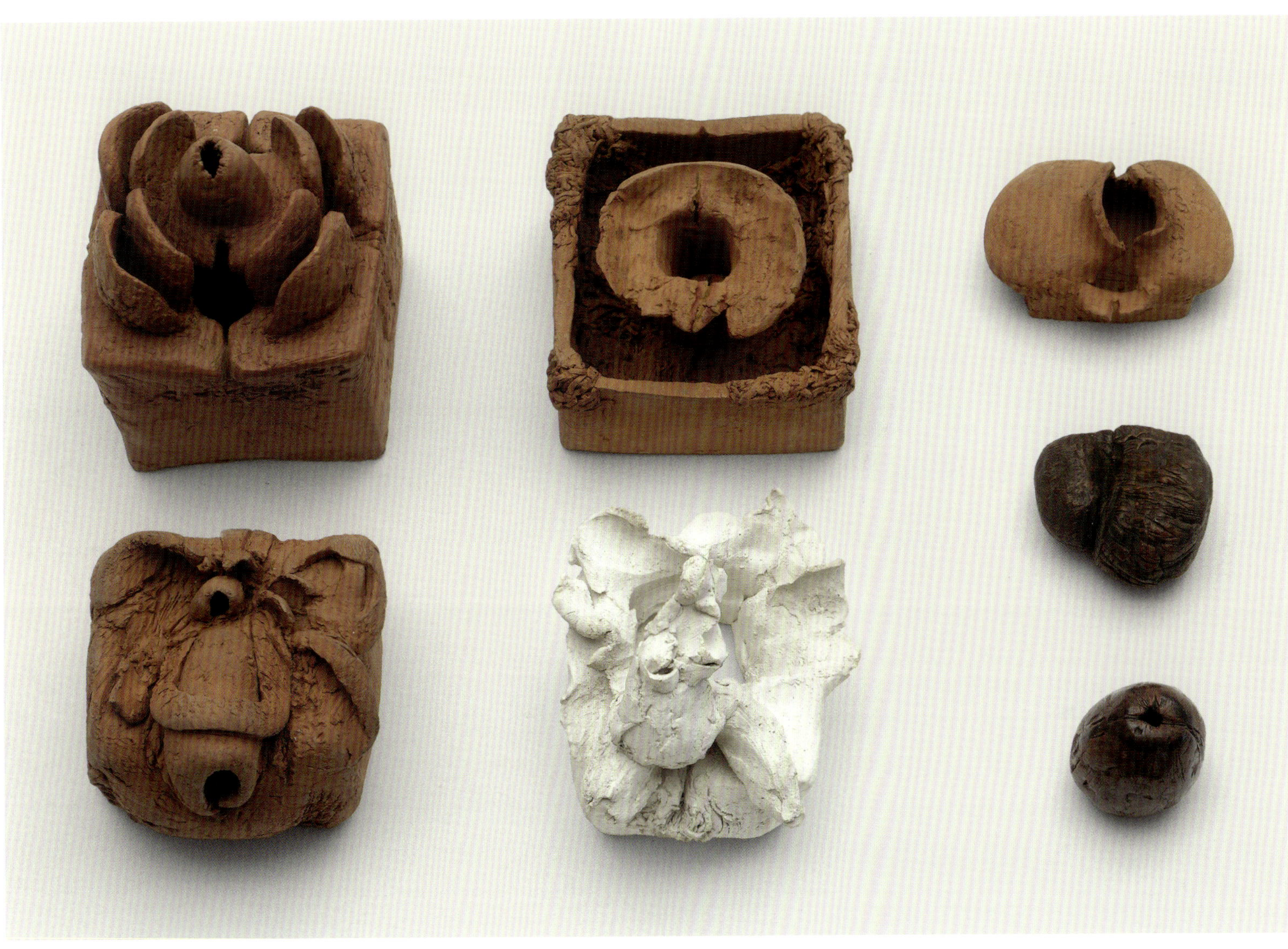

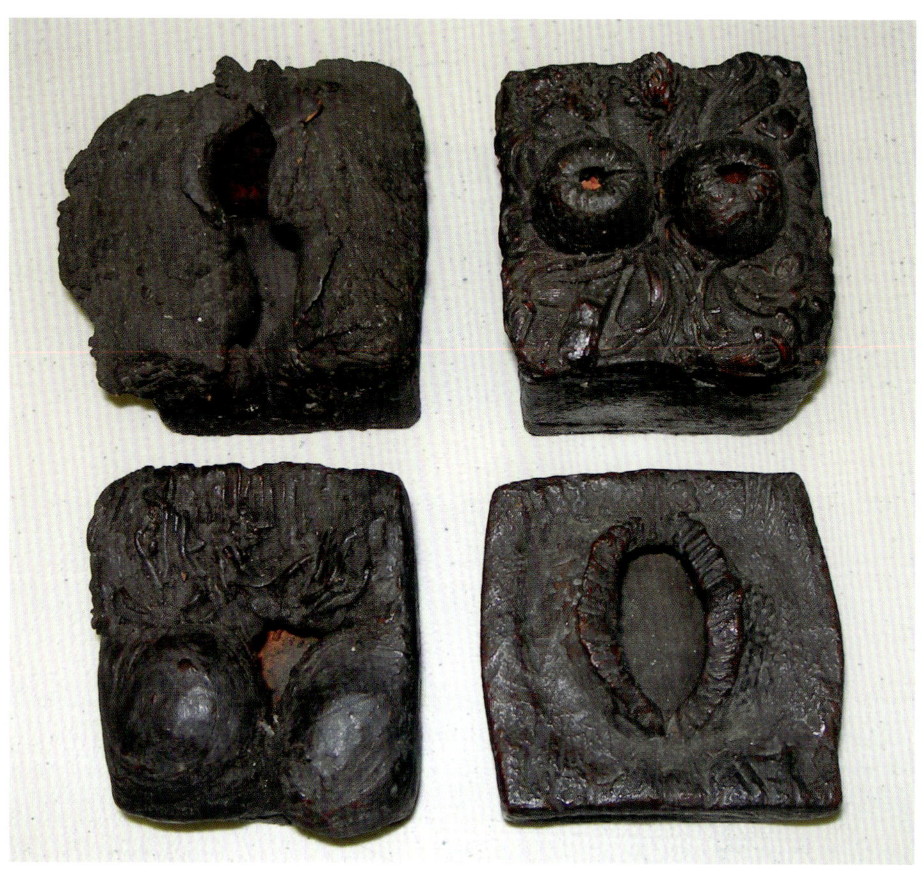

Scharlatt Rousse, 1965. Glazed terra cotta, clockwise from top left: 2¼ x 3⅛ x 3⅛ in.; 3½ x 3⅜ x 3 1/16 in.; 3¼ x 3 1/16 x 2¾ in.; 2¾ x 2¾ x 3⅛ in.

furnished with two penis heads, one poking up from the bottom, one coming in from the side, both slightly menacing, and too abject to be funny. While undeniably sexual in content, they are not by any means straightforwardly erotic. Within a few years, Wilke knew what she was doing. By 1963 or '64, she was making ceramic sculptures "for which I almost got fired"[15] from her high-school teaching job. These ceramic "Boxes" were first exhibited in 1966 in a group show at Castagno Gallery, and also in a 1966 show called "Hetero Is"—one of several erotic art shows that season—at a temporarily rented space on Manhattan's west side; writing for the *Hudson Review*, Lucy Lippard compared a terra-cotta work by Wilke with Giacometti's *Disagreeable Object* (1931), a spiky phallus. Looking back seven years later, Wilke said, "The concept of the disagreeable object had offended me, and I decided to make 'agreeable objects.' I don't feel happy on any level with disagreeable forms—I love beautiful things."[16] These boxes, Wilke recalled in another interview, "were more overtly cunt-shaped than the later Box pieces." Though the language is blunt, much of the work is, by intention, floridly lyrical. "The idea of the vagina image for me," Wilke said, "is primarily about inner feeling, the feeling of getting beyond oneself that one experiences when making love."[17]

Still, many of the works of the mid-'60s remained fairly dark, in emotional

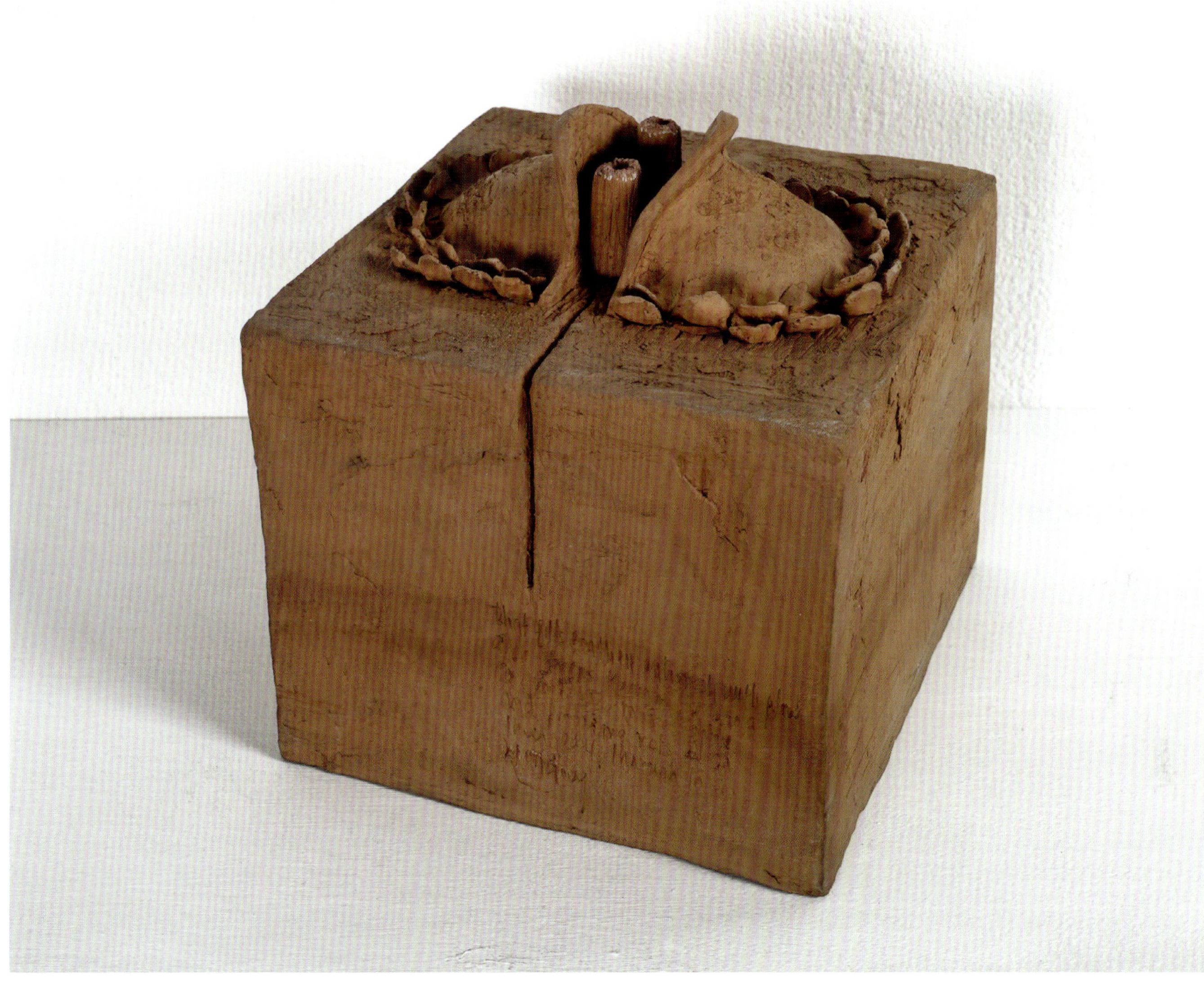

That Fills Earth . . . ., 1965. Terra cotta, 9⅝ x 9¼ x 9¼ in.

tone and often in surface color. *Scharlatt Rousse* (1965) comprises four nearly black terra-cotta vaginal/phallic boxes, each of which would fit comfortably in the palm. (The title is a pun that combines her sister's married surname with the name of a confection they shared as children.) *That Fills Earth* (1965) is a big straight-sided terra-cotta box, the color of unfired clay, with a nearly illegible inscription on the side that begins with the work's title. The two rows of teeth that ring the opening in its top suggest a vagina dentata, though two rods poke up from it like the eye stalks of a clam. The inescapable sexual associations of these early works, their roughly shaped forms, and unfinished surfaces—in a word, their rawness—lend them a particular intensity; they are both more aggressive and more vulnerable, because less sophisticated, than Wilke's subsequent work. The idea that sex is dark and dirty is not altogether dispelled; it is, rather, given a tentative airing.

By the early '70s, a decisive change appeared. The works that appeared in this decade are more regular, more controlled, more finished in every way. And they are significantly more joyous, though some critics noted alternative readings that were surely intended. A group of individually named, pink terra-cotta sculptures was included in a 1971 exhibition at Richard Feigen Gallery, New York, called "10 Painters and One Sculptor" (Wilke was the sculptor). In her 1974 show at the

Foreground: **176 One-Fold Gestural Sculptures**, 1973–74. Painted ceramics, 72 x 96 in. overall. Background, left: **Laundry Lint [C.O.'s]**, 1973. Twelve sculptures, double-fold lint, dimensions variable, overall installation 11 x 96 in. Hannah Wilke Collection & Archive, Los Angeles. Background, right: **Fortunate Cookies**, 1974. Fortune cookies, dimensions variable; no longer extant

Ronald Feldman gallery—her second solo exhibition there—Wilke presented 176 "one-fold gestural sculptures" of pink terra cotta in a range of sizes. Placed directly on the floor, they looked like nothing so much as a field of fresh rosebuds. Edit deAk's review was particularly alert to the work's competing implications. "The new works are small, insignificant, humiliated vaginal evocations. . . . By making hundreds of these little fuckers, she depersonalizes the very body part whose sensual quality depends so much on its individuality. She has made it into an asexual herd of repeated images. . . . I cherish Wilke's expressive potential. I hope she can hold on to it by being hysterical, loud, cheap, silly, funny, formalist, sarcastic, full of sorrow. I hope she can remain a woman artist and hold on to her sense of humor."[18] James Collins's response was more neutral, though it too recognized Wilke's formal ambitions. "What are you to make of her beautifully made, pink ragged edge, 'one-fold gesture' terra-cotta sculpture, of which there are 176 equally spread over the floor?" he asked. "You can either read them as metaphors for genitalia or as Process sculpture—one fold, two fold and so on. Wilke would clearly like both."[19]

The truth of that assertion is clearly borne out in an exchange between the artist and Barbara Rose. Writing in *New York Magazine*, Rose hailed the "self-examination movement" in the course of a review of the 1974 exhibition at Feldman, saying Wilke's work contributed to "an overt assault on the Freudian doctrine of penis envy."[20] Wilke responded rather huffily, in the publication *Art-Rite*, "Well, if I am going to become Pubic Princess of a new movement, I sincerely hope it will also include the awareness of its being innovative sculptural form, and not merely new subject matter."[21] (She also responded by making a small freestanding latex sculpture called *Barbara Rose*.)

Simple (and sensuous) to fashion but subtle in their variation, the labial ceramic sculptures recurred regularly throughout her career, serving almost a ritualistic function, their meaning altering substantially over the years. Throughout the '70s and '80s, they appeared in various mediums, surface treatments, and sizes, though clay remained primary. (Wilke founded a ceramics program at the School of Visual Arts, and sometimes took advantage of the school's ceramics facilities, although she also had a kiln in her studio from roughly the mid-'70s on.) Some of these sculptures are substantial, up to nearly three feet long each; others are diminutive. They were presented singly, in pairs and quartets, and in greater profusion, both chaotically dispersed and ranked in orderly rows. *Elective Affinities* (1978), which Wilke considered particularly important, is composed of eighty-six units laid out in grids on four boards. *The Red One*, dated 1980s, comprises a couple dozen medium-sized bright red forms. In *Raison d'Etre* (1980s; p. 28), the twenty-six components are smaller, and their glazed surfaces are metallic and shiny, almost insect-like. The sixteen moderately sized, uniformly bubble-gum-pink pussies in *Sweet Sixteen* (1977; p. 29) are demurely lined up in four neat rows.

Even more regular in shape and size are the forms in *GeoLogic 4 to One*, from the "Generation Process" series" (1980–82). A game board–like base divided

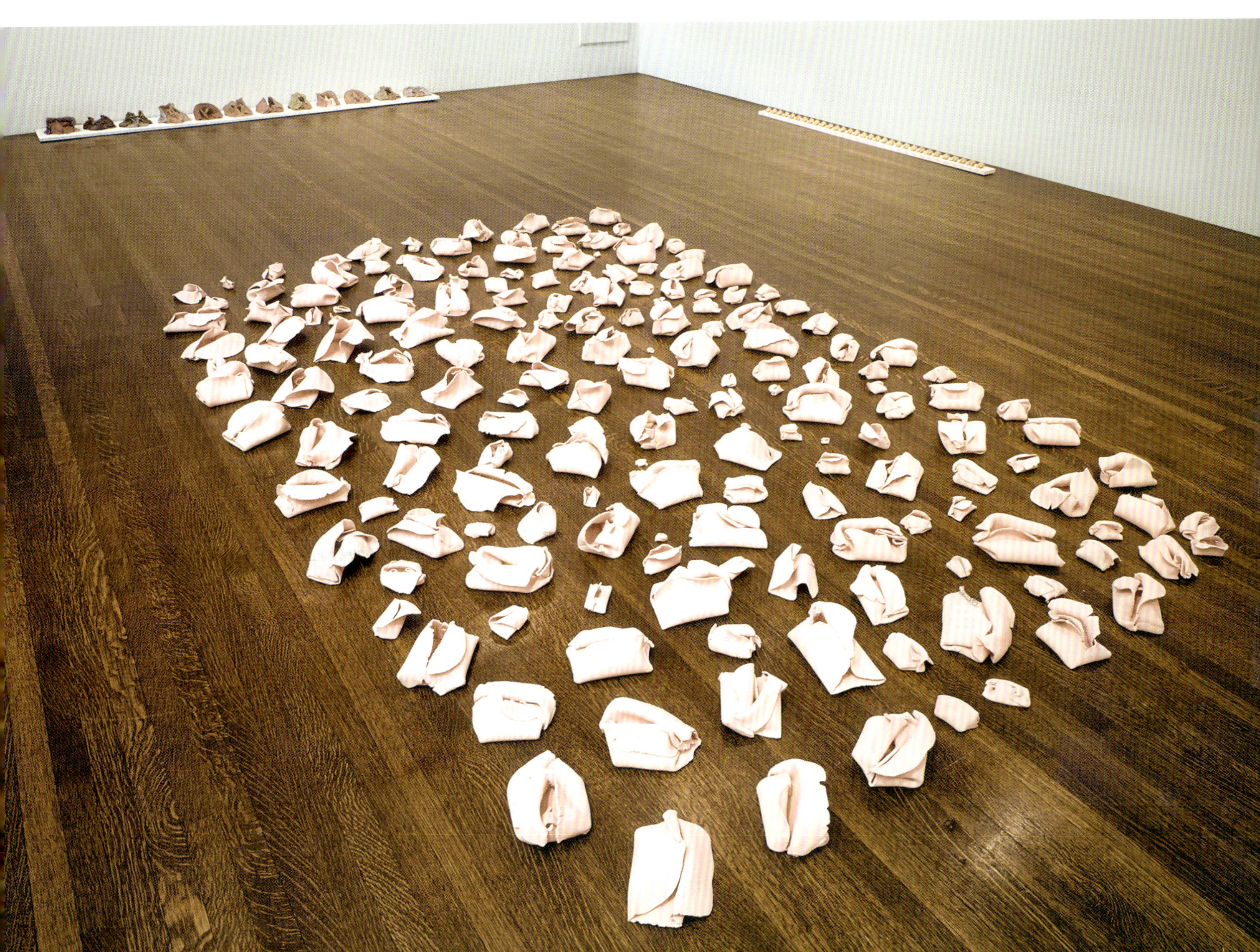

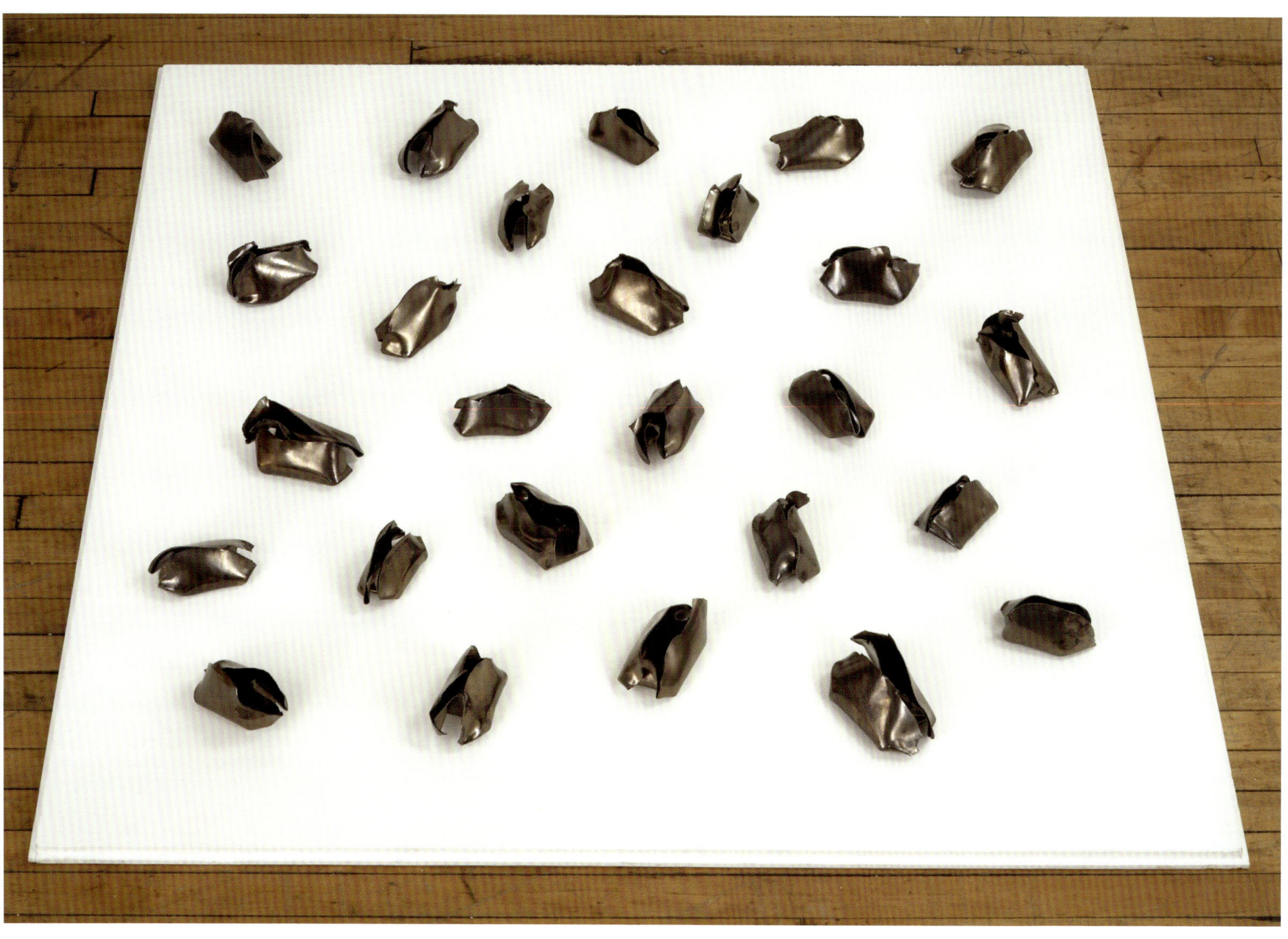

Raison d'Etre, 1980s. Twenty-six glazed metallic folds on painted wood base, 48 x 48 in. overall

into four brightly painted squares—green, red, yellow, and black—supports sculptural units in the same quartet of colors, placed on contrasting fields. The effect is more of a flag or a heraldic shield than of a field of sensuous blossoms. Others in this series involve groupings of twelve or sixteen bright-hued forms, some spattered with paint in a range of colors, others freely brushed. Their proliferation, in works from the late 1970s on, can in some cases be seen as metastatic; the recurrence of Wilke's mother's ultimately fatal breast cancer was diagnosed in 1978; her own lymphoma was identified in 1987. Wilke compared the ranked one-fold sculptures made in this period with cell division in cancer.[22] And some of these sculptures were combined in *In Memoriam* (1979–83), a mixed-medium work with photographs she made in response to her mother's death; in another series that followed shortly, the sculptural components are more closely identified with wombs and motherhood than with erotic vaginal or labial forms. The quite big examples in the "Of Relativity" series—*Snow White* and *Seura Chaya* among them—of the mid-'80s, include some in decidedly fecal earth tones, others with brightly feathered surfaces evoking the bodies of birds, and none remotely suggesting vulvas unless considered in the context of Wilke's other ongoing work. Exhibited on low platforms shaped something like old-fashioned desk blotters, which are painted in complementary or consistent colors and patterns,

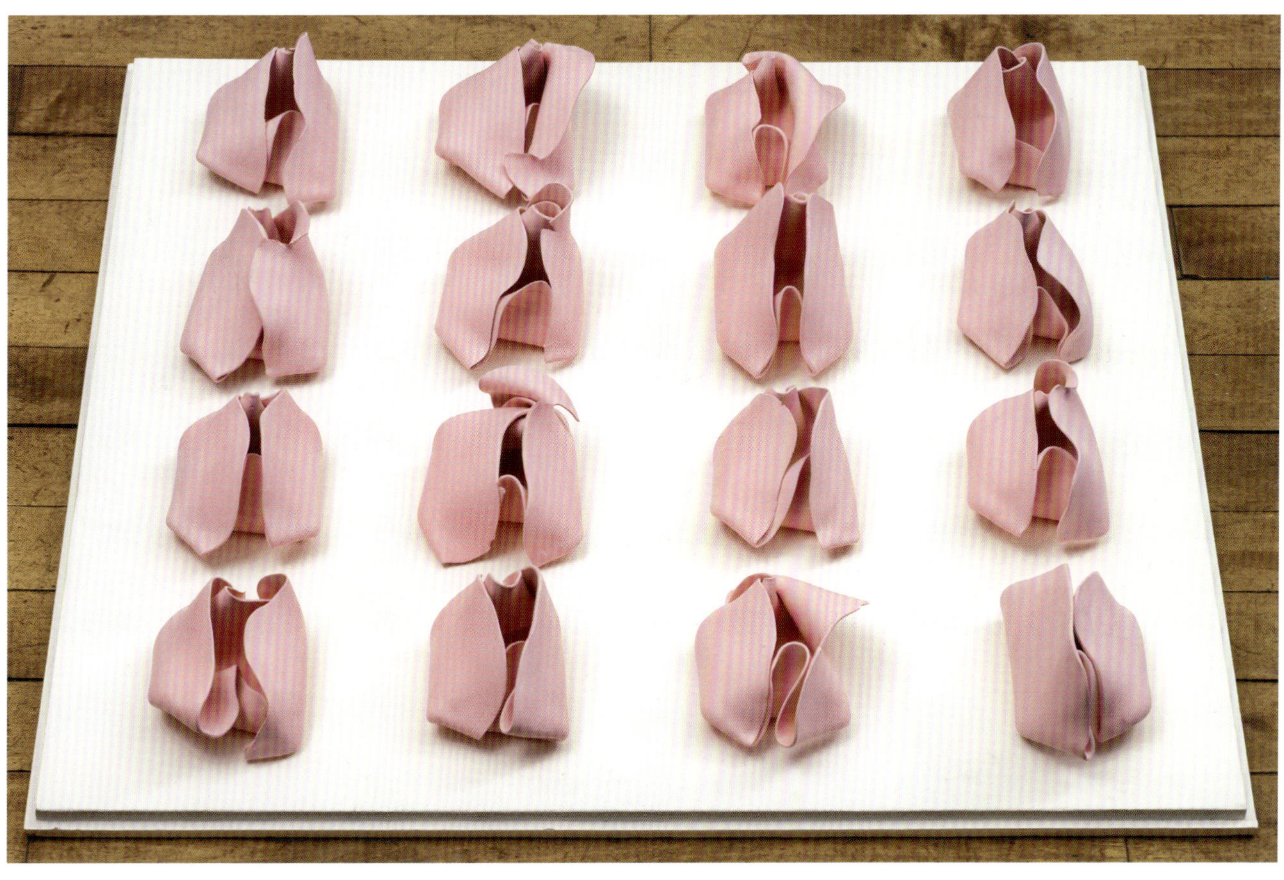

Sweet Sixteen, 1979. Sixteen painted ceramic folds on painted wood base, 32 x 32 in. overall.

are such works as the unitary *Brown Stone #6* and *Chaya #1* (both 1980–84), the latter a single form, brushed red, blue, yellow, white.

Some examples, untitled and undated, are small and beautifully glazed, gem-like; at the other end of the spectrum are proposals for colossal cunts. "Project for a Room Sculpture" (1978), created for an exhibition at the High Museum in Atlanta of small-scale installation models, involved little glazed white ceramic vulvas. Wilke also made proposals for large outdoor sculptures along the same lines, very much in the manner of Oldenburg's oversized lipstick and penknife, and drawn in a manner similar to his drawings; Wilke's, too, are funny and appealingly mischievous. More sober-minded are small bronze models for stepped, band-shell-size horseshoes only vestigially related to female anatomy (*Soft Pyramids*, 1975–80). *Athens* and *Ohio*, 1978, two trios of bronze sculptures, and a group of bronze proposals for large works, identified as "Models for Monumental Outdoor Sculpture," do conform to the female shape of the ceramic sculptures. Wilke's contribution to an exhibition called "After Tilted Arc," of suggested replacements for Richard Serra's dismantled sculpture at Federal Plaza in lower Manhattan, was *Color Fields* (1985), which involved ten contrasting-color pairs of single-fold sculptures, each pair on its own platform. *Hannah Manna* (1985–86), created for Bonnie Sherk's "A Garden of Knowledge" at Central

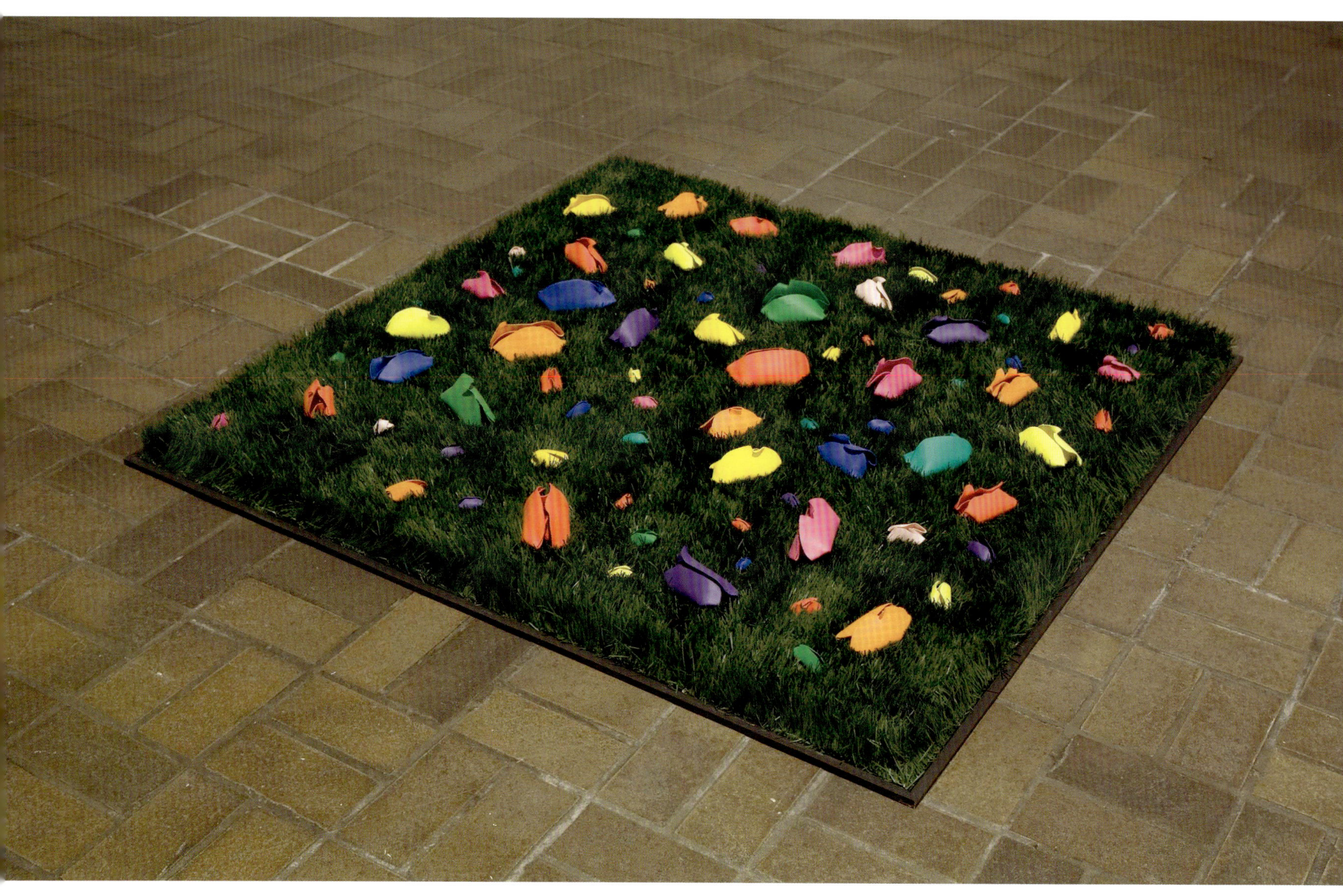

Hannah Manna, 1985–86. Seventy-seven painted ceramic sculptures with wall plaque, dimensions variable. "Hannah Wilke Gestures" exhibition installation on Astroturf, Neuberger Museum of Art, Purchase College, State University of New York, Purchase, 2008

opposite:
Untitled (Could commodities themselves speak . . .), from the **Sotheby's Series**, 1991. Ink on magazine paper, 16½ x 10¹¹⁄₁₆ in.

Hall Gallery in Long Island, New York in 1986, where it was placed on live sod, was recreated on Astroturf for a 2008 exhibition at the Neuberger Museum in Westchester, New York; it consists of colorful painted ceramic cunts in vivid primaries plus greens and purples, variously proportioned. The whole suggests a field of unnaturally bright and not altogether benign flowers.

Perhaps most appealing among these proposals for sited and often-monumental vulvas is a 1991 quartet of drawings in ink, executed on glossy, full-color advertisements for Sotheby's properties in the wealthy community of Southampton, New York. On these storied, monied shores, near where Wilke was renting a (rather more modest) house at the time, her enormous vaginas advance like creatures from the deep, inching toward the waterfront palaces with the implacability of laying turtles. Comic and charming, and not a little truculent, they are marooned intimacies laid at the doorsteps of wealth and power.

Made roughly two years before Wilke died, these drawings use a vocabulary she had developed nearly three decades earlier, at a time when stylized depictions of female genitalia had a completely different rhetorical position and force. Their humor, and the

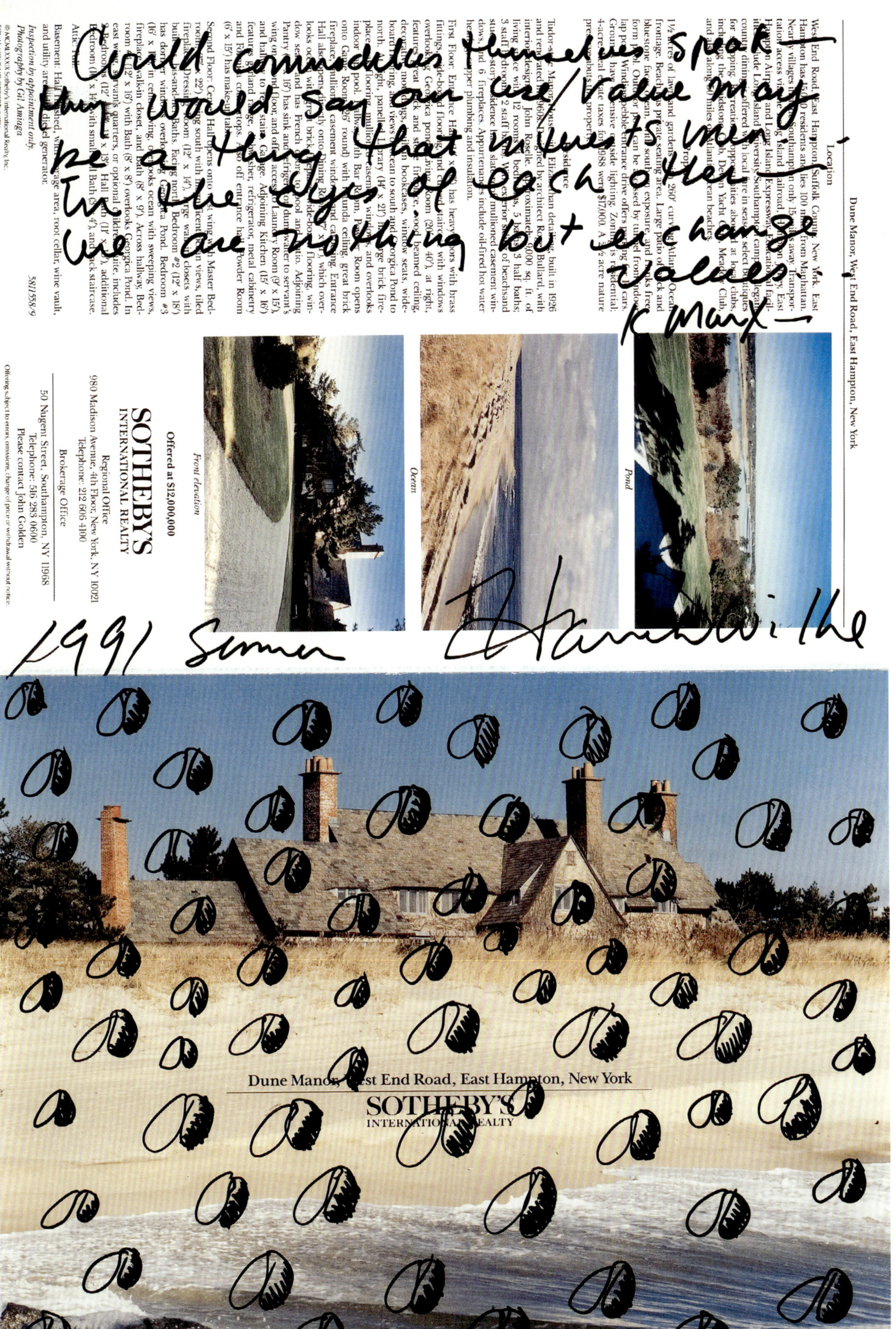
Could commodities themselves speak they would say our use/value may be a thing that interests men. In the eyes of each other we are nothing but exchange values.
K Marx —
1991 Summer
Dune Manor, West End Road, East Hampton, New York
Front elevation
Ocean
Pond
Offered at $12,000,000
SOTHEBY'S
INTERNATIONAL REALTY

Hannah Wilke pouring latex in her Broome Street studio, New York, 1974

nimbleness of the symbolic gesture they make, reflect the nuances with which she had come to endow this signature figure. Alongside claiming a place in the visual culture for an expression of female sexual experience, she remained committed to placing genital imagery within a lineage of formal invention. She also articulated that claim with an extended body of latex wall-hangings that she initiated around 1970 and continued producing through the middle of the decade. The thin, irregularly shaped layers of the rubbery material, which were draped on the wall, were made by pouring liquid latex ("like pancake batter," Wilke said [23]) onto plaster, first in strips and then in circles, and peeling it off when dry.

The early examples were narrow, steeply draped hangings; in the later works, twenty or more sheets of latex would be fastened at their edges with metal snaps, and, as a rule, hung on the wall by pushpins. As she explained the process, "I like one side to be opaque and the other shiny. I pour the liquid latex on a seventeen-foot plaster of Paris floor. The moisture is absorbed by the plaster floor so that the pouring gesture is arrested and caught, and the latex doesn't move any farther. I get a nice bubbly surface, and after a day I can pull the dried latex up and work on it." Notably, she compared the pouring procedure to painting, and specifically to painting of the heroic, Abstract Expressionist mode, continuing in the same interview: "The process was similar to the gestural dance of Jackson Pollock's painting process; I try to draw the holes—the negative space—too. I pour from a cup; it is like making a line drawing."[24]

The similarities in procedure and outcome with the ceramic work that she was making at the same time are clear, and the latex, too, offered considerable versatility. "In the last few years I have only been working in circular shapes which are snapped together like folded petals . . . The pieces I did in 1972 were more tear-shaped and they were longer."[25] The later ones, she said, were more evocative of flesh. The latex was beige when raw; Wilke added pinkish color to it to make it fleshier, and chose the hardware used in each hanging's assembly for its tactile and also symbolic value. "When I developed my latex hangings, I decided to use metal snappers to hold the folds together, but also to combine toughness and softness. . . . I like the shiny, gritty nastiness and the fact that the snaps make the structure possible—as well as vulnerable. You want to unsnap the piece, but that would destroy the shape," she said in a 1974 interview.[26]

Even in comparison with the ceramic work, the sensuality of Wilke's latex hangings is remarkably ripe. The many layers of latex in *Pink Champagne* (1975; p. 34), a four-and-a-half-foot wide latex relief, are irregularly scalloped at the edges and perforated with eccentric holes like freeform lace, or like the macramé and crocheted hangings that proliferated at the time as part of a wave of handcrafted textiles. The pink-flesh surface colors are widely varied, and the work's slightly curved and bowed overall shape make it seem to gush into view, bubbling with the effervescence suggested in the title. Just as Wilke wanted, the snaps give it a slight glinty hardness, and the flash of a reference to the fasteners on garters and bras. *Rosebud*, of the following year (1976; p. 34), is a bit larger and fuller. As wide across as an average arm

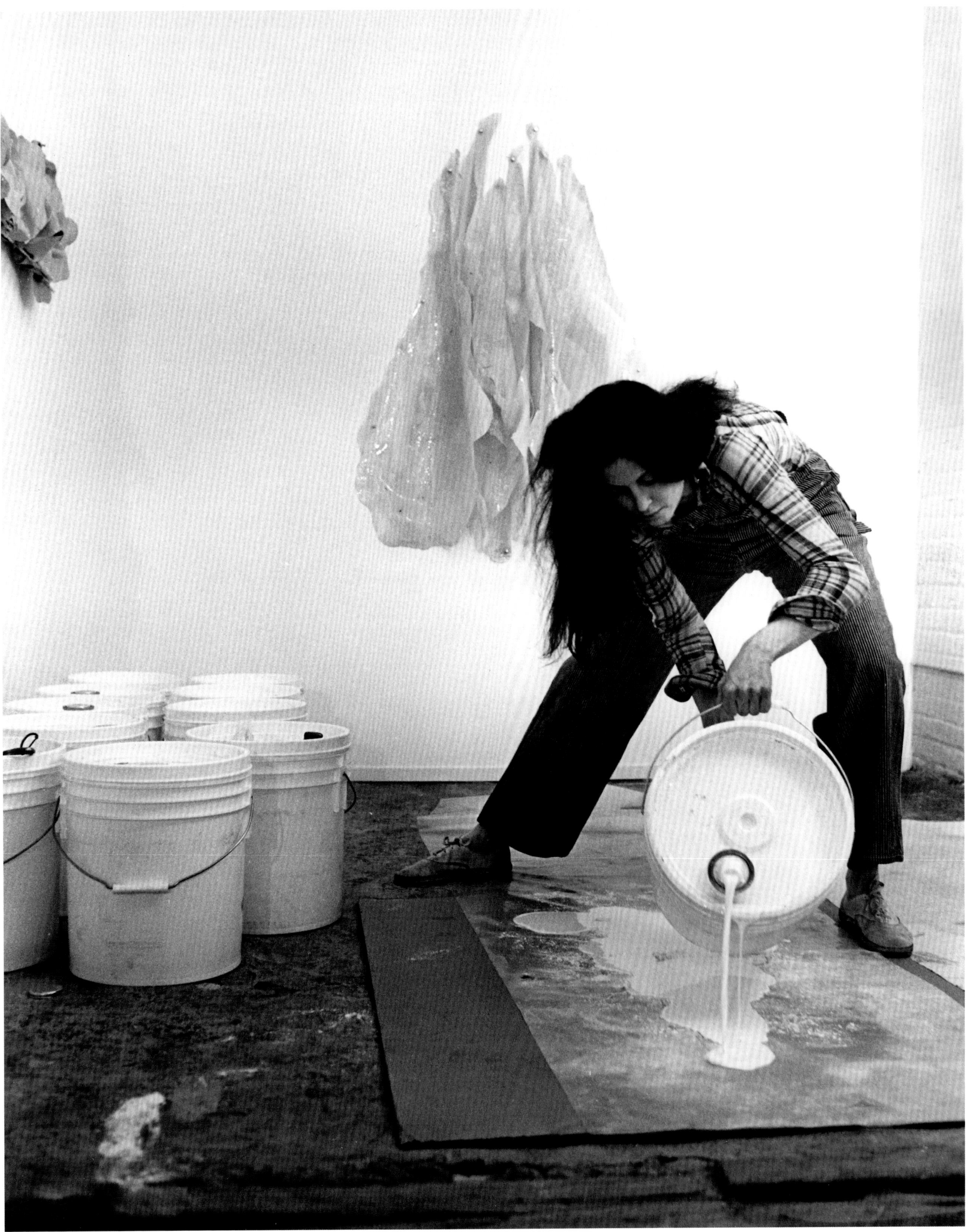

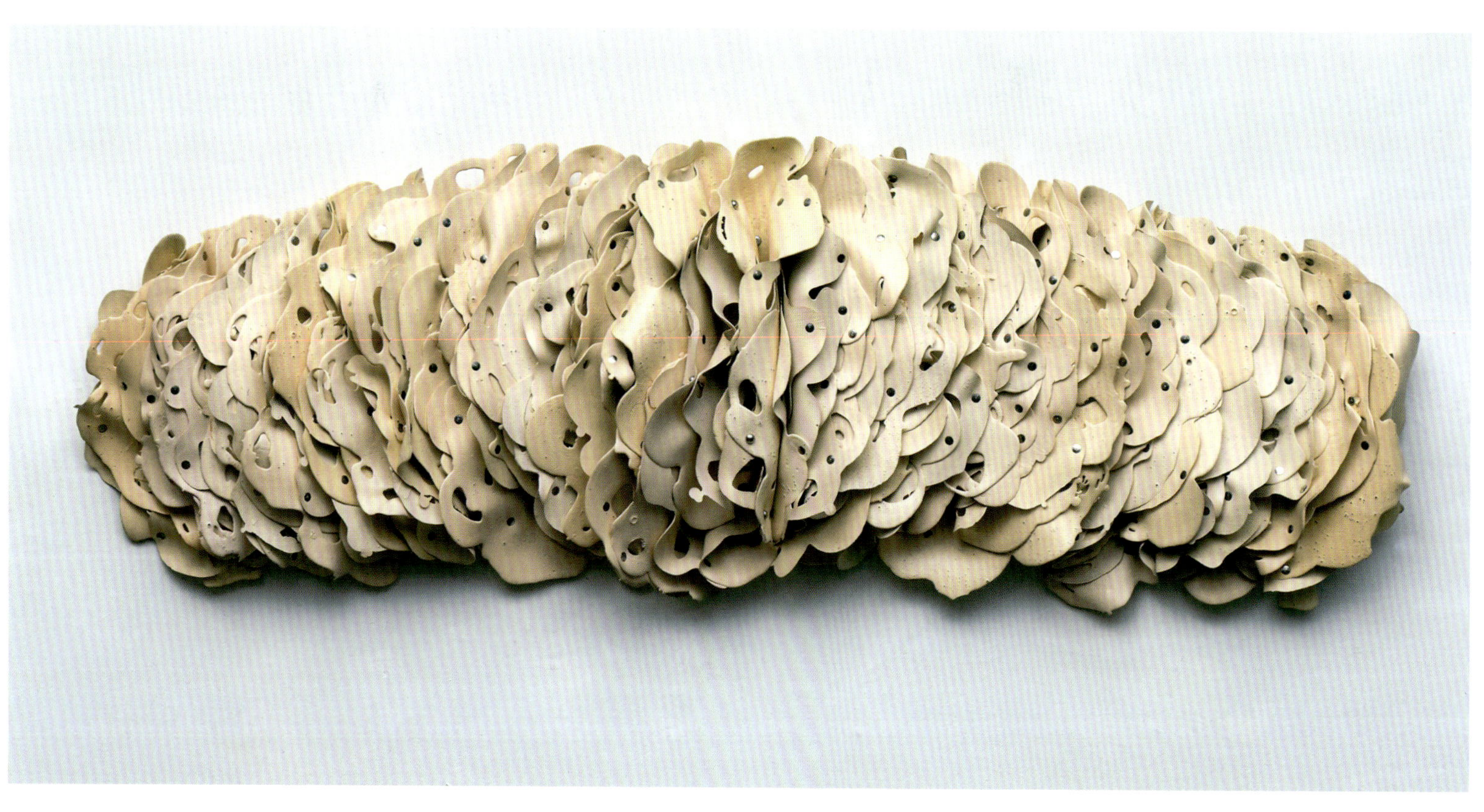

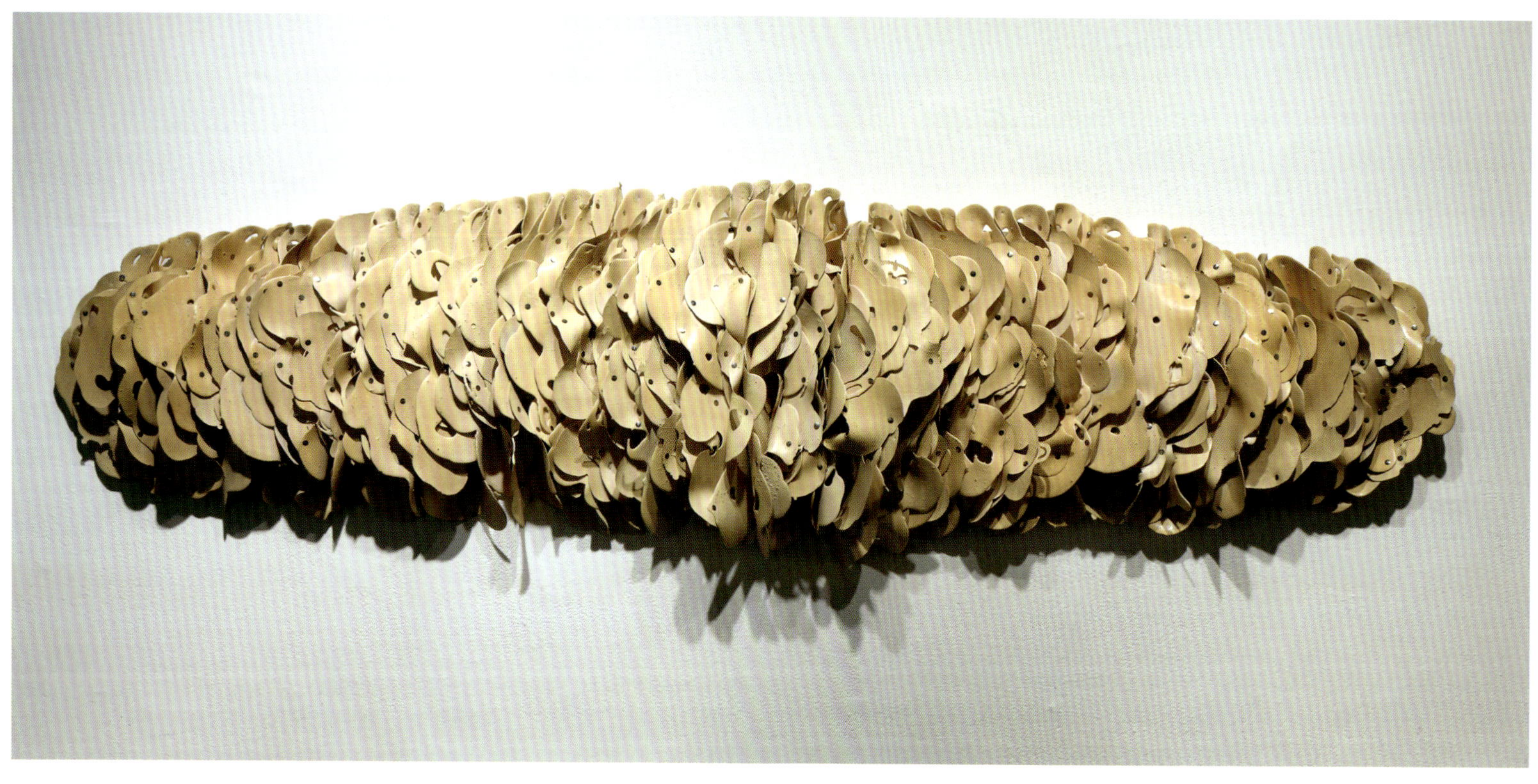

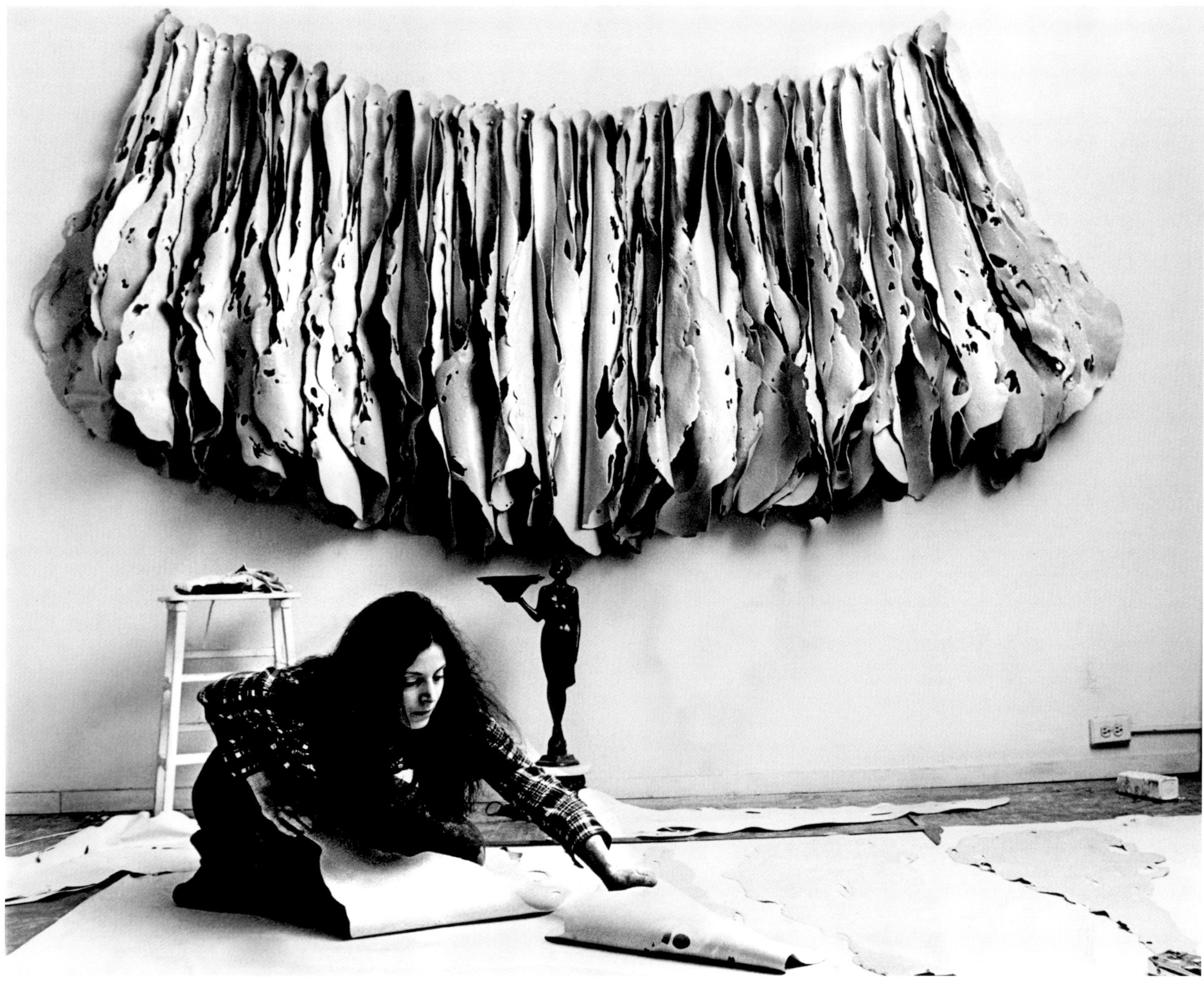

Hannah Wilke in Broome Street studio with **Centerfold** on the wall, 1973

opposite:

Pink Champagne, 1975. Latex with metal snaps, 18 x 54 x 7 in.

Rosebud, 1975. Latex and metal snaps, 24 x 92 x 8 in.

span, and evoking, as do the other lateral works, a bird's outstretched wings, it is organized somewhat asymmetrically around a dark, dense center. Surging outward from a central slit, the lips of pink latex flow in both directions, wave upon wave, in an almost comically vivid evocation of orgasm. One latex sculpture was given the title *Centerfold* (1973); in an article in *Penthouse*, Wilke said, "When you make love and have an orgasm, you experience it in waves, so to me that's like these sculptures: very luscious, very beautiful and opening—opening up like gentle waves, like flowers."[27] In *Viva*, she noted the latex work's "fragile attitude," and also explained that "it expresses a metaphysical feeling related to orgasmic ecstasy."[28]

The interest that these magazines took in Wilke's work (and that of other women using genital imagery; in both articles she was linked with additional artists, including Judy Chicago, Joan Semmel, and Anita Steckel), and Wilke's reciprocal interest in speaking to their readerships, also suggests the clear legibility of the work's feminine—if not actively feminist—iconography. It would never be confused, for instance, with sexually evocative but much blockier flesh-colored resin and

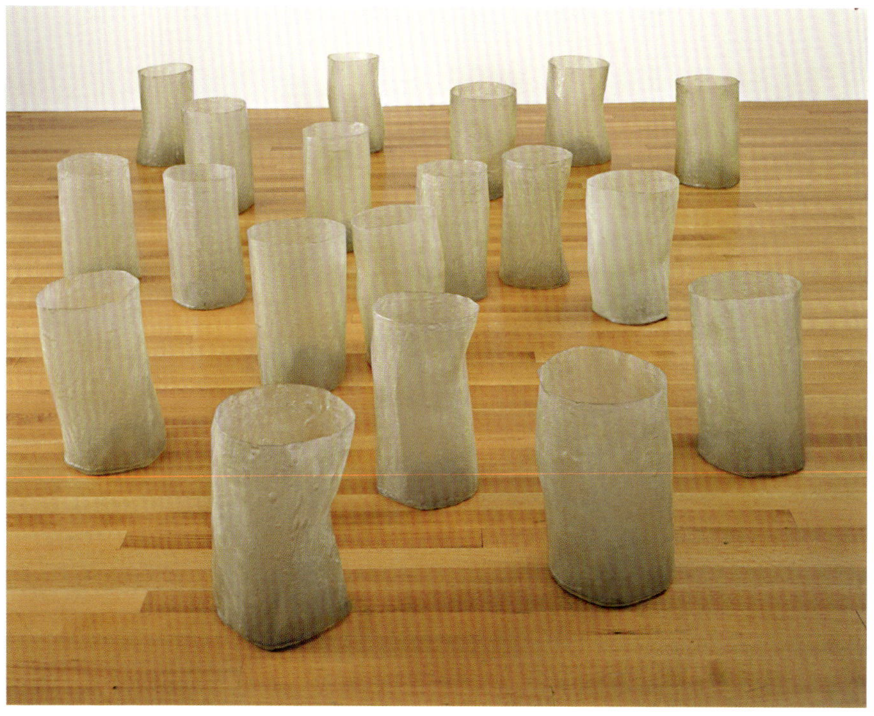

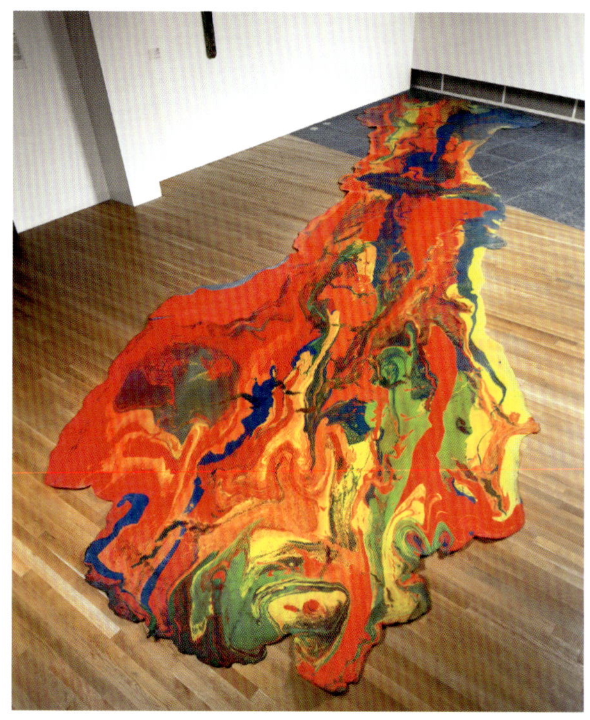

Eva Hesse, **Repetition Nineteen, III**, 1968. Fiberglass and polyester resin, nineteen units, each 19 to 20¼ (h.) x 11 to 12¾ in. (d.)

Lynda Benglis, **Contraband**, 1969. Poured pigmented latex, 116¼ x 398¼ x 3 in. overall (irregular)

opposite:
Vertical Verde for Garcia Lorca, 1976. Latex, Liquitex, and metal snaps, each 48 x 12 x 8¾ in.

latex abstractions made at the time by Gary Kuehn. On the other hand, *Vertical Verde for Garcia Lorca* (1975), is incontestably androgynous. Five lozenge-shaped columns made of layers of small latex rounds, each column varying from assorted shades of green at the ends to a ruddy brown at the center, highlighted with orange and red, are aligned in a row that ascends from left to right. Apart from the title's reference to the Spanish poet, and its vaguely martial coloration, *Vertical Verde* limits its concerns to the field of abstraction. The vaguely phallic forms of the five columns are each analogous to a brushstroke; each is itself an impressionistic canvas of rich colors.

Among Wilke's best-known works, the latex pieces are in the collections of several major museums, although many of the earliest, including several made with twine that runs through them like ribs, succumbed to drying and cracking (an infusion of Liquitex was, she discovered, a way to extend their durability). One notable collector of this work was Willem de Kooning, who, Wilke said, recognized in her sculpture an Abstract-Expressionist peer; in 1972, he purchased *Venus Cushion* (made that same year), which apparently did not survive. Needless to say, that affirmation was enormously gratifying. As with her ceramic sculptures, but more adamantly, Wilke argued for a formal understanding of the latex work. Most critics again demurred. Barbara Rose, for instance, praised Wilke's latex works, faintly, in a review of the 1972 Ronald Feldman gallery show that included these sculptures, as "unpretentious and whimsical . . . not vulgar but endearingly tender."[29] And among the "mostly boring" sculpture Robert Hughes saw at the 1973 WMAA Biannual [*sic*], he singled out only work by Clement Meadmore, Louise Bourgeois, "and a delicately erotic wall piece of pink latex flaps and membranes by Hannah Wilke."[30] In Wilke's response to Rose's later review, of the 1974 floor-works show, she offered, in cumulative exasperation, a list of other artists with whose work she felt an affinity: it includes Robert

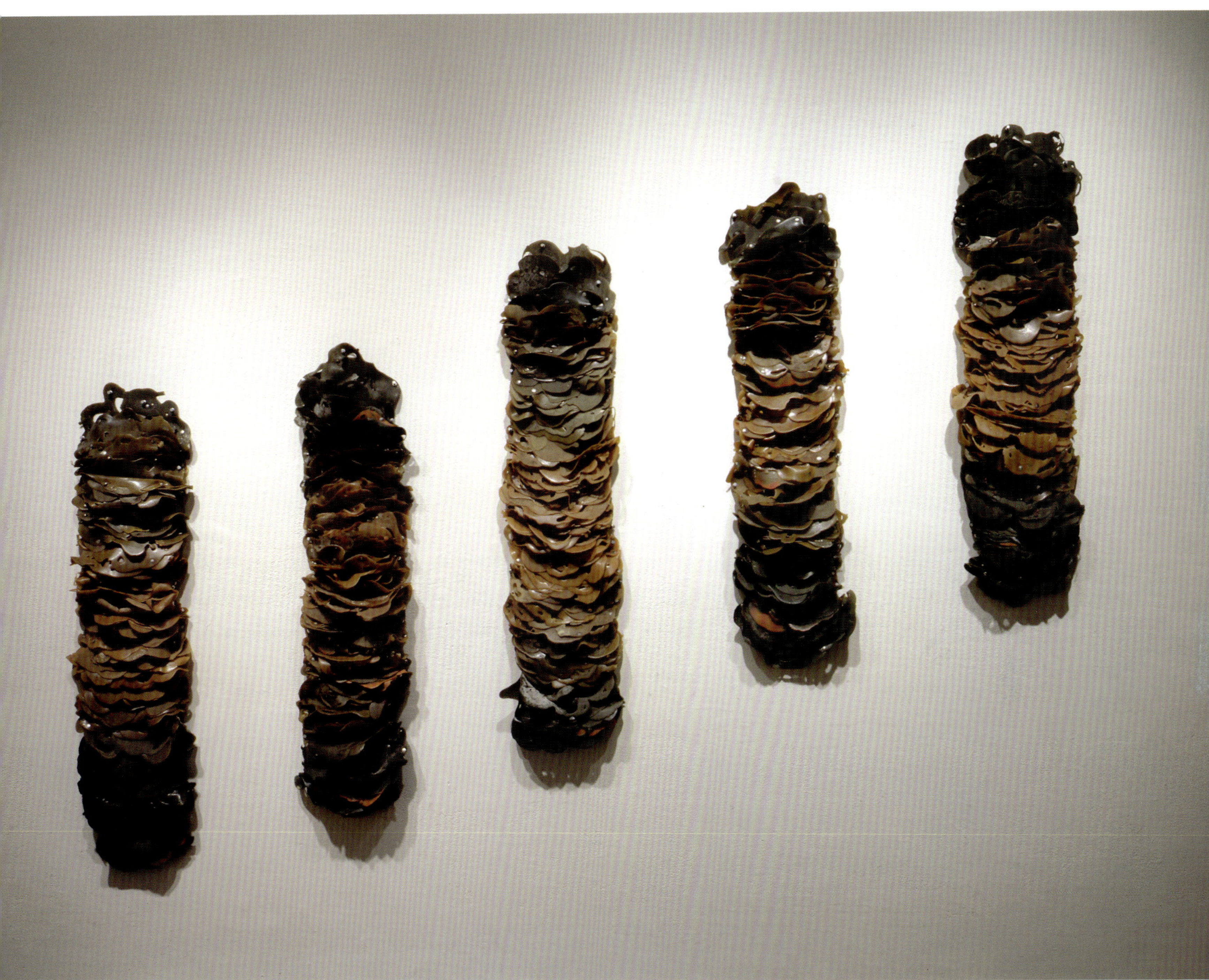

Robert Morris, **House of Vetti II**, 1983. Felt and steel brackets, 88 x 142½ x 47 in.

opposite:
Of Radishes and Flowers, 1972. Latex; no longer extant

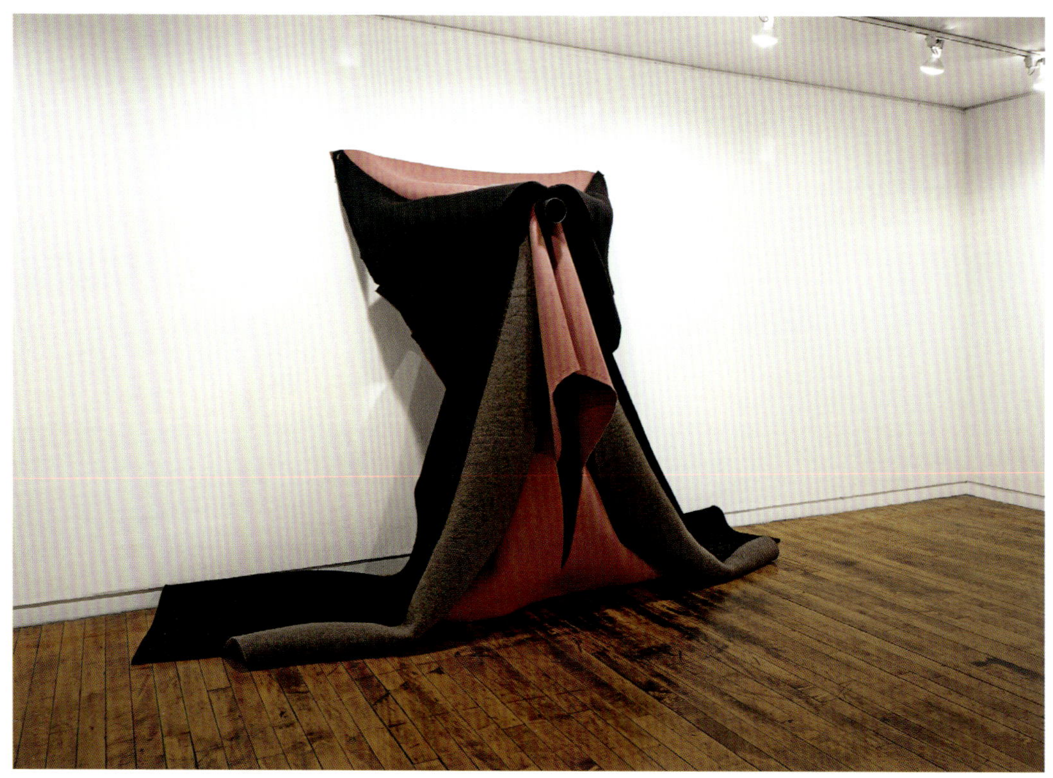

Morris, Richard Serra, and Alan Shields along with Ann Healy, Rosemary Mayer, Nina Yankowitz, and Barbara Zucker.

There is nothing spurious about any of these associations; some of the work that Morris and Serra (to name the two most prominent) made in the '70s, and in the following decade, shared a great deal, in terms of material, process, and form, with Wilke's sculptures. That her concerns with issues central to Post-Minimalism—articulating the properties of process and material—were as deep as theirs, and, especially, that the influences between Wilke and the men she cited ran in both directions are generally shortchanged by critics. Many decline to acknowledge that Wilke's work reflected the same interests and strengths attributed to male Post-Minimalists: the operations of gravity on pliant materials; the deformation of shape as an impersonally physical rather than deliberately expressive operation. Some sympathetic later observers, such as Joanna Frueh, credited Wilke's work's eroticism (Frueh connected the latex hangings, because of their material, to condoms and diaphragms[31]) while also pointing to their affinities with sculptures by bona-fide abstractionists Lynda Benglis and Eve Hesse (p. 36). Benglis's poured-acrylic floor sculptures, the first of which was made in 1969, and the lozenge-shaped beeswax wall-works that she made in the early 1970s, are close kin in terms of process and form. In addition to the sensuous modifications Hesse made to the language of Minimalism, her use of commercial materials like resin are among the links her work has with Wilke's.

Exceptional in its focus on the biases of the critical reception to Wilke's work is a passage in Mira Schor's essay "Patrilineage." Addressing the tendency, among critics, to establish women artists' significance by reference to male forebears while neglecting the influence of women on men, Schor takes Donald Kuspit to task for his review of a Robert Morris exhibition. Kuspit cites Pepe Karmel's description of one

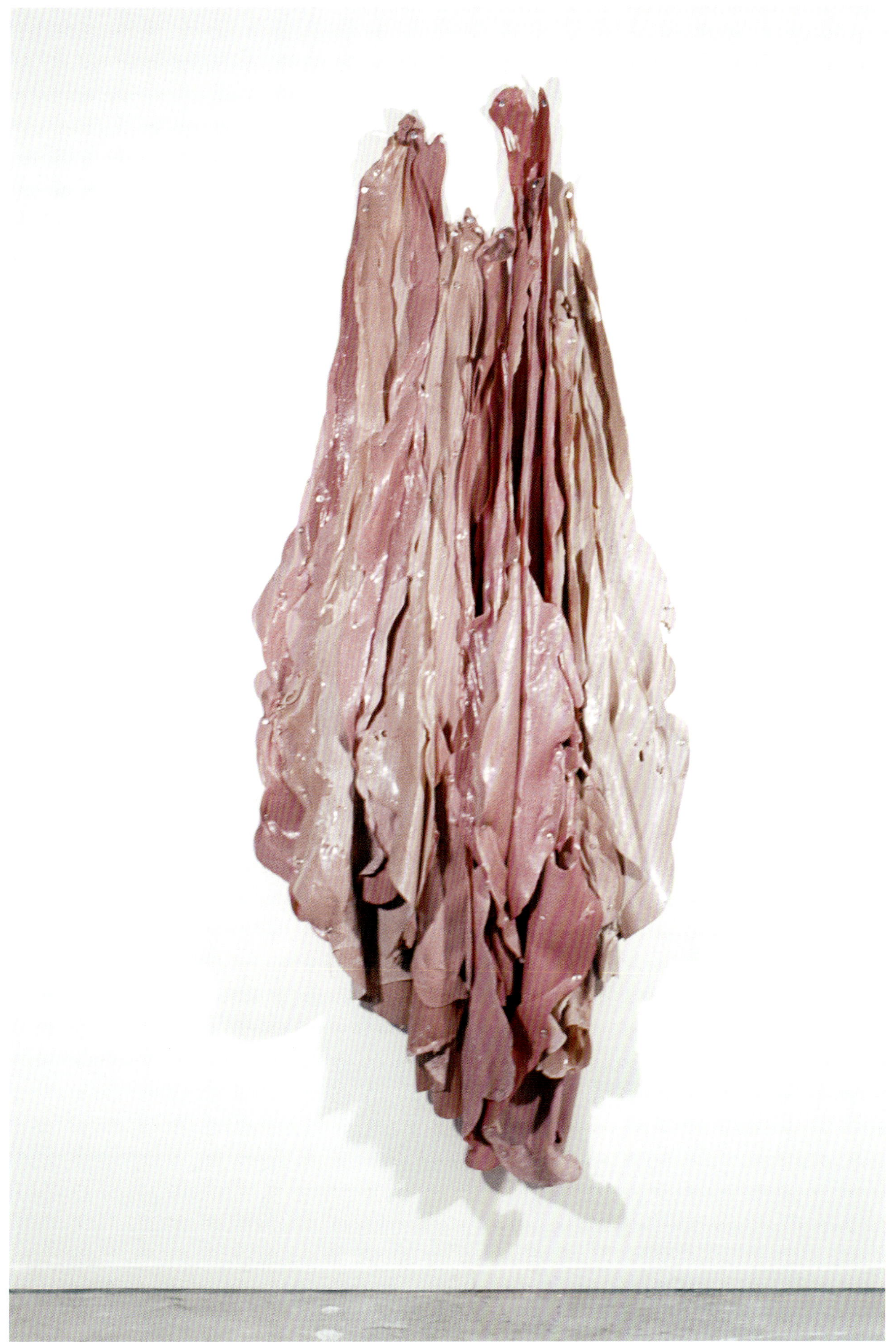

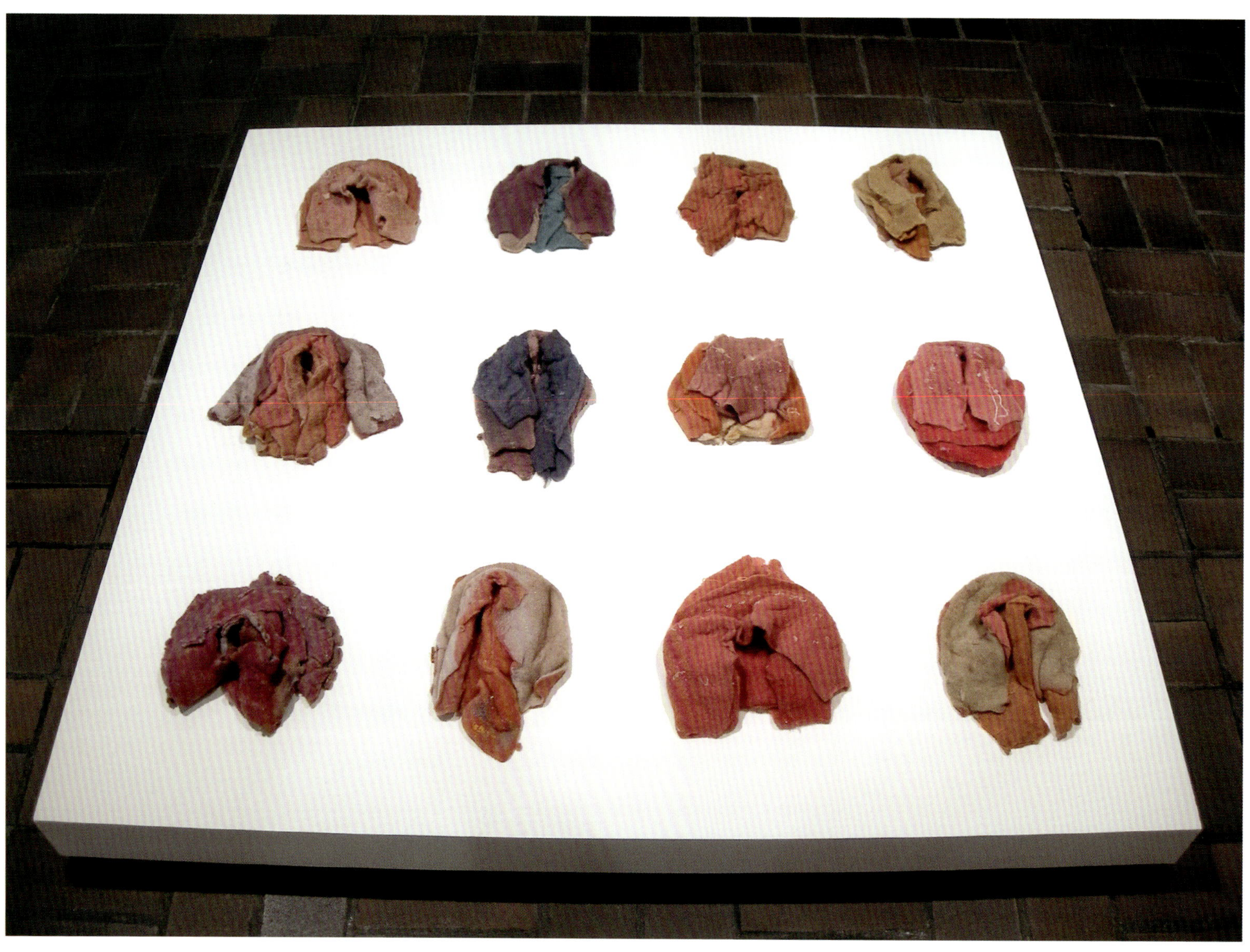

Laundry Lint [C.O.'s], 1971–73. Twelve sculptures, double-fold lint, dimensions variable

work's "central slit enclosed by narrow labial folds of pink felt," but, Schor says, "fails to note the obvious reference . . . to the multitude of 'labial' works done by women artists in the 1970s, which preceded and informed this work by Morris. The description of the work and the work itself, reproduced with the review, particularly recall," Schor notes, "Hannah Wilke's 'labial' latex wall sculptures from the early seventies."[32]

At the same time that the latex wall pieces were being made, Wilke was experimenting with other, funkier materials more firmly grounded in domestic life and bodily intimacies. *Laundry Lint, C.O.'s* (1974) is assembled from layers of lint pulled from the screen of a laundry dryer. Wilke fashioned this lint, each grayish sheet tinted with a distinct hue—some are a surprisingly saturated red or pink—into nested clusters that resemble miniature shrouds or overcoats (one thinks of Charles LeDray's Lilliputian clothing) and also, especially in the context of her ceramic sculpture, vulvas. The "C.O." of the title is Oldenburg, and the work's intimation of their liaison anticipates what was to be one of her most provocative gestures: in later photo-based and performance work, she was quite open about relationships with other men. In the lint works, the connection to her lover, named only by his initials, is otherwise direct and close: spun from almost nothing, these layers of cottony fluff are residue of his clothes, presumably including undergarments; they evoke as well sloughed skin and hair. One imagines them lifted gently from the lint trap, still warm from the dryer, the gesture and the warmth almost humorously tender—and the humor saving them from mawkishness.

Fashioned in simple folding procedures identical to those used for the ceramic vulvas, the lint sculptures were shown with them at Feldman in 1974. In that show, there was also a row of *Fortunate Cookies*: simply thirty-one examples of the cookies served at Chinese-American restaurants, which are made from circles of dough folded in just the way the vulva sculptures were; the cookies were displayed on planks on the floor. As were the lint works, the cookies are formed in heat, which contributes, however subtly, to their eroticism. But like the lint pieces, too, the cookies are unapologetically negligible, and, indeed, irretrievably perishable. The lint works were compared at the time to Joel Fisher's handmade paper and sculptural works, which elaborate on the nearly invisible filaments and hairs that constitute the paper's pulp;[33] many years later, Gabriel Orozco created a room-size installation from sheets of dryer lint hung on clothesline-like cords. But perhaps nothing is as close in spirit to Wilke's lint pussies and fortune cookies as Fluxus experimentations in the '60s with perishable and negligible materials, some of them edible.

The same impulses and associations characterize the more extensive series of vulva-shaped works Wilke fashioned from soft gray erasers. They include a group of collages using vintage postcards (1975). Old tinted photos of the New York Public Library on 42nd Street, the Lincoln Memorial, the Atlantic City boardwalk, a rural lane in Killarney and Franklin's Tomb in Philadelphia are among the backdrops for little bits of gray kneaded erasers (p. 42), which are formed into tiny labia and arranged like troops in formation, or shadow architecture, or thronging pedestrians, or falling rain. Though there is humor here, too, the main impression is of implacability: soft, pliable, diminutive, self-denigrating—indeed, tools of obliteration, as a related series' title insists—the erasers enact a series of maneuvers that cast deep shadows on sites and monuments of history, learning, and tourism. The same material is used to similar effect, if more abstractly, for the works called "Needed Erase-Her" (1973–77; p. 43), a pun on the "kneaded" (more precisely, kneadable) erasers from which they, too were made. For these, row upon row of gray vulvas were lined up in grids on white boards, a seemingly prim but, on closer inspection, delightfully naughty variation on the personalized Post-Minimalist grid: Eva Hesse eroticized. In other examples, the grids devolved into random clusters of eraser buds, like swarming microbes seen through a magnifying glass.

Wilke's recurring use of the grid as an ordering structure for the labial sculptures and her inclination to make facture—fingering, caressing, pouring, kneading—an evident and significant aspect of the work confirm her connection to Post-Minimalism. But it is in some ways easier to argue for her commonalities with the Pop artists. Along with her relationship to Oldenburg, there is the frank sexuality

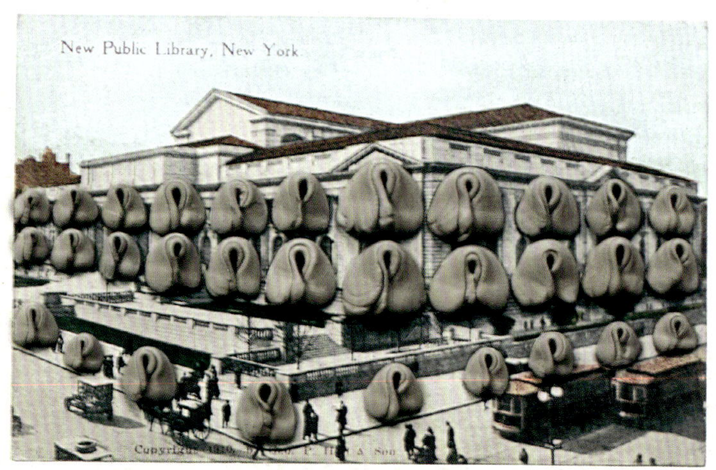

New York Public Library, 1971/73 (detail). Kneaded erasers on postcard on painted wood, 16 x 18 x 2 in.

USS Missouri, 1977 (detail). Kneaded erasers on postcard on painted wood, 16 x 18 x 2 in.

Atlantic City, New Jersey, 1975 (detail). Kneaded erasers on postcard on painted wood, 16 x 18 x 2 in.

opposite:
Needed-Erase-Her, 1974. Kneaded erasers on painted wood, 13½ x 13½ x 2 in. each; four of sixteen

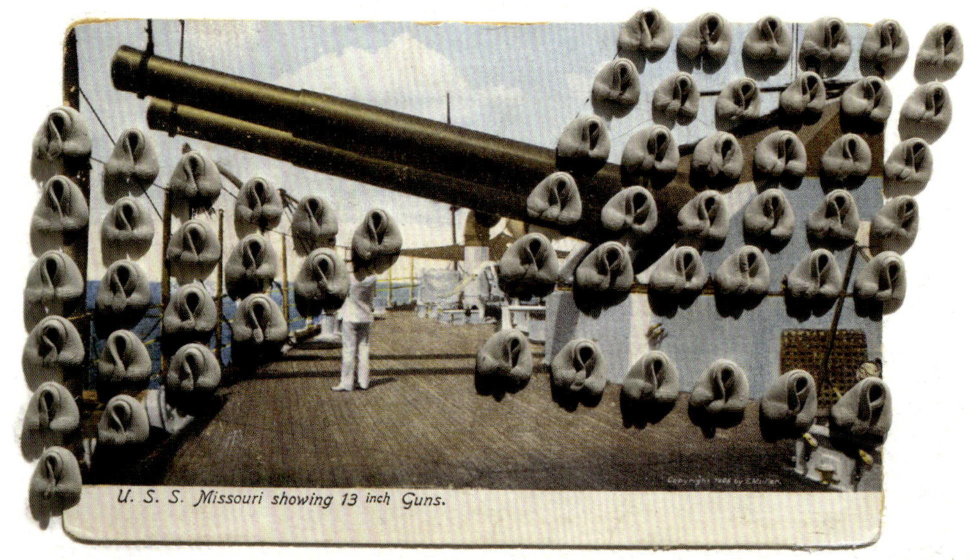

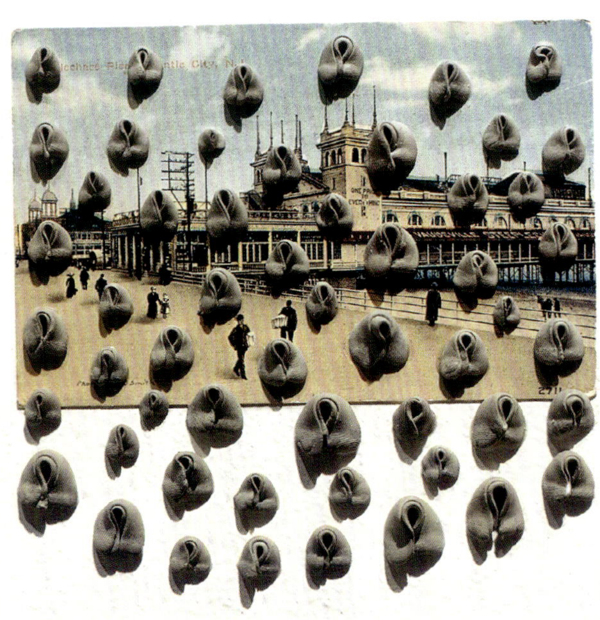

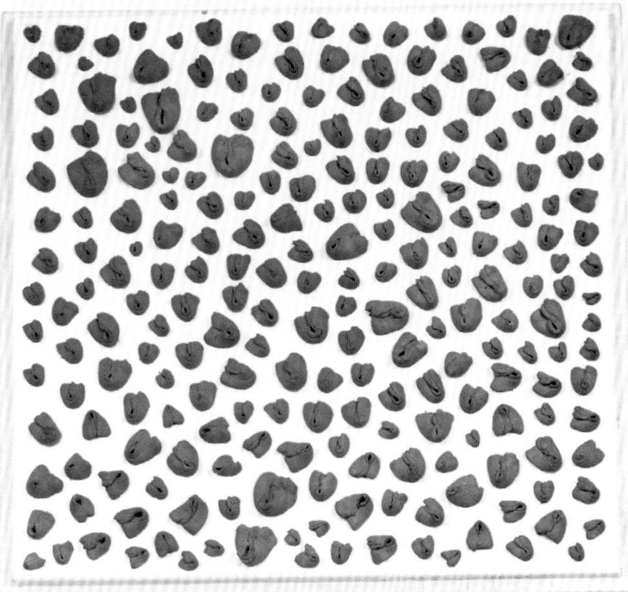

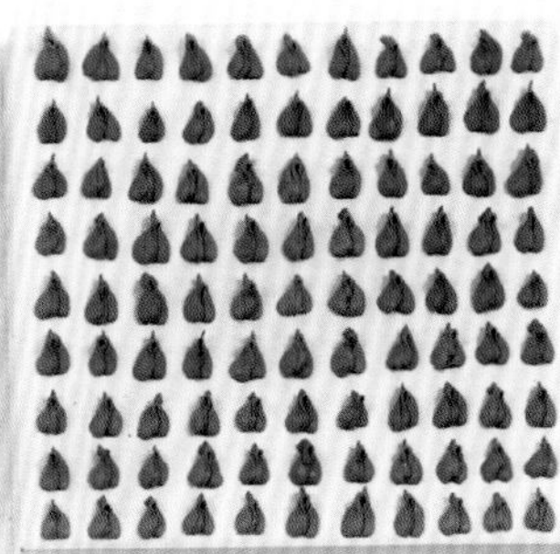

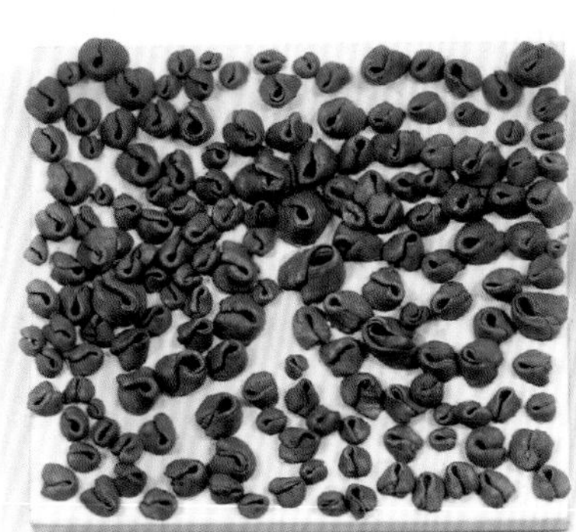

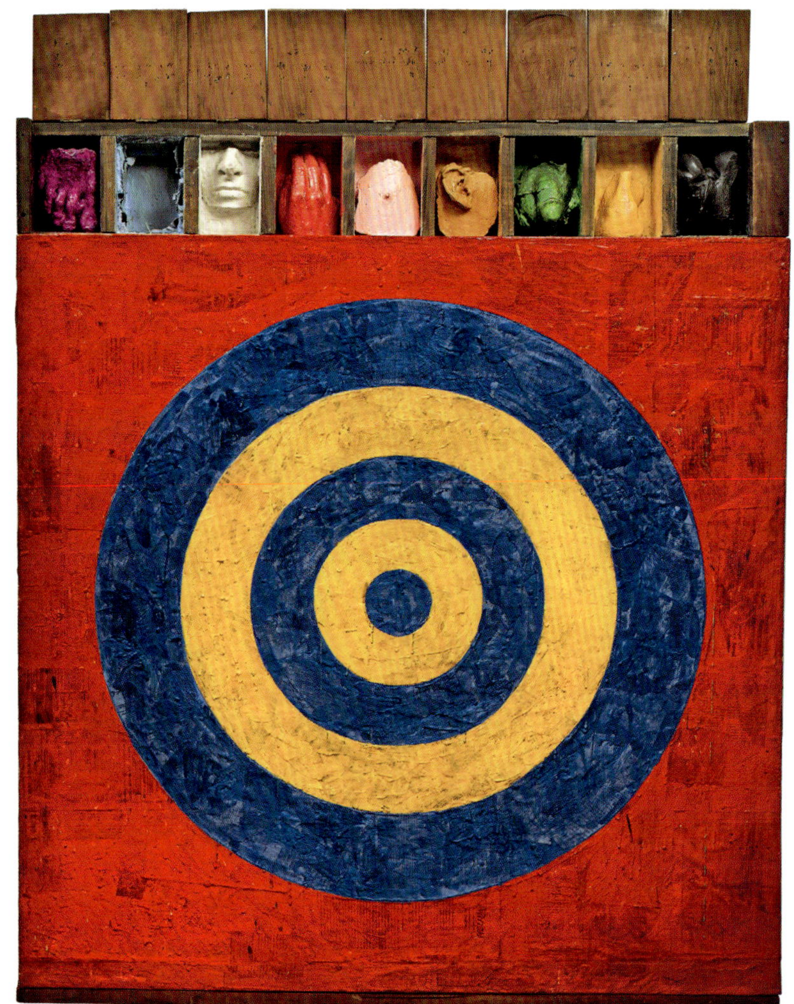

Jasper Johns, **Target with Plaster Casts**, 1955. Encaustic and collage on canvas with plaster objects, 51 x 44 x 3½ in.

that many Pop artists shared with Wilke (and other female and feminist artists of the period). Rauschenberg's paradigm-shifting *Bed* (1955) was, among many things, an eroticization of painterly abstraction; Johns's *Target with Plaster Casts* (also 1955) included in its tidy row of cast body parts a nipple and a penis with scrotum, and overall an unabashed exploration of the naked body; both are surely relevant features of the cultural landscape in which Wilke launched her career. The subsequent course of Pop would find such eroticism richly elaborated, from Warhol's Marilyns to Wesselmann's "Great American Nudes"; it is increasingly evident that Pop's sexual imagery was among its more forceful challenges to the macho cool, mandarin intellectualism and industrial technologies that loomed so large in the story of Minimalism and its successors.

At the outset, these connections were plain to some observers. Lucy Lippard, writing in the *Hudson Review* about the spate of erotic shows in 1966–67 that included the one in which Wilke's ceramic work was included—the shows were concentrated enough for Lippard to proclaim an "Erotic Season"[34]—nominated Oldenburg "one of the purest erotic artists working today."[35] In a revision of that essay for Gregory Battcock's landmark collection of essays *Minimal Art: A Critical Anthology* (where it made strikingly an odd fit), Lippard argued, on the one hand, that erotic art was most potent when abstract. Sex is "the fundamental mystical experience," she wrote, and "the cool tone—deceptively near neutral—of current eroticism is also that of the mainstreams of traditional erotic art." Moreover, "figurative art is at a disadvantage in the erotic arena when lascivious TV commercials, girdle ads, Hollywood movies, girlie, nudist or fetish magazines are available to any American with a couple of dollars in his pocket."[36] But on the other hand, and just as conclusively, she argued that the reigning prince of Pop sculpture was eroticism's exemplary artist. Wilke—whose ceramic work she had cited in passing in the original essay—was left out of the expanded version entirely.

For all the vagaries of Lippard's argument, the eroticism of such Pop artworks as Oldenburg's soft, yielding domestic objects, with their often phallic forms, seems undeniable, and—it seems equally clear—has parallels in the soft sculptures Wilke was making from latex and kneaded erasers. Even in their affection for popular culture, the Pop artists had common ground with Wilke. Donald Goddard, with whom Wilke became romantically involved in the middle 1970s, notes that he and Wilke shared a love of classic, big-budget movies of the 1930s and '40s. The appeal to her of early Hollywood spectacles is reflected, for instance, in several works that use lyrics from such songs as George and Ira Gershwin's "They Can't Take That Away from Me" (1937), introduced by Fred Astaire in the movie of the same year, *Shall We Dance?* ("the way you wear your hat / the way you sip your tea / the memory of all that / no they can't take that away from me" are the lines Wilke quotes). Her sister recalls hearing them sung by their mother and on the radio; the girls sang them together as they got older.[37] Goddard laughingly concedes that an unacknowledged source of Wilke's erotic "central-core imagery" might have been Busby Berkeley's movies, with their extravagant, colossal blooming flowers of women's legs.[38]

If anything blurs the line connecting Wilke to Pop, it is her own tacit denial. Unflaggingly, she insisted on playing for the biggest stakes, which at the outset of her career were firmly identified with Minimalist abstraction, and then devolved to its heirs, including Conceptualism as well as Post-Minimalism. The formal intelligence of her sculpture and, later, the theoretical reach of her photography were what she most wanted acknowledged. A contributing factor, perhaps, was the popular success—and critical condemnation—that greeted the internationally touring *Dinner Party*, which became, for many, an object lesson in what a feminist artist should avoid doing and saying. Labeled "kitsch" and "vulgar," both used as terms of unequivocal disdain—though with respect to certain Pop efforts, these very words could imply successful provocation—the *Dinner Party* can be seen as a benchmark for everything Wilke would avoid, including its inescapable sanctimony. Wilke never practiced feminism as a religion, but neither was she comfortable framing her work in the language used to situate Pop art within either the consumer marketplace or the visual culture.

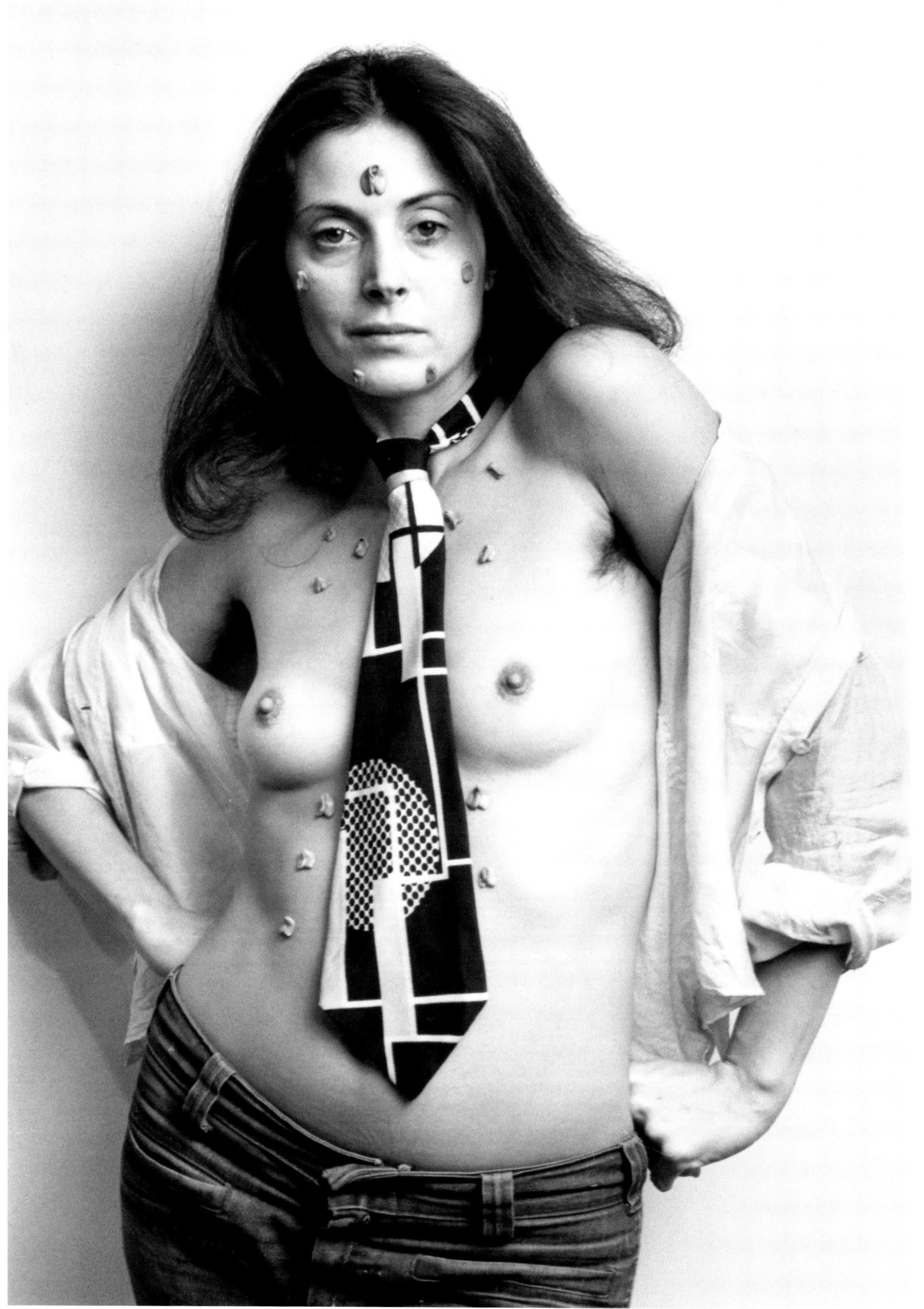

CHAPTER TWO

In Full

Whatever Wilke's qualms about Pop art, nothing could be more insouciantly Pop-like than bright-colored sticks of sugary chewing gum. And Wilke embraced the serendipity involved in its appearance in her work. As she explained it, "I was making gray sculptures . . . of kneaded erasers. When Edit deAk commented in a review about their anonymous grayness, I wondered how I could make them less depersonalized, and decided to buy some bubble gum." Its use presented itself spontaneously: "I was coming home and saw Peter Frank and Irving Sandler on the street. I picked them up and offered them a piece of gum. Peter was generous enough to take one and I said, 'Peter, you have to save it for me; I want to make an art piece from it.' He respected my seriousness and saved the chewed gum for me. That was when I made my first gum piece."[1]

Chewing gum became for a time as versatile and prominent a part of Wilke's material repertory as ceramics. Singly or severally, chewed sticks of gum were shaped, again with the quickest of maneuvers, into little, surprisingly delicate and subtly colored cunts that dotted grids demurely lined up on paper, stood in for berries and blossoms on color photographs of verdant foliage, and, everywhere they appeared, shifted her expressive language to embrace oral and as well as genital eroticism. Like the cake-decoration-based work that Pat Lasch began doing shortly thereafter, applying paint to canvas with pastry tubes, Wilke crossbred the seductions of eating, sex, and sugar. Her most notable application of gum, however, was not in faceless grids

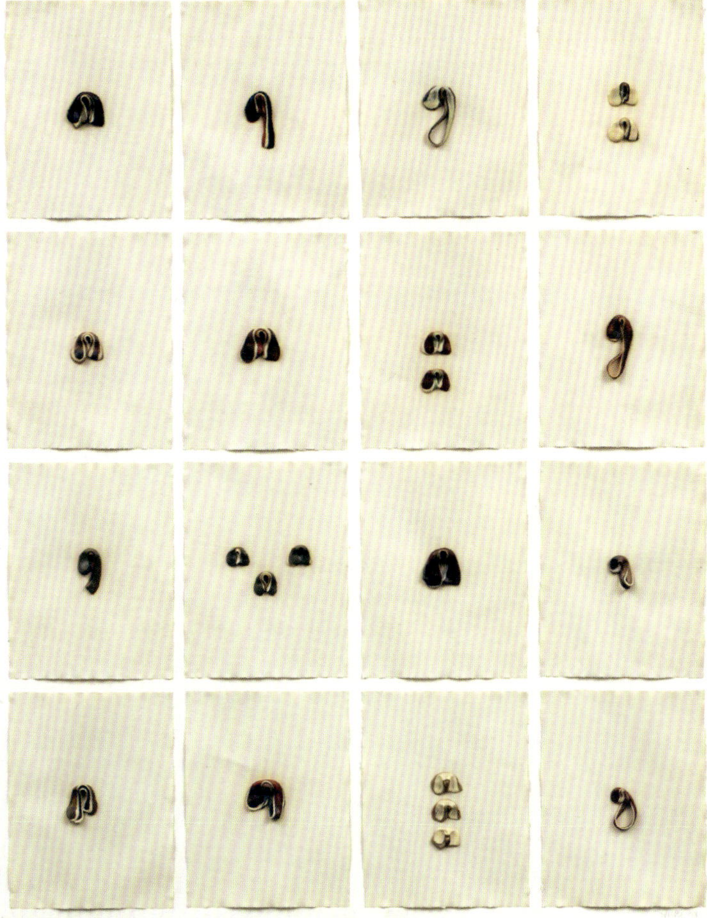

S.O.S. Starification Object Series #1, 1975. Chewing gum on rice paper in Plexiglas frame, 33¾ x 26 in. overall

California Series [Gum with grasshopper], 1976 (detail). One of six Kodachrome photographs mounted on board, 32½ x 28 in. framed

opposite:
S.O.S. Starification Object Series [Tie], 1974. Black-and-white photograph, 40 x 28 in. Part of **An Adult Game of Mastication** installation, 1974–75

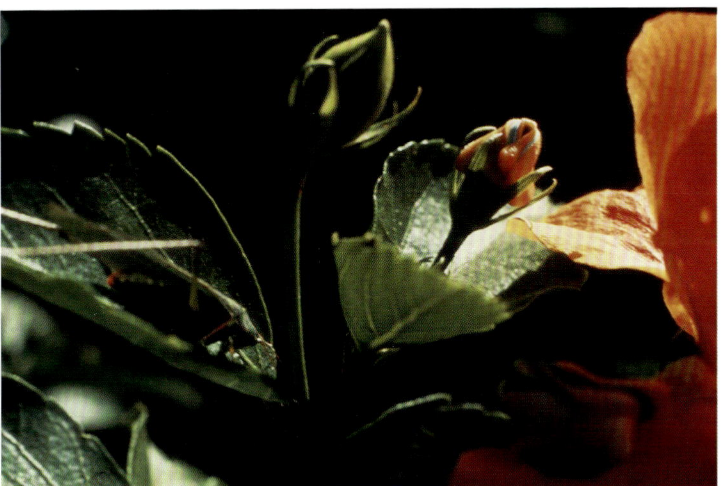

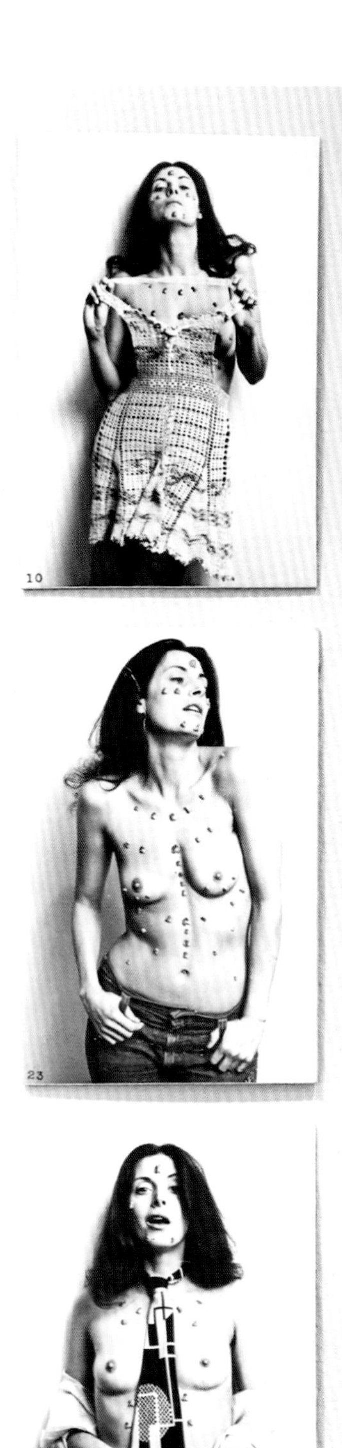

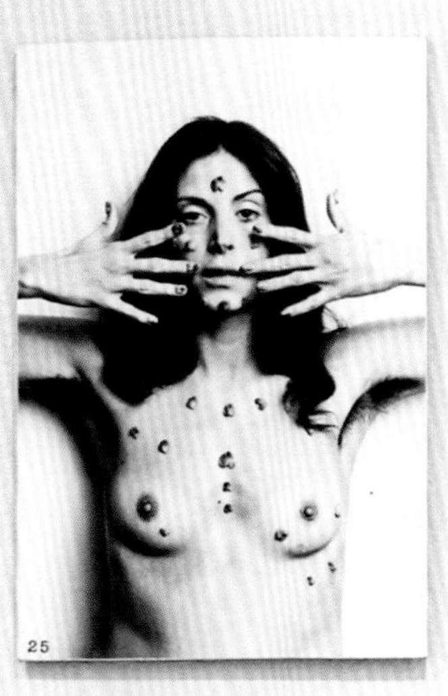

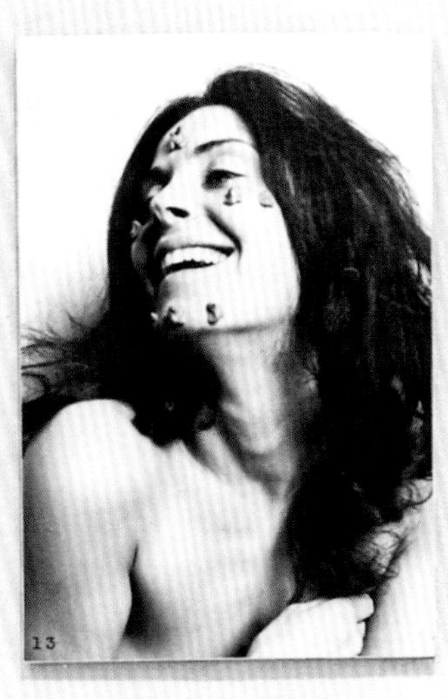

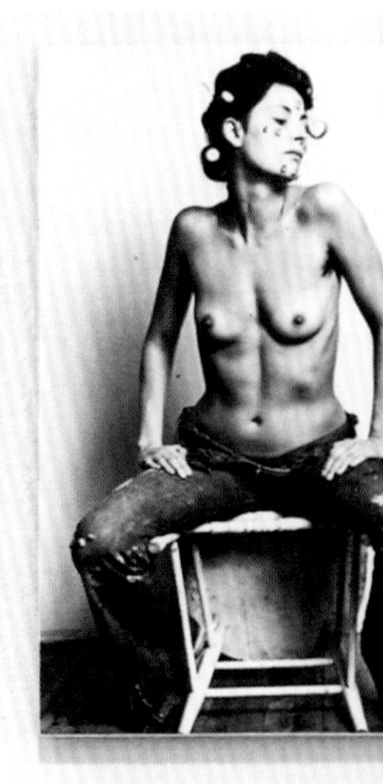

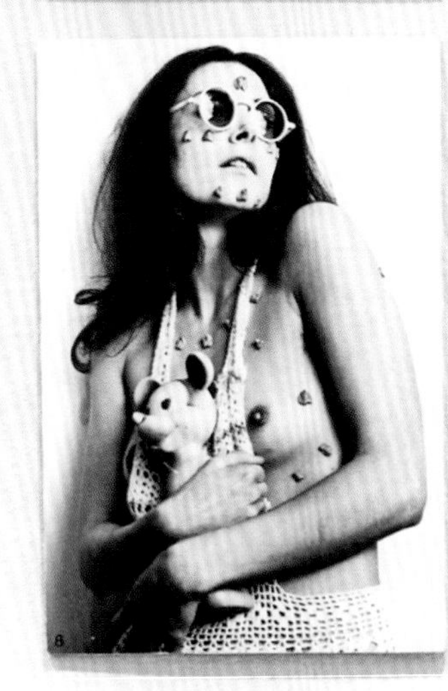

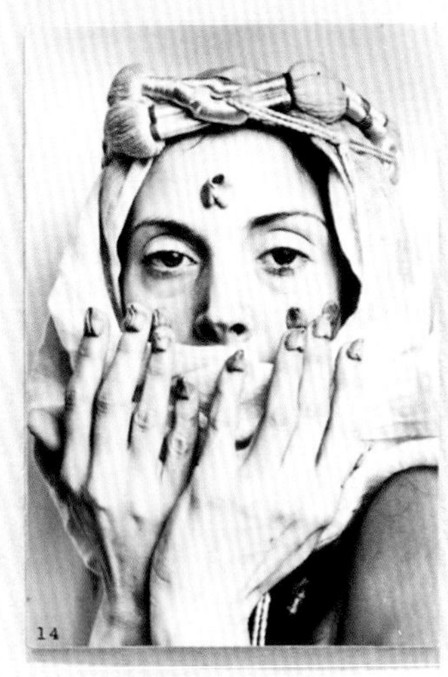

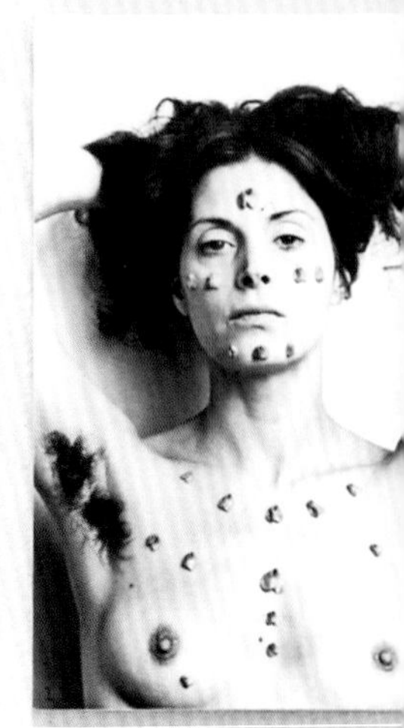

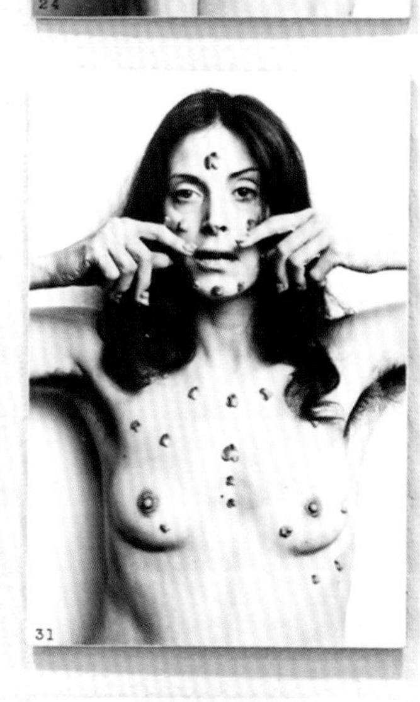

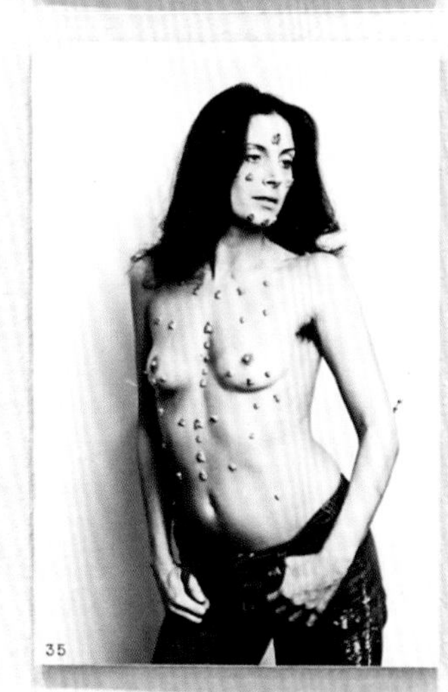

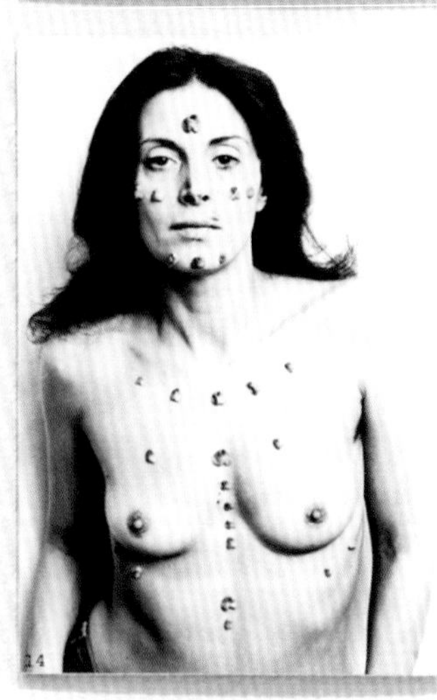

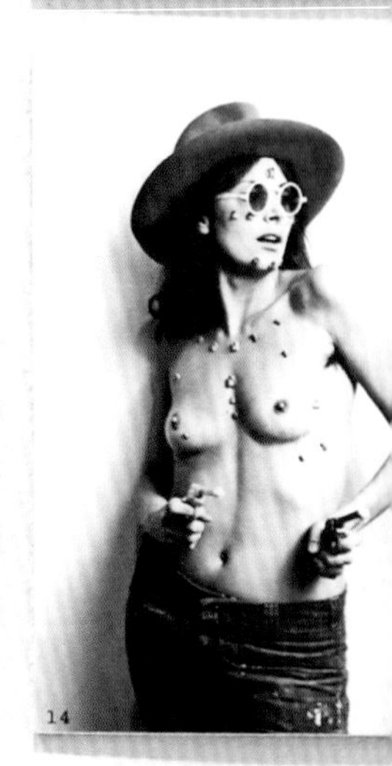

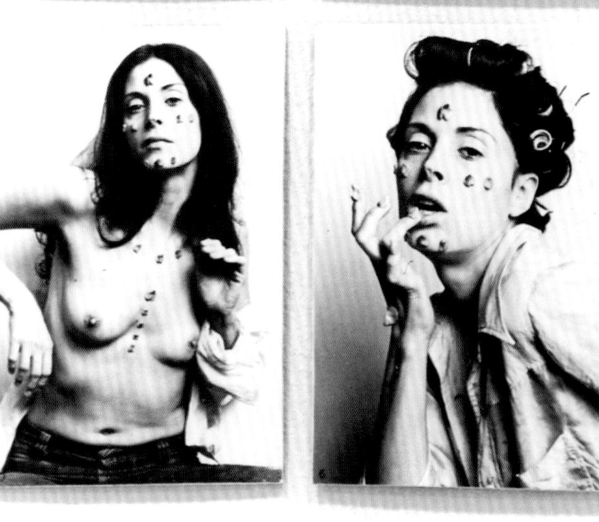

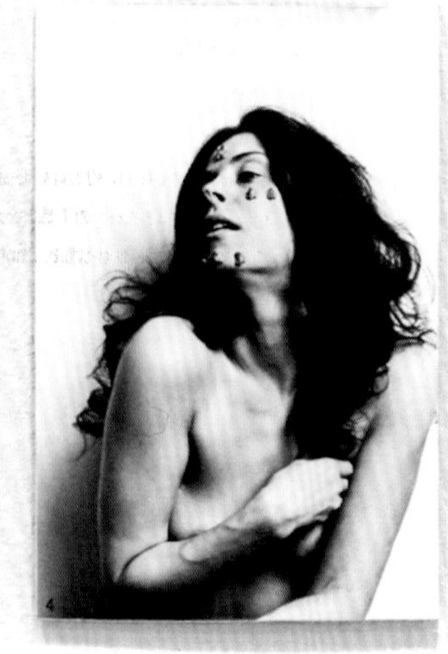

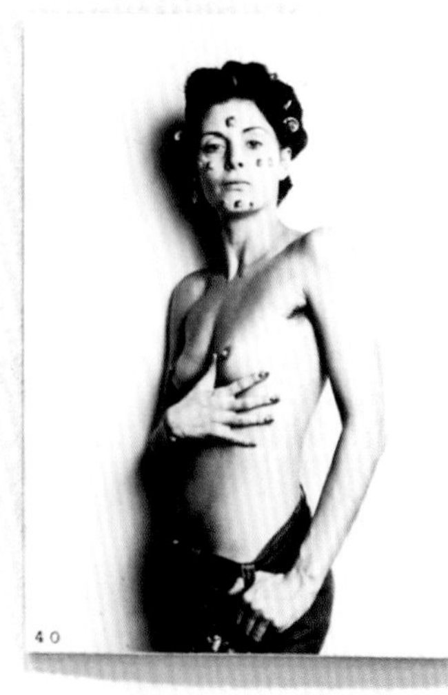

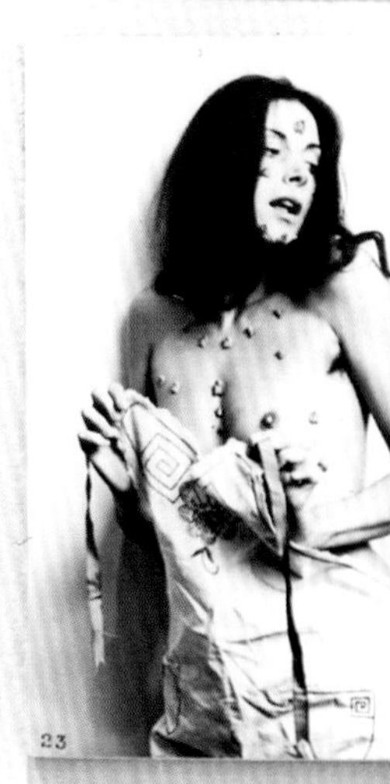

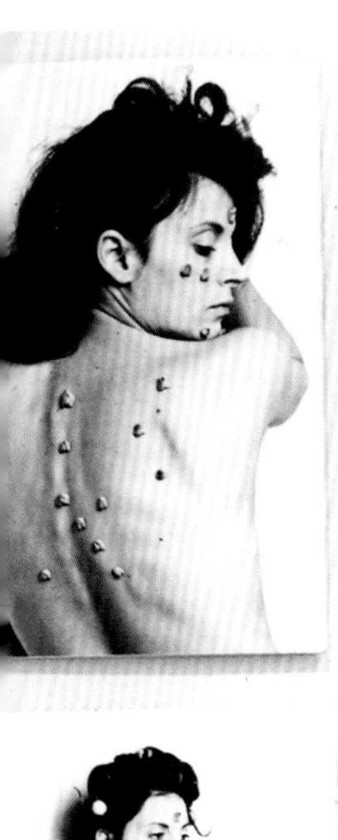
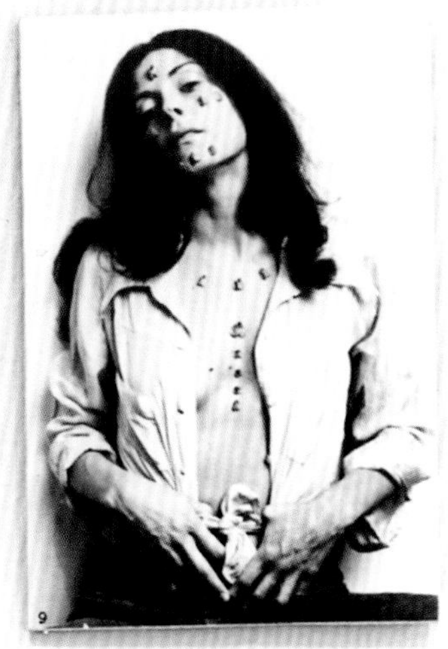
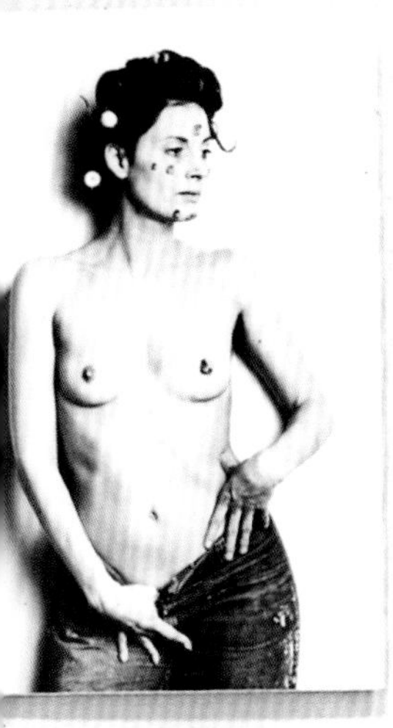
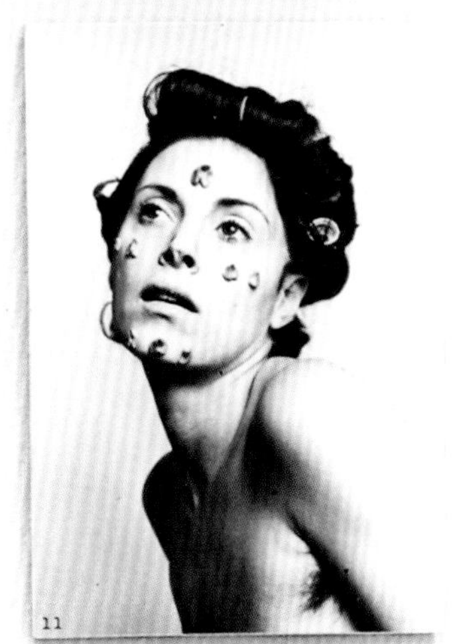
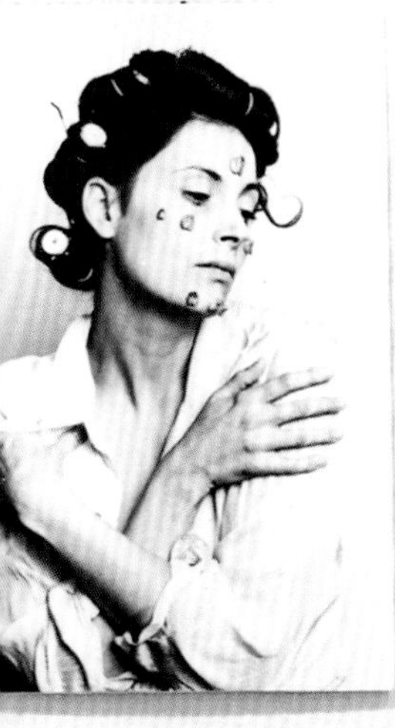
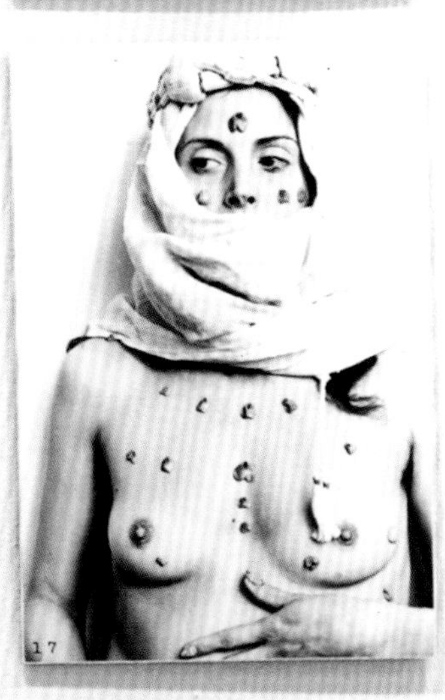
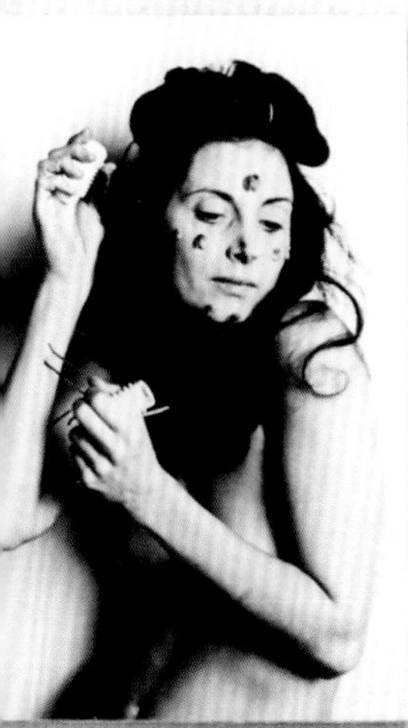
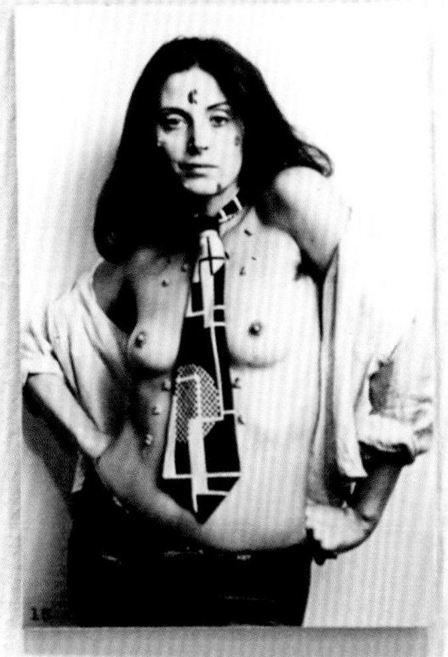
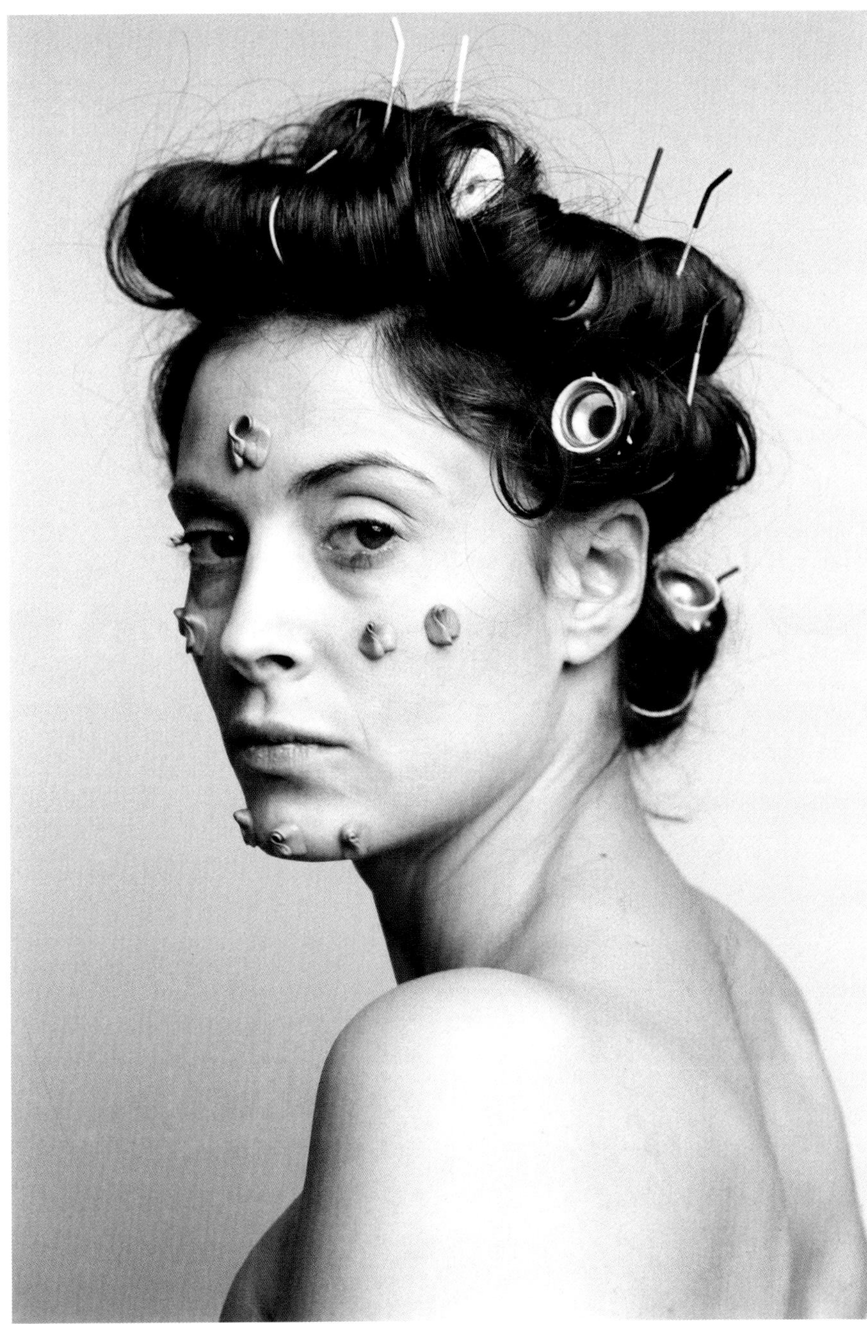

left:
S.O.S. Starification Object Series, An Adult Game of Mastication, 1974–75. Twenty-eight black-and-white photographs, 7 x 5 in. each, 35¾ x 42¾ in. framed

above:
S.O.S. Starification Object Series (Curlers), 1974. Black-and-white photograph, 40 x 27 in.

S.O.S. Starification Object Series [Guns], 1974. Black-and-white photograph, 40 x 28 in.

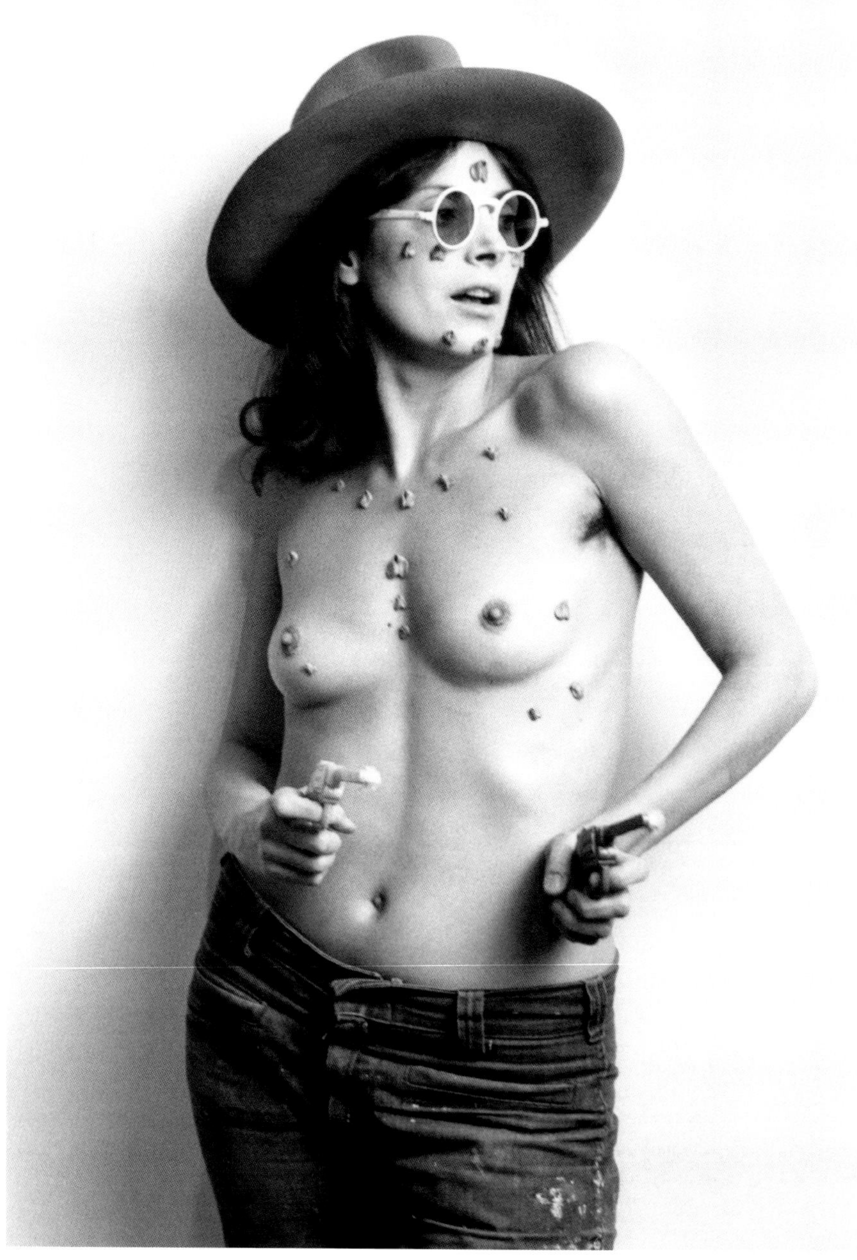

or photographs but on her own living body. With the "Starification Object Series" and other performance-based photographic work that she began to do at the same time—1974 and '75—Wilke stepped back from a narrow focus on the iconic attributes of female sexuality to explore, again as a fairly lonely pioneer, the implications of bringing her full naked body into public view. And, not for the last time, she spoke with slightly eerie fatefulness of the mortality the work represented: In a 1975 panel discussion, she observed, "One strength of American art right now is that we're involved with a culture that's about destructiveness. Some of the best art has a planned obsolescence. I alternate between the idea of some of my works disintegrating," an experience she'd just had with the early latex sculptures, "because it's hard to admit that you're going to die yourself." When Alan Saret, another participant, interrupted, "You identify your existence with your material. Your body is a material," Wilke replied, "That's what my chewing gum sculpture is about."[2]

The best known component of the "S.O.S." is a group of photographs Wilke

S.O.S. Starification Object Series (Veil),
1974. Black-and-white photograph, 40 x 28 in.

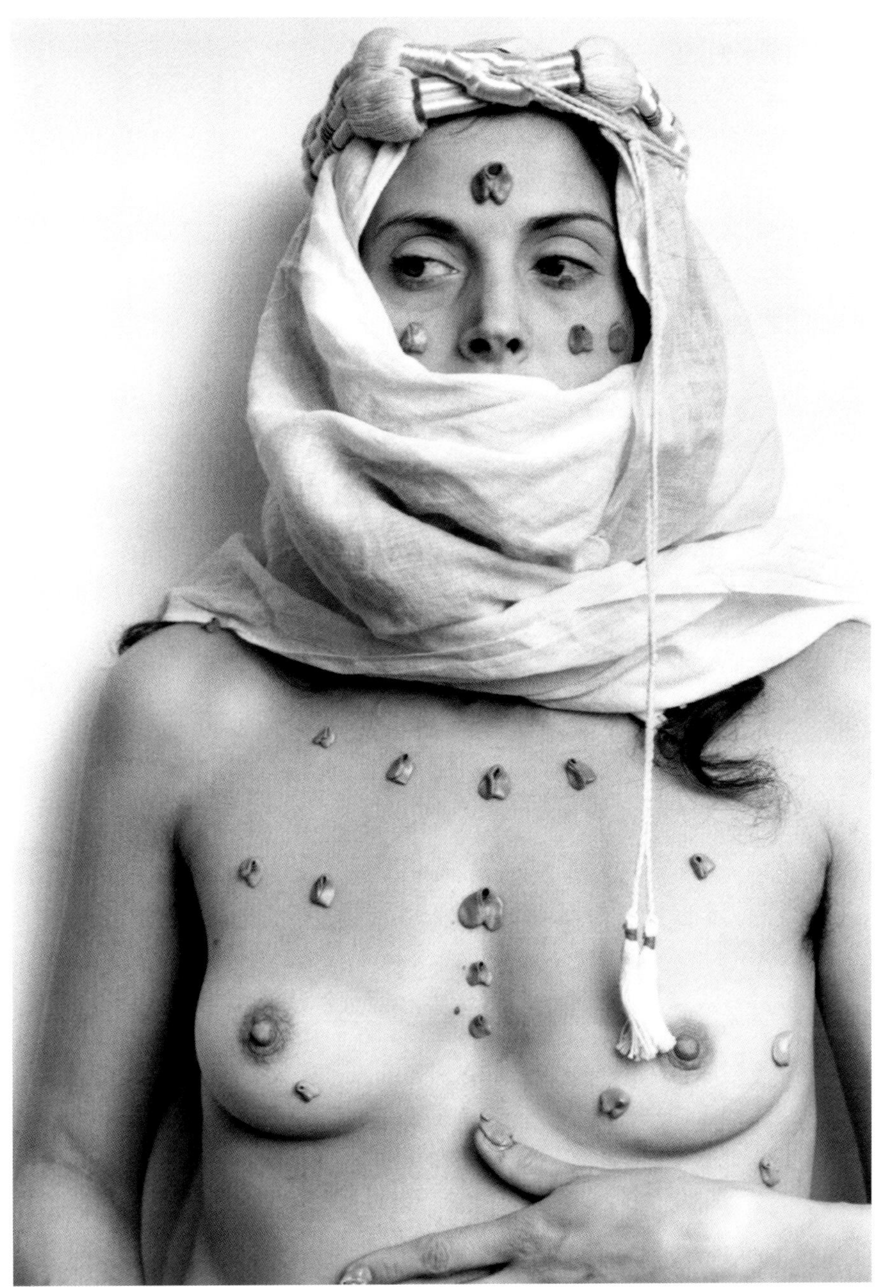

staged in 1974 (they were shot by Les Wollam), in which she struck a variety of fashion-model poses. She was topless in most, ornamented from chest to forehead and fingernails with shaped pieces of gum, sporting accessories ranging from an Arab headdress to a cowboy hat and two toy guns to hair curlers—the labors of female beautification were also the subject of work at this time by Annette Messager, Martha Rosler, Eleanor Antin (p. 66), and others. In some poses looking like jewels, in other like blemishes, or sores, the gum is, always, a beckoning license to touch. A work shaped by both mouth and hand, these tender buttons, scattered all over Wilke's body, suggest themselves as a means for operating the body they adorn—a very sticky form of connection between viewer and subject. The "S.O.S." photographs, like many of those Wilke had made for subsequent projects, were put to a number of different uses, including *Having a Talent*, a proposed subway poster for the School of Visual Arts in New York, where Wilke taught; in this image, she is wearing big sunglasses and a crocheted apron that reveals much of her body, and clutching a

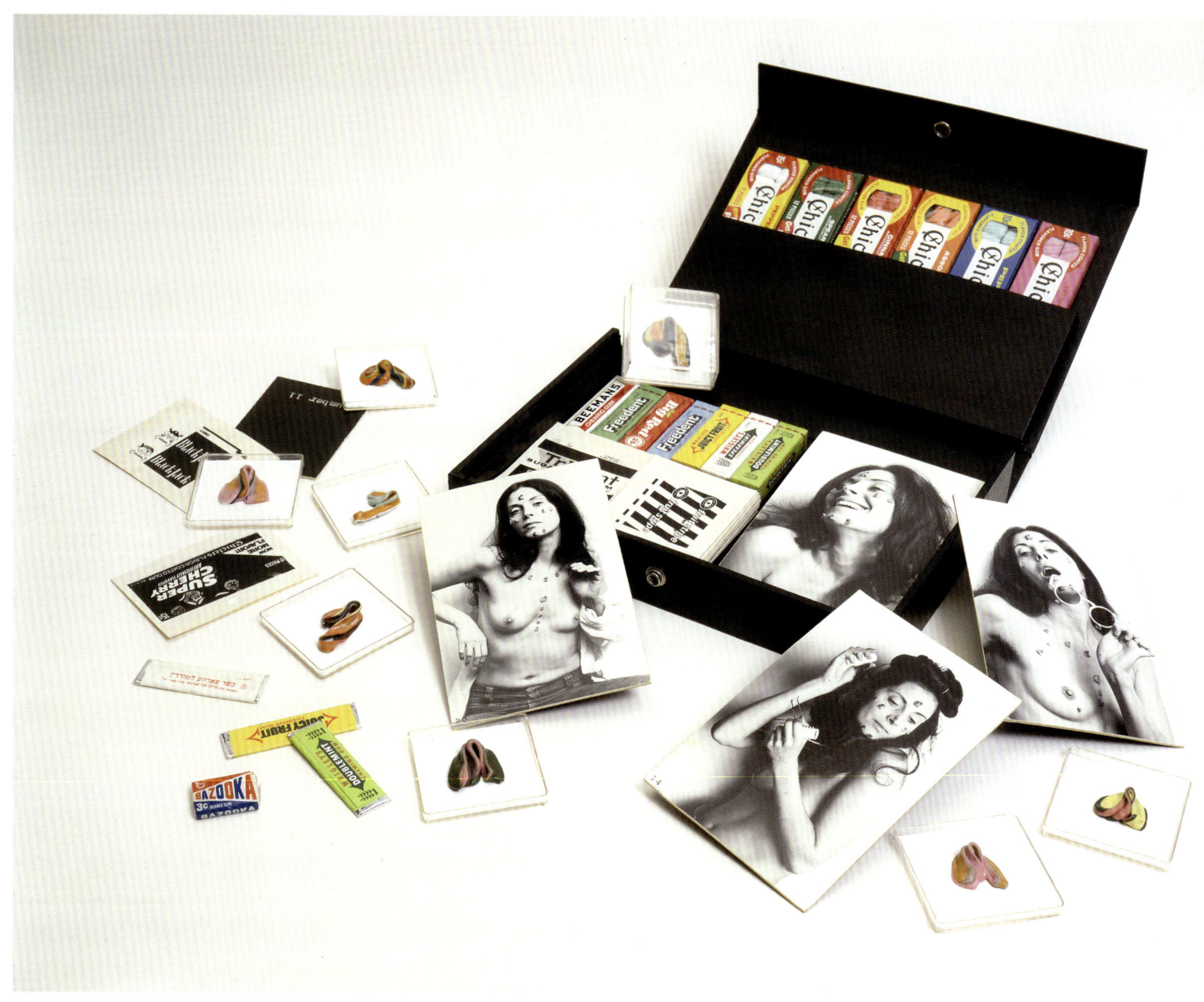

S.O.S. Starification Object Series: An Adult Game of Mastication, 1974–75. Game box, 12 x 8½ x 2 in., with photographs, chewing-gum sculptures, playing cards, and chewing gum, dimensions variable

Mickey Mouse doll; the decidedly mixed message includes signals of Pop and handicraft, childishness and adult eroticism, along with traditional female roles and their dismissal.

But as her exchange with Peter Frank suggests, the "S.O.S." works were fundamentally interactive. An early and especially important project in the series was a board game created for a January 1975 exhibition at the Clocktower (a then-new alternative art space in New York, of which P.S.1 soon became an outpost) called "Artists Make Toys." *S.O.S. Starification Object Series: An Adult Game of Mastication* (1974–75), a proposed multiple which exists only in a single prototype, was originally a boxed set of forty-eight numbered playing cards, twenty-eight photographs that were hung on the wall in a grid, a large single image, eight loose photographs of Wilke, six boxes of Chiclets, sixteen packs of stick gum (Juicy Fruit, Doublemint), and instructions for their use: each player was to choose a flavor and keep the package for identification, then chew, turn over a card to determine a pose, and give the

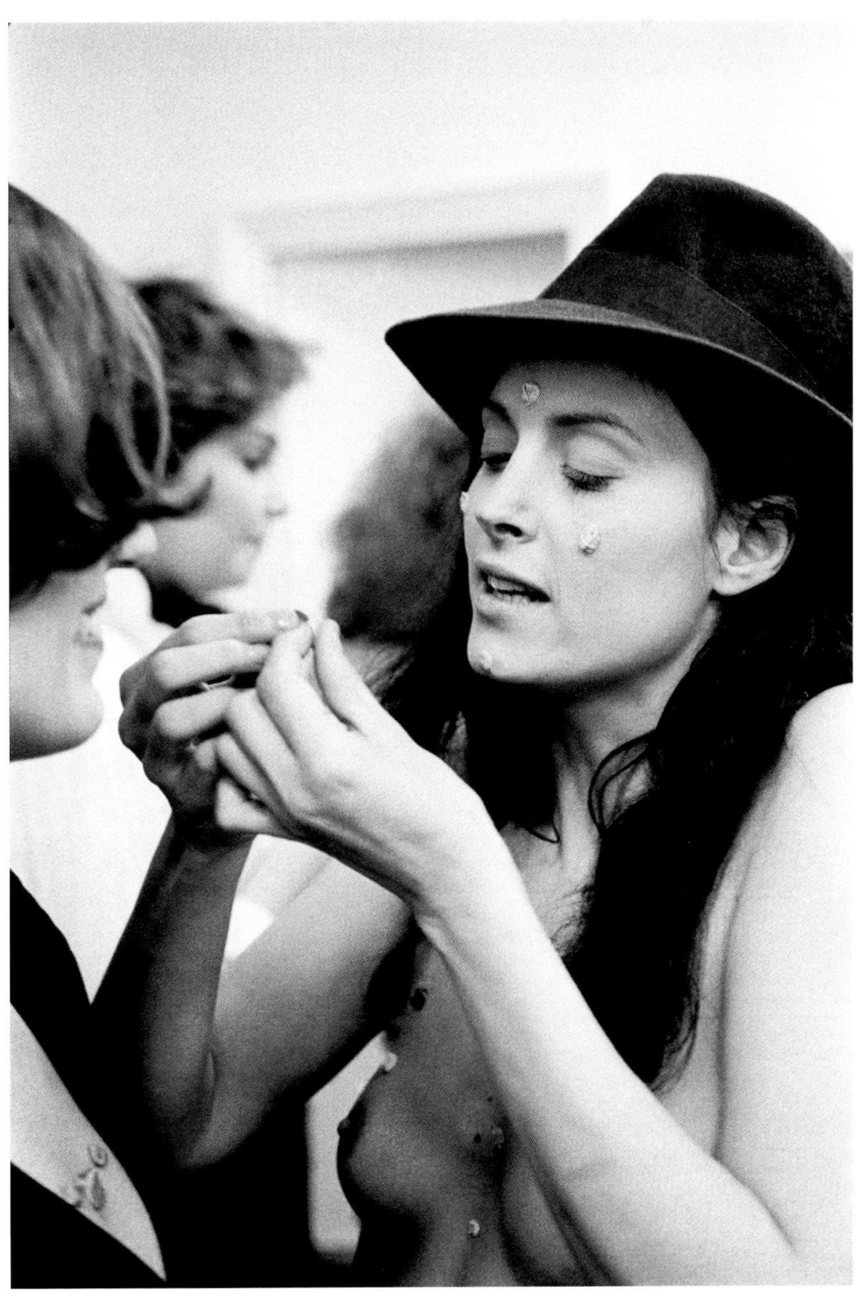

Hannah Wilke at **S.O.S.** performance, in the exhibition "5 Américaines à Paris," Galerie Gerald Piltzer, Paris, 1975

spent gum to the "starification object" (Hannah Wilke) to form and place on her body. (The installation also contained twelve chewing gum sculptures in Plexiglas boxes that Wilke later added to the box.) More radical than any other of its sexual innuendos was this last condition of the game, one that was never realized: to play it properly, one would "rent" the artist for $1,500 (a rather exorbitant sum, and more so then). As play progressed, she would grow increasingly "starified."

Other participatory works involving chewing gum were more public. For her contribution to the exhibition "5 Américaines à Paris" at the Gerald Piltzer Gallery in February 1975, Wilke, as a kind of emissary of American popular culture, brought 3,000 pieces of chewing gum for a three-hour performance at the opening. "Amid non-stop television cameras and flashing bulbs, she offered Super Cherry, Apple Green and chocolate flavored gum to the elegantly attired guests; the chewed pieces were either returned to Wilke who rapidly molded them into 120 'sexual sculptures' push-pinned to the wall or fastened to the artist's half nude body. The only jarring

My Count-ry 'tis of Thee performance in the exhibition "Four for the Fourth" at the Albright-Knox Art Gallery, Buffalo, July 4, 1976

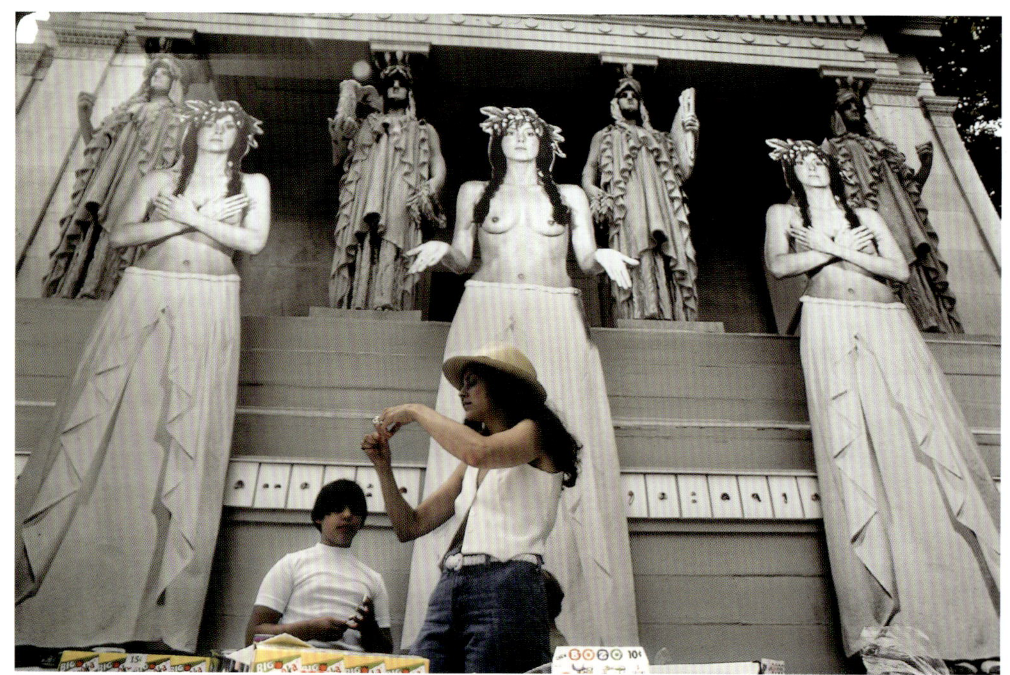

note was the intrusion of two male artists," reported the *Feminist Art Journal*.[3] For her solo show at Feldman in September of the same year, she put out a table full of gum for viewers to experiment with (and "use all five senses"); she also showed latex, ceramic, and kneaded-eraser work, as well as "S.O.S." photographs.

In keeping with its occasion—the nation's bicentennial Independence Day—Wilke's July 4, 1976 reprise of the "S.O.S." Paris performance dispensed with the darker aspects of the board game shown at the Clocktower and the subsequent participatory event, though not with their punning sense of humor or their spirited transgressions. An open-armed, unbuttoned declaration of independence, her *My Count-ry 'tis of Thee* (1976), performed/presented at the Albright-Knox Art Gallery in Buffalo, again involved communal chewing, this time mostly by children. Wilke collected the used gum for a frieze she created around the base of the museum's neoclassical portico, where eleven-foot-high cutout photographs of the toga-clad, bare-breasted artist, a garland of laurel leaves on her head, alternated with the caryatids by Augustus Saint-Gaudens supporting its pediment. (It was on this appearance by Wilke that Cindy Sherman, a 1976 graduate of SUNY Buffalo, might have first encountered her work.)

As usual with Wilke's provocations, the gum events were challenging on several levels. Writing about the Feldman show, the critic Mark Savitt mused, "One imagines . . . the reprimanding reaction of hostile parents, 'Didn't I tell you never to accept candy from a stranger?'"[4] The comment suggests the breach of boundaries she staged between the public encounter and intimate exchange; it also gets at the event's latent (and perhaps unintended) sexual menace: we all know what those strangers offering candy are really after. Other kinds of propriety were challenged as well—Savitt might have added, "Didn't I tell you that chewing gum in public isn't polite?" Wilke, whose own gum chewing was mostly done on camera, never tried to cover up or apologize for her background, her family, or her slight but unmistakable "New York" accent (though the inflection has as much to do with class as region);

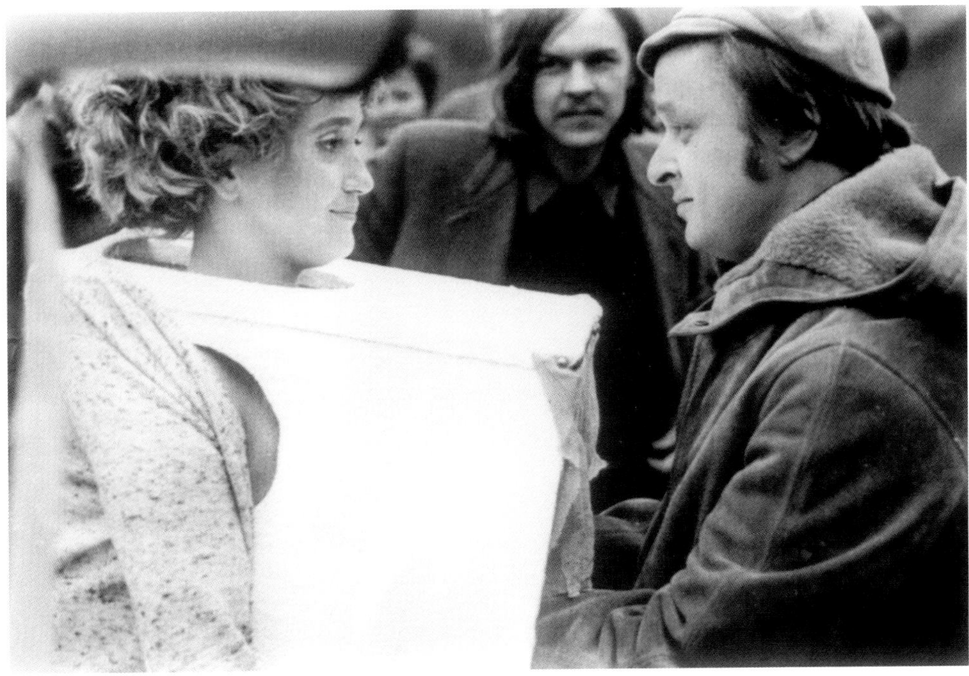

VALIE EXPORT, Tapp und Tast-kino, 1968–71. Still from black-and-white film, 2 min.

her self-exposure was, if not comprehensive, certainly unsparing. If she felt like chewing gum before an audience she would, whether or not it evoked a streetwise middle-class adolescent in an art world that then, as now, was run by a moneyed elite.

Of the many kinds of discomfort the chewing gum exchanges caused, one was, arguably, less acute in the mid-1970s than it would be if staged a generation later. The ravages of AIDS, and the specter of deadly untreatable viruses spreading inadvertently—or otherwise—in a world grown exponentially more connected, have made the kinds of physical exchanges enacted by Wilke and others seem almost unthinkable today. (It is hard to imagine a contemporary production of Carolee Schneemann's famous *Meat Joy* performance of 1964, for instance, which involved not just fairly indiscriminate physical contact but also an abundance of raw meat.) Having become more health conscious and, at an even steeper rate of increase, more litigious, we have also become more squeamish. Though fears about germs and sanitary conditions may seem unrelated to sexual prudishness, the inclinations have grown together. They are part of a dauntingly knotty complex of cultural concerns —religion certainly comes into the mix; so does greater sensitivity to non-Western sensibilities, which are as often conservative as otherwise—that has reshaped, or at least complicated, the rules for acceptable self-display and interpersonal contact.

Characteristic of Wilke's work is the range of associations she invoked with the "Starification Object Series" title, from self-celebration (as a star) to subjection to the kinds of elective ritual injury that tribal cultures sometimes practice (scarification) with their ties to Western forms of painful beautification procedures, and including other, far more brutal forms of damage. (So obviously that it is seldom remarked, "S.O.S." is, after all, an urgent call for rescue.) In a later text, she linked the chewing-gum "scars" to the branding of numbers onto the arms of Nazi concentration camp victims: "as a Jew, during the war, I would have been branded and buried had I not been born in America. Starification-Scarification."[5] Comparisons can be made

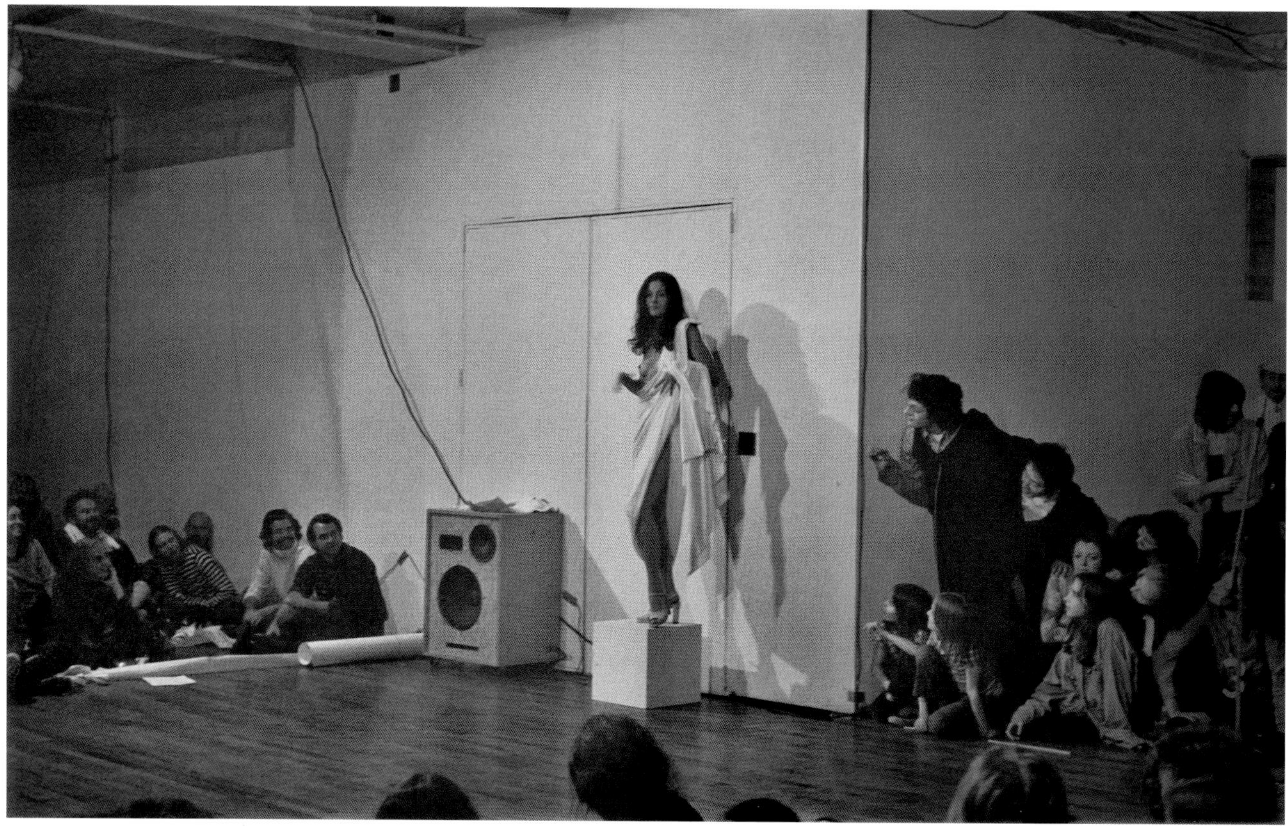

above:
Hannah Wilke performing **Super-t-Art** at the Kitchen, November 1974

opposite:
Hannah Wilke Super-t-Art, 1974. Twenty black-and-white photographs, 6½ x 4½ in. each, 40¾ x 33 in. framed

between the chewing-gum game and several roughly contemporary important performances, including Yoko Ono's *Cut Piece*, first presented in 1964, in which she invites audience members to cut off pieces of her clothing; VALIE EXPORT's touring *Tapp- und Tast-Kino* (Tap and Touch Cinema) (1968–71; p. 55), in which a cardboard box with an opening in front, worn around the artist's torso, allowed pedestrians in various European cities to touch her chest in public; and Marina Abramovic's *Rhythm O* (1974), in which she allowed gallery visitors to use a range of objects—a rose, a chain, an axe, a gun—in any way they wished. As in these precedents, Wilke's chewing-gum works, the *Mastication* game especially, invited the audience into a chancy encounter, and (literally) put all the cards all in their hands.

At roughly the same time that she developed the "S.O.S." works, Wilke created another series of striking and widely circulated photographs; these arose from what she described as her first performance, which was presented on the occasion of a November1974 event called "Soup & Tart." Organized by Jean Dupuy at the Kitchen (another young New York nonprofit space), it included roughly three-minute performances by more than three dozen artists, including Philip Glass (as an unaccompanied vocalist); Gordon Matta-Clark (sawing open a cardboard box to reveal a house-shaped cake, which he sawed in turn into slices, to much affectionate laughter and wild applause); and Alan Saret (playing an acoustic guitar and looking soulful). The nearly 400 guests were served soup and tarts, and there was much milling around; seating was on the floor. On the evidence of a documentary videotape, performers appeared more or less alphabetically; Wilke was last. When she appeared, in high-heeled sandals (earth shoes were the order of the day) and nothing else apart

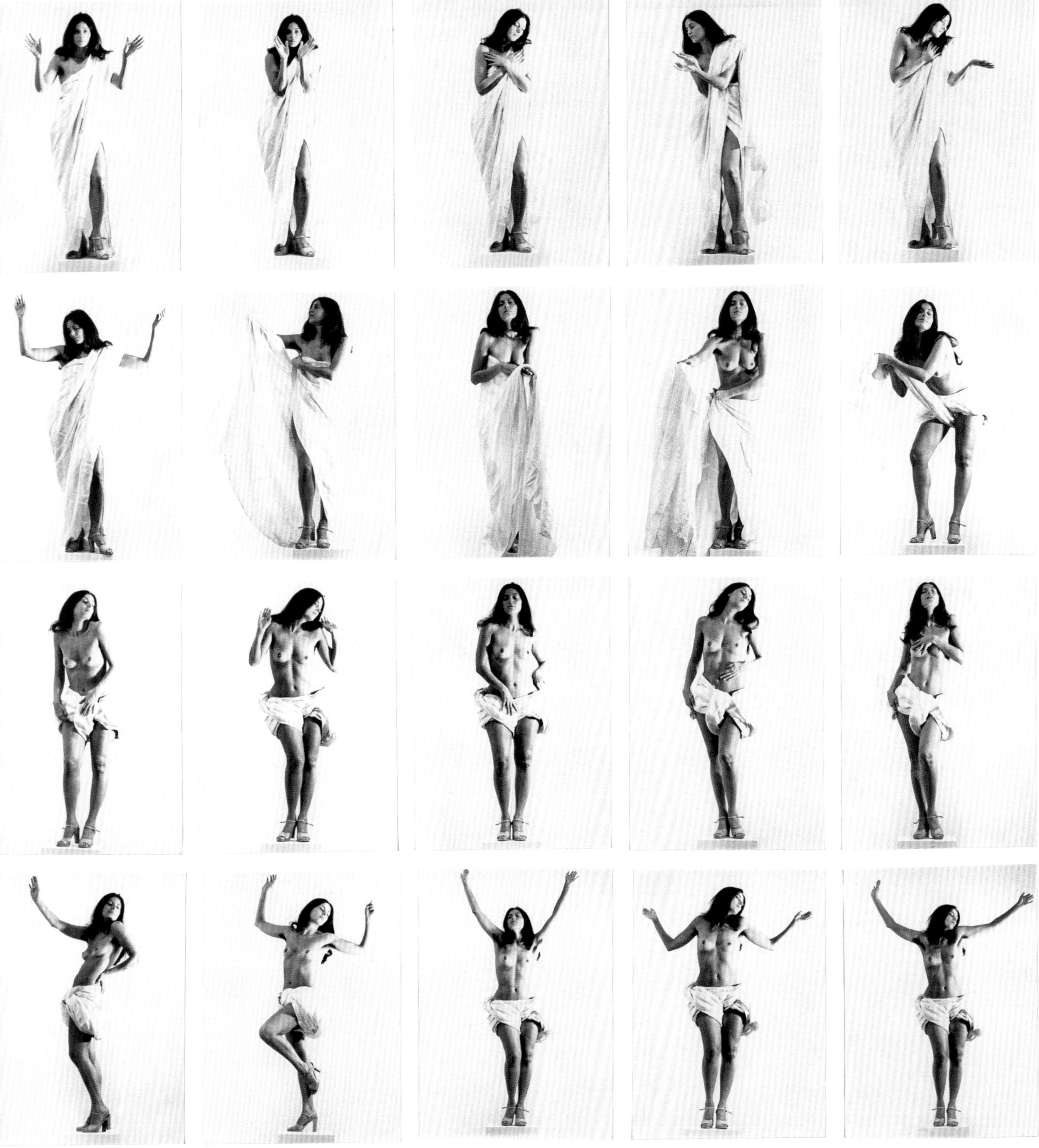

from a large cloth subsequently identified as both a tablecloth and a bed sheet, she was greeted with a few loud, isolated guffaws, then nervous silence. As she stepped onto a spotlit pedestal and progressed through a series of exaggeratedly sexy moves, pausing for each, there was intermittent laughter, mostly male. At the end, when she spread her arms into the shape of a cross, a brief spell of deadly quiet was followed by resounding—relieved?—applause (admittedly, the entire performance program was being cheered).

This event, which Wilke called *Super-t-Art*, was restaged for twenty photographs taken by Christopher Giercke; for these images, Wilke struck a series of calculated poses that progress from chaste Greek goddess to ecstatic innocent to crucified Christ; the cloth variously becomes a toga, diaper, lingerie, and loincloth (pp. 56–57). In one of the sexiest and most triumphant, Wilke strikes a pose very like Botticelli's famous Venus. It may be relevant that Wilke wrote a term paper, which survives, on Botticelli; it begins by drawing attention to "the growing personal pride both he and his contemporaries sought in their work," which "caused Botticelli to add his signature to the paintings he created, distinguishing himself from both the other artists during this period and the past." She also noted "the wistfulness of the mood" of the renowned Venus, which "seems to recall the Florentine fear of a loss in beauty."[6] Noteworthy, too, is another historical comparison, made by the *New York Times* critic John Rockwell in his review of the Kitchen event, where he singled out "Hannah Wilke's not entirely parodistic re-creation of semi-nude Victorian erotic tableaux-vivants."[7] One can't help thinking of Wilke's appreciation for the novels of Thackeray and Goethe featuring such tableaux. Another connection that comes to mind is more contemporary, and perhaps more likely to have been on Wilke's mind as well: her final, arms-out pose recalls Chris Burden's headline-grabbing self-crucifixion on the hood of his Volkswagen Beetle in a piece he called *Trans-fixed*, performed just months before Soup & Tart. (Earlier in 1974, Burden exhibited at Ronald Feldman gallery, just before Wilke's show there.)

One sequel to *Super-t-Art* was *Give: Hannah Wilke Can. A Living Sculpture Needs to Make a Living*, staged at the Susan Caldwell Gallery in 1978 as part of a fundraising event for the Public Art Fund. A documentary photograph shows Wilke seated on a stool, which is on a low platform; she is wearing a sleeveless, low-cut black dress and pointy shoes, and looking sultry—hardly an emblem of need. Dollar bills and coins are scattered about, and a boom box sits in front of her. But arranged around the perimeter of the platform are examples of *Hannah Wilke Can*: tin cans with slots in their tops, of the kind used for soliciting change for worthy causes like UNICEF and the Salvation Army; these are wrapped with a *Super-t-Art* photo in which Wilke looks especially radiant. Perched on her heels in a curvy contrapposto, the sheet draped around her hips, she gazes skyward and smiles, fondling one breast.

The dismal economy of the mid-1970s, particularly in New York, is the background for the flowering of both non-commercial, "alternative" art spaces and non-traditional art forms, including performance, and also, more particularly, for

Hannah Wilke Can, 1978. Photo reproduction on coin collection can, 6 x 3 in.

Give: Hannah Wilke Can—A Living Sculpture Needs to Make a Living, 1978. Photograph from a benefit performance for Public Art Fund for City Walls at Susan Caldwell Gallery, New York, May 22, 1978

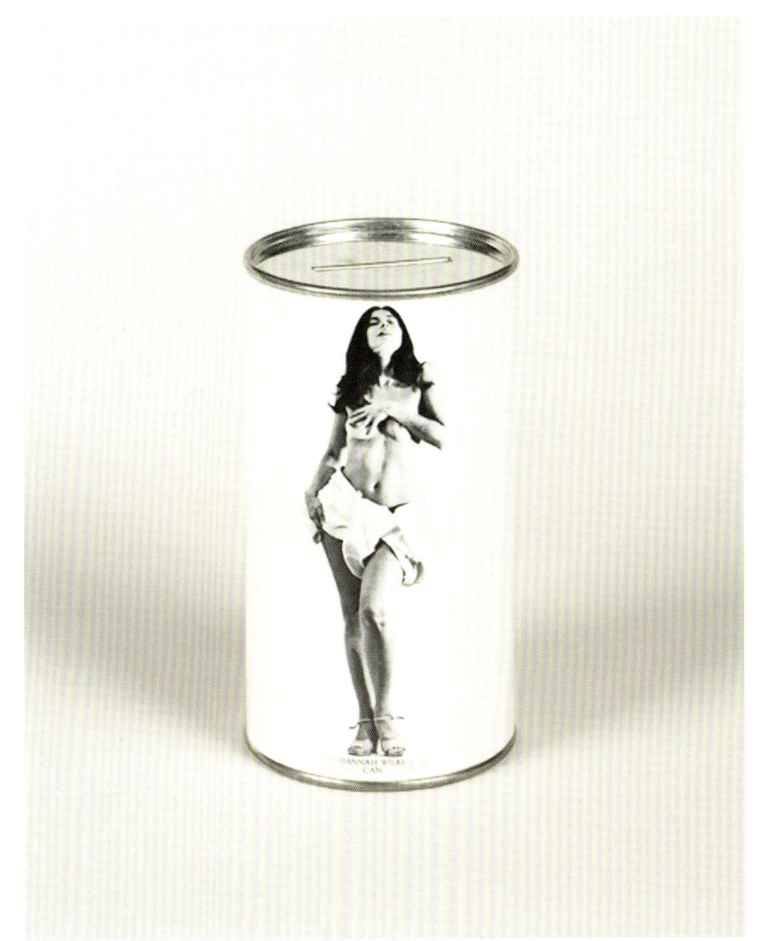

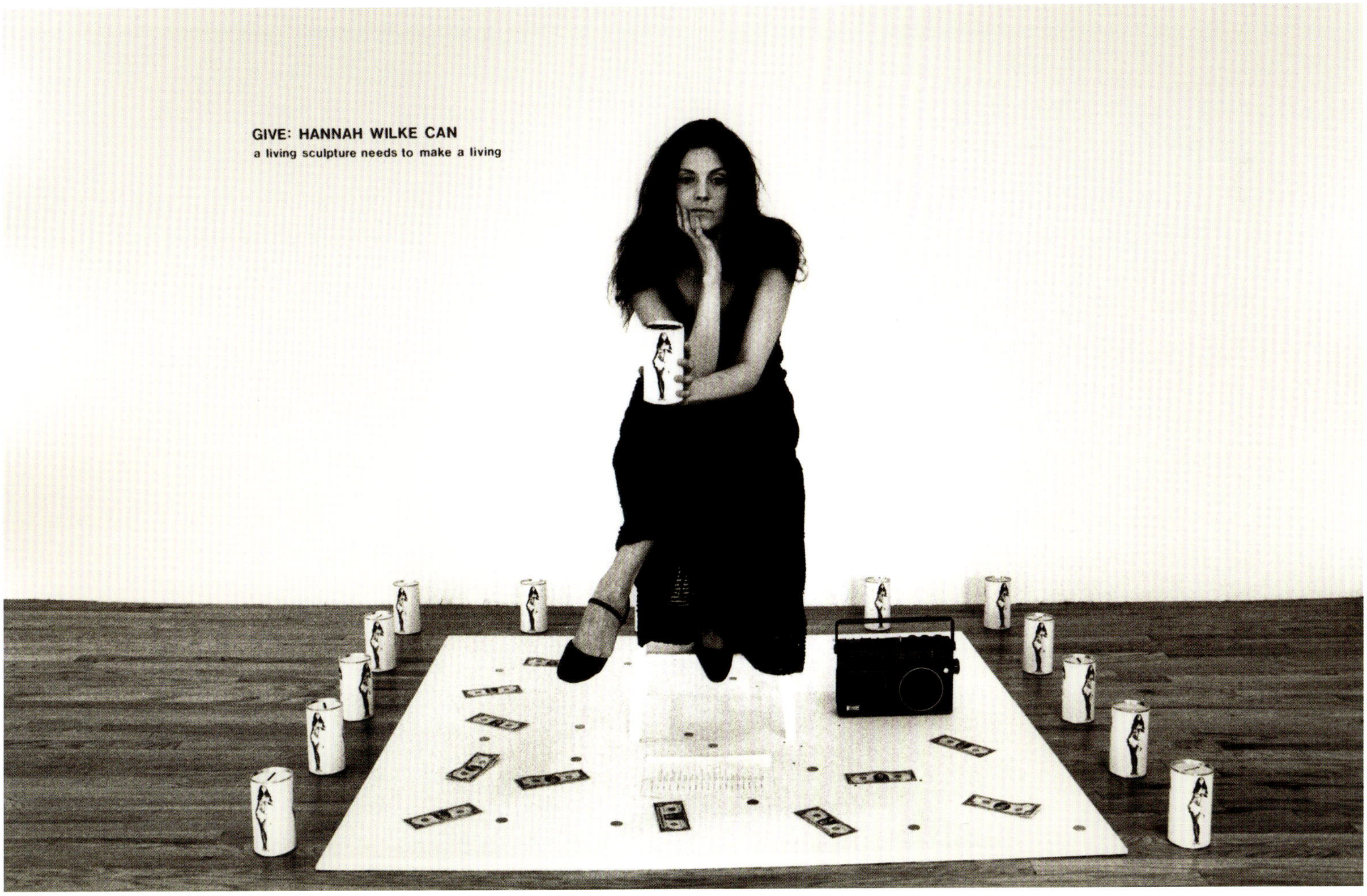

GIVE: HANNAH WILKE CAN
a living sculpture needs to make a living

Conceptualist work that focused on the mechanisms of the art market. Among the most relevant to *Give: Hannah Wilke Can* is Dan Graham's "Income (Outflow) Piece" (1969–73), a series of text pieces that invited viewers to invest in Dan Graham, Inc., at $10 per share, and participate in a commercial experiment that would circumvent the gallery system. But Wilke's inclinations were less toward the kind of oblique Marxism expressed in the projects undertaken by Graham, Robert Smithson, and others, and more toward the heavily ironic self-merchandizing of Gilbert & George, the British "Living Sculpture" duo whose first success came with the performance of the vaudeville song "Under the Arches" in 1969. Like them, Wilke was negotiating several kinds of desire—her own and her audience's, for material and sensual satisfaction—while seeming to occupy a position outside the circle in which those deals would be struck.

If maintaining this ambiguous position depended on the protocols of the art world, Wilke, like Gilbert & George, and like Graham as well, was also determined to address an audience far more diverse and unpredictable than the one that would appear at a New York art gallery. Witness an occasion on which Wilke took a *Hannah Wilke Can* with her for an academic speaking engagement. "I went up to Ithaca and Cornell University," she reported in 1978, "and, after my lecture, I was on the street with my can . . . and I just stopped the first car and begged, at the red light, and this older man gave me the money and started to laugh, he said, laughing, 'that's some can. That's pretty good.' I asked this hippy guy, he turned out to be an art student, and he gave me all his money . . . he just kept putting it in, . . . He understood immediately, he was as drunk as could be, and he just took all his money out of his pockets. It was a very beautiful thing."[8]

That the spirit of these and other similar actions is perhaps better characterized as guerilla-style street theater than sober social analysis—and that as much as she cared about professional success, she was capable of fairly bold provocations against her colleagues—is evident in such incidents as the one that took place at Lynda Benglis's 1975 opening at Paula Cooper Gallery in New York. Benglis had already posed for a 1974 announcement card in a pants-around-her-ankles cheesecake shot taken by Annie Leibovitz when she ran an instantly notorious ad, at her own (considerable) expense but titled to look like it was paid for by Paula Cooper, in the November 1974 issue of *Artforum* magazine. It shows Benglis naked except for novelty sunglasses and holding a giant double-headed dildo between her legs, an image (and a use of magazine pages that was an uncomfortable hybrid of the commercial and the editorial) that aroused considerable controversy. A letter signed by five of the magazine's six associate editors, including Rosalind Krauss and Annette Michelson (both of whom shortly thereafter resigned to launch the journal *October*), condemned the ad's "vulgarity," and lamented that while "*Artforum* has, over the past few years, made conscious efforts to support the movement for women's liberation," the publication of the image "reads as a shabby mockery of the aims of that movement."[9] The episode still arouses strong feeling. In a series of interviews con-

Lynda Benglis, **Artforum** advertisement, November 1974

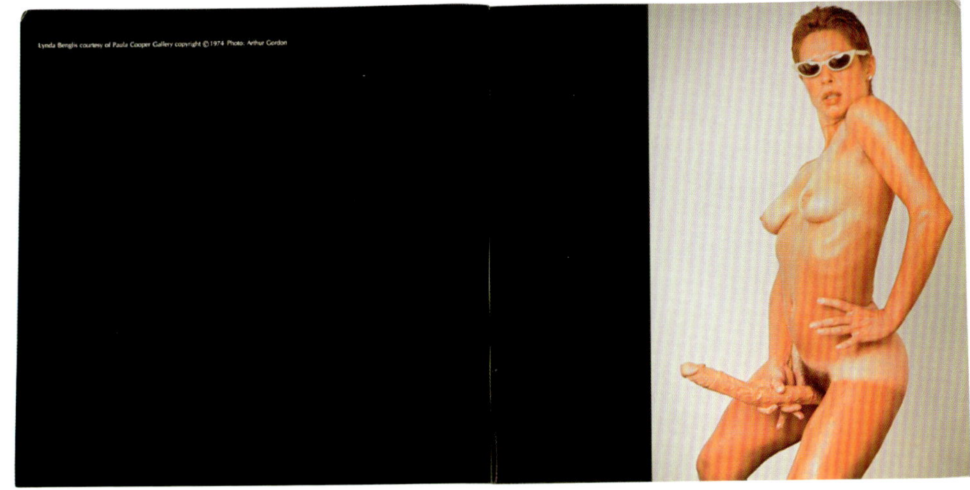

ducted between 1993 and 1999 for an oral history of *Artfourm*, Krauss reflected, "I felt that publishing that ad was tantamount to saying that we were all hookers together, the writers as well as the artists, that we were all for sale."[10] It is striking that Krauss felt the ad reflected on her integrity; pertinent, in this respect, is her involvement at the time with Robert Morris, who had produced a beefcake publicity poster of himself in a spiked collar, chains, and military helmet for which Krauss had been the photographer. Benglis, also then close to Morris, said twenty years later, "People said I was doing it because of him, but I was *not* doing it because of him, you know. I wanted to do a centerfold, alone."[11] She also noted that "much later, *Penthouse* wanted I think Hannah Wilke and myself to do something," but they could not agree on terms. (In Goddard's recollection it was *Playboy*.) Summarizing the contretemps (which was the subject of a spring 2009 exhibition organized by David Platzker for the Susan Inglett gallery), Robert Rosenblum said two decades later, "this was incredible chutzpa to come out as a woman with a dildo, vying for power in the art world . . . I particularly loved the editorial response because it got all of the thought-control police out of their closets and, there they were, the voices of intellectual freedom, liberalism and so on, turning into McCarthy-era censors."[12]

At the reception for the Benglis show this "ad" promoted, Wilke took off her clothes, was photographed, and called it *Invasion Performance*. "I did it," she later said, "because I felt, in a way, her using her body was sexually negative, very macho . . . it didn't really have anything to do with real feminism; and, I really don't even know if it had anything to do with her art, per se. But it was 'au currant' [*sic*]; whereas, I had been doing this vaginal symbolism for twenty years, and was getting into a lot of trouble for it . . . I didn't stay around. . . . It was very funny, 'cause I knew I was being bad; it is interesting that people should not upset other people's art shows, yet, people can upset other people's lives."[13] Wilke was not only protesting a distinction she believed to be indefensible between professional and personal behavior, she was, more pointedly, establishing the priority of her own claim to the use of frankly sexual nudity as a way of contesting conventions of self-expression and advocacy. The announcement Wilke had run in the magazine *Avalanche* for her own 1972 exhibition at Ronald Feldman used a photograph taken in 1970 by Oldenburg showing

Hannah Wilke in her studio, Chateau Marmont, Los Angeles, August 1970. Black-and-white photograph as used in photowork and advertisement for exhibition at Ronald Feldman Fine Arts, Inc., in **Avalanche**, Summer 1972.

opposite:
Hannah Wilke performing in window of Washington Project for the Arts, "Performalist Self-Portraits" exhibition, 1979

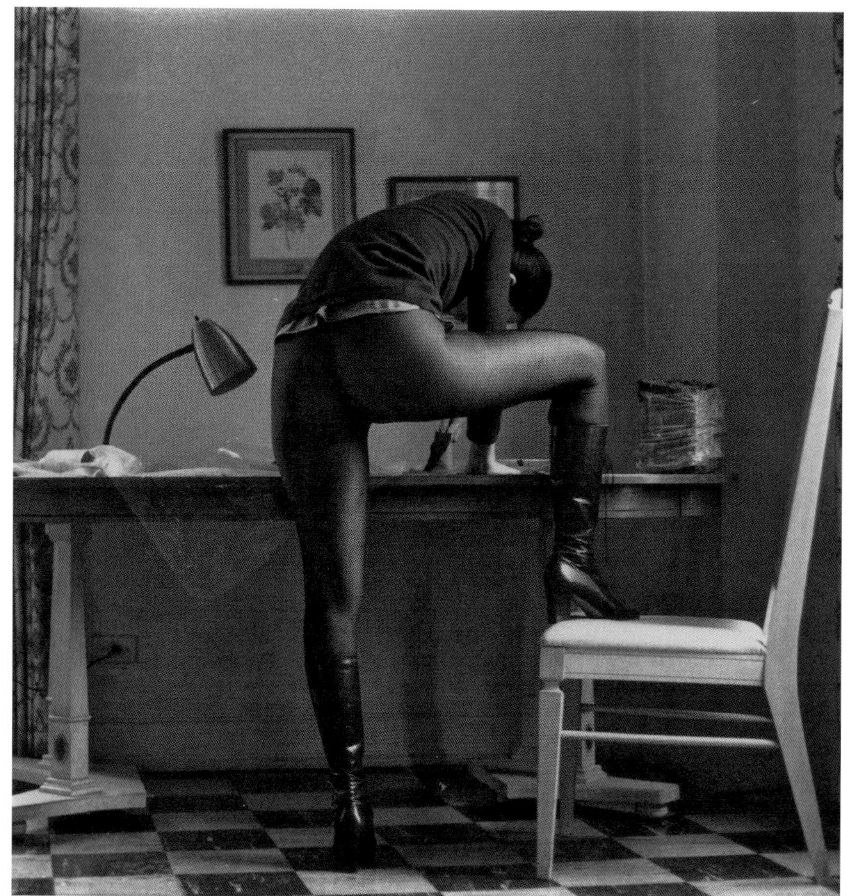

her from the back, bent over a desk in a room at the Chateau Marmont hotel in Los Angeles, wearing sheer pantyhose and no underwear, one high-heeled-boot-shod foot hoisted on a chair. Provocative though it was, it did not generate anything close to the outcry caused by Benglis's ad. When Wilke's 1975 show at Feldman opened, she asked the photographer for *Art News*, which was running a review, to take installation photos that included her, topless. The magazine declined those shots (one ran in *Playboy* in 1979, with a short article about Wilke and her work). For the opening reception of her own 1979 exhibition at the nonprofit Washington Project for the Arts in Washington, D.C., Wilke posed nude in the storefront space's windows.

In 1975, Wilke was asked to share ideas on feminism in art with the Center for Feminist Art Historical Studies. (A substantial exhibition in 1976 at the University of California at Irvine, "Hannah Wilke: Scarification Photographs and Videotapes," her first solo show in a public space, would bolster her presence in southern California.) Wilke's response, first exhibited at the Women's Building in L.A, in 1977, was a poster using an "S.O.S." photograph in which her opened shirt reveals a bare chest dotted, like her face, with chewing-gum vulvas; a boldly patterned necktie—it looks like it was designed by Roy Lichtenstein—hangs between her breasts; and her level gaze is aimed right at the camera (p. 65). Her fists are on her sassily cocked hips. "Marxism and Art," reads the boldface legend at the top. "Beware of Fascist Feminism," it reads below. Look at me, says the picture; I defy you to resist the simple truth of my beauty, to keep your ideological wits about you when your senses are so clamorously engaged.

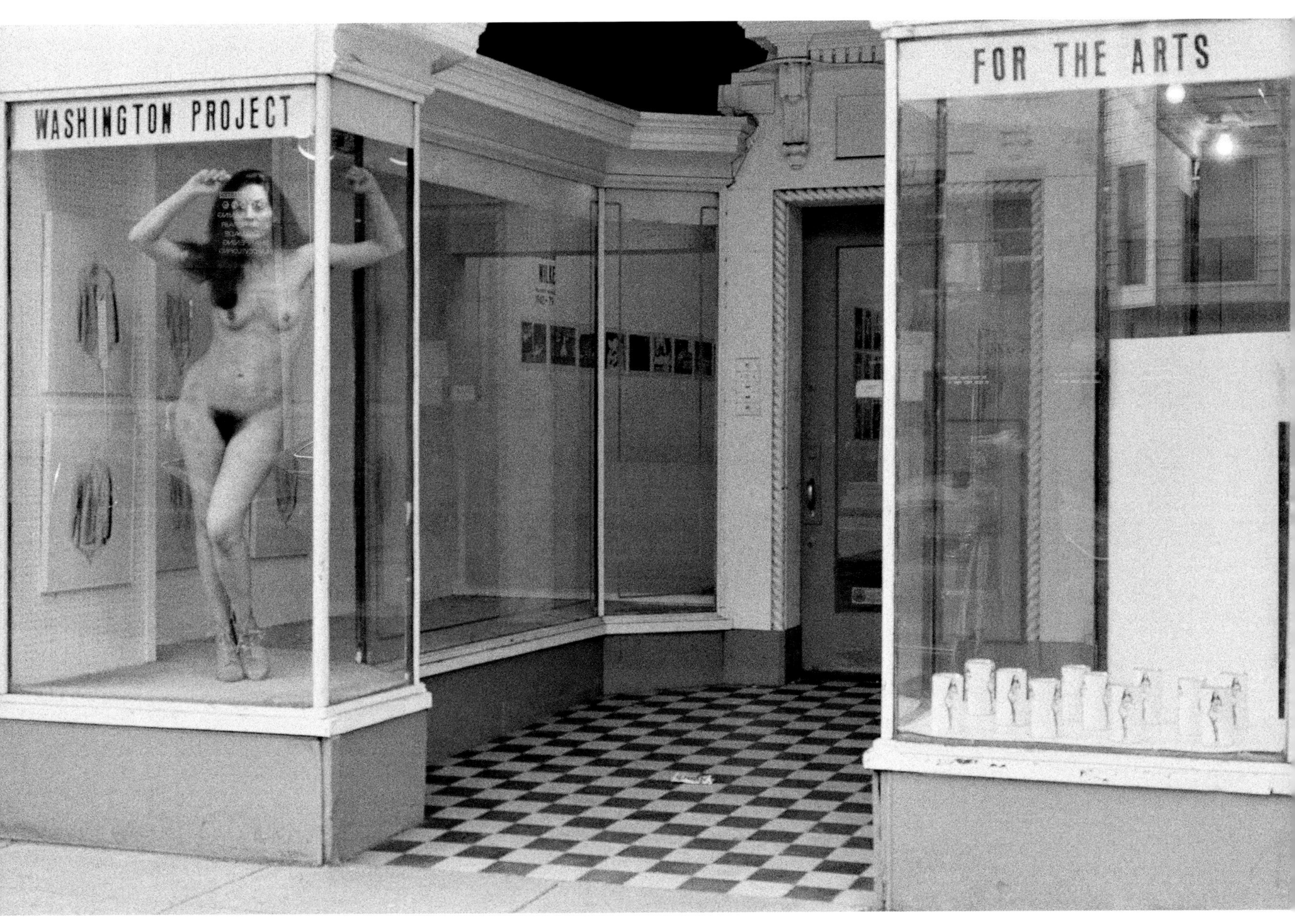
WASHINGTON PROJECT
FOR THE ARTS

Marxism and Art: Beware of Fascist Feminism, 1977. Silkscreen on Plexiglas, 36 x 27½ in.

This poster was not meant, nor taken, as a substantive academic statement. But Wilke's struggle with "fascist" feminists was protracted. In 1980, she wrote in the third person but surely of herself: "To be the artist as well as the model for her own ideas, whether sexually positive or negative, she must resist the coercion of a fascist feminism, which devolves on traditional politics and hierarchies in feminist guise rather than self-realization with respect to the physical superiority of woman as the life source."[14] In another text of the same year, she spoke up for art by women with formal rather than political concerns: "I hope that women will not sacrifice their biological superiority to doctrinaire collectivism, or their intellectual equality in an artistic arena dominated by male ideology. In the narrow politics of feminism, art is only a weapon, which may endanger women's art that is formally and humanly relevant but does not adhere to a specific political or commercial concept."[15] These are among her most explicit remarks on the politics of feminism, and they represent a heartfelt indictment of judgmental sectarianism among women making art. But many of Wilke's political formulations, as articulated in the scripts she used for performances, are essentially impressionistic collages of ideas that are structured as much for cadence as for coherence, and they seem to have been accepted—or dismissed —as rhetorical gestures.

Neither did Wilke's invocation of ritual scarification in her use of chewing gum and, even more uncomfortably, of crucifixion, elicit much response. At a time when *Jesus Christ Superstar* (1971), with music by Andrew Lloyd Weber, was a hit play on Broadway and a successful movie (1973), a time before religious conservatives had become a powerful political force and when identity politics in America hadn't extended much beyond the most fundamental struggles of the civil rights movement, these were not red-button issues. That Wilke could propose, without significant opposition, a link between Jesus and fertility goddesses—"I created a performance where I was first dressed as Mary Magdalene, changing to the Christ. . . . I really feel the crucifixion is a female fertility figure in disguise. . . . It's woman's blood that creates life, not Jesus"[16] — speaks of the enormous cultural divide separating the 1970s from the first decade of the twenty-first century. Similarly telling is the tolerance that greeted what may have seemed a rather cavalier reference to the Holocaust (though it was certainly meant in deepest earnest). Nor, for that matter, did the spectacle of a middle-class woman with sufficient resources presenting herself as a panhandler provoke criticism.

But Wilke's uncontested beauty was a different story—more even than her nudity, it was provocative from the first. Reflecting on her early use of her body, she said in 1989, "I looked too young for the artworld in the 1960s; I didn't fit in. I looked very glamorous and pretty, and the social irritant of it made me create for my first piece *Hannah Wilke Super-t-Art*, which was a female crucifixion. 'Cause I was being, I probably didn't realize it, being crucified for my looks."[17] A decade earlier, she had said in an interview that her *Super-t-Art* persona was "like a whore, or something, or, a Primal Prostitute of Art, as Mona da Vinci said of me, once. . . . After that . . . people . . . like Peter Frank would say, 'Oh, she takes her clothes off at the drop of a hat,' but, I do it only politically."[18]

Marxism AND Art

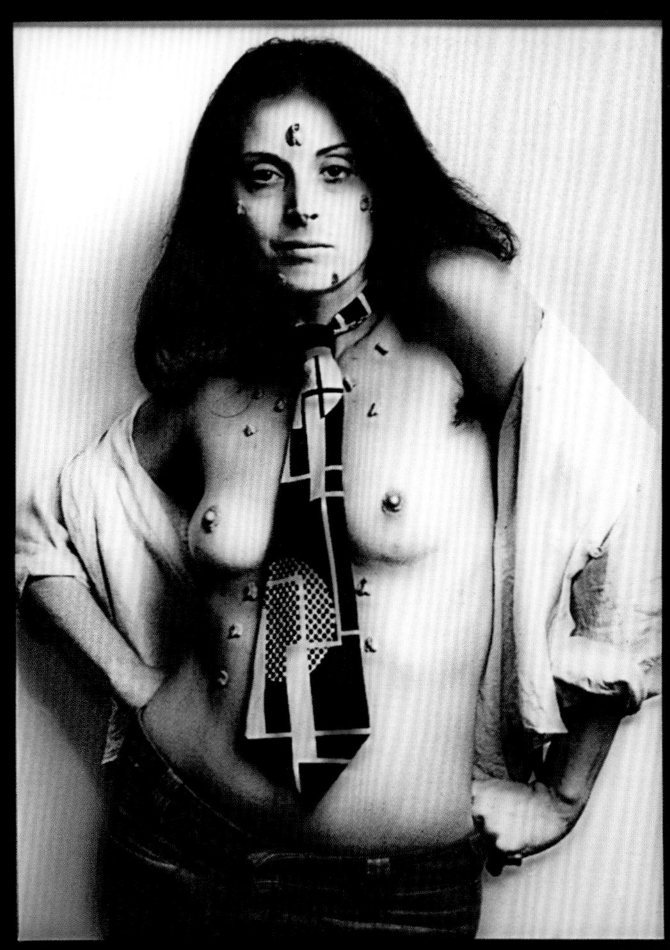

BEWARE OF Fascist Feminism

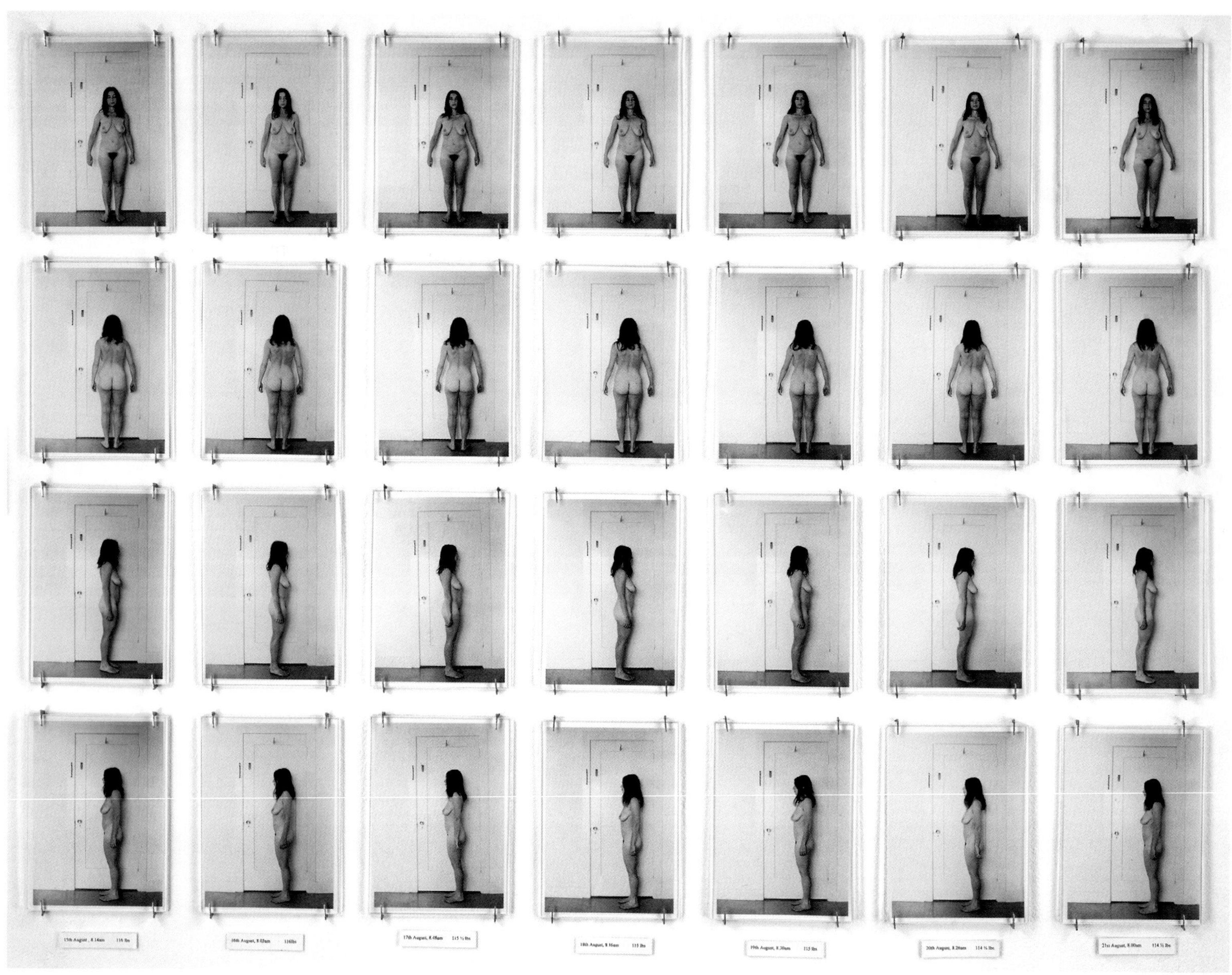

Eleanor Antin, **The Last Seven Days from Carving: A Traditional Sculpture**, 1972/1999. Black-and-white photographs and date labels, twenty-eight photos, 7 x 5 in. each; seven date labels

In other words, from early on in her career and until its end, Wilke used her body as a social barometer, and for a long time what it measured was how comfortable people were with raw female allure. Edit deAk wrote as early as 1974, "One of the rarest things in life is to see a physically beautiful person with a sense of humor," which Wilke clearly had. "And she needs it," deAk continued, 'because, in spite of the excellence of her work, people talk about her."[19] Looking back, Laura Cottingham observed twenty years later: "Perhaps more than any other post-war American artist, Hannah Wilke situated beauty at the center of her practice. . . . Wilke's work approaches the idea of beauty from various and divergent expectations and perspectives: her own (female) beauty; the patriarchal use of and abuse of (her) beauty and the activation of (her) beauty as a generative, self-empowering quality construed to resist and subvert male appropriation."[20] A powerful magnet that she used to attract those who were open to it, and repel those whom it made uneasy, or suspicious, or envious—and also, most productively, to measure the strength of both forces—beauty was at the center of her identity. It was also its most fragile aspect, of which she was perfectly aware. "People often give me this bullshit of, 'What would you have done if you weren't so gorgeous?' What difference does it make? I was still alluding to the suffering of humanity. Gorgeous people die as do the stereotypical 'ugly.' Everybody dies,"[21] she said in 1985, with what again seems sad prescience of her own premature death.

Inevitably, it was other women who were most skeptical about her motives. In 1976, Lucy Lippard wrote, "her confusion of her roles as beautiful woman and artist, as flirt or feminist, has resulted at times in politically ambiguous manifestations which have exposed her to criticism on a personal as well as on an artistic level."[22] Though Wilke was stung by these often-quoted words—her sensitivity to criticism was acute—they were actually quite circumspect, suggesting (a little disingenuously, perhaps) that while Wilke lay "exposed" to such attacks, Lippard herself wasn't the one to launch them. The emphasis shifts slightly but significantly in the light of the remarks that preceded them: "Hans Peter Feldmann can use a series of ridiculous porno-pinups as his art, but Hannah Wilke, a glamour girl in her own right who sees her art as 'seduction,' is considered a little too good to be true when she flaunts her body in parody of the role she actually plays in real life."[23] And later, Lippard retracted unequivocally, telling Saundra Goldman, "She was constantly preening herself in public. I was in my combat boot period. That didn't appeal to me much."[24]

However guarded, the admission clearly exposes the fault lines that ran through the women's movement of the late '60s and early '70s, in which the exigencies of solidarity often came into conflict with artists' equally urgent needs for individuation, and in which falling in line could mean accepting leadership that itself later came under suspicion. Thus in her reappraisal of Wilke, Lippard stated quite simply, "I did like her work . . . she was really the forerunner of Judy [Chicago]'s vaginal stuff."[25] (Wilke, of course, had long said the same, though without much credence in her lifetime.) Similarly, while Ann-Sargent Wooster criticized Wilke in the '70s, by 1990 she had revised her opinion: "In 1975 she exhibited the S.O.S. Starification Series . . . I wrote at the time I could not understand why she needed to 'vulgarly accessorize herself with personal portable leprosy.' I was offended by Wilke's use of unnecessary nudity to 'sell' her art." As did Lippard's, Sargent Wooster's reevaluation involved acknowledgment of a revised understanding of lineage: "Scenes of [Wilke] being menaced in often sado-masochistic poses, such as those found in the *So Help Me Hannah* series, were a form of image making that anticipated Cindy Sherman's early work."[26]

Writing in Wilke's defense, Joanna Frueh cites the notion that a beautiful woman is "hostage to her beauty," a truism whose potency is often lost on those less favored. Of the many women who exposed their bodies in the service of feminist art in the late '60s and early '70s, most were attractive, and all were young. Even among that cohort, Wilke stood out, glaringly; her appeal was on the order of movie stars and fashion models. More to the point, these other women presented themselves matter-of-factly; they took their clothes off as much to forestall erotic responses as to engage them—see, for example, Eleanor Antin's landmark exercise in public dieting, the photo-documented *Carving* of 1972; Wilke, on the other hand, vamped

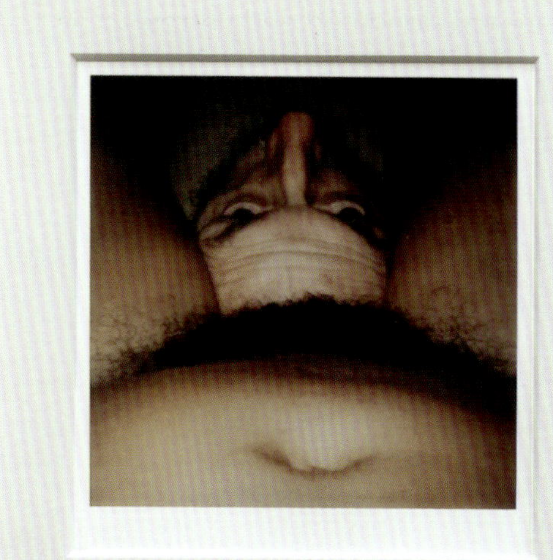
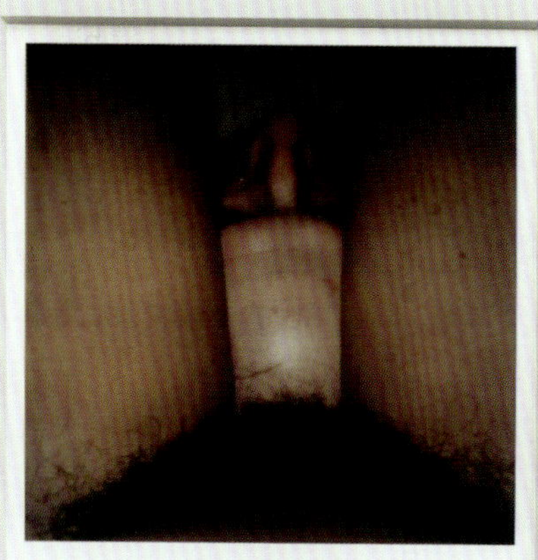
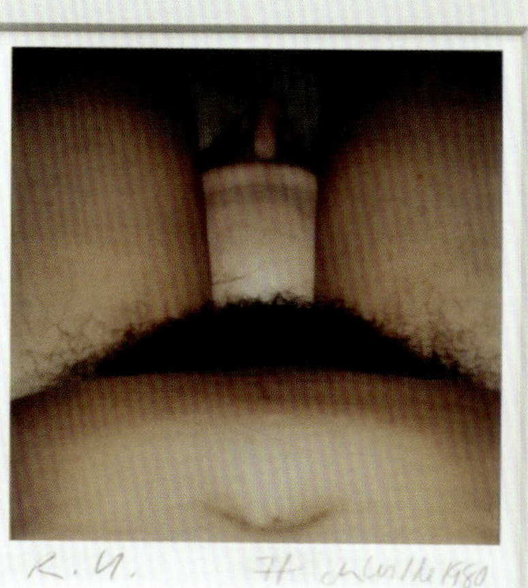

Venus Envy, 1980. Triptych: three unique Polaroid photographs, 13 x 21 in. overall, framed

and aroused. Among her many provoking attitudes, perhaps the most controversial was her presumption that men were as likely to respond to her work as other women, and that she welcomed their appreciation. Just as there was an Oldenburgian impulse in her ceramic sculpture, there was more than a hint of Warhol in her deployment of her own glamour. The robust sexiness of his Marilyns and, equally, their newsprint-thin tragedy are both important coordinates for Wilke's work. They plot a field in which beauty, as a category historically understood to be coterminous with the esthetic, is on one axis, and celebrity the other. The American pinup can be charted on this grid, with all its zesty vulgarity, but elegy has a place there too. So do the least-exalted outlets of the mass media. While she insisted on her hard-earned right to be ranked among the formal and intellectual heavyweights of her generation—the Post-Minimalists, the Conceptualists—she accepted coverage (respectful, to be sure, and featuring her art as well as her body) in *Playboy* and *Oui*[27] as well as *Penthouse* and *Viva*.

Just as important, though, were contemporary counterparts to Wilke's use of nudity in the work of men. Indeed, men were seen by some observers to have claimed the territory of nudity as their own, spoiling it for women. After citing Hans-Peter Feldmann's pinups, Lippard also wrote, in 1976, "It was not just shyness, I suspect, that kept many women from making their own Body art from 1967 to 1971 when Bruce Nauman was 'thighing,' Vito Acconci was masturbating, Dennis Oppenheim was sun bathing and burning himself and Barry LeVa was slamming into walls. It seemed like another very male pursuit, a manipulation of the audience's voyeuristic impulses, not likely to appeal to vulnerable women just emerging from isolation."[28] And Wilke, it is important to note, made considerable numbers of photographs of nude men, most of them intimate friends. Very few, even more significantly, have been shown; Ronald Feldman notes that Wilke made pinup-style photographs of her lovers that remain unexhibited. The imbalance of power represented in this disparity is expressed with delicious concision in a triptych of Polaroids Wilke took in 1980 called *Venus Envy (with Richard Hamilton)*. In each shot, Hamilton's face is framed by Wilke's naked thighs and her pubic hair crowns his head, which is in turn "crowning," as in childbirth (though coming out chin first). At the same time, his forehead, elongated and narrowed by her legs (which obscure the sides of his head) resembles the shaft of a penis and, progressively over the three-image sequence, his nose/chin become the penis's pointed head. It is much funnier than it sounds, and also more affectionate: Hamilton, a pioneering British Pop artist with whom Wilke was then intimate, looks up at her (or at the camera she was holding) with sweet helplessness. His willingness to play along in this scenario is supported by his apparent acceptance of the photos' public exhibition.

Also worth noting with respect to the proliferation of naked bodies in art of the '60s and early '70s is that nudity found its way, in those years, into mainstream entertainment, including Broadway theater and Hollywood movies. Two prominent examples are *Hair* (1967) and *Oh! Calcutta!* (1969), both striking for their popularity and their capture of a zeitgeist in which the new sexual freedoms associated in part with reliable and widely available birth control were being in turn established, explored, and exploited in popular culture, all at a dizzying pace. That these freedoms were not an unmitigated boon for women is, at most, a deep undercurrent in either commercial entertainment or serious art. Wilke's work is no exception, though her candor about her own promiscuity is unusual. And while the men and women who celebrated the new sexual license would soon be labeled the "me" generation and scorned as having contributed to a "culture of narcissism," (notably by Christopher Lasch, in a 1979 book of that title), the moral laxity and self-absorption against which conservative critics aimed these barbed terms were of a different order than the particular transgressions of which Wilke stood accused when she was called, as she not seldom was, narcissistic.

Harriet Senie, for instance, writing in the *New York Post*, called Wilke "lovely" and spirited, but concluded that her work was "so laden with narcissism as to all but obscure any other point."[29] Even the sympathetic Joanna Frueh, describing photographs and drawings Wilke made of herself as early as her mid-teens, calls these exercises precocious examples of "autoerotic narcissism." In the clinical term used by Freud, who borrowed it from classical myth, narcissism is an inability to see others except as reflections or extensions of oneself; in common usage, it designates a variable place on a spectrum that centers on self-possession (which is simply a kind of healthy poise and containment), and runs at the extremes from self-consciousness (a close cousin to shame) to self-absorption (with which narcissism is most commonly identified). In her work and in her character, Wilke seemed to occupy all these positions in turn. And to present them, deliberately, as pressure points in the exploration of how art engages audiences; how visual appeal, when personified, plays havoc with measured, intellectual responses; how naked beauty makes people confused, suspicious, envious, alert, and deeply curious about the character of the person thus exposed. The dream of exposure is often a nightmare: to imagine oneself naked in public is, most commonly, to picture oneself profoundly humiliated. For Wilke, it was fundamentally a gesture of celebration.

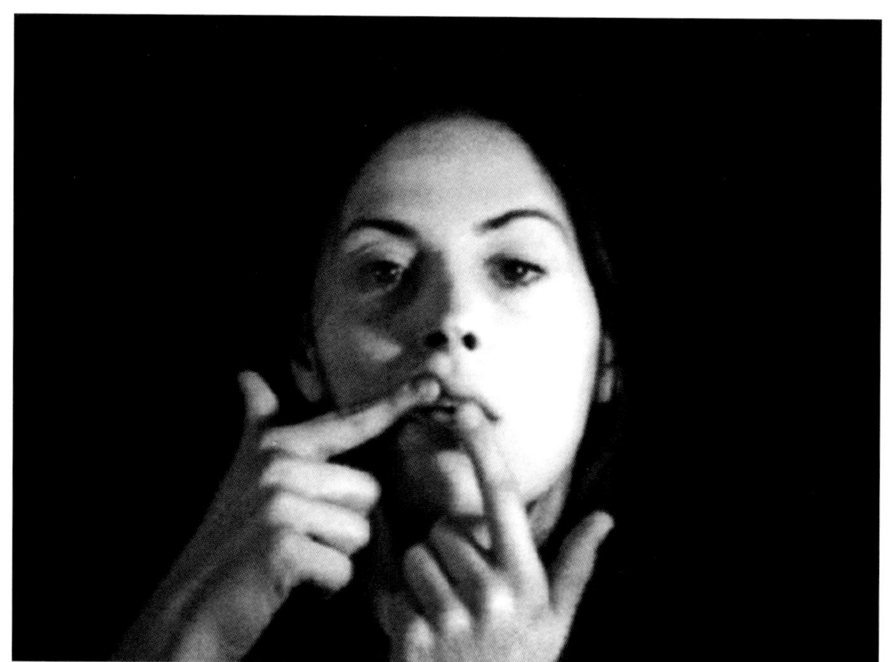

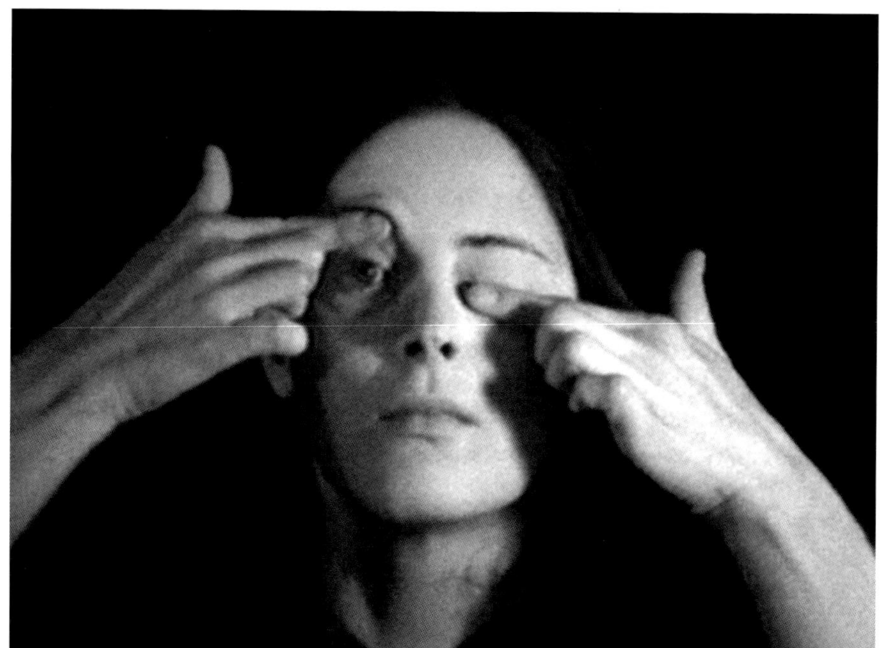

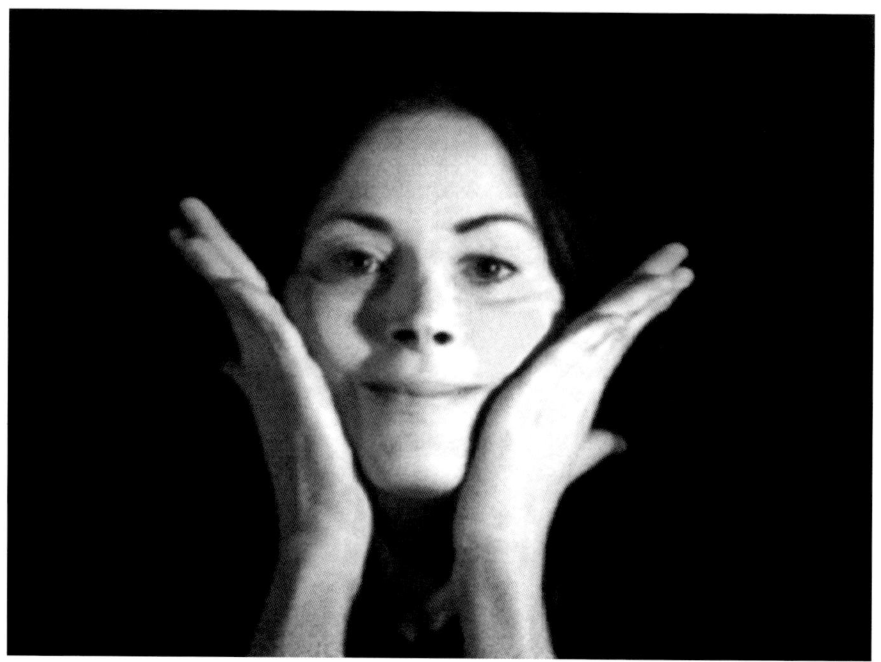

CHAPTER THREE

In Motion

At roughly the same time that she began to use photographs of herself, Wilke made the first videos she would exhibit publicly, and the themes explored in the "S.O.S." imagery are expanded on in these performance-based works. They were also preceded by personal projects undertaken when she was living with Oldenburg in California. "At that time," she recalled, "I . . . did some 8mm films. They were early performances for Claes. He was the cameraman, so I was always switching roles to make the woman—myself—the artist rather than the model. Actually I met Claes first when one day, in 1967, I walked into Leo Castelli's Gallery with a crash helmet on and no motorcycle. It was a 'life performance.' I enjoyed causing all that flourish . . . . Another time I came in with a fake wig on, and—would you believe it—Leo Castelli tried it on. We had a good time. I guess these were private performances."[1]

The "flourish" she describes would bloom in later performances and videos. But the earliest video she conceived as a freestanding artwork is the rather decorous, minimalist *Gestures* (1974), a wordless, thirty-five-minute black-and-white work that never leaves the artist's face. At some points the camera is a little closer than at others, and she moves her head to either side and back, but most of the action, such as it is, involves the expressions she shapes, for the most part manually, using her fingers to stretch her mouth, and cover it and her eyes, to slap her face and touch it tenderly, pull her lip down, touch her tongue, ears, eyes. Saundra Goldman notes[2] that Wilke treats her face like a slab of clay, and there is in fact a strong character of dissociation in this work, as if she is teaching herself emotional expressions that should be instinctive but aren't.

It is a quality shared with other artists experimenting with this new medium and using as subjects those nearest at hand. Vito Acconci's *Passes*, a twenty-minute black-and-white videotape of 1971 in which he passes his hand over his face, and *Prying*, another black-and-white video of the same year, in which he tries to pry open the closed eyes of his female companion, similarly present themselves as clinical data for the study of facial expression as social and psychological phenomena. Bruce

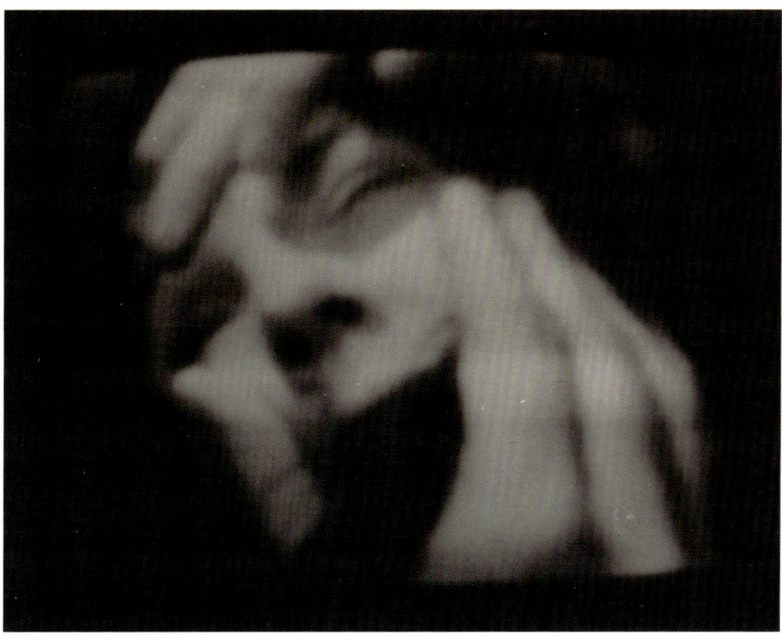

Vito Acconci, **Pryings**, 1971. Live performance at Eisner Auditorium, New York University. Black-and-white video, sound, 20 min.

opposite:
Gestures, 1974. Stills from videotaped performance; black and white, sound, 30 min.

Nauman's hologram series *Making Faces* (1968) is also closely related. Wilke's *Gestures* shares with these explorations a studious tedium; a reflexive focus on the passage of time was a critical dimension of the new performance-based work. But many features of this first video are distinctively Wilke's: one is her relationship with the camera, which is as rapt and unselfconscious as someone looking in a mirror. This intensity and intimacy make us, the viewers, her reflection, a peculiar and deeply unsettling relationship that she sustains throughout her photo-based work. Also characteristic is the frequency with which she touches her mouth, not only distorting it but, more often, covering it; even later, when she performed with her whole body and made explicit reference to the conventions of fashion-runway strutting and striptease, and had become far more controlled about her movements and expressions, this gesture recurred, seemingly unbidden. And because it does seem unintended, or at least unintentionally repeated, it is—ironically, given her overall candor—particularly revealing, and personal. It is of course a gesture of embarrassment, of fear one has said too much. In *Gestures*, her most tentative video work, it is most prevalent.

Wilke's next, still-experimental work is the twelve-minute black-and-white video *Hello Boys* (1975). As in Nam June Paik's *Video Fish* of the same year, in which footage of fish plays on twenty monitors, in front of which are small aquariums containing actual fish, a fish tank occupies the foreground of *Hello Boys*. Behind it, Wilke rises like a giant mermaid, her face floating up hesitantly into the field of vision. She moves slowly, as if underwater, and holds her hair up, to make it look like it is floating around her. Less beatifically, she wraps it around her face, as if she's drowning, a Pre-Raphaelite vision of etiolated beauty that reverts to a healthier sensuality as the video progresses and it becomes more frankly erotic. Her breasts are revealed, and she touches, then caresses them, as, all the while, rock music plays (it is The Who's "Can't You See the Real Me"; those Pete Townshend beseeches include his father, a doctor, and a preacher). *Hello Boys* is perhaps the most innocent of Wilke's videos, a trippy vision of sensuality that is playful and full of grace. But at the same time, it invites seeing the aquarium as a metaphor for the unwelcome social visibility that has long been characteristic of the art world, and was especially true of the relatively small one of New York in the mid-'70s: a fishbowl with as many sharks as angelfish.

The next year, an exceptionally busy one (in which the "S.O.S." project continued), she took on the legacy of perhaps the most conceptually powerful figure in twentieth-century art, Marcel Duchamp, in a number of projects. The first was the striptease she performed behind his *The Bride Stripped Bare by her Bachelors, Even* (1915–23), also known as the "Large Glass" (it was performed during filming at the Philadelphia Museum of Art of a ninety-minute special program for German television on Duchamp called *C'est la Vie Rrose*, in which Wilke was featured as herself). Something of a Rosetta Stone for Duchamp's cryptic oeuvre, the "Large Glass," a free-standing, double-paned, metal-framed glass panel, bears the symbolic narration, delineated in wire, lead foil, and oil, of the titular bride's last night as a virgin. In the upper panel, she is shown (abstractly) disrobing before the suitors who are repre-

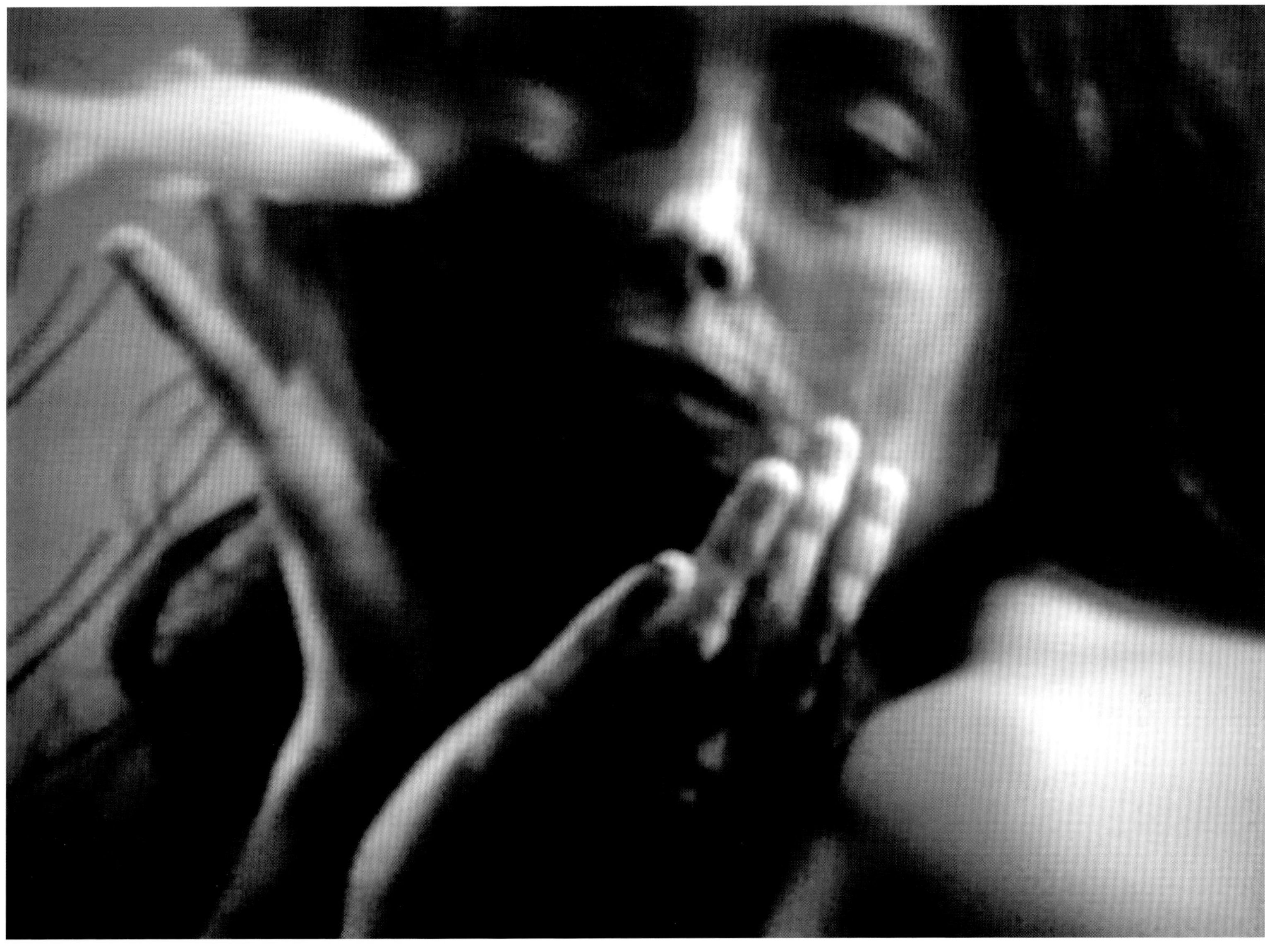

Hello Boys, 1975. Still from videotaped live performance, Paris; black and white, sound, 10 min.

following pages:
Hannah Wilke Through the Large Glass, 1976. Stills from live performance filmed at the Philadelphia Museum of Art. 16mm film, color, silent, 10 min.

sented (also abstractly) below; the "Malic Molds," water mill, chocolate grinder, and squares of cloth disposed by chance that appeared in previous Duchamp works are here brought together, in a window-like composition that was, notoriously, shattered in transit and repaired by the artist, who as always welcomed the intervention of unforeseen circumstance. An elaborate allegory of sensual desire and mechanical depersonalization, it was meant to frame—to render transparent—not only its own erotic tale but also the viewers who, passing behind it, become entangled in the tableau.

When Wilke undertook her performance and video work *Through the Large Glass* (1976; pp. 74–75), she was, then, in some sense doing something altogether literal: taking the master at his word, she stripped bare, for whichever bachelors (and bachelorettes) might choose to watch. As the silent, ten-minute color video of the performance begins, she walks on camera and stands behind the glass, wearing a three-piece white suit, fringed white scarf, and white fedora—attire that evokes both Tom Wolfe's trademark whites and the men's haberdashery made instantly fashionable by Diane Keaton the next year in Woody Allen's *Annie Hall* (the fedora was a Wilke trademark, too). Striking poses associated with fashion photography, Wilke struts, thrusts her hips sideways, touches her hat and, again, her face, her mouth

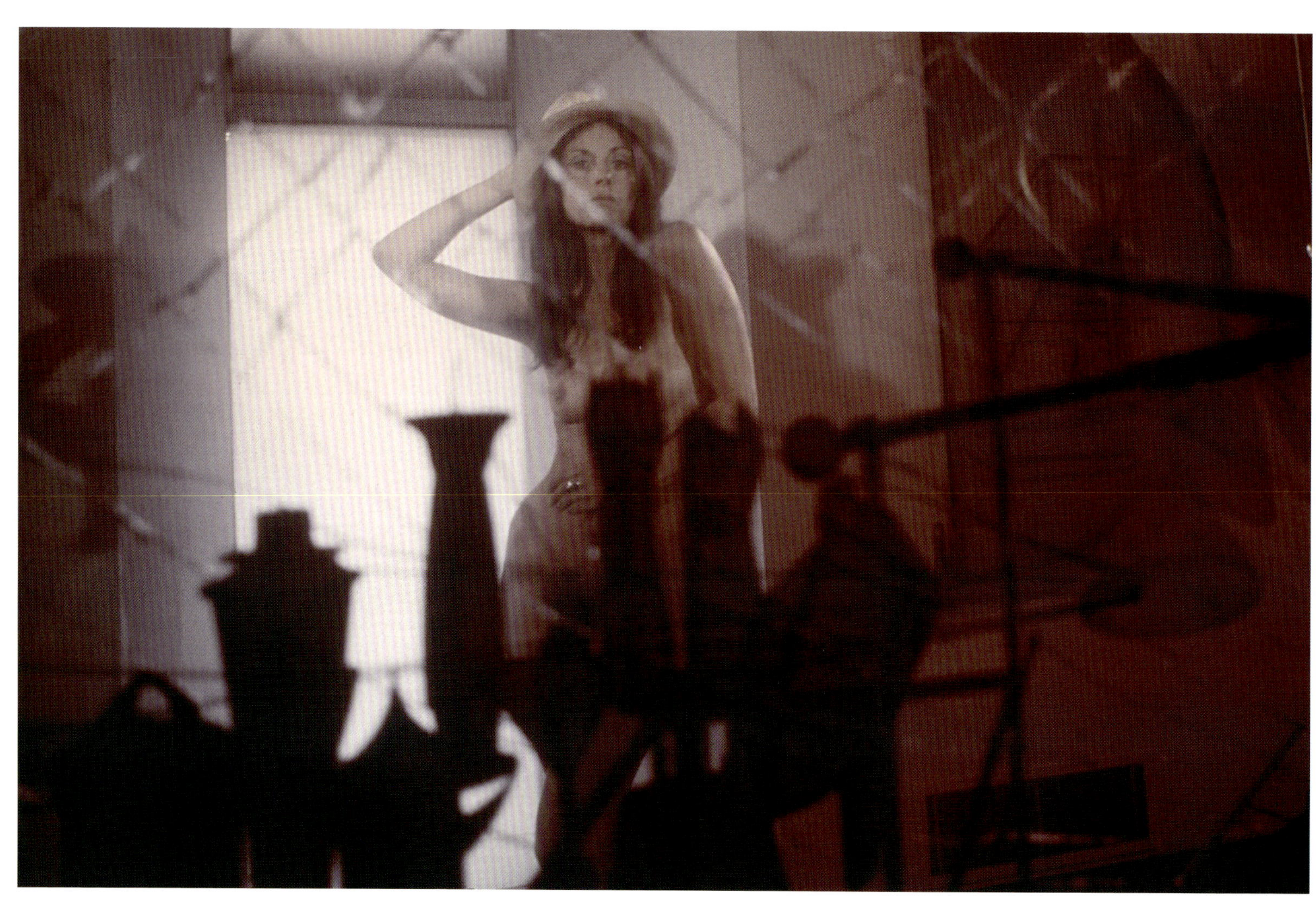

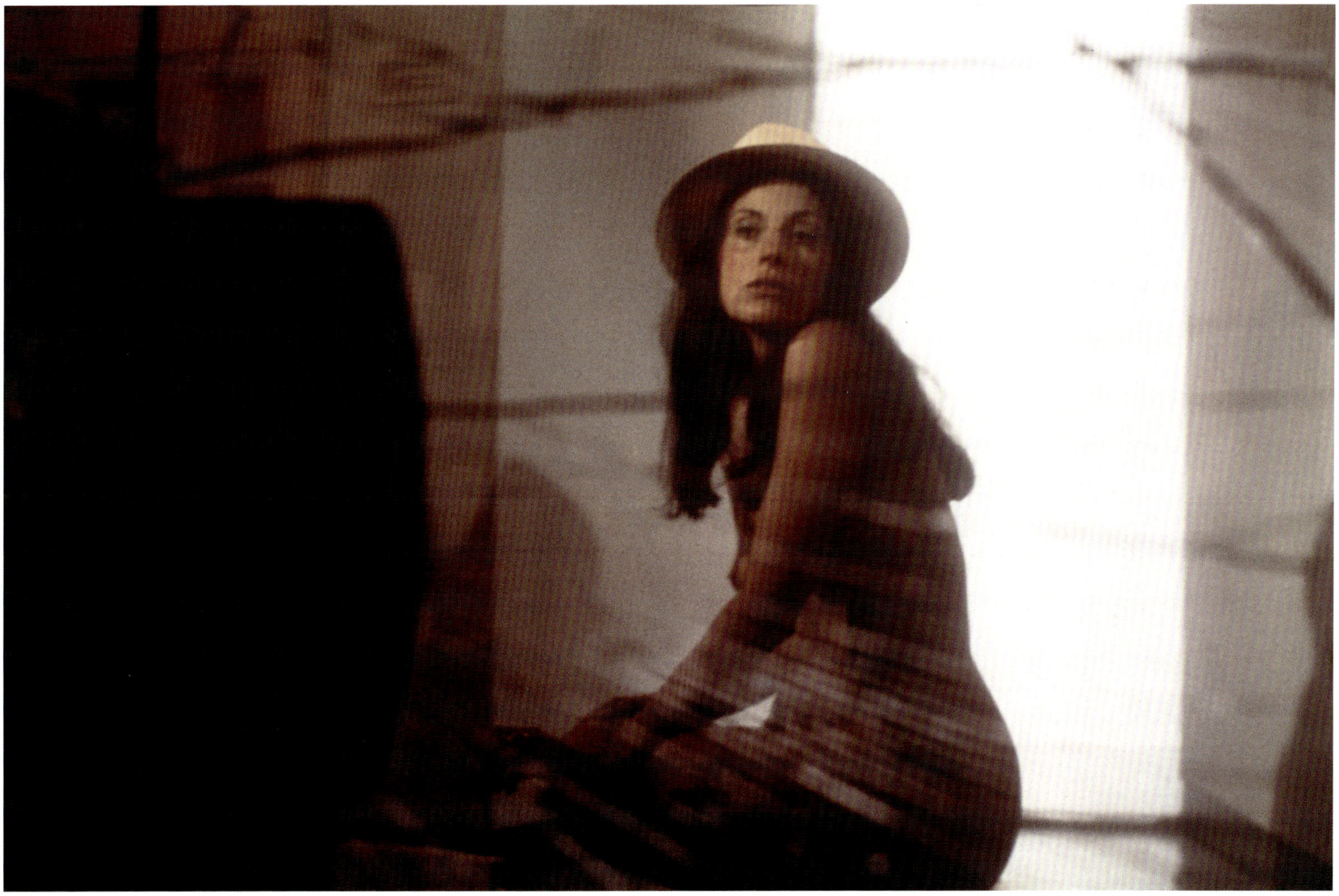

HANNAH WILKE: PHILLY

An auto-documentary of her performance at the Philadelphia Museum of Art for the films "Through the Large Glass" and "C'est la vie rrose"

produced by Hans-Christof Stenzel for German television
Video camera by Andy Mann. Editing by John Sanborn and Hannah Wilke.

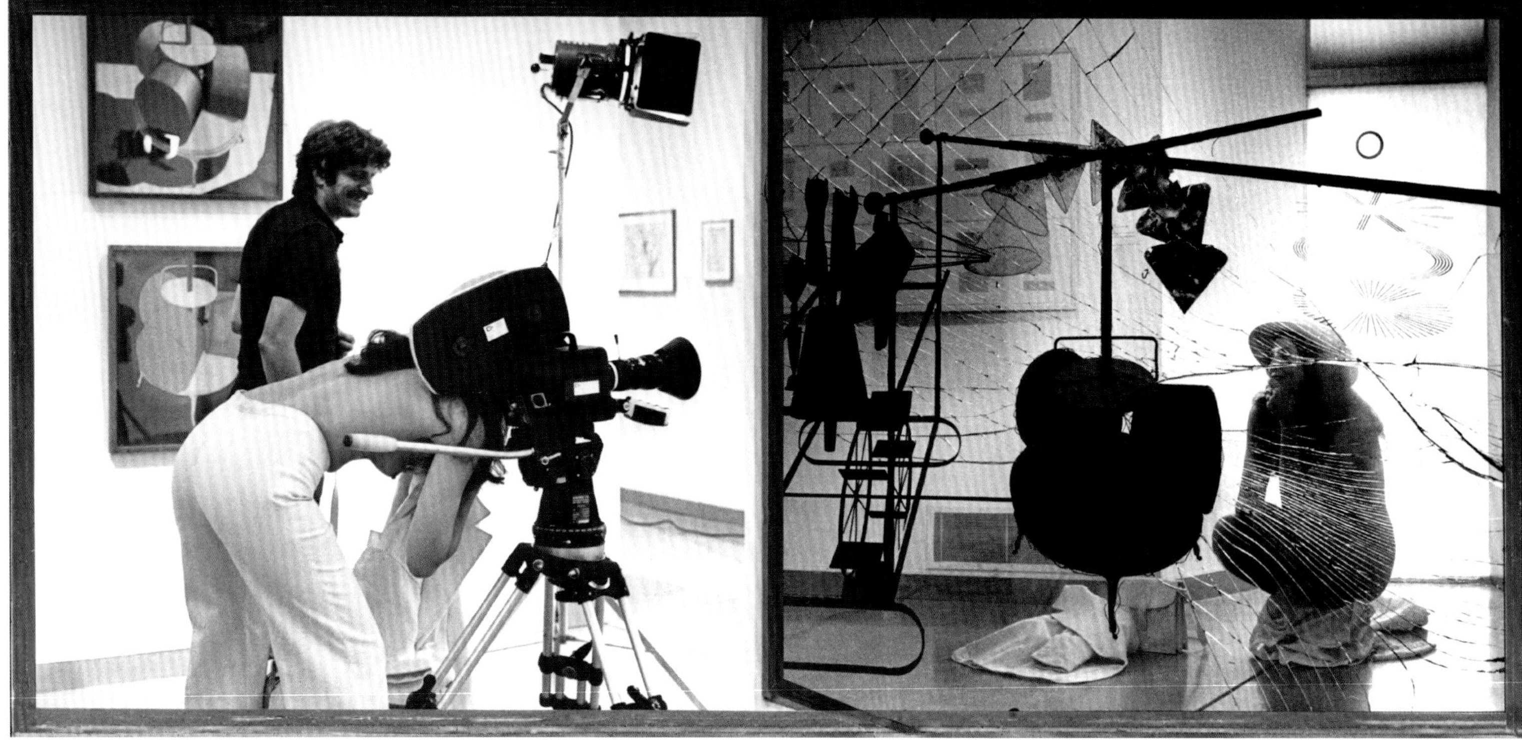

Philly, 1976–78. Black-and-white photographs with text, 27⅛ x 40 in. framed

opposite:
Hannah Wilke and I Sa Lo at the Philadelphia Museum of Art, 1976. Black-and-white photograph used by Hannah Wilke in poster for **C'est la Vie Rrose**, a film directed by Hans-Christof Stenzel for German television, 1976

especially—often, what seems an unintentional gesture is converted, as we watch, to a more deliberate caress. Slowly, with great panache, she takes off her jacket, unzips her pants, adjusts her hat. One or another of the cones pictured on the "Glass" is often centered on her crotch as she removes her jacket and coyly shields her breast with a shoulder, then reveals it, slides off her pants, stripping and teasing, moving slowly, pausing as if for a still camera to capture a pose. At the end of the tape's first segment, she assumes a stance that, again, descends directly from Botticelli's most famous Venus, her crumpled pants substituting for the clamshell. In the video, the performance is repeated twice, the camera closer the second time; the third, which combines footage from the first two, ends with her putting her clothes back on.

The thirty-two-minute video *Philly* (1977) also resulted from the German filming; Wilke framed her performance behind the glass with some preliminary footage: she is seen walking hand-in-hand with the Duchamp film's director, Hans Cristof Stenzel, romping through the Philadelphia Museum of Art (which owns and permanently displays the Large Glass), playfully putting her hat on a portrait bust, and taking a piece of gum out of her mouth and fashioning a little cunt with it that she shows to Anne d'Harnoncourt, then a Philadelphia Museum curator, and holds out in front of a framed artwork. Entering the gallery that holds Duchamp's work, she talks to the cameramen, suggesting ways the shots might be framed, then goes into the ladies

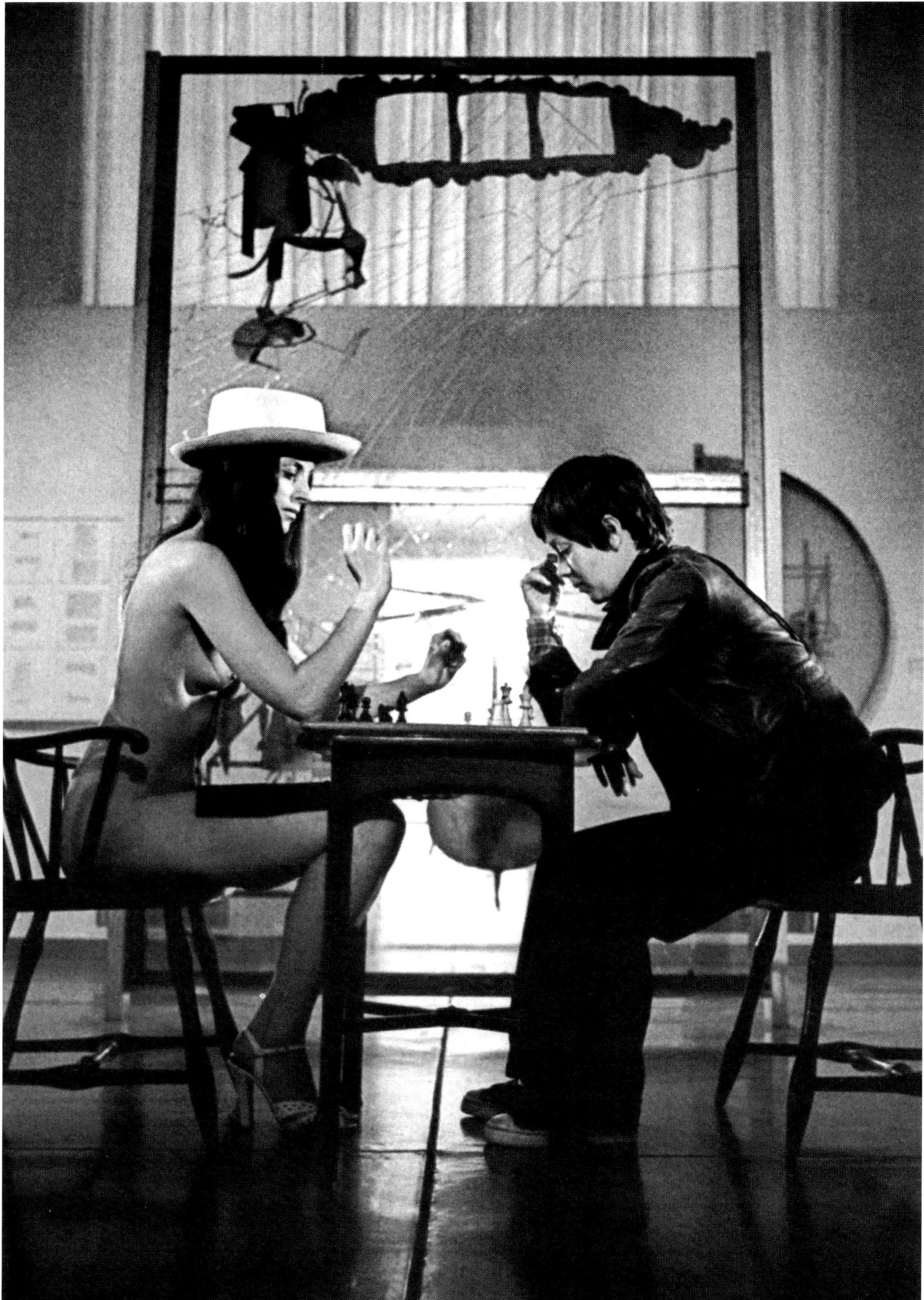

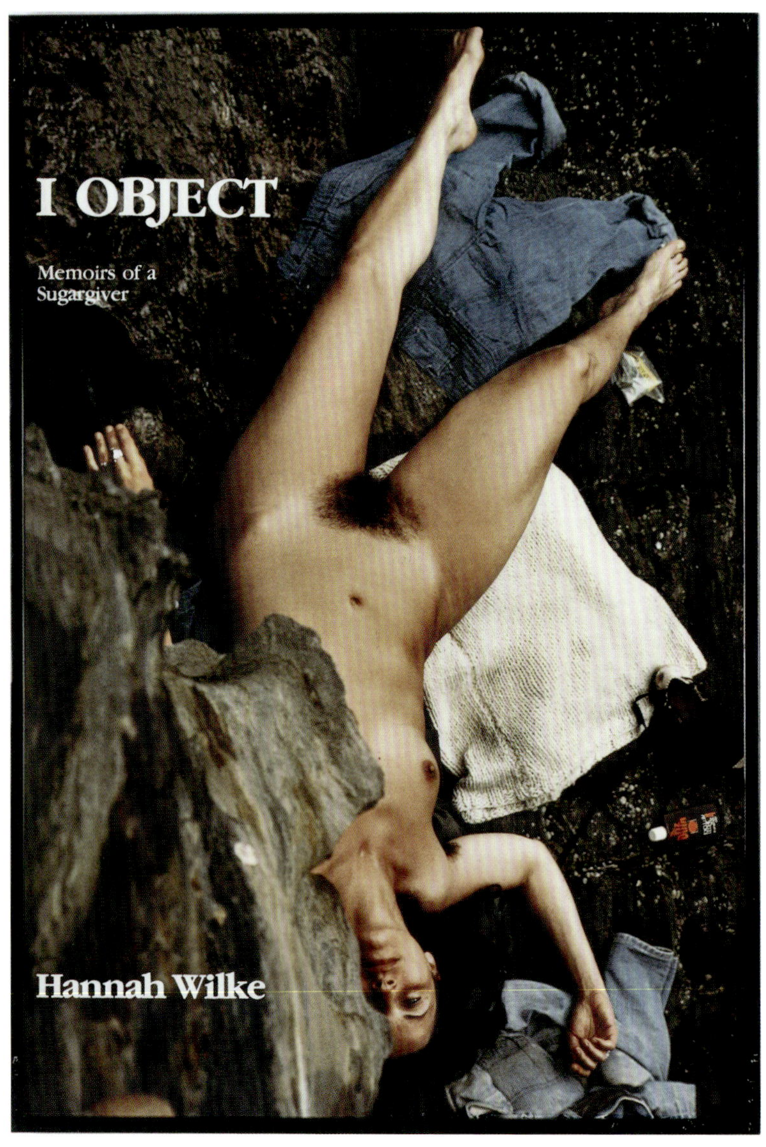

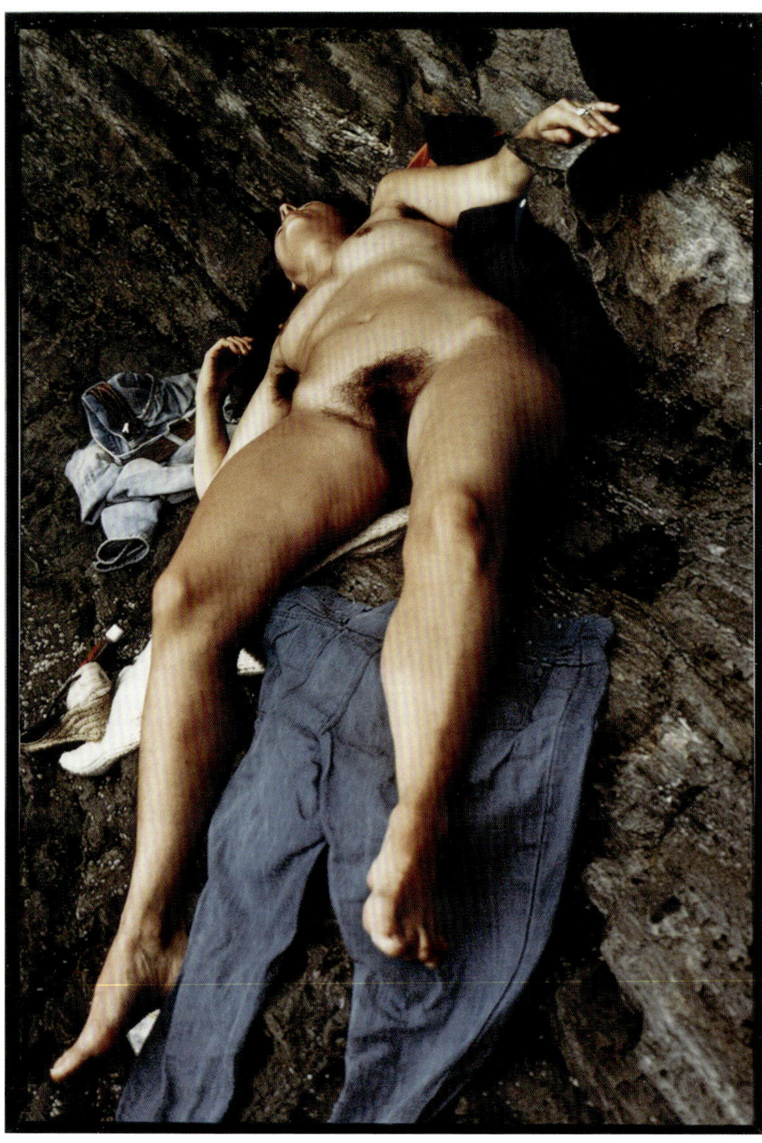

I Object: Memoirs of a Sugargiver, 1977–78. Cibachrome diptych, each photograph 24 x 16 in.

room to put on her white costume. Wilke allows herself to be filmed urinating, taking off her clothes and dressing ("very Humphrey Bogart," one of the cameramen says of her suit), but asks the cameras to be turned off while she puts on makeup—a telling moment in which she protects the privacy of whatever arts she uses to enhance her beauty. Out in the gallery again, she rehearses several gestures and poses before, finally, performing the striptease. At the end of the film, she sits naked at a chessboard, opposite a clothed player (the German actress I Sa Lo), enacting a famous 1963 photograph of Duchamp playing chess with a similarly unclothed opponent (a twenty-year-old art student and Duchamp fan named Eve Babitz), a photo staged on the occasion of his retrospective at the Pasadena Art Museum. "Check, checkmate," we hear Wilke say, before she puts the pieces away.

Her steady (though not unbroken) and solemn engagement in these films with the camera, which she seems to consult, again, as if it were a mirror, lends support to the first work's titular reference to Lewis Carroll's looking-glass world, with its capricious laws governing social deportment and physical presence; arguably, too, there is a trace element of Alice-ish naiveté, or at least of childlike wonder, curiosity and self-absorption, in Wilke's performance. Certainly she shared with both Carroll

Marcel Duchamp, **Étant Donnés: 1° la chute d'eau, 2° le gaz d'éclairage . . . [Given: 1. The Waterfall. 2. The Illuminating Gas . . .]**, 1946–66 (detail). Mixed-medium assemblage, 7 ft. 11½ in. x 70 in.

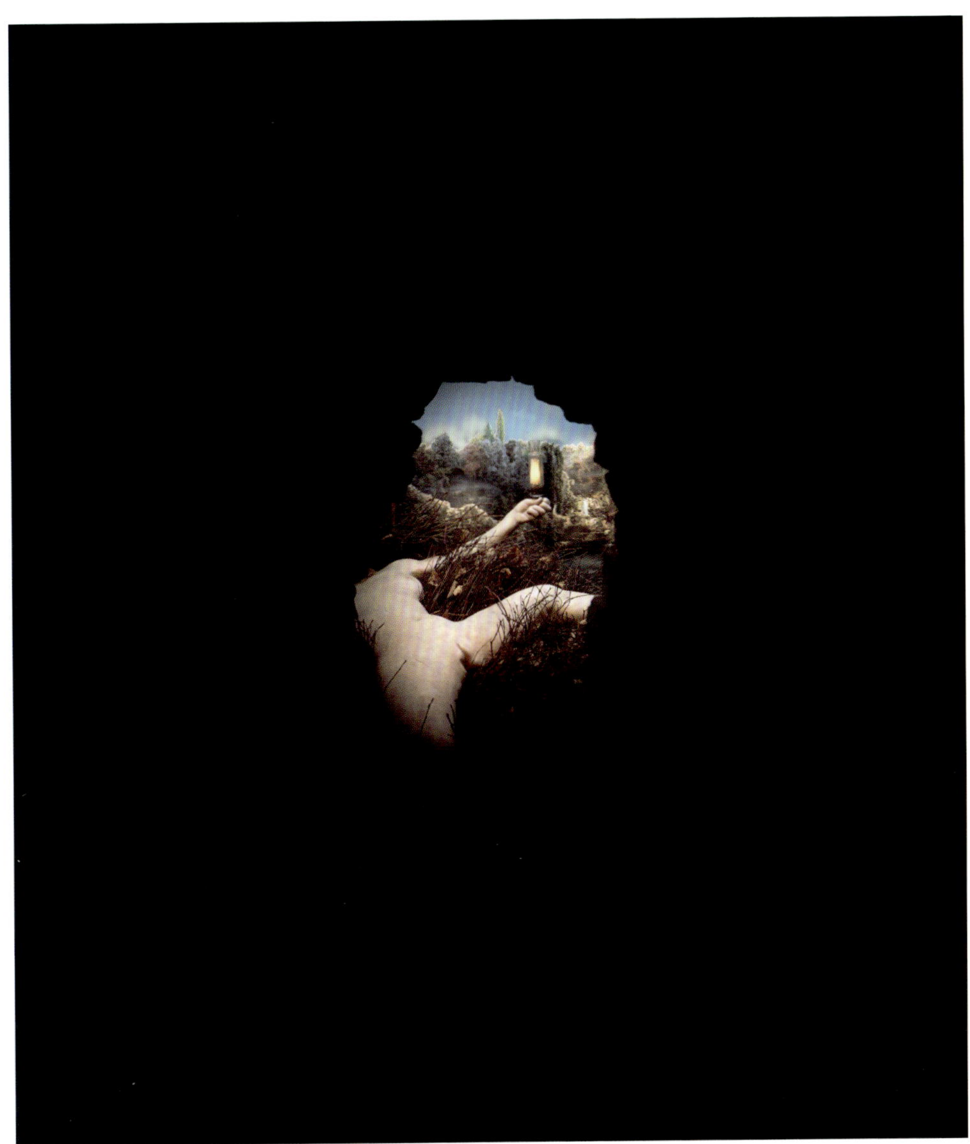

and Duchamp a love of wordplay of every kind, and a chess player's appetite for testing the limits of rule-bound games. But if, taking Duchamp at his word, she reinvigorates the cracked image that is among his most important works, subverting its nominal narrative by seeming to conform to it, she does not appear to be playing so much to him, or to Carroll—or, really, to spectators/voyeurs of either sex—as to her own reflection; again, we, the viewers, help her complete herself.

Wilke addressed Duchamp's work again (and not for the last time) in *I Object, Memoirs of a Sugar Giver* (1977–78), two photographs in which she lies naked on the boulders of a rocky beach in precisely the position of the subject of Duchamp's last work, *Étant Donnés: 1. La chute d'eau, 2. Le gaz d'éclairage* (1946–66). The photographs were taken in Cadaques, Spain, where Duchamp's wife Teeny lived, by Richard Hamilton, who had worked closely with Duchamp and was then romantically linked with Wilke. The pose Wilke assumes is troublingly ambiguous: indolent sunbather or pitiable victim, she is positioned, with respect to the camera, in a debased and slightly foreshortened perspective like the one viewers are offered by *Étants Donnés*. In that work, the female subject, a lifelike mannequin imprisoned behind a heavy wooden door through which two peepholes are drilled, is radically disadvantaged with respect to the viewer (or, rather explicitly, voyeur). Though *I Object* shows Wilke liberated from this kind of confinement, she remains passively, if not submissively, prostrated. Moreover, the memoirs to which the title refers didn't then exist (although a sequence of varied texts, most of them borrowed, later appeared under that name); these images, for the front and back covers of a story not told, may be testaments to the purest sun-soaked pleasure, but they can also be read as documents of subjection. Hence the title's double entendre: in *I Object*, the second word functions as both verb (I protest) and noun (I, a plaything). (In another play on words, she would later refer to the role as a "ready-maid."[3]) If Wilke's posture retains some of the provocative uncertainty of Duchamp's helpless subject, she places the viewer in a very different situation. We are fully liberated, by being granted total visual access; neither jailers nor johns—two of the options prominent among those suggested by *Étants Donnés*—but instead something like equals, we are given to judge the sensuality on offer from a position as exposed and embodied as Wilke's.

In the great majority of her photo-based works (for which she used a variety of photographers, generally credited), the poses Wilke strikes are of women as seen by, and marketed to, the commercial world. Sometimes, her enlistment of fashion photography's glamour found her in proximity to popular films. In many striking (if perhaps superficial) ways Wilke's work is echoed in the 1978 thriller *Eyes of Laura Mars*, which concerns a beautiful female photographer whose career straddles the worlds of art and fashion (and also, unlike Wilke, of fairly nasty pornography). A closer connection can be made between Wilke's reliance on the camera to probe reality—and shape it—and Michelangelo Antonioni's 1966 *Blow-Up*, in which a handsome young British fashion photographer captures with his camera a crime he's not sure has occurred. But it was the imagery found in advertising itself that Wilke's photo-based works most closely tracked. (In 1979, she coined the term "Performalist," to emphasize that she posed and directed them herself.)

She was not alone in her reliance on commercial imagery. In the middle 1980s, in response to the emergence of a considerable body of photography by women that involved stylized self-presentation, Craig Owens wrote a series of essays on uses of the "pose." In the 1983 essay "The Discourse of Others: Feminists and Postmodernism," Owens noted, "In order to speak, to represent herself, a woman assumes a masculine position; perhaps this is why femininity is frequently associated with masquerade, with false representation, with simulation and seduction."[4] The insight, which draws on French psychoanalytic theorists Jacques Lacan and Joan Rivière (the latter's *Womanliness as a Masquerade* appeared in 1929), is crucial for such approaches to Wilke's work as that taken by Amelia Jones. So is Owens's observation, about female artists, that they "are not primarily interested in what representations say about women; rather, they investigate what representation *does* to women."[5]

Crediting women with using photographic self-portraiture not simply to document the roles women took, voluntarily or otherwise, but also to examine the ways that photography itself participated in defining those roles, Owens offered an approach to work like Wilke's that honored its intelligence. Assuming the aspect of a seducer—conventionally, a masculine aspect—some women like her were taking possession of erotic engagement from a female perspective, thereby helping to complicate the simple binary definition of female and male, which was another target of Owens's critique. (In this regard, Duchamp, who cross-dressed as Rrose Sélavy, is again a key precursor; it is worth noting that when Wilke performed behind the "Large Glass," the clothes she took off—the three-piece suit, hat and scarf—were androgynous.) But Owens did not mention Wilke. The artists to whom he referred, including Dara Birnbaum, Louise Lawler, Martha Rosler, and Cindy Sherman, shared a guardedness about self-exposure altogether at odds with Wilke's inclinations. Their analyses of how commerce and entertainment shape women's self-perception and social options were astute, often caustic, and not infrequently (especially in the case of Birnbaum's video *Wonder Woman*, 1978, its footage appropriated from the popular TV show) devastatingly funny. By and large, they abjured the vulnerability—the uncompromising nakedness, in every sense—that was at the core of Wilke's practice.

The year after he wrote "Feminists and Postmodernism," Owens refined his thoughts about the "pose" in an essay on "The Medusa Effect," in which he invoked Lacan's ideas about the operations of the always presumably male, because authoritarian, "gaze" (these ideas had already been put to use by theorist Laura Mulvey in her celebrated 1975 essay, "Visual Pleasure and Narrative Cinema"). "To strike a pose is to present oneself to the gaze of the other as if one were already frozen, immobilized—that is, already a picture," Owens wrote. "For Lacan, then, pose has a strategic value: mimicking the immobility induced by the gaze, reflecting its power back on itself, pose forces it to surrender. Confronted with a pose, the gaze itself is immobilized. . . . To strike a pose is to pose a threat."[6] Like Medusa, in other words, who turns anyone who looks at her to stone, the artist who confronts the possessive (i.e., male) gaze on its own immobilizing terms has a powerful weapon in her hands. Owens organizes this discussion around the work from the early '80s of Barbara Kruger, and concludes with, "Against the immobility of the pose, Kruger proposes the *mobilization* of the spectator."[7] Kruger's pairing of archival images with blunt language and bold graphics had the force of a sophisticated ad campaign (p. 82); the voice in which the works' terse statements speaks, often the second-person "you," is deliberately indeterminate about whether it addresses some offstage listener (or, culprit), or us, the viewers; the only person explicitly excluded by this voice is Kruger herself, who never uses the first person. The contrast with Wilke is clear.

In a third essay on the subject, Owens temporized. This time citing Roland Barthes, he wrote, in the 1985 essay "Posing," "*to pose* is, in fact, neither entirely active nor entirely passive; it corresponds, rather, to what in grammar is identified as the middle voice . . . Both the active and the passive voices indicate activity or passivity vis-à-vis an external object or agent; the middle voice, on the contrary, indicates the interiority of the subject to the action of which it is also the agent."[8] This, perhaps,

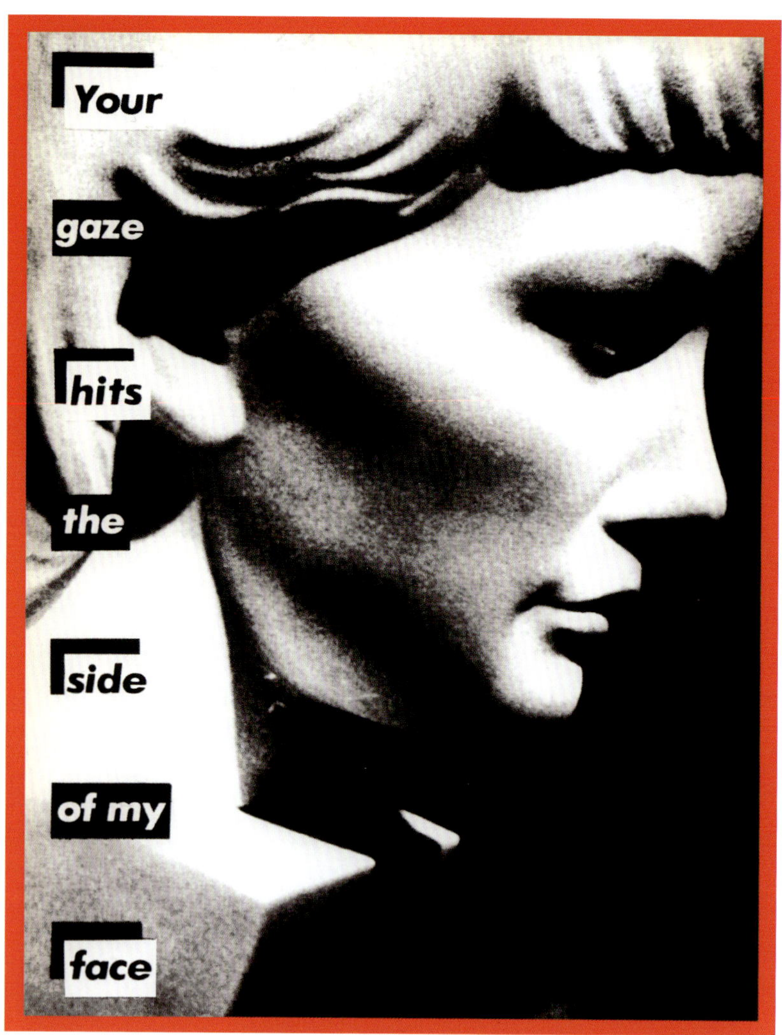

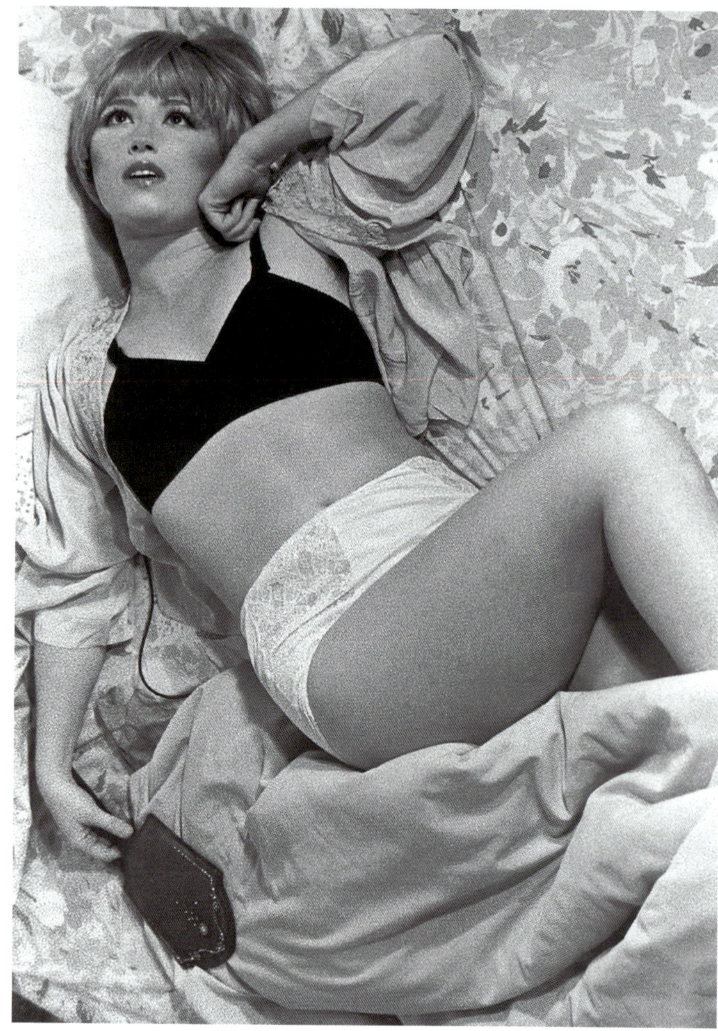

Barbara Kruger, **Untitled (Your gaze hits the side of my face)**, 1981. Photograph, 55 x 41 in.

Cindy Sherman, **Untitled Film Still**, 1977. Black-and-white photograph, 10 x 8 in.

opposite:
Intercourse with . . . , 1973–75 (detail). Black-and-white photograph used on cover of documentation accompanying two-hour audiotape of recorded telephone messages

comes closest to describing Wilke's use of poses borrowed from the conventions of entertainment and enticement. Speaking in her own voice, using her own body, she positioned herself squarely in the middle of the action. If, as Owens also offered, in the second of these essays, "Stereotypes . . . disavow agency, dismantle the body as a locus of actions and reassemble it as a discontinuous series of gestures and poses–that is, as a semiotic field,"[9] then Wilke's relationship to stereotypy was one of wary distance. She never relinquished agency; on the other hand, she did step inside stereotypes to stage gestures and poses that constitute a semiotic field of considerable richness.

Owens's essays exemplified a shift in the critical zeitgeist. Having embarked on the project of photographic self-presentation as a way of exposing how female eroticism looks when its expression is undertaken by a woman, and proceeding with an eye toward the (mostly) recent history of art, Wilke found her work framed by a discussion about the means and ends of representation, a discussion informed by psychoanalysis and deeply attuned to the commercial media. This broad change in art-theory paradigms may be one reason—others were personal—for her shift in emphasis from the more strictly feminist question of female sensual self-possession to the broader issue of how power circulates through the art world, and through images in the wider culture.

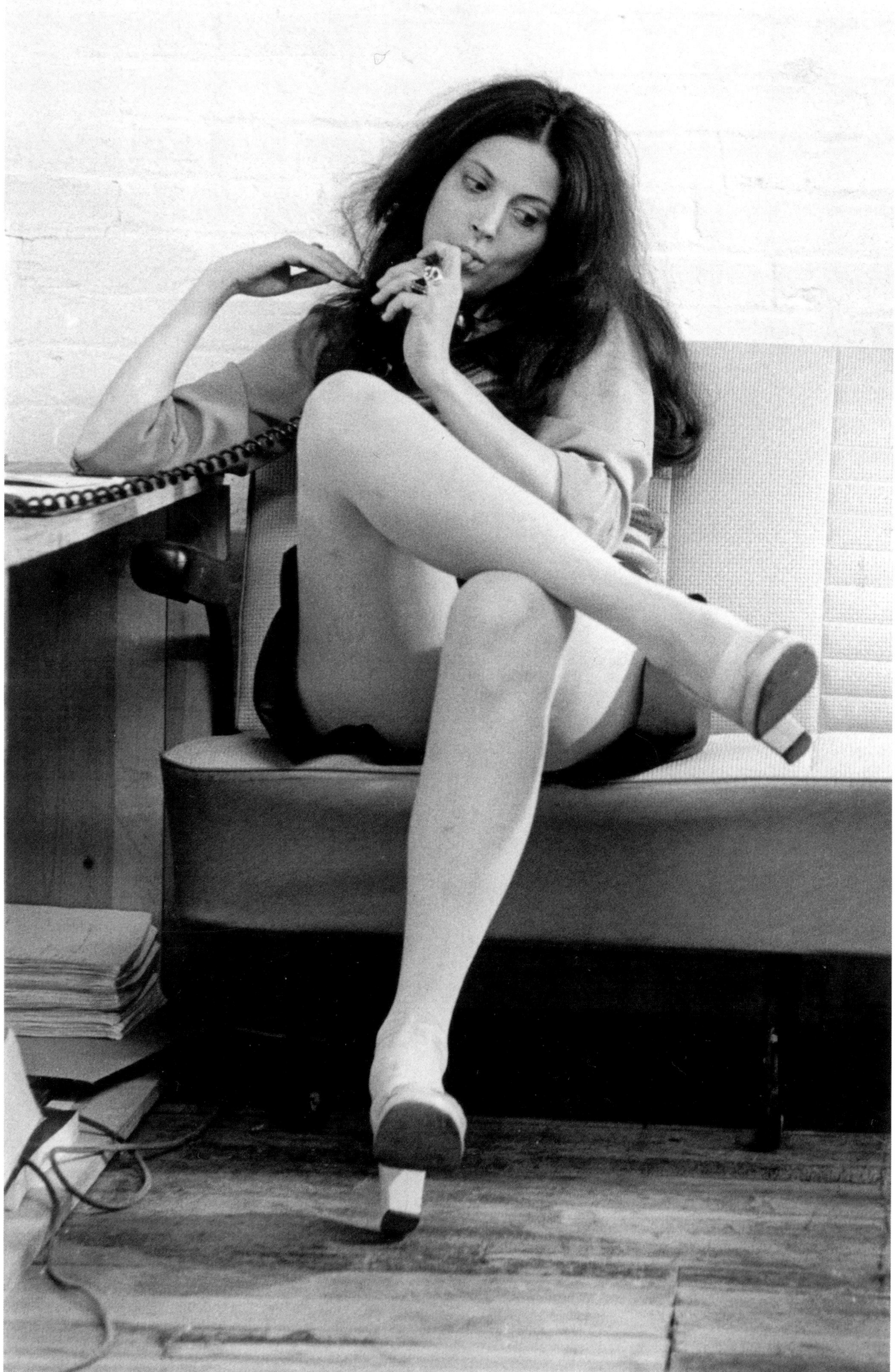

Though Wilke is firmly identified as an artist who used her own naked body as an expressive and investigative tool, some of her most potent work involved no visible bodies (or parts thereof) at all. "Intercourse with . . ." is the name she gave to several works, one a nude performance, preserved on videotape. But its first instance was an audiotape compiled from messages left on Wilke's telephone answering machine, accompanied by a typewritten list of the callers, presented in a ring binder; it was first shown in 1975, in an exhibition called "Lives" organized by Jeffrey Deitch for the Fine Arts Building in New York. The earliest of the messages date to 1973, when the technology was new—and, as is true of online social media these days, some callers quite obviously found it intrusive, impersonal, and annoying. The original exhibition format was a big reel-to-reel tape player, which allowed everyone in hearing distance to watch each other listening to messages they were never meant to hear. On the cover of the binder is a black-and-white photo of Wilke, looking down thoughtfully and sucking a lollipop, one leg crossed over the other ankle at the knee, the camera held low and aimed sharply up. Among the callers are Louise Bourgeois, Bill Jensen, Tod Williams (repeatedly, sounding very lovesick), Oldenburg (always identifying himself by first and last name, and sounding archly professorial), Tony Shafrazi, Francis Ford Coppola, an unidentified heavy breather, Barbara Rose, Barbara Haskell, Donald Goddard, Marsie Scharlatt, Emmy Scharlatt, and, several times, Wilke's mother, Selma Butter, who leaves messages imploring her daughter to visit, and offering inducements ("I've got a big pot of stuffed peppers"; "a meatloaf"; "love you, kiss kiss"). There is even a message from Wilke herself, who leaves an exasperated message ("Jesus Hannah, I don't know, you can do better than this"). Often the callers comment on the outgoing message, which evidently changes regularly; it seems that one asks the caller to say something funny, another is a little racy, and at least one involves music: for Wilke, everything in life that could be a performance was seized on, every boundary between public and private was tested.

From Ad Reinhardt's spoofs of Alfred Barr's famous flow chart mapping the progress of the twentieth-century's major modernist styles to Mark Lombardi's meticulous, chilling diagrams of the connections between big business, covert national security programs and politicians to Simon Patterson's reconfigured map of the London subway system, in which station names are replaced with celebrities, the circulatory systems for cultural power have been a subject for artists with a Conceptualist bent. Wilke's approach was, characteristically, by far the most personal. Placing her own network of connections on public view, she freely admitted her eager traffic in art stars; her promiscuous "intercourse" with well-known artists, gallery owners, curators, and critics both male and female; her willingness to let distinctions between work and pleasure blur. Or, more important, her willingness to make that blur a matter of public record, forcing listeners to examine their own alliances. But as usual, there is nothing remotely defensive or bitter about these maneuvers. Wilke is clearly tickled by the heft of her Rolodex, amused at the jealousies she arouses among rival suitors (sexual or otherwise), and, patently, willing to take the consequences of full disclosure. And though her callers didn't know she would use their messages in public, they toyed self-consciously with the new electronic barrier to personal contact, posing, strutting, joking, ruing the machine's presence and pining for the live voice it mimicked: in a word, they performed. This may be one reason why, twenty years later, the seemingly endless audiotapes are so engrossing.

The *Intercourse with . . .* tapes also became part of a performance, presented in 1977 at the London Art Museum and Gallery, in London, Ontario (p. 87). For this event, she entered wearing a black mink, and listened thoughtfully to the tape before removing her coat and proceeding with the kind of striptease she had staged previously. Moving back from a close-up on her face, a videotape of the performance takes in her full figure as she takes off her hat and clothes, this time black. Baroque chamber music plays as the various declarations of love made to her answering machine are heard ("I really want to talk to you not your machine, I love you very very much," one caller says). Wilke strips slowly, pants first, pulling her sweater over her head and letting it cover her face for a long moment, exposing her chest and the little black stick-on letters that cover it: they spell out Claes, Eddie, Donald, Richard, Arthur, Francy, CO, RH. Blindly, she starts peeling them off, then finishes taking off her sweater, to melancholy strains of music. A monologue begins: Wilke intones, "Since 1960 I have been concerned with the creation of a form of imagery that is specifically female . . . . Its content is always related to my own body, reflecting pleasure as well as pain, translated into an art close to laughter, . . . continually exposing myself to whatever occurs." Her voice is girlish but serious. "Starification, scarification" she says, and recites the names she has branded herself with. "Labeling people instead of listening to them, judging according to primitive prejudices to make objects instead of being one, to be a sugar giver instead of a salt seller," she continues. (The last phrase is a reference to Duchamp; the title *Marchand du Sel*, a near-anagram of his name—it means "salt seller," itself a homonym of the more common term "salt cellar"—was given to a volume of his writings edited by Michael Sanouillet and Elmer Peterson.) At the end of the performance, Wilke is naked, half smiling, half smirking, leaning back in her chair, one arm thrown over its back.

It is perhaps not a coincidence that Wilke's relationship with Oldenburg ended in 1977, the year the *Intercourse with . . .* performance appeared. Their mutual professional support was significant to both Oldenburg and Wilke, but only she was willing to make it a matter of public record. After their rupture, Oldenburg (who married Coosje van Bruggen the same year) sought to suppress all evidence of their connection, though it was manifest in several artworks that had already circulated fairly widely. For the 1975 Clocktower exhibition "Artists Make Toys," to which Wilke had contributed the game *Starification*, and Oldenburg a proposal for a "moving sculpture" in the form of a tractor that would roam forever, driven by an operator hired for life—a job that would devolve, dynastically, to that operator's sons, in perpetuity—a poster was made featuring a color photograph of Oldenburg and Wilke in bed together; the same photo appears on the cover of the show's catalogue. It is a

Intercourse with . . ., 1977. Stills from video of live performance at London Art Museum and Library, London, Ontario; black and white, sound, 30 min.

happy—a playful—image: both artists are covered to the waist by a quilt, and otherwise naked, except for Oldenburg's billed cap; both are propped on their elbows; Oldenburg has an arm around her. One of his soft sculptures is visible on the wall behind them. Wilke looks very happy and a little dazed. The black-and-white photographic diptych *Dear Claes*, dated 1970–82, is a big (twenty-nine-by-eighty-one-inch) composition featuring the close-cropped head of a dappled, dewy-eyed fawn on the left and, on the right, an unflattering picture of Oldenburg lying on a rumpled bed, again propped on an elbow but with his face invisible. Most prominent are his naked rump, and his penis, which lies on the bed in a comical echo of the fawn's outthrust, inquisitive muzzle. The light that plays around the fawn makes it look like it's got a ring through its nose.

If these images of Oldbenburg are merry, teasing testaments to a loving relationship, they are also candid snapshots of a power couple. It seems that Wilke was never unaware of the complexities, including frankly exploited advantages as well as, surely, jealousies and disappointments, of being in a romantic partnership with a professional peer. Then as now a common working condition for artists, it has seldom, if ever, been examined as forthrightly. Nor was her willingness to go on record about its vicissitudes limited to flaunting her ties to a man of formidable art-world clout. (It is worth noting in this regard that apart from Oldenburg's prestige as a Pop master, he is the brother of Richard Oldenburg, director of the Museum of Modern Art from 1972 until 1994.) For her 1978 solo exhibition at Feldman, Wilke wanted to include photographs she had taken of men who had been part of her life, but wasn't able to secure permission from all of them. In *Advertisements for Living*, a grid of nine big color diptychs from photographs dated as early as 1966 and continuing through 1984, Wilke paired the names of various prominent men (Karl Marx, David Smith, Henry Geldzahler) with photos of people to whom she was (or had been) intimately connected, including Oldenburg, Hamilton, and Donald Goddard. As the series title suggests, these diptychs, not quite billboard-size, are meant to read as ads: they flaunt Wilke's happiness, her ambition to be associated with the brand-name artists emblazoned on the paired images—David Smith, Sol LeWitt, [Carl] Andre (represented by his last name only)—and, just as important, her lifestyle (including its gritty urban milieu). The very brazenness with which this bounty is broadcast suggests a degree of irony. Advertisements are not generally associated with unvarnished truths, and the good life Wilke shows us is surely meant to arouse skepticism as well as approval or envy.

At least as bold was her willingness to speak out, in her work, against a man who spurned her. She initiated legal proceedings against Oldenburg in 1979, asking for payment of unmet financial obligations and the restitution of her work in his possession.[10] Oldenburg, for his part, took successful legal action, in 1989, to prevent the University of Missouri from reproducing, in a catalogue accompanying the only major survey in her lifetime of Wilke's work, pieces that included his image, or any other reference to him. To take photographs of *Advertisements for Living* at the St. Louis

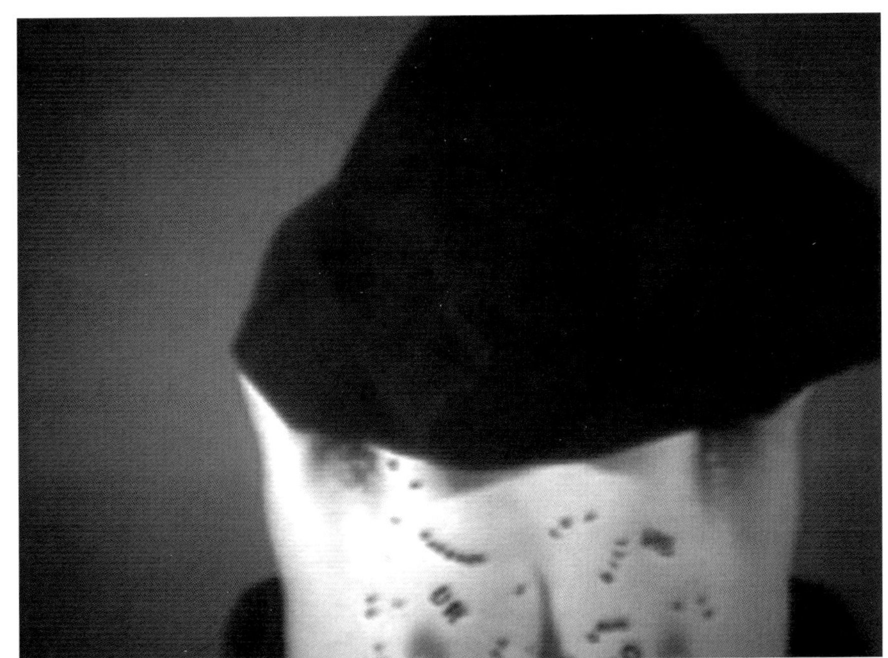

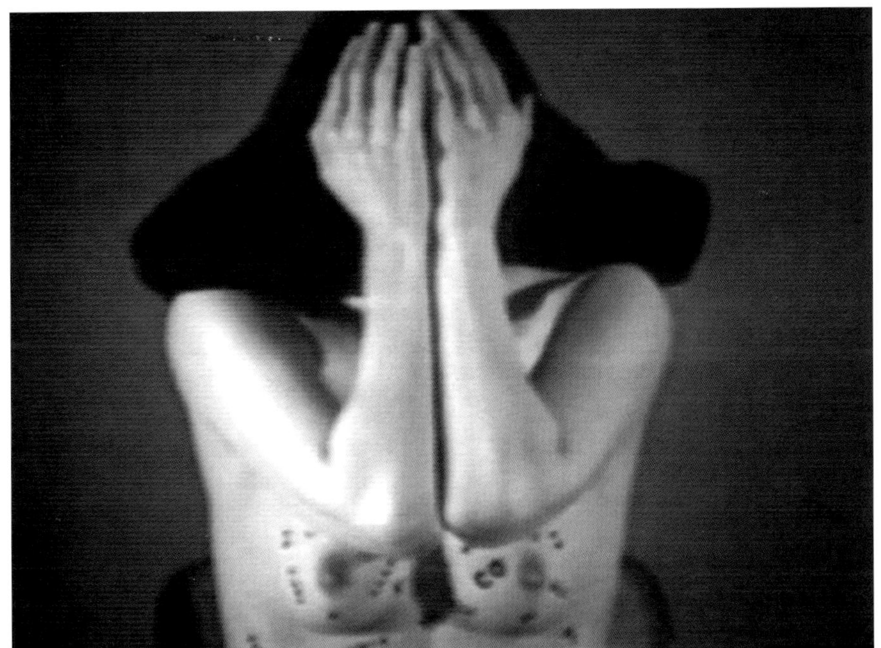

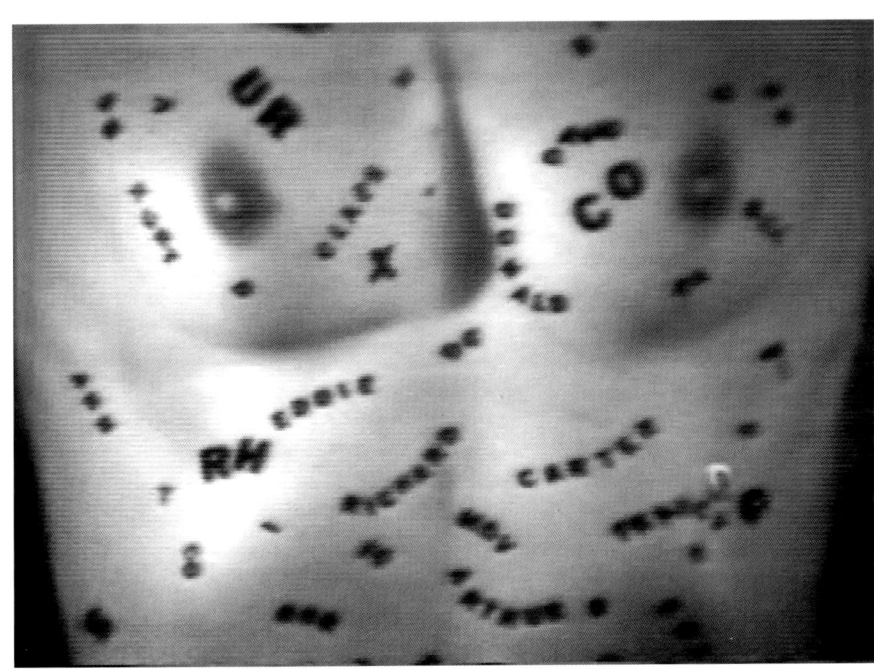
UR
CO
X
DONALD
EDDIE
RH
RICHARD
CARTER

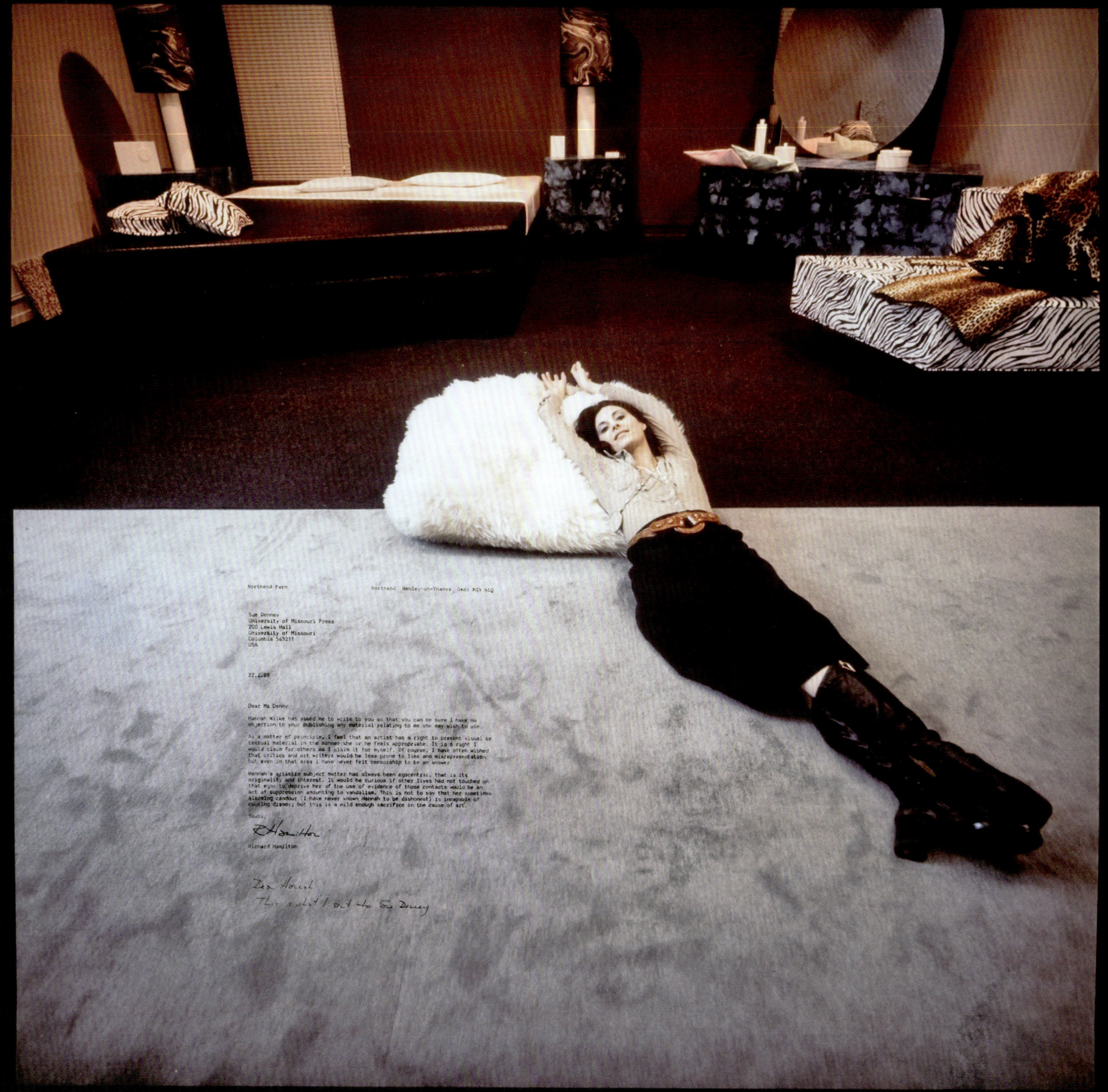

Northend Farm Northend Henley-on-Thames Oxon RG9 6LQ

Sue Denney
University of Missouri Press
200 Lewis Hall
University of Missouri
Columbia 565211
USA

22.2.89

Dear Ms Denny

Hannah Wilke has asked me to write to you so that you can be sure I have no objection to your publishing any material relating to me she may wish to use.

As a matter of principle, I feel that an artist has a right to present visual or textual material in the manner she or he feels appropriate. It is a right I would claim for others as I claim it for myself. Of course, I have often wished that critics and art writers would be less prone to lies and misrepresentation but even in that area I have never felt censorship to be an answer.

Hannah's artistic subject matter has always been egocentric, that is its originality and interest. It would be curious if other lives had not touched on that ego; to deprive her of the use of evidence of those contacts would be an act of suppression amounting to vandalism. This is not to say that her sometimes alarming candour (I have never known Hannah to be dishonest) is incapable of causing dismay; but this is a mild enough sacrifice in the cause of art.

Yours,

R Hamilton

Richard Hamilton

Dear Hannah
This is what I sent to Sue Denny

Even-tu-ally, 1969–91. Cibachrome with silkscreen imprinting of text, 21 x 21 in.

show, curator Tom Kochheiser had someone stand in front of the image of Oldenburg, and this is how it appeared in *Arts Magazine*, where attorney Tim Cone explained that Oldenburg was able "to assert his right of privacy in the photographs," and also, because he is a "celebrity of the art world," could claim "a separate, 'right of publicity,' the right to control the commercial use of his name or likeness." The issue at stake was whether Oldenburg relinquished these rights when he agreed to be photographed in the first place. "Balanced against the harm to Wilke" that would follow losing control of her own work, Cone concludes, "Oldenburg's recently discovered qualms do not weigh very heavily." Cone also notes that "It is fitting that Wilke should stumble upon these legal issues, since her art challenges the very notions of privacy that Oldenburg relied on to prevent publication of the photos."[11]

Two years later, in 1991, Wilke created a print, published by Juni Verlag, that uses a photograph made in the mid-1970s of the artist lying on her back, fully clothed and smiling, on a shag rug that is part of the classic Oldenburg installation, *Bedroom Ensemble* (1963). Superimposed on the photo is the text of a letter written by Richard Hamilton to the University of Missouri in which he defends, graciously and forcefully, Wilke's right to her own work. "Hannah Wilke asked me to write to you," the letter says, "so you can be sure I have no objection to your publication of any material relating to me. As a matter of principle I feel that an artist has to present visual or textual material in the manner she feels appropriate." Hamilton continues, "Hannah's artistic subject matter has always been egocentric, that is its originality and interest. It would be curious if other lives had not touched upon that ego: to deprive her of the use of evidence of those contacts would be an act of suppression amounting to vandalism."

Wilke undertook a different sort of defiance in the black-and-white photographs that comprise the first element of a body of work called "So Help Me Hannah," which were shot at P.S.1 in Long Island City, New York in 1978 by Goddard. Then in its second season as an art space, P.S.1 (now affiliated with the Museum of Modern Art) had been an abandoned public school building, its old-fashioned classrooms, narrow stairwells, and dank basement offering, at the time, appealingly derelict contexts—rich with peeling paint and rusted fixtures—for artists to make site-related works. With the camera as her guide, Wilke stalked its hallways, rooftop, and bathrooms, nude except for her high-heeled sandals, posing as a vamp, a thief, a waif, a goddess of the machine age, and a melancholy child, alone in the corner, with her discarded playthings—toy guns, like those she helped Oldenburg collect for his Ray Gun museum—scattered on the floor in front of her.

In their initial exhibition, as part of a 1978 installation at P.S.1 called "Snatch Shots with Ray Guns," forty-eight of the photos were accompanied by a collection of the "ray guns," arranged on the floor. On a chalkboard were 100 postcards with typed quotes of notable writers, artists, philosophers and critics, from Edmund Burke to James Joyce and including both Marxes (Karl and Groucho). Six of the photographs

Exchange Values (Marx) from **So Help Me Hannah**, 1978–84. One of six black-and-white photographs, 60 x 40 in. each

were enlarged in 1984 for an exhibition at the New Museum in New York, the photographs all captioned with shorter versions of the postcard quotes. Straddling a toilet as if to urinate, Wilke looms above the words "His Farced Epistol," from James Joyce. Standing in the posture of a runner about to start a race, she graces the top of a compressor in the basement in a photo that bears the legend, from Karl Marx, "Exchange Values." Leaning her head into the frame, which is cropped to her open-mouthed face and shoulder, she is labeled "Annihilate Illuminate"; the words are Oldenburg's. Lying prostrate on a gritty floor in a particularly dark image, she is the victim of a noir film murder; the quote, "Opportunity Makes Relations As It Makes Thieves," is from Goethe. In every picture she is armed with a small silver handgun; often she seems unaware she's got it in her hand.

Wilke called this series one of her earliest collaborations, in an interview in which she noted, "I reappropriated back 'ray-guns' that were gifts to Oldenburg from 1969–78."[12] (Oldenburg's work was on exhibit at the Whitney Museum at the same time as the P.S.1 installation; Wilke clearly hoped that viewers would make the connection, though Oldenburg, who credited by name friends who had helped him collect the toy guns, identified Wilke's finds only as "Group W.") While the project was undertaken in part as a frontal assault on a man who had exploited ("Help Me, Hannah") and then hurt her, the images Wilke produced are deeply ambivalent. Melancholy, fatigue, and even helplessness alternate with poses that present her, albeit ruefully, as an armed avenger or martial goddess. As so often, she caught the contradiction with neat economy in the series' title, which, like "S.O.S.," is, first among many other things, a telegraphed call for help. But "So Help Me Hannah," a rather old-fashioned locution, is also a kind of shorthand imprecation, in which the missing word is God and the tone is, as a rule, one of affectionate complaint. We can easily imagine someone—an alter-ego to her unfailingly supportive mother, for instance—saying in exasperation, "So help me God, Hannah, if I find out that you've been dressing up in my mink stole, or taking your clothes off in front of a camera, or sleeping with all the legions of men who call you on the phone . . . ." And if Oldenburg was on her mind while she was making these images, so was her mother, who found in 1978 that her cancer had recurred. Mrs. Butter also needed, and received, Wilke's help, and clearly provoked a reciprocal sense of vulnerability. If the bold sexual posturing in Wilke's work was easier for her feminist peers to swallow than the kittenish coyness she just as often enacted, nothing was less politically acceptable than this frank invocation of childlike need.

In the performances that were also part of the "So Help Me Hannah" series, these competing inclinations are if anything exaggerated. Presented five times between 1979 and 1985, each about a half-hour long, they were staged simply. For a 1979 performance at D.C. Space in Washington, D.C., Wilke entered the room like a thief and stalked it slowly, toy pistol in hand. Slender, graceful, absurdly beautiful, wearing nothing but extravagantly high-heeled sandals, she maintained—as the videotapes of the event document—a mostly solemn face, sometimes engaging the camera,

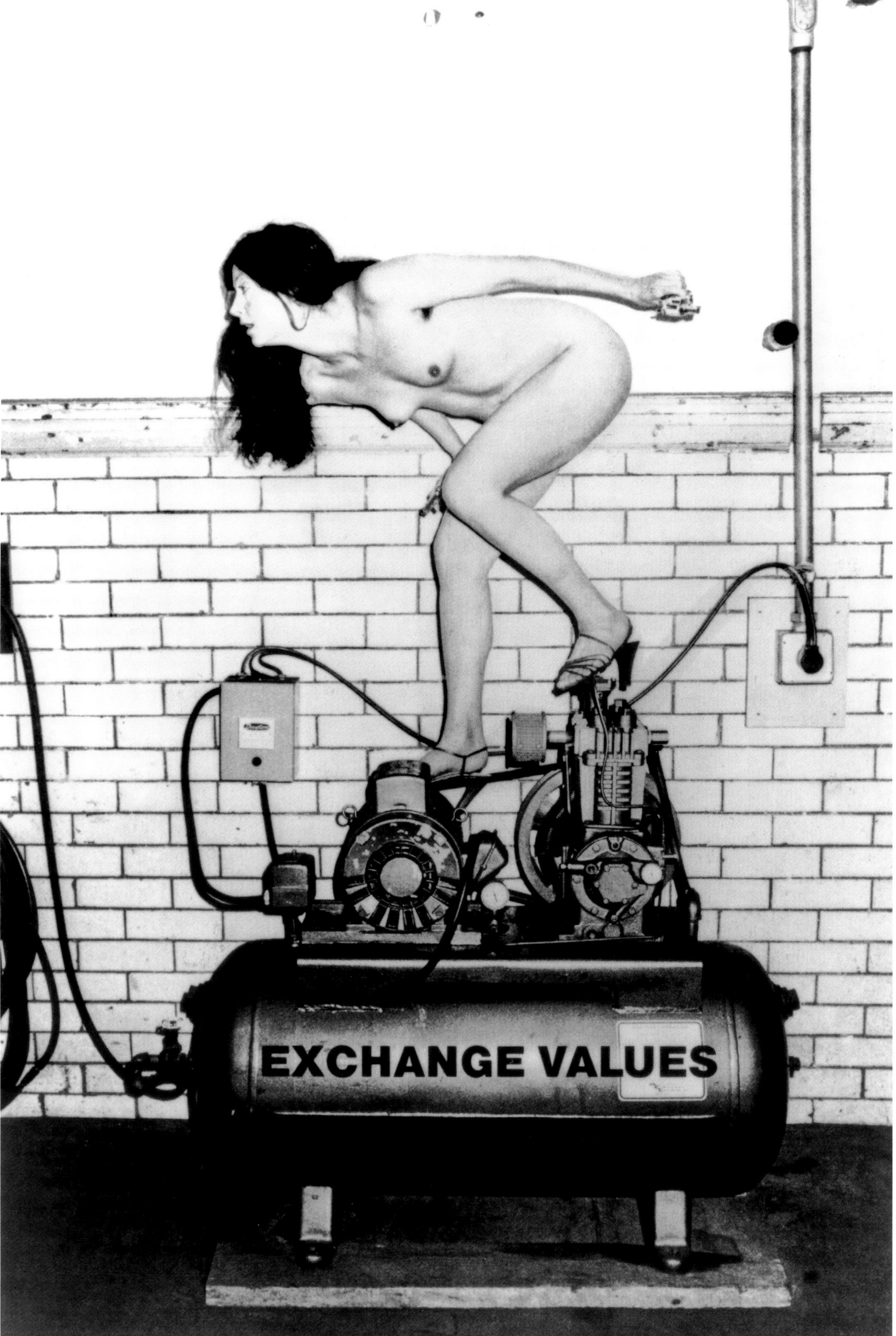
EXCHANGE VALUES

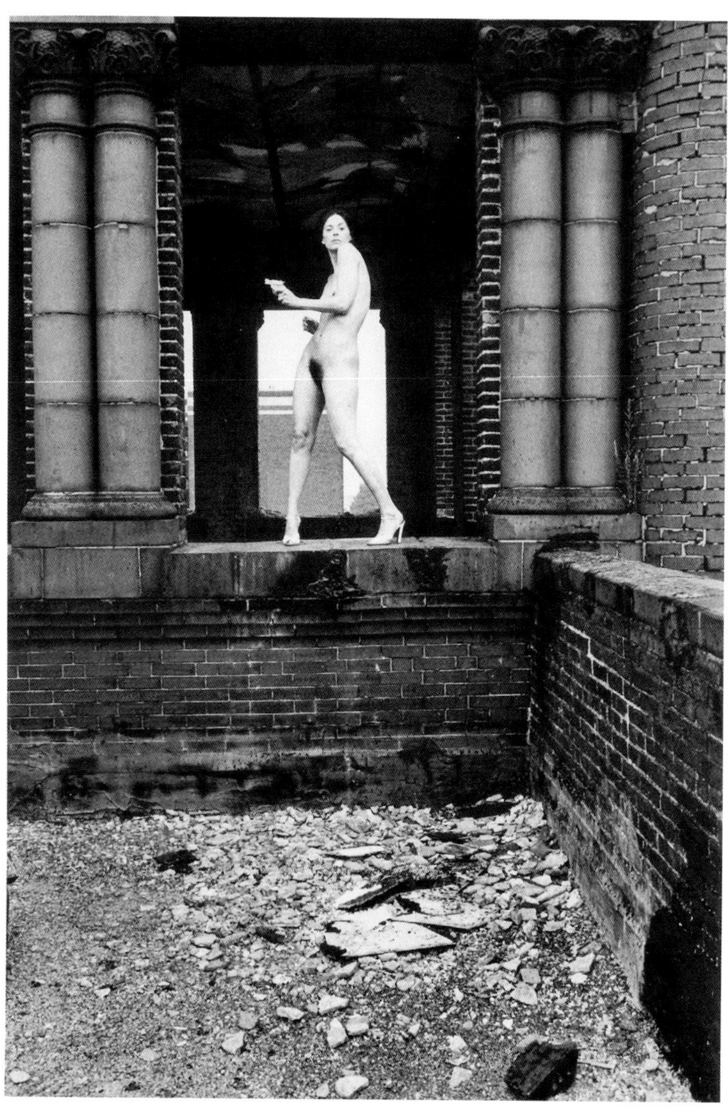

So Help Me Hannah, 1978. Four of forty-eight black-and-white photographs, 14 x 11 in. or 11 x 14 in. each

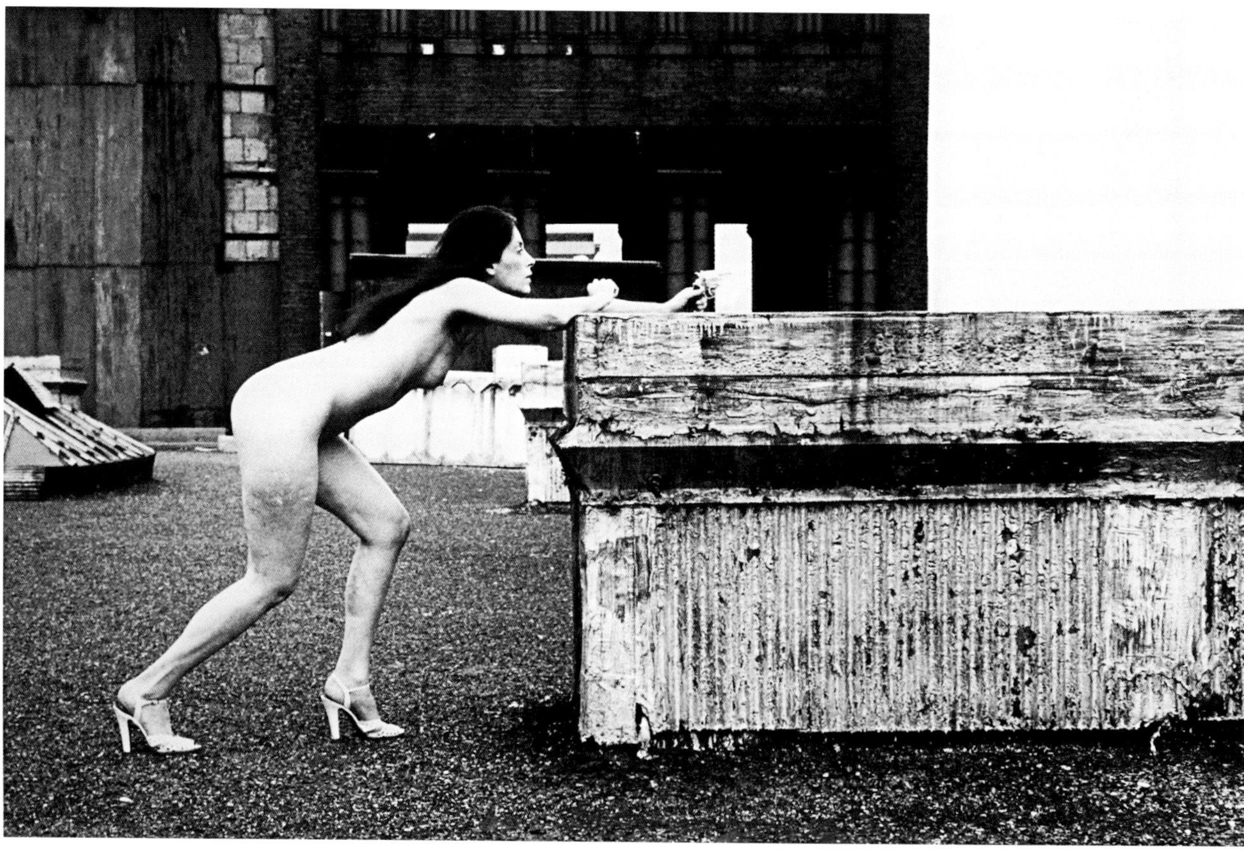

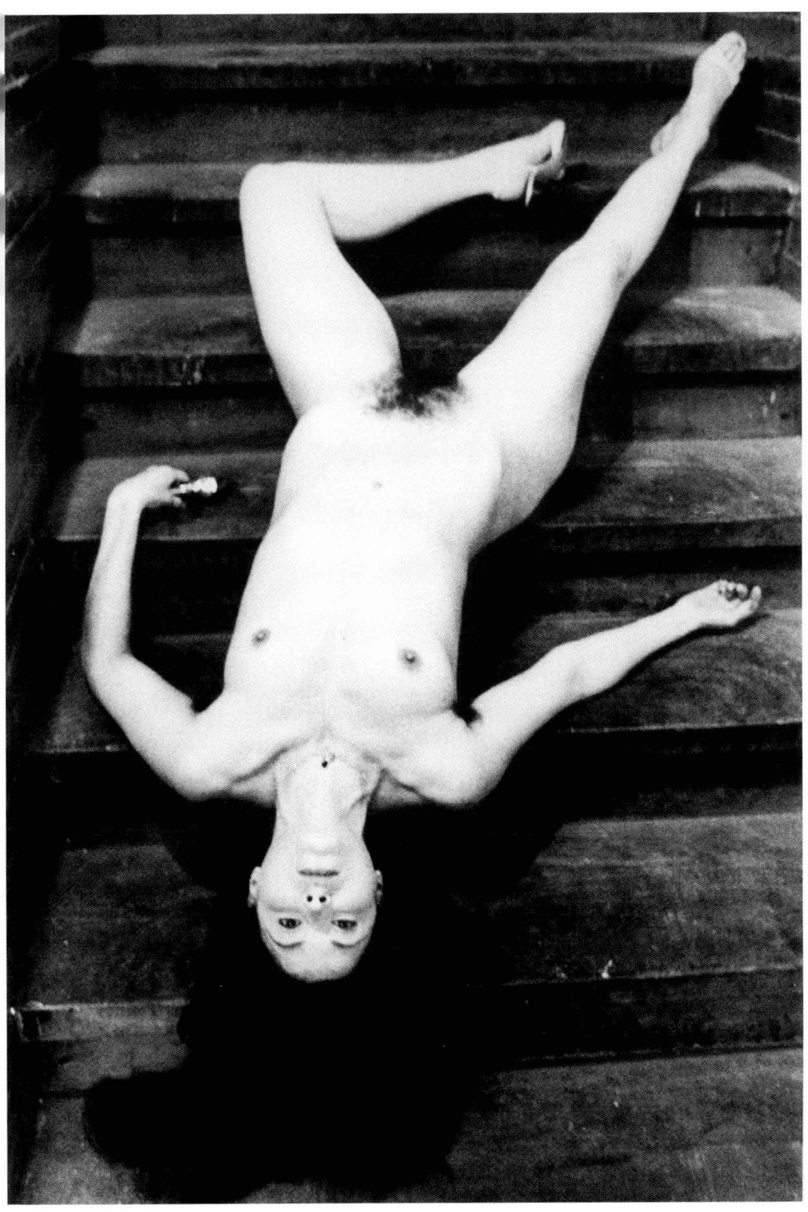

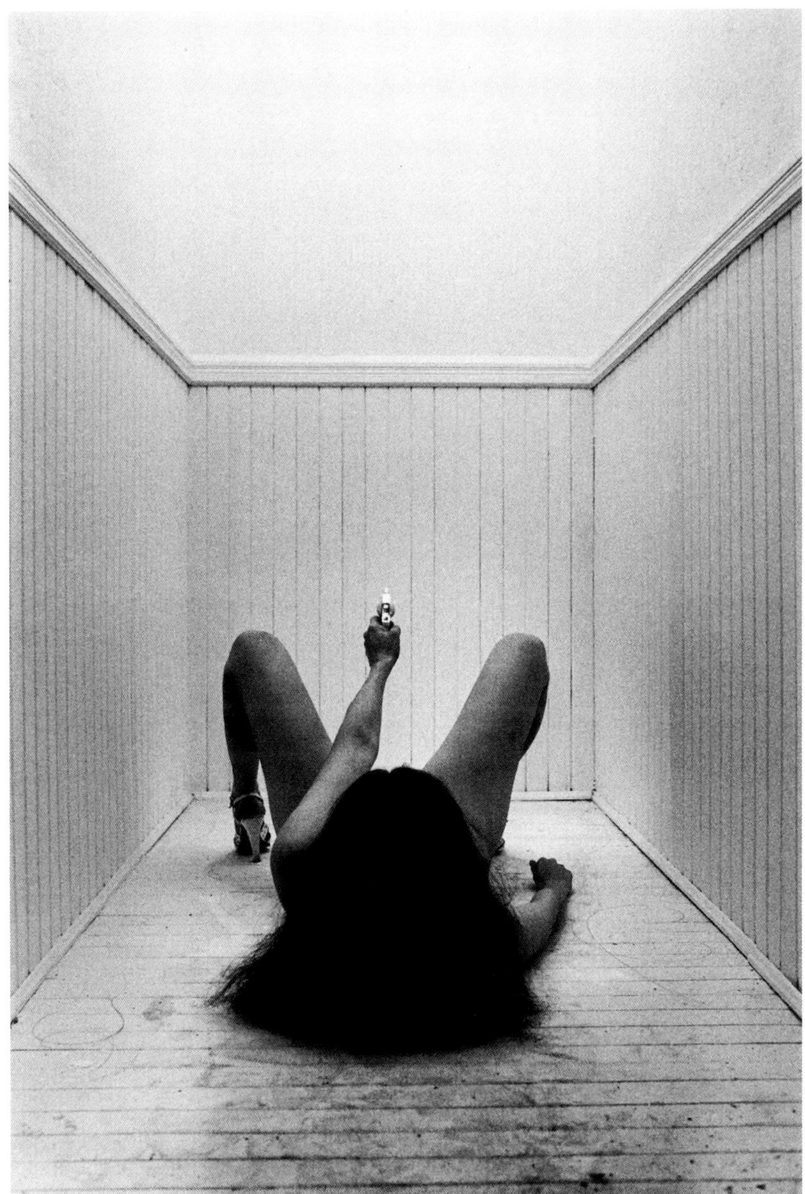

Hername, 1978–91. Black-and-white etchings on paper, 36 x 26 in.

sometimes looking away. The performance is slow and silent, an erotic thriller in mime; she advances and retreats, shrinks and crouches, stands and confronts. Occasionally, she wields the gun menacingly, though for the most part it seems an almost negligible accessory; at one point, she backs up against the wall, hands up, and slides down it as if shot. Twice she subsides to the floor and leans on her elbows, her back arched and head thrown back to expose her neck in just the manner of Giacometti's *Woman with Her Throat Cut* (1932). At the conclusion of the performance, she lies on the floor, defeated, the gun lying on her hip.

Three years later, at A.I.R. in New York, Wilke, again nude but for the high heels and armed with a toy handgun, looks noticeably older and more tired. The expressions she projects are often sexy, but just as many are raw and weary. Moving slowly, sometimes on her hands and knees, at others erect, she arches her back, rolls slowly on the floor, crawls on her stomach. Her exposure is complete, and ranges from seductive to shaming; she does not always ask the camera to flatter her. Her expression is fixedly blank; at one point she strokes her face tenderly with the gun. The videotapes of this performance are in color and share an audio track, which plays her recorded recitation of unattributed quotes, expanded from those included at P.S.1: "The ideal of freedom has retreated to an implosive autistic flight from outside stimuli"; "I don't believe the artist has a professional responsibility to the audience"; "a puzzle is harder to love than a fact." Behind the quotes are sounds recorded from television, including the intermittent sound of a typewriter. At the outset of the performance and also later, a man's voice is heard whispering "I'm sorry." Among additional prose and poetry included in the "So Help Me Hannah" performances is writing by Henry Geldzahler, John Ashbery, Frank O'Hara, Sol LeWitt, Lucy Lippard, Gilbert & George, Vito Acconci, Hans Haacke, Susan Sontag, Henry Miller, Goethe and Karl Marx. We hear Nietzsche ("What must these people have suffered, that they might become thus beautiful?"); Oldenburg ("If you love something very much and are very hungry for touching, you probably could crush or dissolve it out of affection."); Hitler ("Success is the sole earthly judge of right and wrong."); and Harold Rosenberg ("The photograph leads the mind to the actual world . . . if it is of a nude, it will make one think of women, not art."). Ad Reinhardt's "What does this represent, what do *you* represent," is a kind of motif. Goddard, who took the photographs (and is an art writer who was managing editor of *Art News* from 1974 to '78), wrote in 1982 of the "So Help Me Hannah" performances, "The evolution of the work, its emotional and erotic substance, depended on the particular interaction that emerged between the primary cameraman and Wilke. . . . The interplay became an existential game—symbolically, as well as actually, between life and death."[13]

Like Wilke's early and ongoing commitment to ceramic sculpture, which has been eclipsed by her better-known photo-based work, her involvement with literature, and, more concretely, with language—evident in her work's titles as well as in her incorporation of quoted texts—has been obscured. Just as the grids that appeared in her early work were put to uses too personal for Wilke to accurately be called a

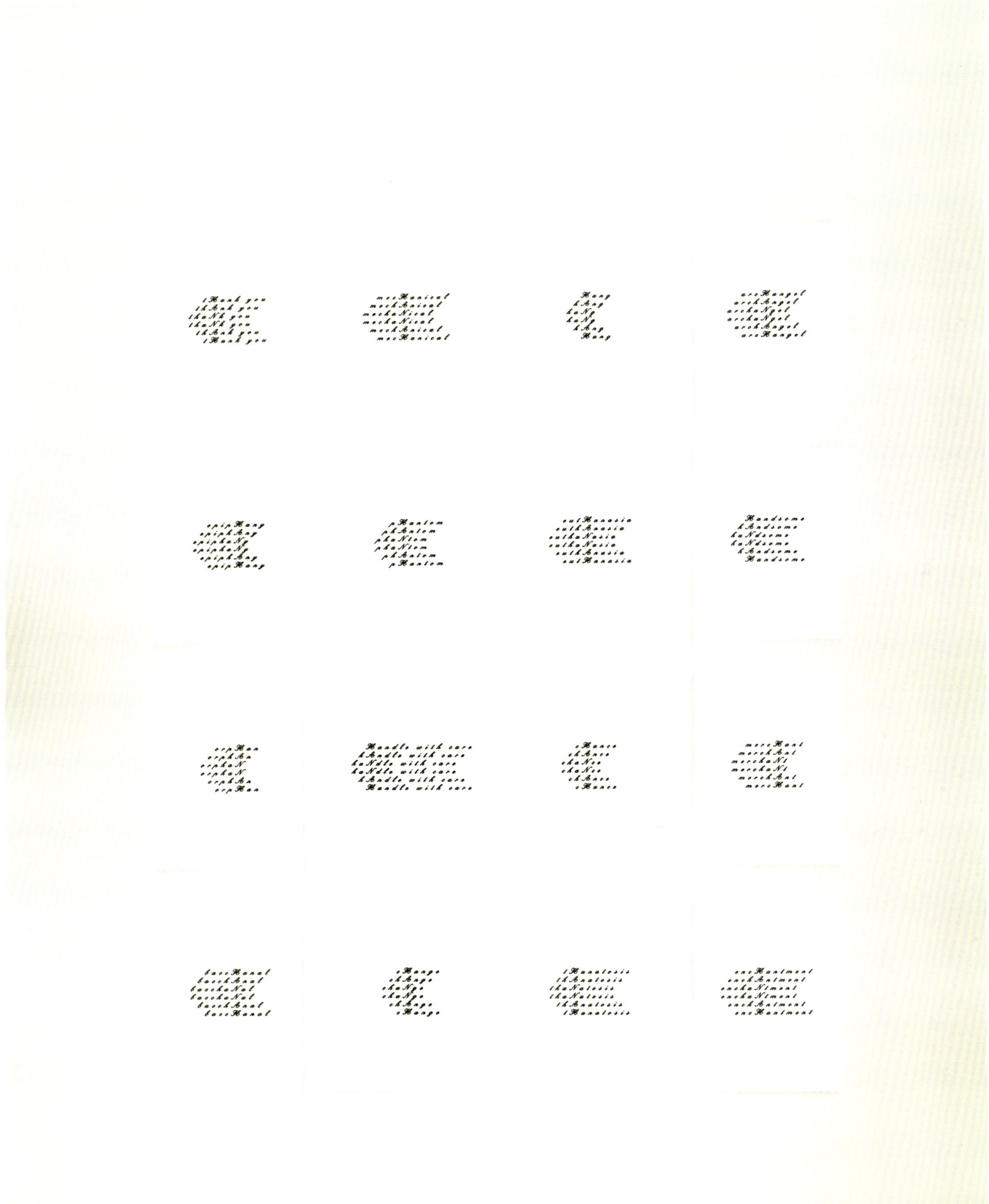

26/30

wilke 78-91

Minimalist, her use of language was far too subjective to merit the term Conceptualist. Nonetheless, her interest in words was genuine and deep, and it resulted in textual formulations that are novel and revealing, even if they don't reach the level of challenge that her work in other mediums does. The instability of language, its easy slippage from sense to nonsense, or to other meanings, as in good puns, is very much like the instability of good looks. Wilke made the analogy a sustained theme. In one passage of a text published in the catalogue accompanying an exhibition of Duchamp's heirs (in which Wilke was one of only two women among nearly sixty men), she moved without pause from children's rhymes to Hollywood-musical lyrics to political theory: "Marxism and Art. Fascistic feelings, internal wounds, made from external situations. Sticks and stones break our bones, but names more often hurt us. . . . Yet to name a thing wherein I caught the conscience of the king, as well as the queen . . . to keep on naming a thing . . . to where [*sic*] my hat, the memory of all that, until that thing is really something. To exist instead of being an existentialist [ellipses in the original]."[14] Goddard says the statements she read in "So Help Me Hannah" "were advertisements of the self, and yet they thematically and rhythmically evolved into a single statement about social contracts, visual prejudice, political and psychological violence, complexities of interchange between art and life."

Word games using her (assumed) first name in elegant but rather compulsive repetitions are the subject of such works as *Hername* (it was the painter Knox Martin, a friend in the early 1960s, who had proposed that she use Hannah, her middle name, rather than her given first name, Arlene, making even that first integer of identity a rearrangement of fact[15]). Realized both as a series of drawings on graph paper (1978; p. 95) and as a suite of sixteen etchings (1978–81) printed in formal wedding-invitation-style cursive script, *Hername* involves aligning the letters H, A, N, N, A, and H vertically within stacks of words or phrases that contain all three letters: they include thank you, archangel, phantom, euthanasia, handsome, orphan, handle with care, chance, merchant, bacchanal, thanatosis, and enchantment. As sometimes seems true of the photographs and videos, such word works circle around Wilke's self-understanding with a relentlessness that ultimately erodes the subject of its focus.

The puns can be seen as a kind of inadvertent, preemptive joke on post-structuralist linguistics and its theorization of the mutability of meaning; a latter-day Joycean, Wilke was in her way also a precocious Derridean, alive to the tendency of words to slip their moorings, and of fixed significations to shift under the pressure of neighboring terms. As has been observed with respect to the Surrealists' frequent use of anagrams and other kinds of wordplay, they are also a link, forged in full consciousness, with the language of dreams and psychoses. Playful if compulsive word repetitions, inversions, rhyming, and echoing are probes of social and linguistic connective tissue that in the normal course of things goes undisturbed. It is also probably pertinent that Wilke's autographic writing could be erratic in the extreme, as handwritten documents show, and her spelling atrocious—bad enough to seem deliberate, as if even the simplest linguistic conventions were worth a good hard shake.

All are among the ways of worrying the language that can be practiced by those it worries right back.

Of course another way of describing her verbal and visual provocations and calls for help is that they were meant to be taken at face value. As scared as anyone else—neither more nor less—she kept pushing her limits, flaunting both her power and, more unsettling to many women, her weakness, dependency, and need for attention. The too-muchness of everything she did is, in this light, not a symptom but a choice. And if there was a blurting, deeply discomfiting expression of vulnerability to some of Wilke's actions and work, there was more often—and sometimes simultaneously—a sense of surpassing confidence. Certainly no one who knew her describes her as anything less than brimming, spilling over, with vivacity—with glee, anger, pride, curiosity, courage.

Wilke's studio habits were irregular; long periods without obvious art-making activity alternated with others of intense productivity; at the same time, things that happened in life were often later recovered as art. In her continuum of talk, her surfeit of ideas, her reluctance to differentiate between street smarts and serious discourse, or to distinguish one body of work from another, or to separate life from art, there was, nonetheless, the consolidation of a distinct and highly self-aware personality. Perhaps of greatest importance, with respect to her personal history and its impact on her work, is that for all her broadcasting of need, she never portrayed herself as a victim. As she said with respect to *Hannah Wilke Can*, ". . . it is easier to give to somebody than to take . . . to ask, is the most difficult of all."[16]

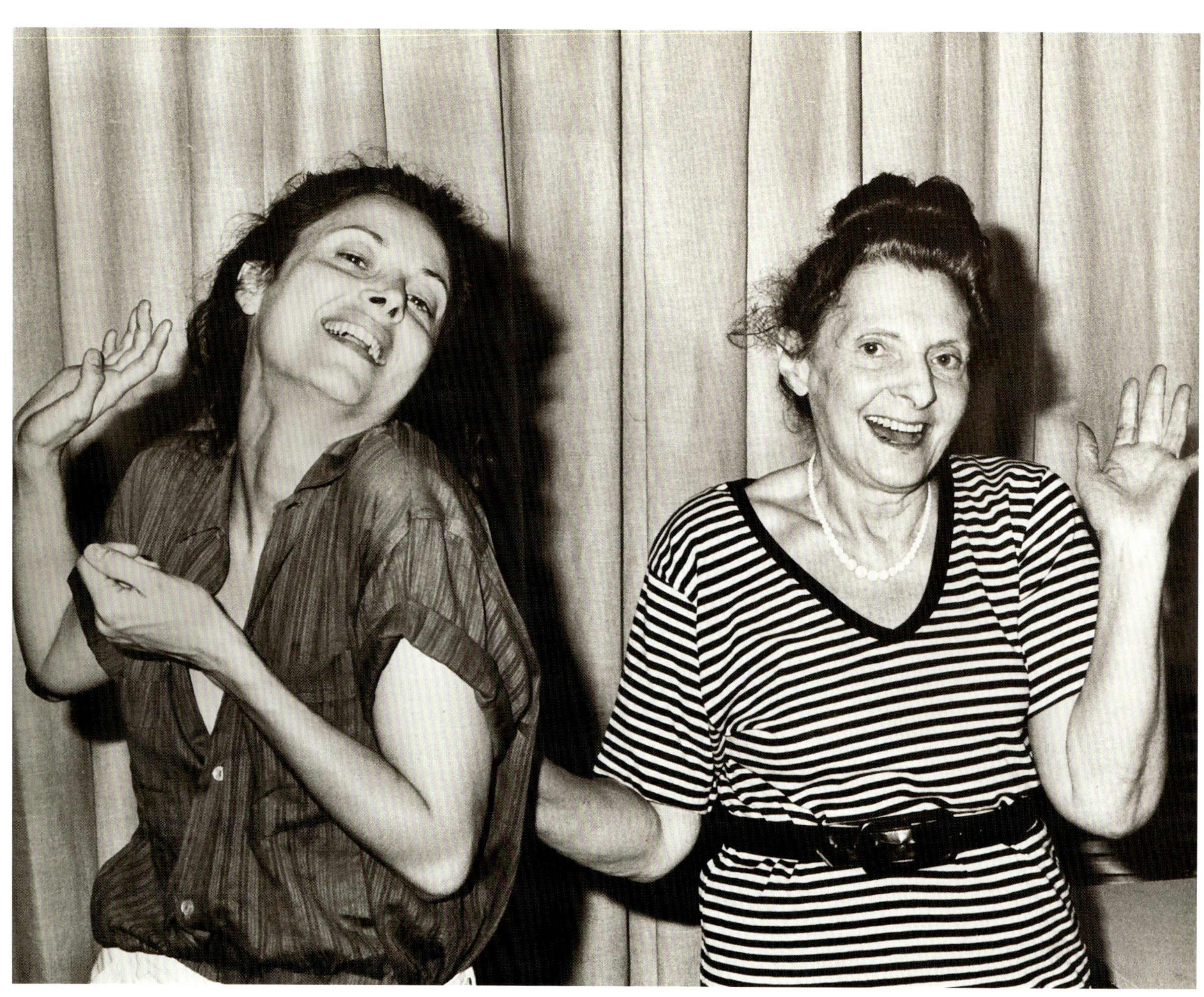

CHAPTER FOUR

In Extremis

A 1988 text by Wilke called "Seura Chaya"—it is titled after her mother's Hebrew first and middle names—begins plaintively: "My mother never let me have a pet," Wilke writes, in the tone of an aggrieved child. There is also language borrowed from fairy tales: "She grew up as a great beauty on the Lower East Side and married the 'Prince of Fourth Street,' Emanuel Butter. They lived happily ever after until he died of a heart attack one morning in her bed, in 1961, seven months after my own marriage." The text's bifurcated focus, one eye on her mother and the other on herself, is sustained. "On my 30th birthday, in 1970, my mother had a mastectomy,"[1] Wilke writes. She doesn't say how old her mother or father were at these junctures. She does relate that after a period of remission, Selma Butter's cancer returned, in 1978, following a stroke. Wilke, living not far from her in downtown Manhattan, became involved in her mother's care; their relationship was by all accounts close and loving. Wilke would say afterward that she gave up art during this period to look after her mother, but the truth, by her own description, is more complicated. In a 1985 interview, she recalled, "I seduced [my mother] into allowing me to be with her during her battle with cancer. My going to the hospital and sitting with her nine hours a day made her feel guilty. So in order to absolve herself, she let me take the photographs, because then, somehow, I was still doing my art."[2] In "Seura Chaya," Wilke says, "I took thousands of photographs of her over the next four years, hoping the images of her would keep her alive." In the following sentence, her attention again wanders: "I had taken thousands of photographs with Claes also, but these too were lost to me when he got married in 1977. The images I made of myself and my mother kept me alive. Art is a distraction, so is life."

Wilke had already introduced Selma Butter in the *Intercourse with . . .* audiotapes. That first fleeting audio appearance gave a good indication of what was to follow: a revelation of a relationship—between a mother and her adult daughter—seldom explored so deeply in art, and the plotting of another coordinate in the map of Wilke's character. As was true of Butter's voice and the contents of her phone messages, the mother's appearance was more marked by ethnicity than was the daughter's. (In fact, Wilke had cosmetic surgery to alter her nose shortly after her first marriage, to Barry Wilke; the photos of her mother are, perhaps, one clue she leaves to this self-modification.) Wilke's decision to celebrate her mother in photographs was, then, also a kind of self-exposure, even when she was not in the frame. But if Wilke subjected her mother to her own project of self-exploration, she also implicitly submitted to Butter's authority as a parent, to the degree that the photos extract a kind of approval. If the Hannah of "So Help Me Hannah" caused exasperation, and expressed it right back, these documents of a solicitous daughter's attentions seem aimed at mitigating both effects.

They are also a certificate of the mother's blessing on a career that most first-generation Americans would discourage in their children because of its poor prospects for financial security. Another is provided in a story Ronald Feldman tells. "I've seen a lot of artists with their parents," he says, "and in most cases, the parents

Dancing in the Dark, 1978. Black-and-white photograph, 15½ x 19½ in.

In Memoriam: Selma Butter (Mommy), 1979–83. Photographic triptych with sculpture. Triptych: three groups of six gelatin silver prints, each with press type and art paper, mounted on board, 41 x 61 in. each. Sculpture: three groups of two acrylic-painted ceramics on acrylic-painted Masonite, 13 x 20 x 4 in. each.

have no idea how they had a child like this. They don't know who this is. . . . Mrs. Butter was different. Very different." On the opening day of one of Wilke's shows, Mrs. Butter arrived early and waited patiently for her daughter. When Wilke appeared, her mother asked if she planned to perform at the reception. Wilke said no, and Mrs. Butter said, "Oh fine, I'm going home." That was the opposite of what Feldman expected, and he asked her why. "She said, 'If Hannah was going to perform, I wanted everyone to see and know that I was there, and I don't think there's anything wrong. But since she's not, I'm going home.' She wanted to give Hannah cover."[3] Describing the exceptional closeness of Wilke and her mother, Feldman also notes with humor Mrs. Butter's belief in the weight her judgment would carry, for the public and for her daughter. But he does not dismiss its importance, or its audacity, and neither did the artist. Like "Intercourse with . . . ," then, Wilke's photographs of her mother are about a very volatile mix of need, respect, competition and deep affection.

When we first see Mrs. Butter, in the black-and-white photograph *Dancing in the Dark* (1978; p. 98), she looks great. Mother and daughter stand in front of a curtain—a metaphorical concealment of the dark toward which, the title intimates, they turn their backs. Both women are laughing, and both are holding their hands up—it is the only dance gesture visible; presumably their legs are moving too, though they're outside the frame. But while Butter looks simply happy and happily engaged, Wilke is acting; her gesture is theatrical, her head is thrown back, her smile is less cheerful than seductive. Both women look straight at the camera; Wilke's eyes are partly closed, just shy of sultry. By the end of that year, Butter would be deep in cancer treatments; her glossy hair, still dark and piled atop her head in *Dancing in the Dark*, is all gone by the time the photos that make up *In Memoriam, Selma Butter (Mommy)*, (1979–83) were taken. In this substantial work, three big framed compositions each contain six photographs of Butter in various states of illness. Each composition also includes a trio of arrangements of paper scraps that, careful scrutiny reveals, represent fragments of the negative space around the subject in the photos. Beneath these collages are triads of words: Form, Cause, Make; Support, Foundation, Comfort; Bond, Intimate, Part. Finally, placed on the floor below the wall-hung compositions are three big ceramic sculptures—wombs more than vulvas, at this scale and in relationship to these photographs; like the edges of the paper scraps, they are colored in various paired permutations of the primaries.

The complexity of this work announces its seriousness and importance—it has the heft and solemnity that a memorial requires. But the formality of the arrangement, uncharacteristic for Wilke, is a little stiff, almost dutiful. The individual photographs, on the other hand, are eloquent. In some Butter seems hale and spirited, strolling across the street and waving, seated behind a table groaning with plates and bottles, smiling gamely even though her hair is gone; in others she looks exhausted, grim and terribly sick. One shows her seated at the corner of the image, staring at a wig that she has taken off her small bald head; she faces, without consulting, a mirror that reflects her to the camera as a malevolent gnome: a moribund but deathless

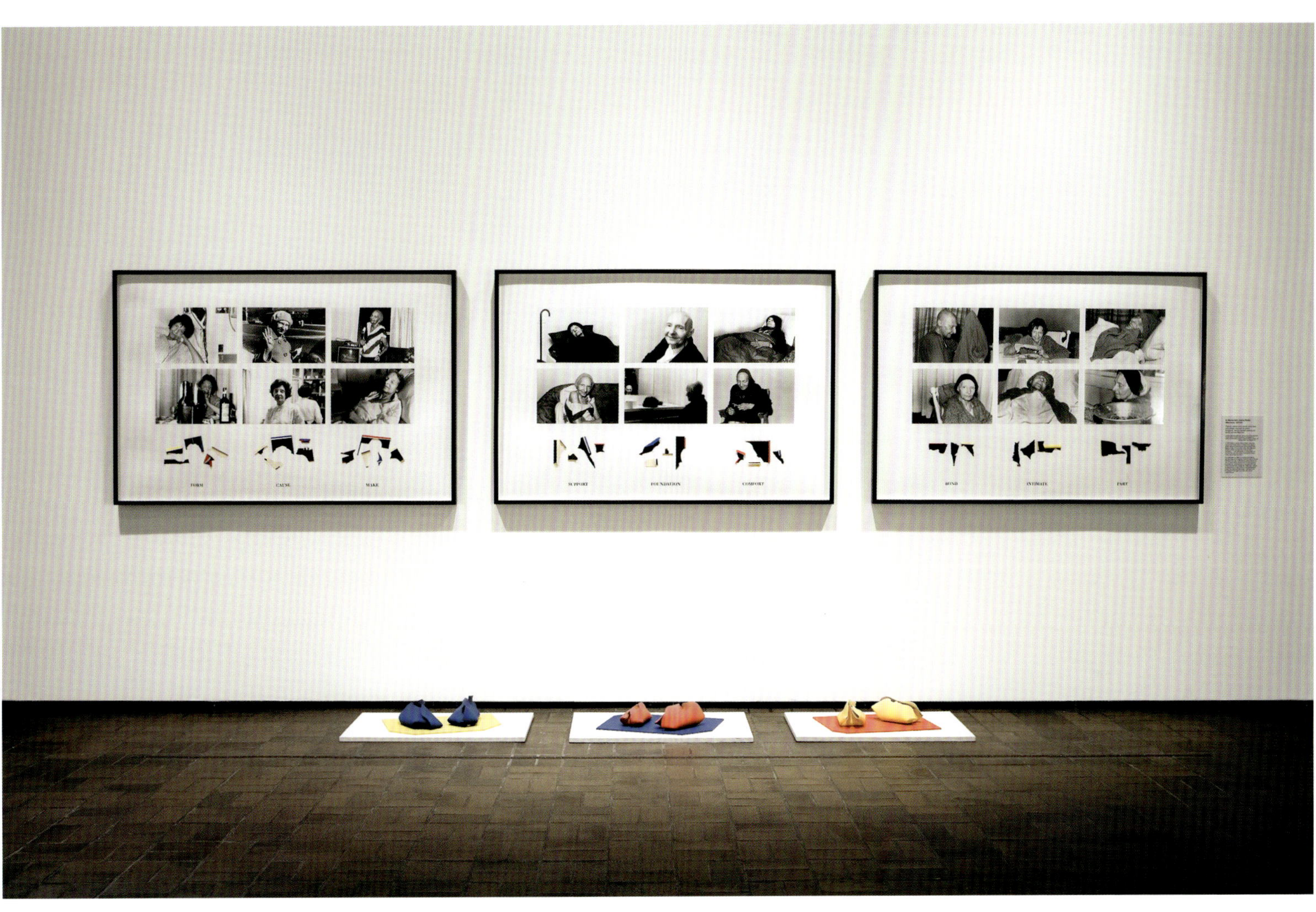
FORM
CAUSE
MAKE
SUPPORT
FOUNDATION
COMFORT
BOND
INTIMATE
PART

Seura Chaya #1, 1978–89. Black-and-white photograph with watercolors, 59 x 63 in. framed

opposite:

Seura Chaya #2, 1978–89. Black-and-white photograph with watercolors, 59 x 63 in. framed

Seura Chaya #4, 1978–89. Black-and-white photograph with watercolors, 59 x 63 in. framed

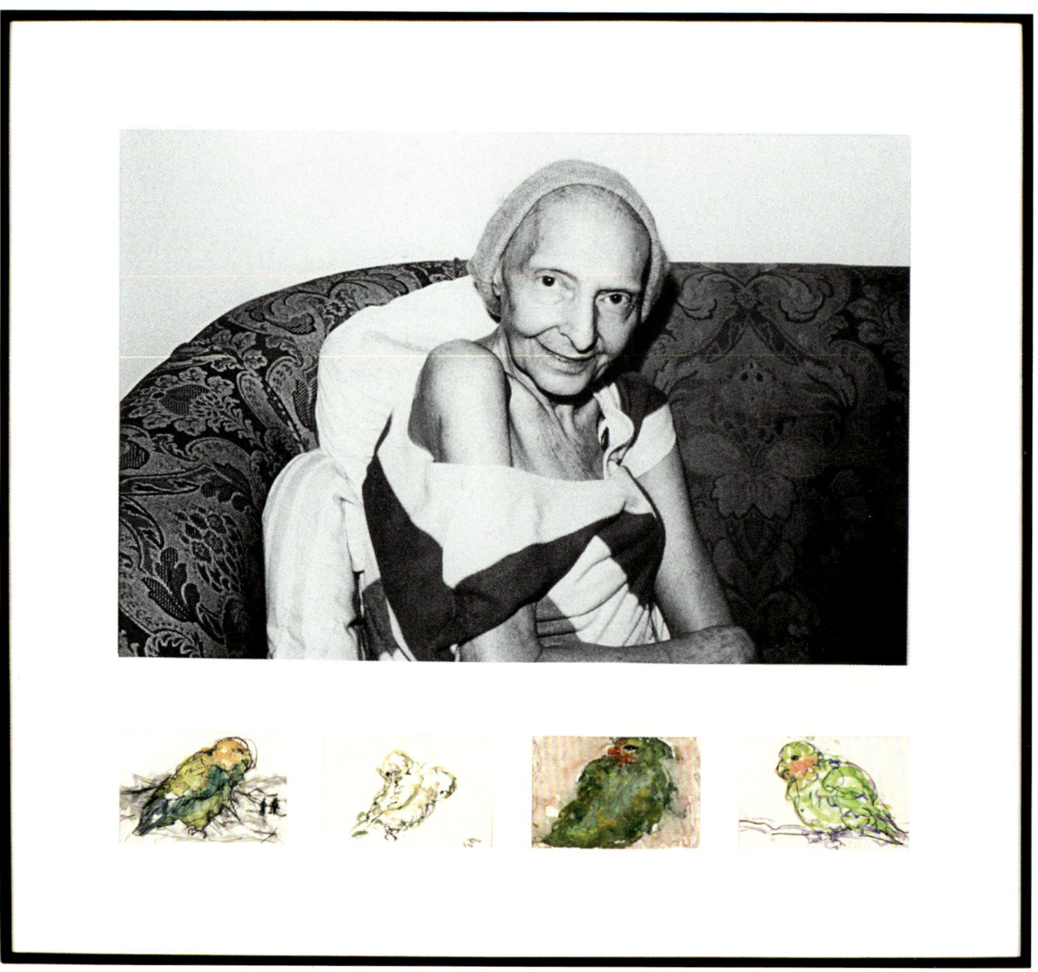

Nosferatu. The range of expressions the photos evoke—or reveal, in the artist who made them—includes fear, sadness, a deep sense of betrayal, and, certainly not least, enormous empathy.

Three of the photographs that appear in *In Memoriam* are each the centerpiece of a quartet of photo works called *Seura Chaya* (1978–89). In the first of these (above), Butter is nestled into one side of a brocade couch, propped up with pillows. The couch looks enormous, but so does a sweater that is draped over her shrunken frame. A knit cap doesn't conceal quite all of her nearly hairless scalp. She smiles widely—if also, it seems, with considerable effort. Most disconcertingly, she allows the sweater to fall off one shoulder, which is turned toward the camera in a terrible parody of the coy, sexy pose Wilke uses, often and powerfully, in the "S.O.S." photographs and *Through the Large Glass*. Beneath the photo, which is large (the work's overall dimensions are fifty-nine by sixty-three inches), are four small watercolor drawings of a green lovebird, lively and vivid. The bright-eyed bird variously looks ahead, preens, settles, and, in a mottled blur, rises aloft. In *Seura Chaya #2*, *#3*, and *#4* (1978–89), the same format is followed: a big black-and-white photograph of Butter with four watercolor drawings of birds beneath, like the predella of an altarpiece. In *Seura Chaya #2*, however, the photo's subject is standing and in profile, wearing slacks and a brassiere, and holding a wig in her hands; she is more naked but less exposed, and her bald head and black pants neuter her image. Looking down, she ignores the camera completely. Only slightly less ambitious than the earlier

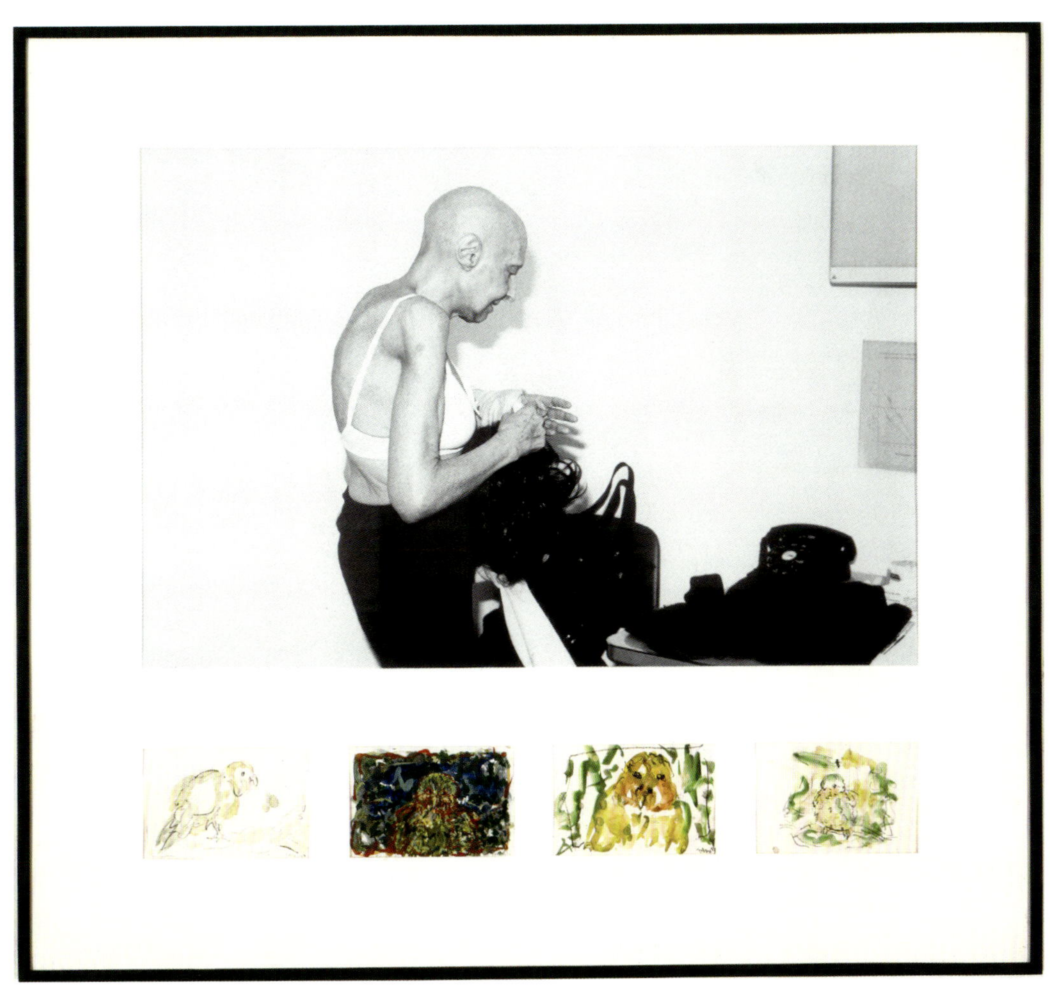

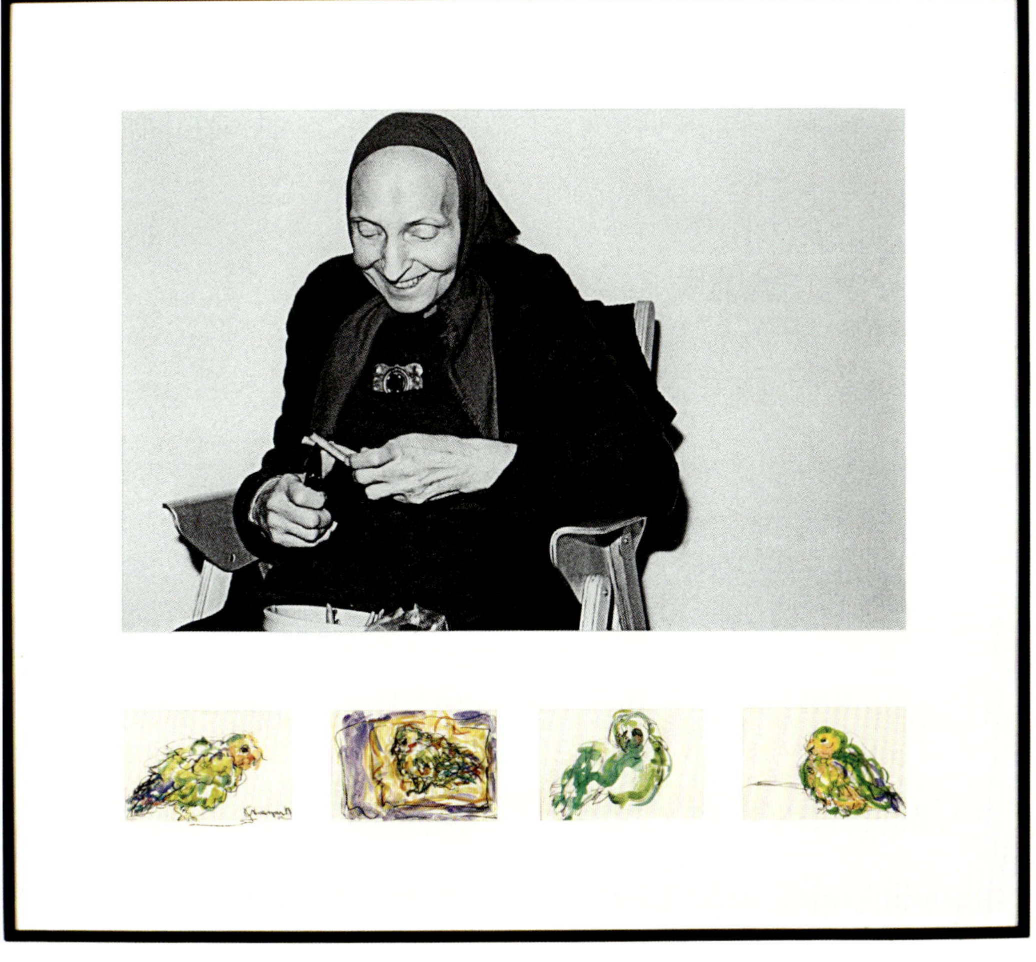

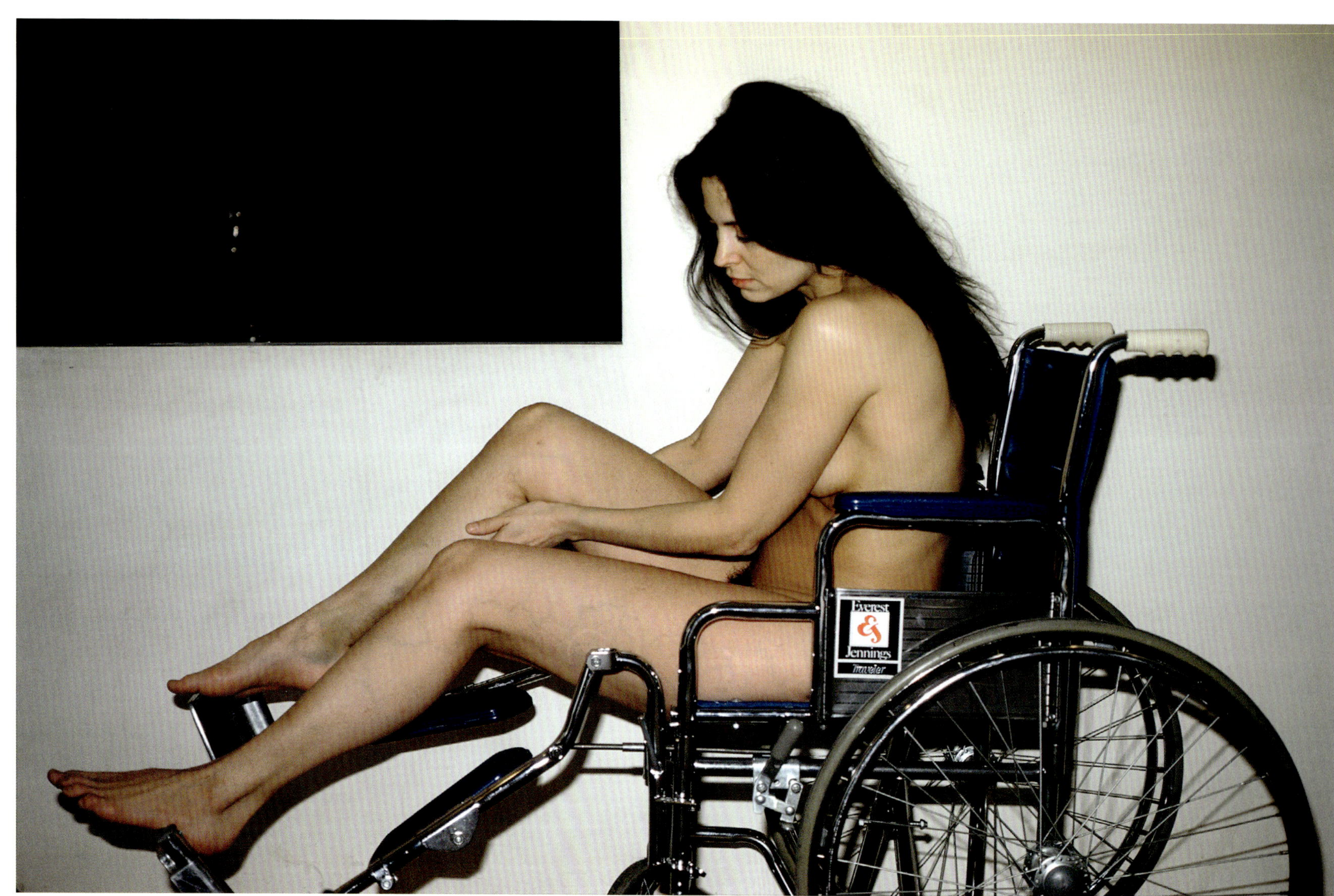
Everest
&
Jennings
Traveler

Nancy Fried, **Self-Portrait**, 1994. Terra cotta, 13½ x 19 x 11 in.

opposite:
Vein Attempt—Broken Blood Vessels from Heel Kicking Hannah, 1981

following pages:
Portrait of the Artist with her Mother, Selma Butter, 1978–81. Cibachrome diptych, each photograph 40 x 30 in.

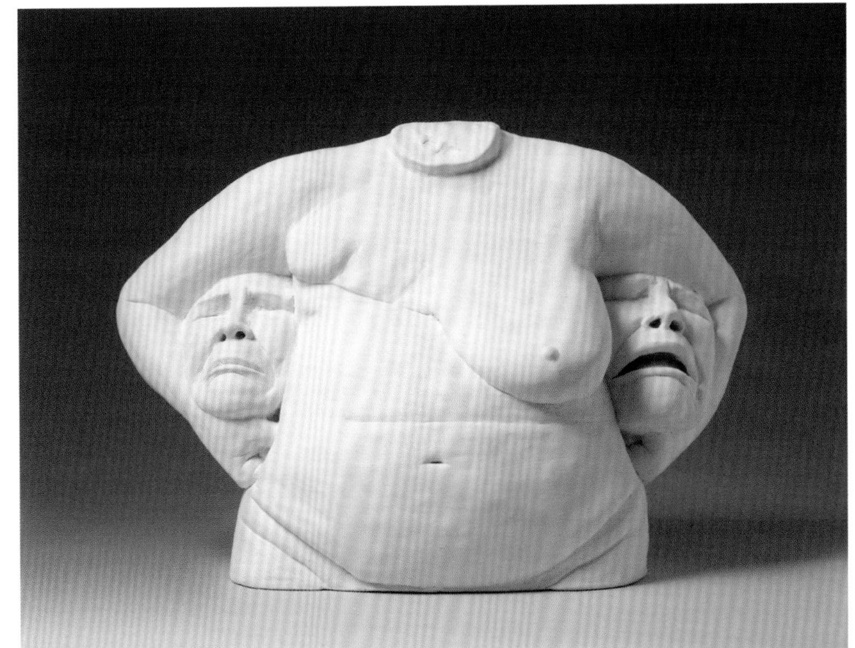

memorial composition, the "Seura Chaya" works are more richly suggestive. They invite speculation about Mrs. Butter's role in creating these photos that the less intimate *In Memoriam* inhibits. Was she entirely passive, merely following the artist's instructions? Or active in a way that sharply illuminates Wilke's own character, but from the oblique perspective of maternal influence? Or, most likely, did she occupy a position complicatedly between these poles?

Wilke used other photographs of her mother during her final illness, some of them in color, as single, freestanding images. There are also photographs Wilke made of herself during the four-year period of "withdrawal" from art-making. *Breastplate* (1981) is a black-and-white diptych: on the left is a shot of a cake Wilke had made for an artist's auction, adorned with chewing-gum cunts and surrounded by fern leaves; on the right, Wilke is lying on her back, one arm raised to expose luxuriant underarm hair, one breast covered with this cake, which becomes a shield; the overhead perspective and prostrate pose flattens the exposed breast and contributes to an effect of near androgyny. In *Vein Attempt–Broken Blood Vessels from Heel Kicking Hannah* (1981), Wilke matches her beauty against the cold metal of a wheelchair, into which she has settled with particular delicacy and grace.

But none of the photographs Wilke made of her mother and herself during this period offer comparisons as provocative as *Portrait of the Artist with Her Mother, Selma Butter* (1978–81; pp. 106–07). On the right of this color diptych, Butter is shown cropped just below her chest. She has a full head of rich brown hair—perhaps it is a wig—and red lipstick. But this time her eyes are averted. In fact, they seem to be closed—understandably so, since Wilke has convinced her mother to pose topless, revealing the livid scars of a radical mastectomy. On the left, Wilke lies back in an image of insolent health. Indeed, she has accentuated the bloom of her (relative) youth with almost clownish makeup: circles of rouge, baby-blue eye shadow, pink lipstick. Her plucked and shaped eyebrows are arched; the gaze she directs straight at

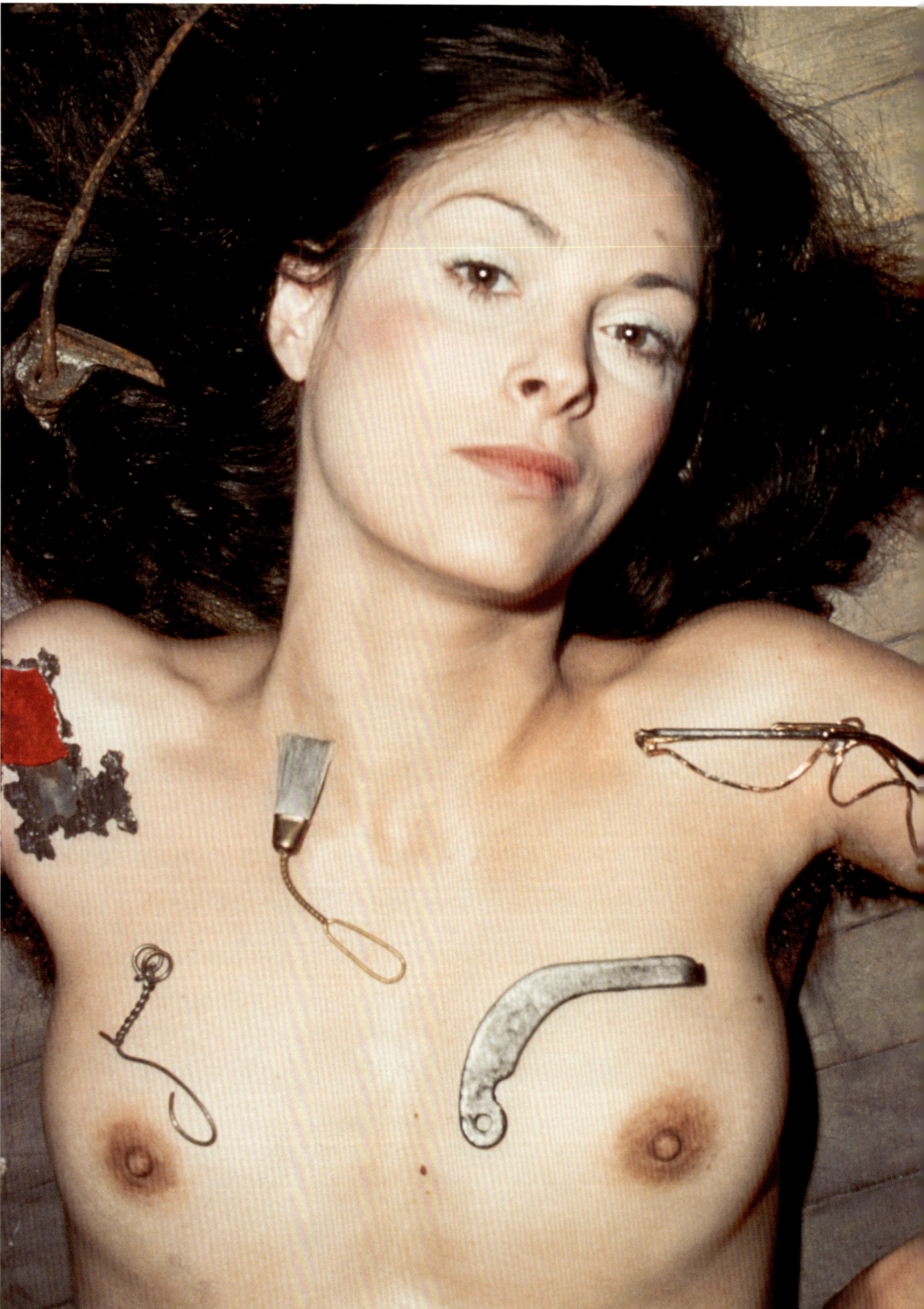

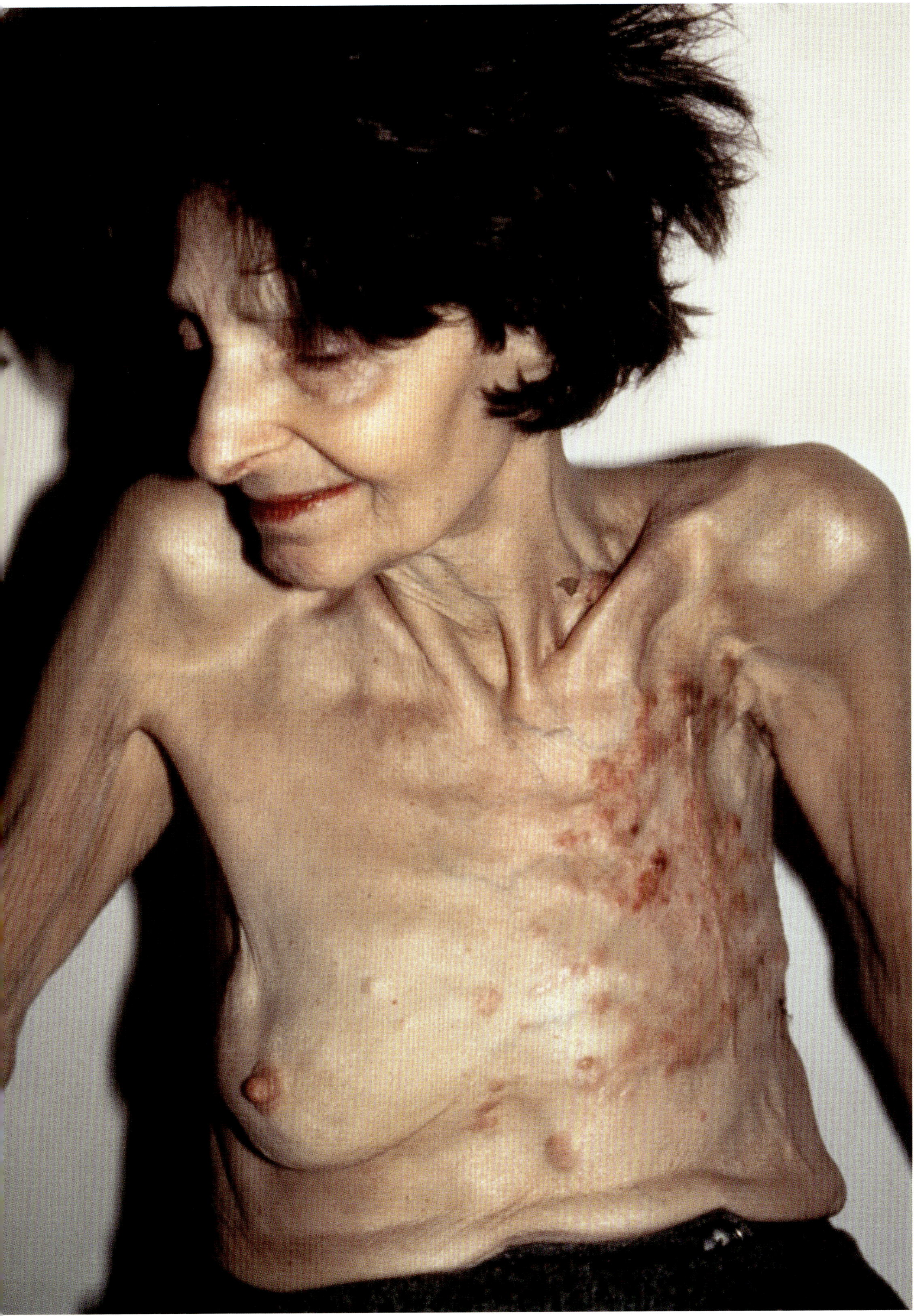

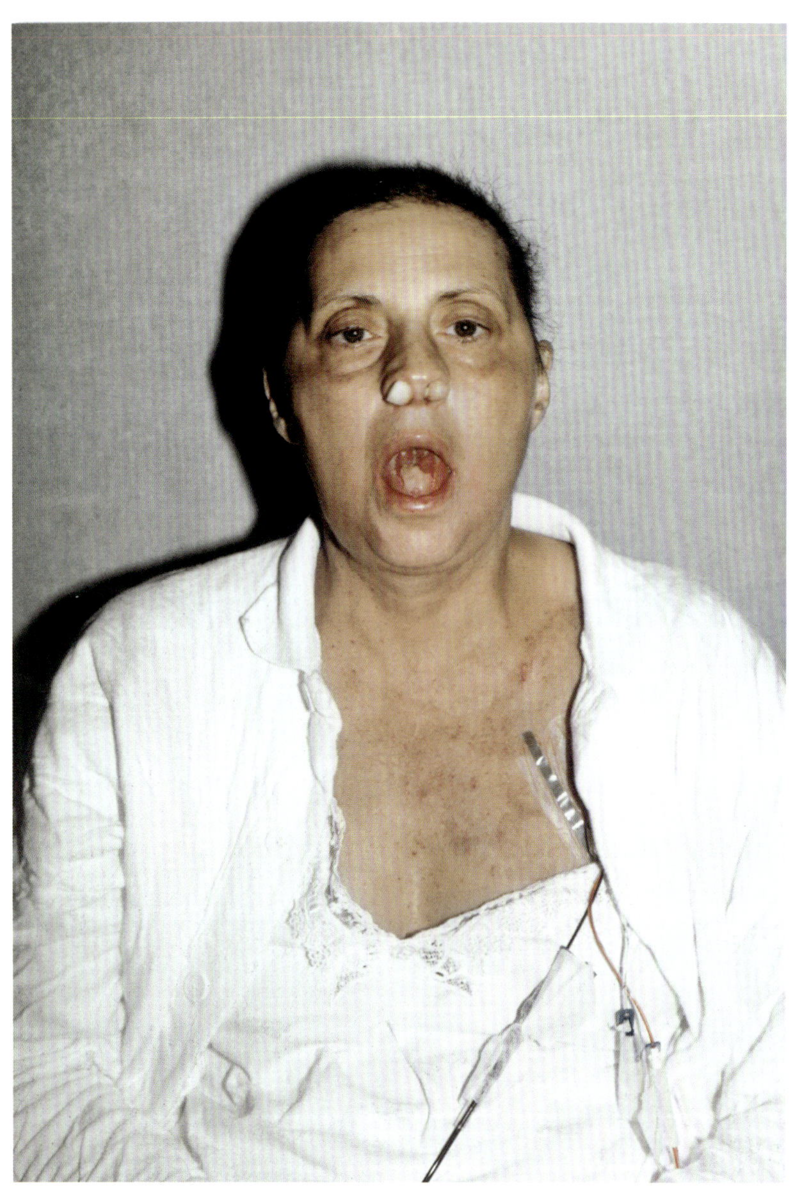

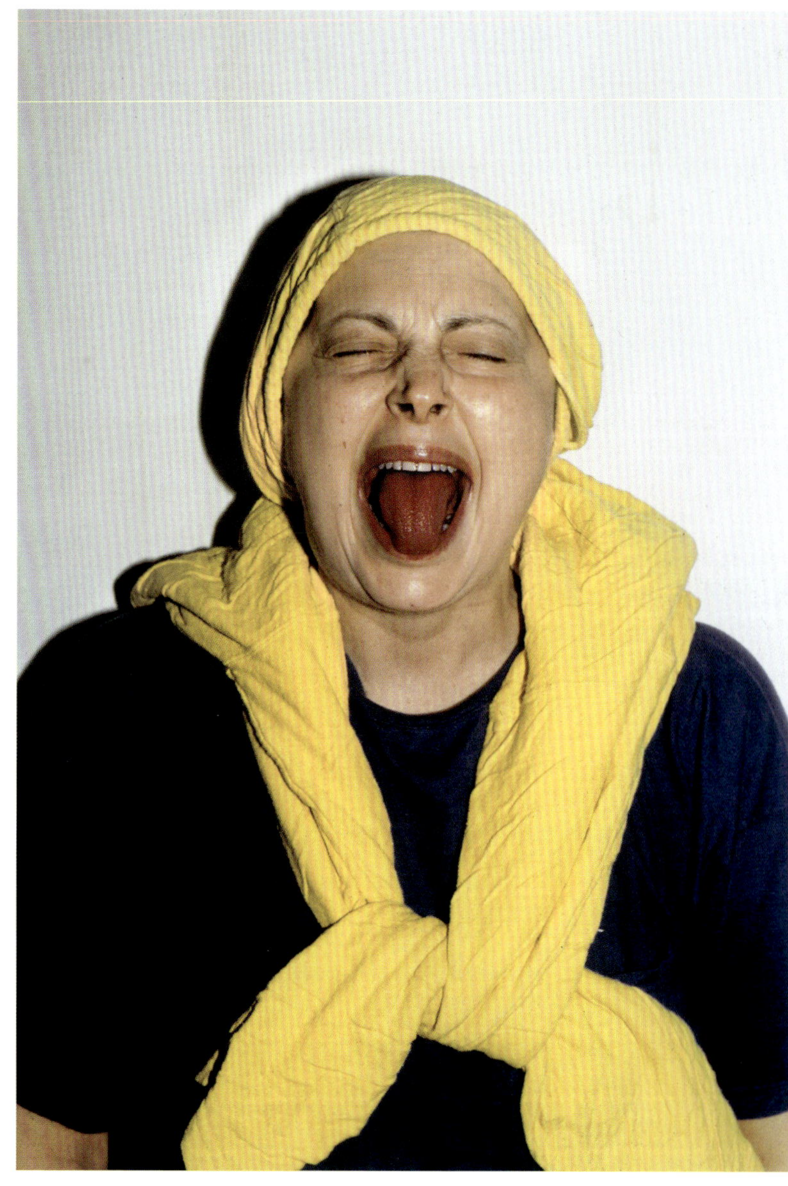

Intra-Venus #5, June 10, 1992/May 5, 1992. Two chromogenic supergloss prints, 71½ x 47½ in. each

opposite above:
Intra-Venus #1, June 15, 1992/ January 30, 1992. Two chromogenic supergloss prints, 71½ x 47½ in. each

opposite below:
Intra-Venus Series #4, July 26 and February 19, 1992. Two chromogenic supergloss prints, 71½ x 47½ in. each

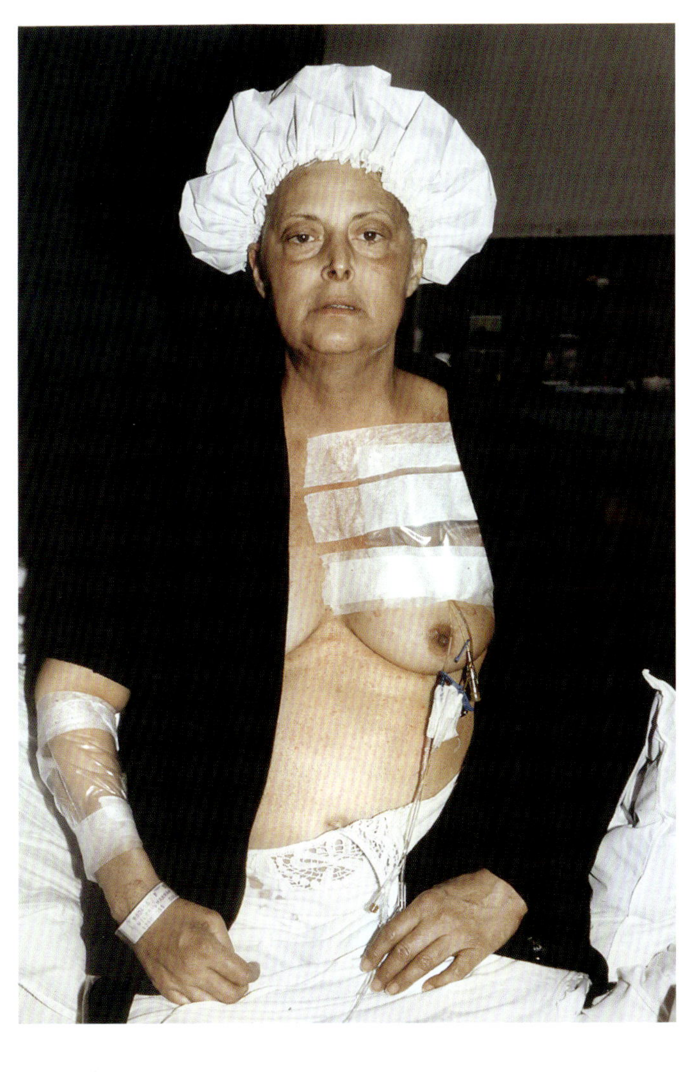
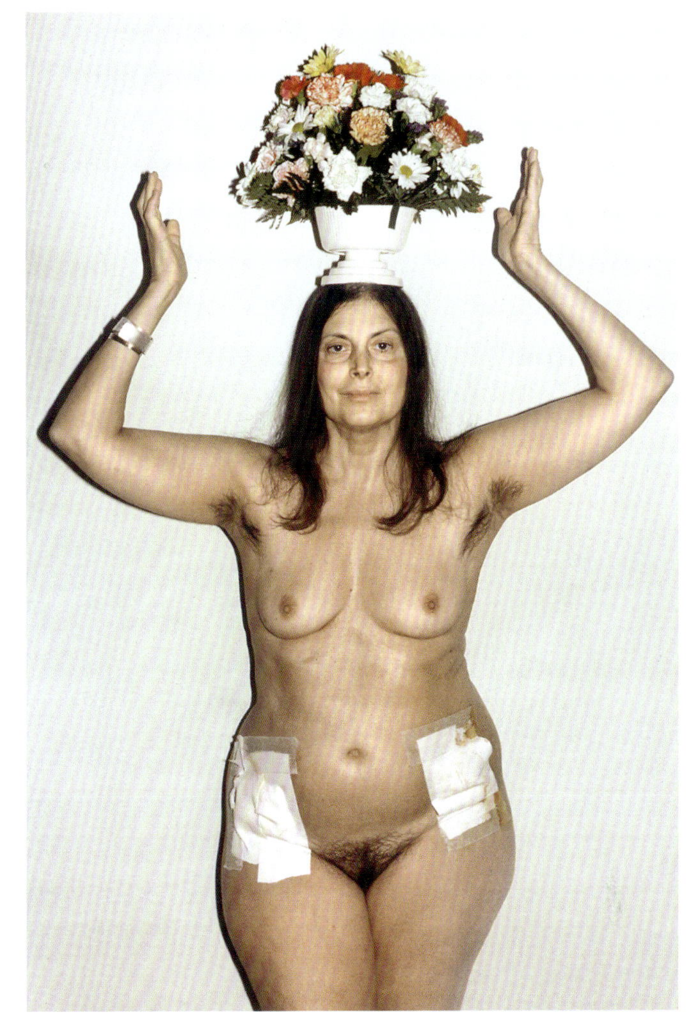
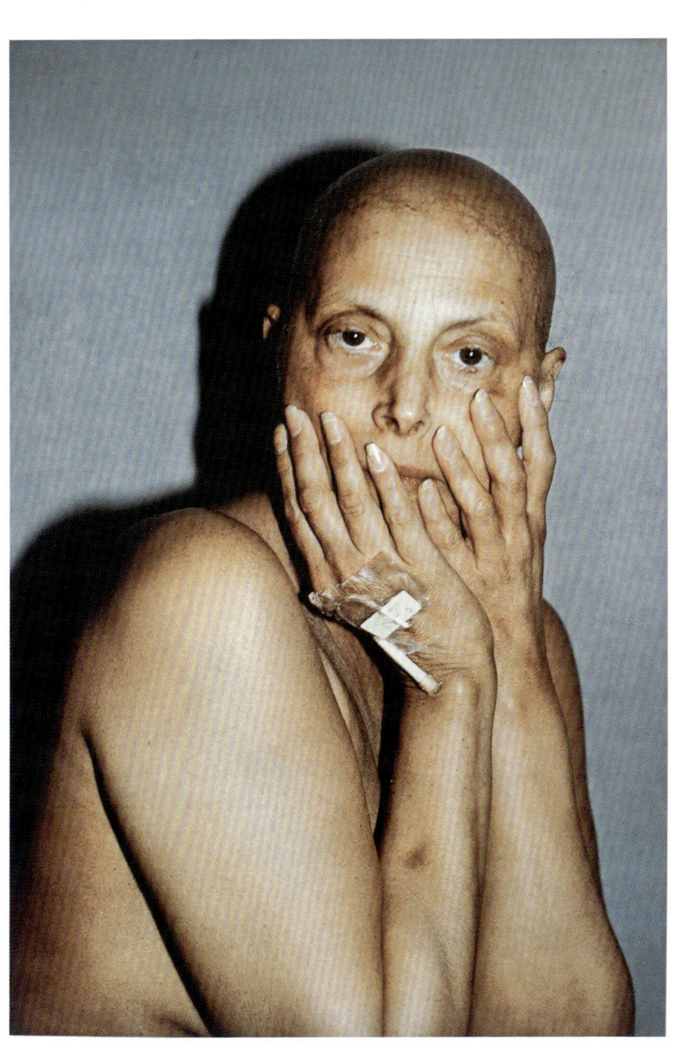
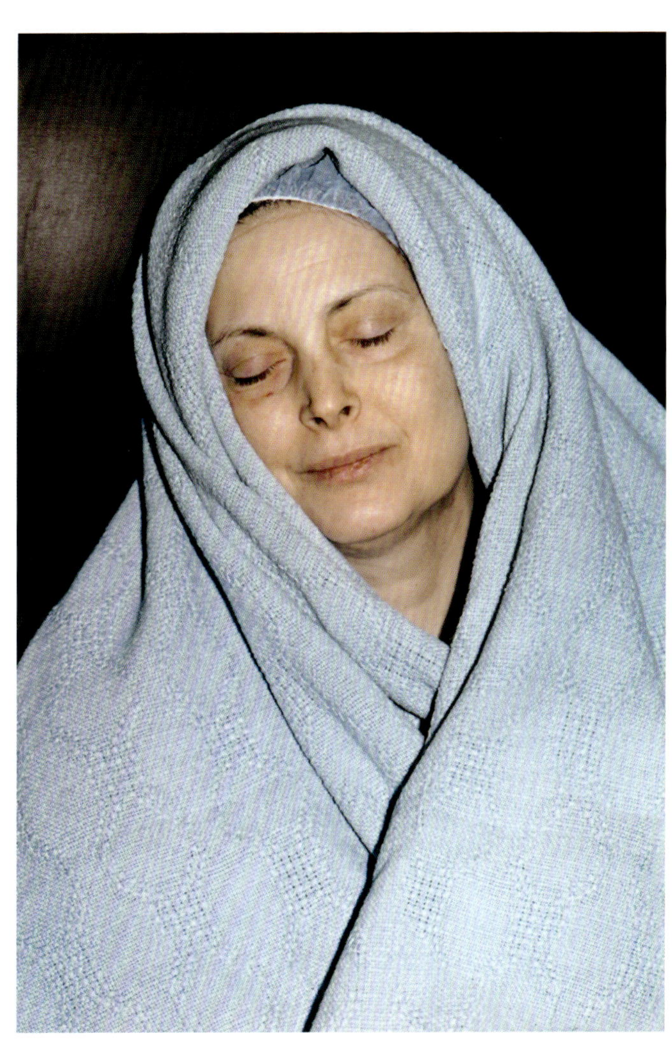

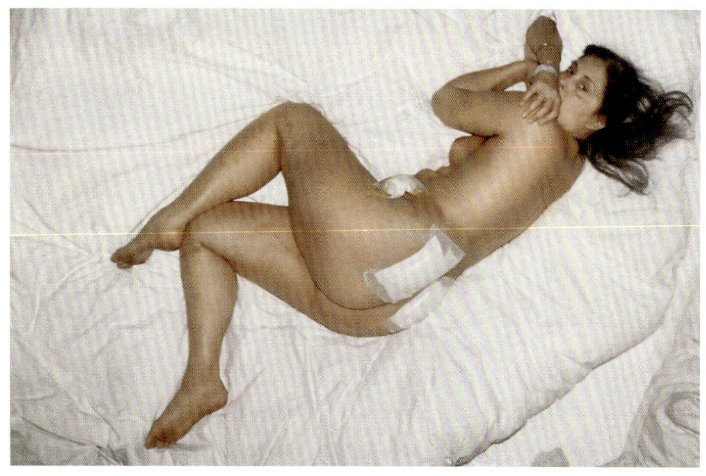
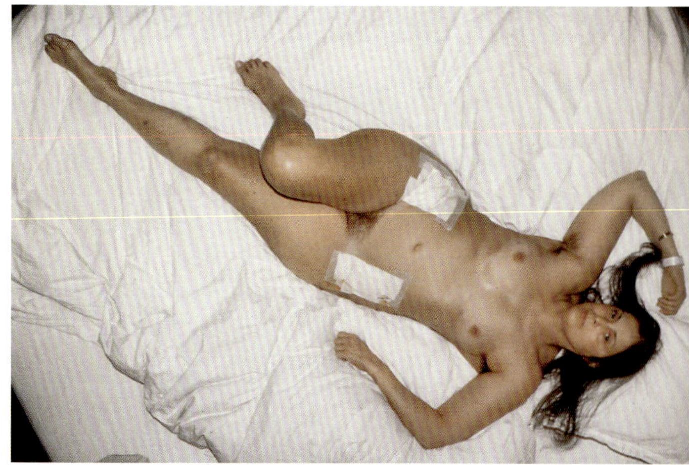

Intra-Venus Triptych ["Marilyn Monroe"], 1992–93. Three chromogenic supergloss prints, 26¼ x 39½ in. each

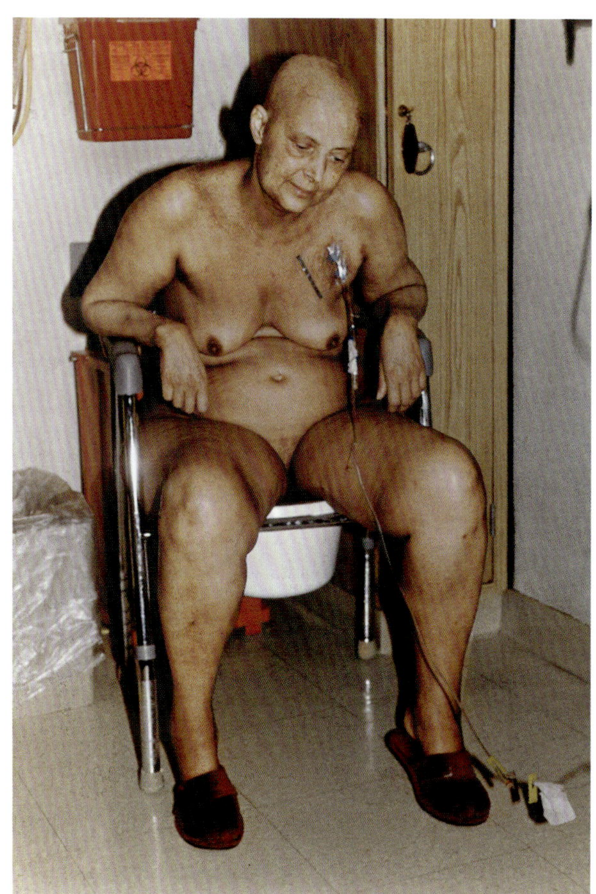
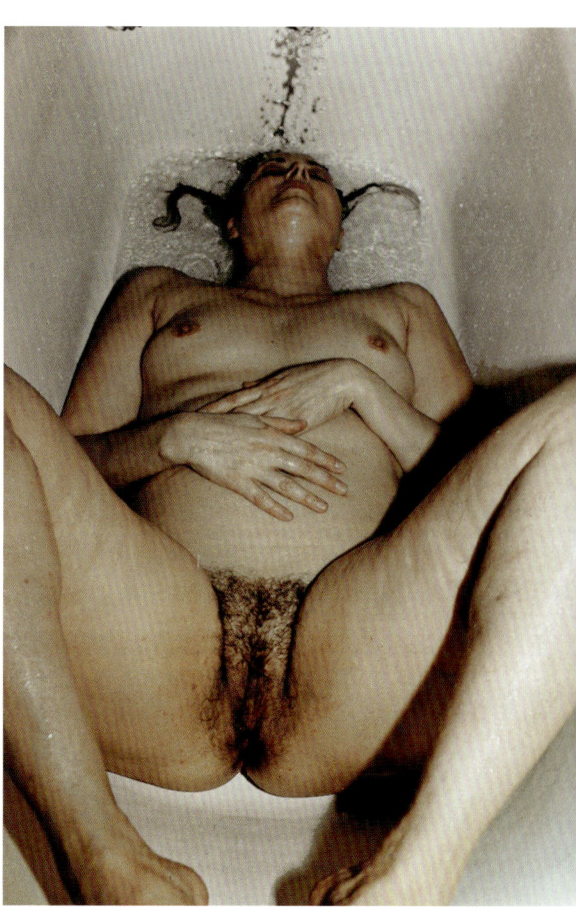

Intra-Venus #3, August 17, 1992/ February 15, 1992/August 9, 1992. Three chromogenic supergloss prints, 71½ x 47½ in. each

the camera is challenging and almost smug. The smooth, perfect skin of her breasts is adorned—armed—with odd, frail little examples of her ray gun collection. The emotional complexities of this work are manifold (again, they seem to include Wilke's anger at her mother for getting sick and threatening to leave her); rather astonishingly, she seems in full possession of all of them.

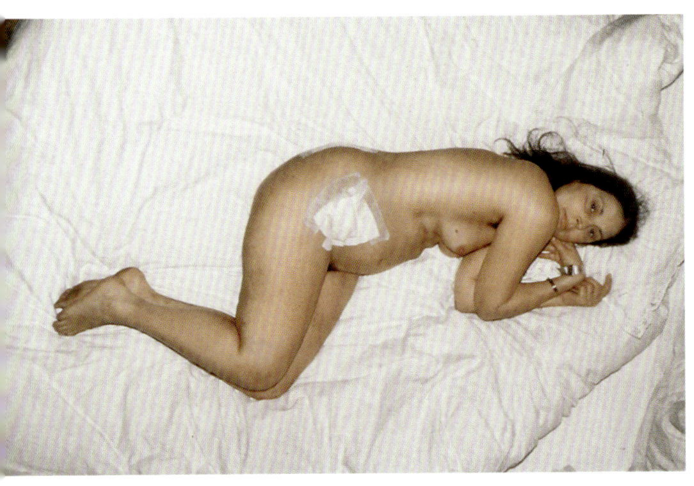

That mastery is substantiated in the work that concluded Wilke's career, the "Intra-Venus" series. Wilke's own diagnosis of cancer—lymphoma—was made in early 1987. For the first four years or so, it progressed slowly, and was treated with a mild form of chemotherapy. Then the cancer became more aggressive. Wilke died in January 1993, at fifty-two. The ravages of the disease, and of the treatments Wilke received to defeat it, were documented in photographs and videotapes (taken by Goddard, Wilke, and others). In many ways, these images are the most challenging she made. As with her pioneering use of her sexual allure as a subject, she was not working in total isolation. Between 1982 and 1986, the British artist Jo Spence created a series of frank and militant photo-based works, "A Picture of Health?," that document her struggle with breast cancer, and with the medical establishment in the U.K. Beginning in 1986, Nancy Fried made terra-cotta torsos of women who'd undergone radical mastectomies (as she had), truculent little figures that, whatever their physiques, deliberately invoke the Amazons who, according to myth, cut off one breast to maximize their prowess as archers. Relevant, too, are the unsparing, if deeply romantic, color photographs Nan Goldin made in this period, beginning with her famous *Ballad of Sexual Dependency* (1979–86). The scourge of AIDS makes an early appearance in Goldin's photographs; in 1987, Nicholas Nixon put AIDS at the center of a series of black-and-white photographs he undertook to represent its victims.

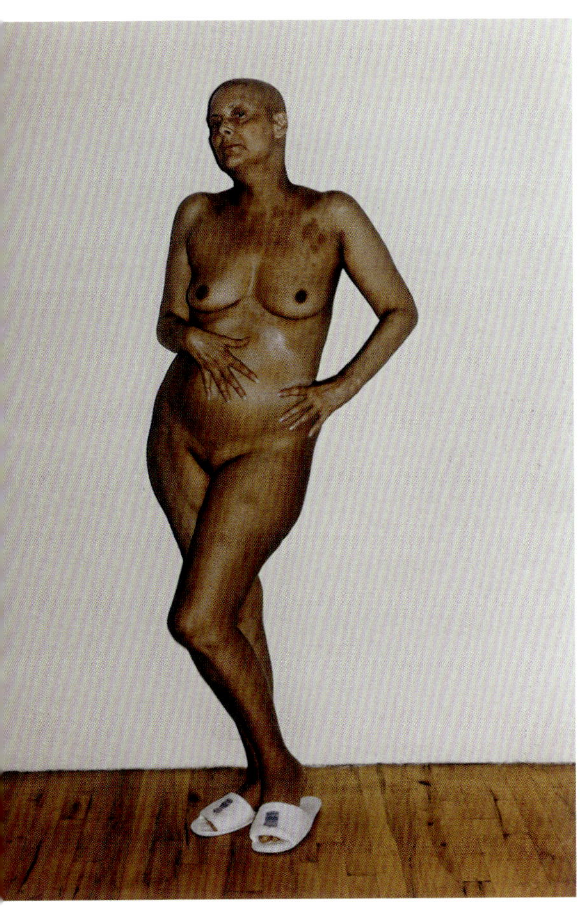

However affecting, none of these compare to the brutality, the openness, or, most unnervingly, the moments of raw beauty in Wilke's "Intra-Venus" photographs, which she began making in 1991. Some of the big color photographs are presented as diptychs. On the left in *Intra-Venus Series No. 5, June 10, 1992/May 5, 1992* (p. 108), Wilke appears in a worn-looking nightgown and robe, both white. Shown seated in front of a gray background, her body and face look blasted: her eyes are blank, her chest mottled with broken blood vessels and crisscrossed with plastic tubes; her hair is a rim of black fuzz. In her nostrils are plugs of slightly discolored cotton; her mouth is open and, most ghastly of all, her tongue is partly

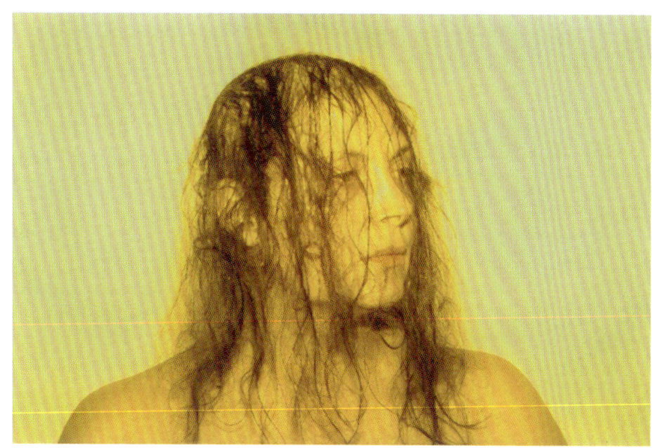
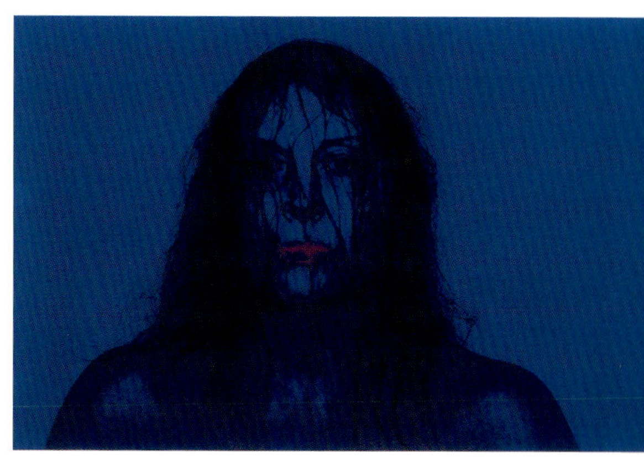

Tree of Life: Red, Yellow and Blue, 1992.
Triptych: three colorized photographs, 14 x 38 in. framed

following pages:
Brushstrokes No. 7, January 19, 1992.
Brushstrokes No. 6, January 19, 1992.
Artist's hair on Arches paper, 30 x 22½ in. each

skinned by chemotherapy. The photo on the right is this image's polar opposite. A bright yellow cloth is wrapped tightly around her head, like a turban, and draped almost jauntily across her shoulders; she wears a bright blue T-shirt, and, to complete the triad of primary colors, her tongue, a preternaturally bright shade of red, sticks way out of her bright-red, wide-open mouth. Her eyes, on the other hand, are squeezed shut; her expression is of outrage, and is itself outrageous. Her fury, most explicit in the Medusa-like out-thrust tongue, feels truly apotropaic. But it is powerfully life affirming, too, especially in contrast with its partner image—clearly, she is not capitulating. As in all the "Intra-Venus" works, Wilke's refusal to seduce by inviting pity—or, more challenging still, her denial of more empathic responses—retroactively reconfigures the previous work. Even when her eyes are closed, her complicity with the camera is lively. The jokes she once shared with it—the raised eyebrow, the heels, the strutting and slinking—are now a form of gallows humor. But the laughter is real, the hope not gone. She intended to title the exhibition of the "Intra-Venus" works "Cure."

And as long as she was making art, she was thinking about her work's place in art history. The trio of primaries in *Intra-Venus #5* was in part an answer to Barnett Newman's *Who's Afraid of Red, Yellow and Blue* (1969–70), itself a response to the color preferences of arch-modernist Piet Mondrian. The studies of extreme facial expressions represented in the character studies of the eighteenth-century German sculptor Franz Messerschmidt were also, Ronald Feldman says, source material for Wilke; Messerschmidt's bust of a man with his tongue thrust out is a close antecedent of Wilke's expression in *Intra-Venus #5*.[4] Seventeenth-century Dutch portraiture lurks behind *Intra-Venus #1, June 15, 1992/January 30, 1992* (p. 109) in which Wilke appears naked on the right, nearly full figure and frontal, gauze patches from bone-marrow harvesting marking each hip. Her arms are raised, like caryatids', though only to parenthesize a white plastic vase of fake flowers balanced on her head—a generic, rather saccharine arrangement that, along with Wilke's joyless smile, speaks for the clichéd gestures of concern to which hospital patients must submit; her response is full frontal nudity, a defiant Venus in extremis. In the companion photo, she is utterly defeated. Seated, her eyes unfocused, she wears a clownishly big white shower cap—a grim parody of a Dutch hausfrau's bonnet. The hospital ID around her wrist, like the tubes, clamps, paper tape, and patches of clear plastic adhered to and pen-

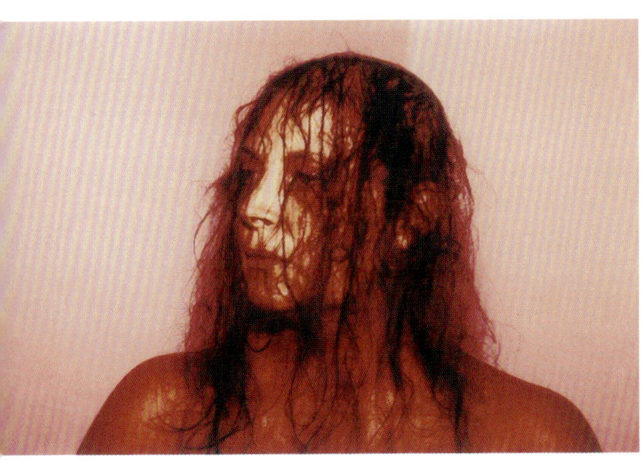

etrating her body, thoroughly objectify her. The dehumanizing effects of male desire to which Wilke referred in *I Object* is given a new meaning in the late work: here, her body is incontrovertibly reduced to an amalgam of active, protesting personhood and inert medical equipment. The diptych *Intra-Venus Series #4, July 26 and February 19, 1992* (p. 109) again looks to art historical prototypes, this time with a Madonna-like image of Wilke's head and shoulders draped modestly in a blue hospital blanket, her head slightly inclined, eyes reverently closed, lips chapped. On the right, she is naked and completely bald, and her long, elegant fingers are raised to her mouth; still taped to the back of one is an IV needle, though it is attached to nothing. Here, she stares balefully at the camera, her lashless lids making her eyes seem unnaturally big, and transfixing.

Other photos in the series show her in every variety of degradation and resilient dignity. She lies in bed, naked, nearly hairless, bloated, asleep, her mouth slightly open, her chest laced with tubes. She sits on a portable toilet, again fully naked, eyes downcast. Still graced with a head of hair, she stands, with some effort, supporting herself on the back of a chair. She lies in bed, a big teddy bear squeezed between her legs. Her head slightly turned, she regards the camera askance from luridly bloodshot eyes, her face curtained by the thin, wet strands of her remaining hair. Perhaps most disturbing is the triptych *Intra-Venus Series #3, August 17, 1992/February 15, 1992/ August 9, 1992* (pp. 110–11). The image on the right, a full-figure nude, presents her in an almost saucy pose, a classic contrapposto with one hand on her hip, elbow cocked. She is seated naked on a hospital toilet in the image on the left. In the center, Wilke is shown on her on her back in the tub like some monstrous baby, what's left of her hair trailing into sadly silly pigtails, her knees wide and the camera looking straight at her now nearly hairless vulva. The Courbet who painted the spread legs and foreshortened torso that is *The Origin of the World* (1866) would surely have run screaming; perhaps Lacan (who once owned it) would have fled as well. This is what it comes to, Wilke seems to say. Take a good look. Elaine Scarry writes that intense pain is wordless; being exceptional, it isn't well represented in memory, and can't be accurately evoked by verbal description, however graphic. Of course, oceans of ink have nonetheless been spilled in the effort. The same might be said of pictures: when about pain, they refer us to an experience that, even for those who have shared it,

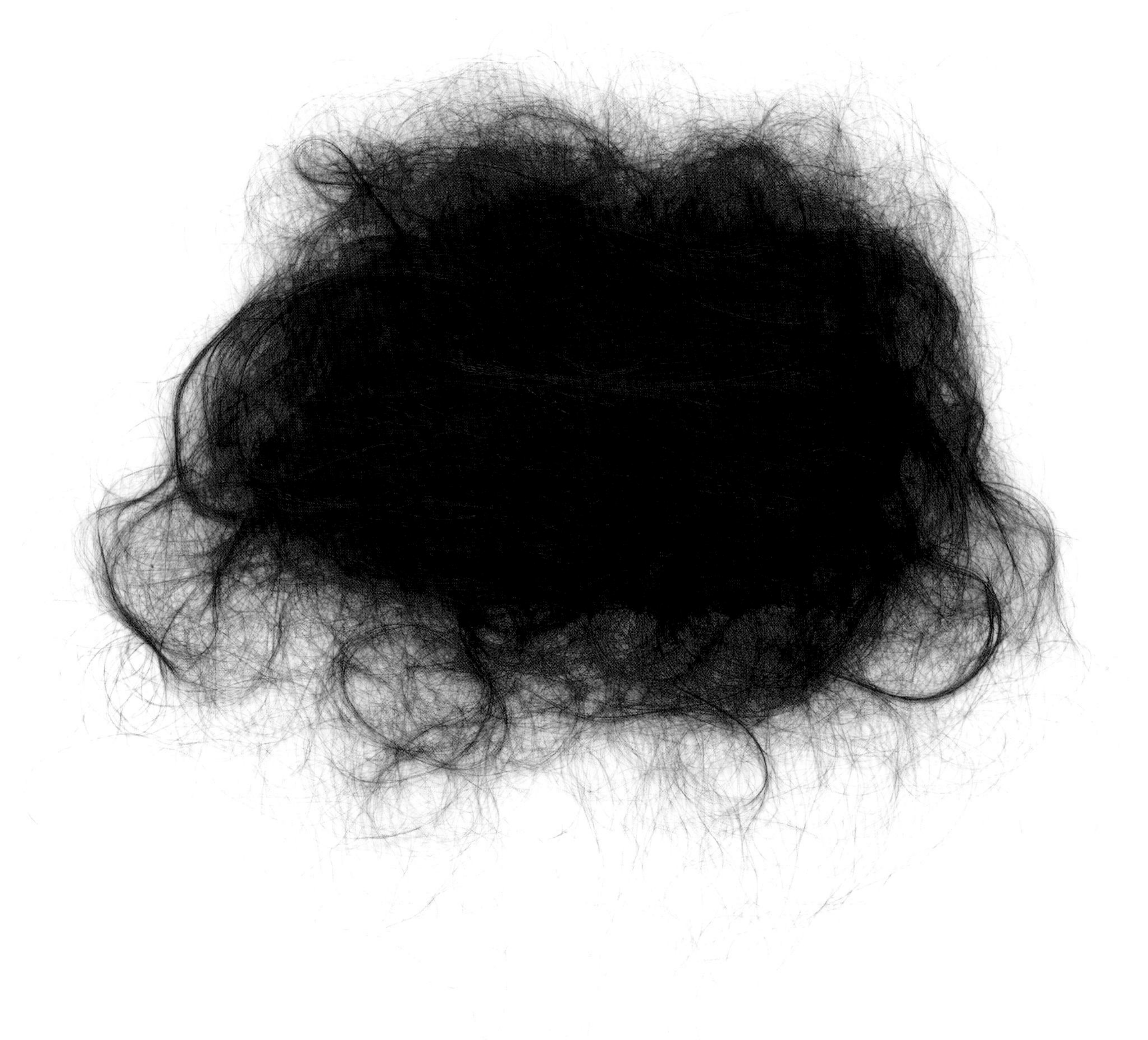

Jan 19 1992 Hannah Wilke

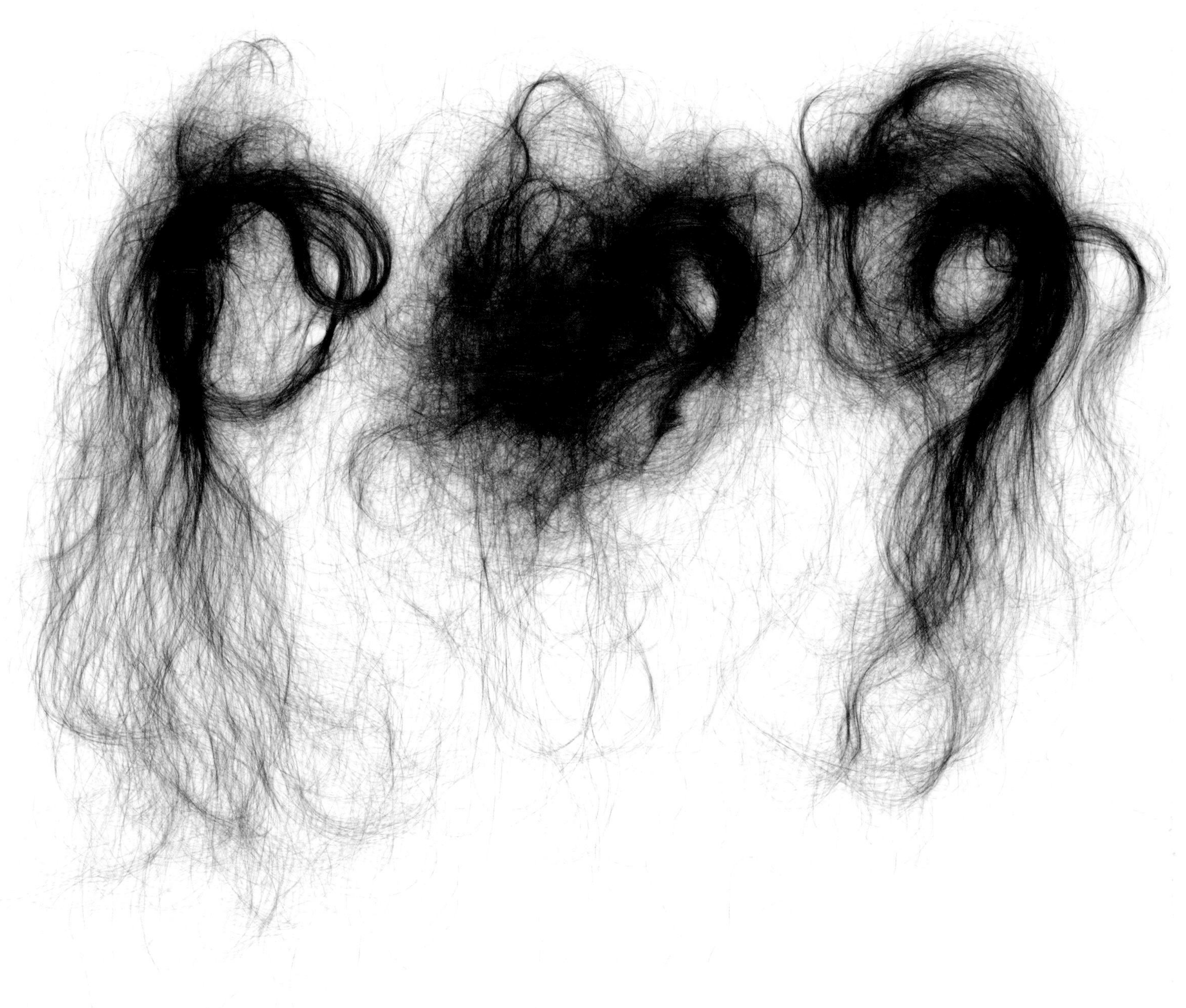

Jan 19, 1992

Wilke

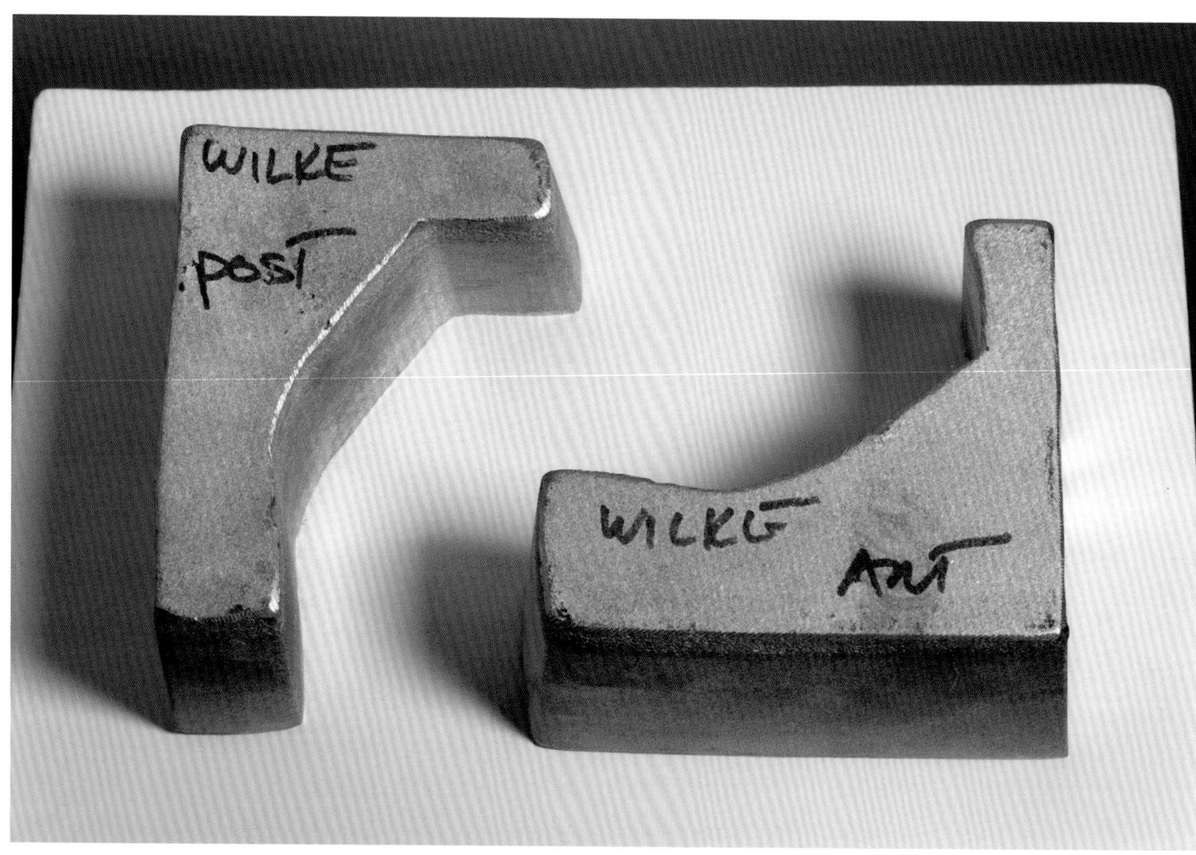

Wedges of . . ., 1992. Two lead alloy radiation blocks, 3 x 6½ x 6 in. each

isn't readily available for recall. Wilke made an end-run around this impasse, going straight through pain to the soul-shattering business of being required to surrender your sense of physical integrity—and then refusing to give in.

Sometimes, in the "Intra-Venus" works, she did this by the hurricane-force strength of her candor. In other cases, she chose artfulness instead. A series of small square photographs made in 1992 employ experimental techniques, including solarization, to heighten color and electrify the imagery. *Tree of Life: Red Yellow Blue* (pp. 112–13) is a trio of photos that shows Wilke facing right, left, and center, her hair an iridescent tangle against contrasting neon backgrounds of cyan, ruby, and sallow gold. Another similar-size triptych, in naturalistic color, presents Wilke in full face, from the back and in profile; her head is Yul-Brynner bald. In the full-face image she flashes a diabolical, clenched-teeth grin; in profile, her jaws are jowly, and a nearly invisible halo of baby-fine hair can be traced at the top of her forehead. A four-image composition brings together a pair of shots, each repeated, of Wilke shown front and back, her hair sticking up in stiff witchy shapes, her face grim, and a little disgusted. These photographs, for all their careful formal considerations, evoke sets of mug shots; their revelation of detail and their invitation to come in close have a forensic aspect, inviting, uncharacteristically, a dispassionate, clinical inspection.

The "Intra-Venus" works were preceded by an extended series of watercolor drawings of faces called "B.C.," for "before cancer," which were begun when she suspected she was ill but before she knew the diagnosis; they were followed by smaller watercolor drawings, some made in the hospital, of bandaged faces and hands. During treatment, Wilke also executed a series of eighteen *Brushstrokes*

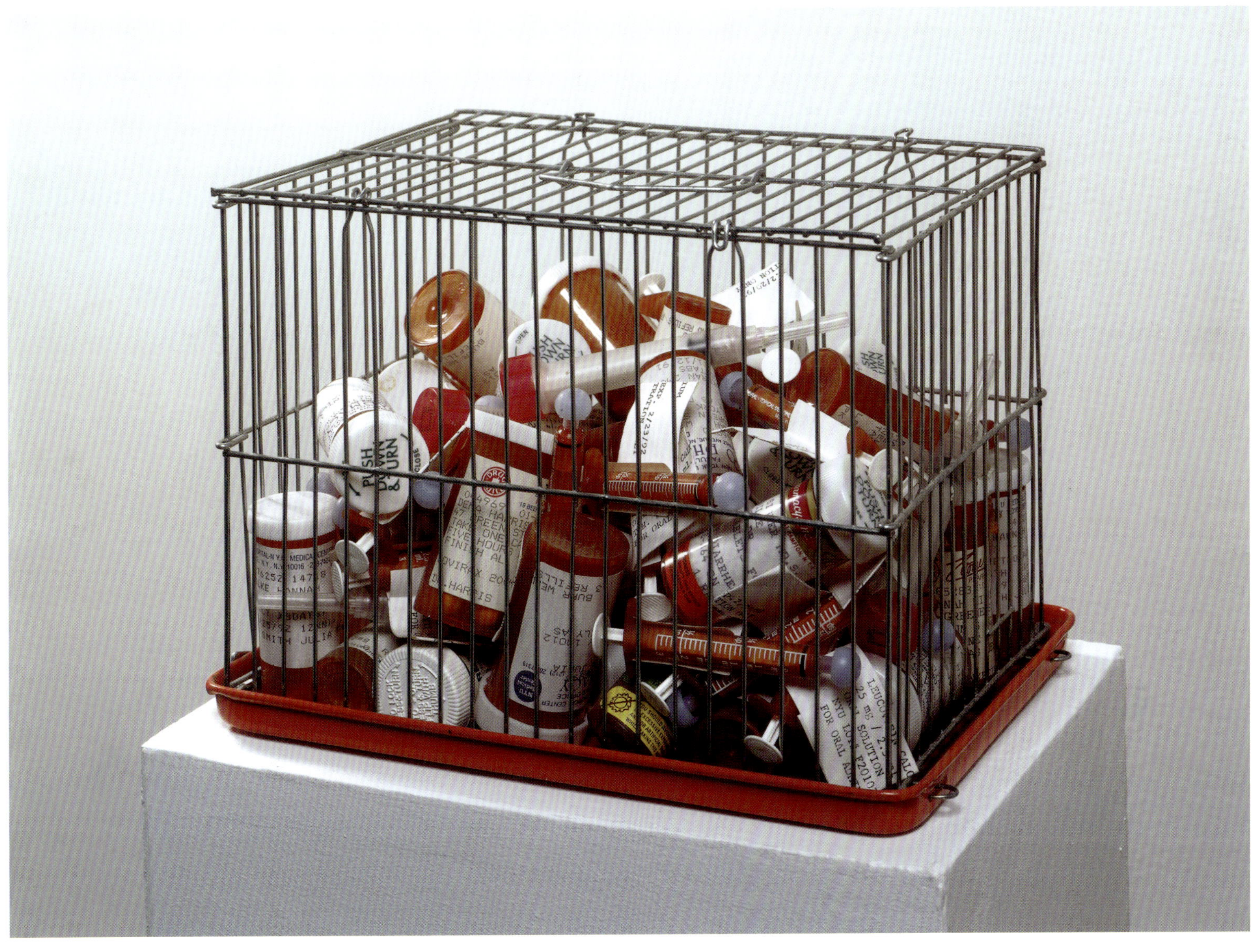

Why Not Sneeze . . ., 1992. Wire bird cage, medicine bottles, and syringes, 7 x 9 x 6⅞ in.

(1992; pp. 114–15), so called because they were made from her hair as it fell out from the chemotherapy and was caught in her brushes. Attached to paper with invisible (and fragile) adhesive, the hair forms linear deposits that vary considerably, some wispy, others lush, "Like distant, infinite nebulae and the inevitable, random movements of life, all at once," in Goddard's description.[5] Recalling the preserved tresses of loved ones that in Victorian times were kept in lockets or woven into jewelry, or the cherished first hair cuttings from a baby that many parents still keep, the *Brushstrokes* speak with unnerving intimacy about mortality and loss.

As if intentionally tying up the strands of her career in an omni-media gesamtkunstwerk, Wilke also made a number of "Intra-Venus" sculptures, both hand-formed ceramic pieces and found-object assemblages. Two are final homages to Duchamp: *Wedges of . . .* (1992) consists of a pair of lead-alloy neck radiation blocks, cousins of Duchamp's bronze and plastic *Wedge of Chastity* (1954). And Wilke's *Why Not Sneeze . . .* (1992), a rectangular wire birdcage filled with medicine vials and syringes, looks back to Duchamp's *Why Not Sneeze, Rrose Sélavy* (1921), in which a similar birdcage contains simulated sugar cubes made of marble, along with a cuttlefish bone and a thermometer. Duchamp's typically enigmatic work has been explained as the

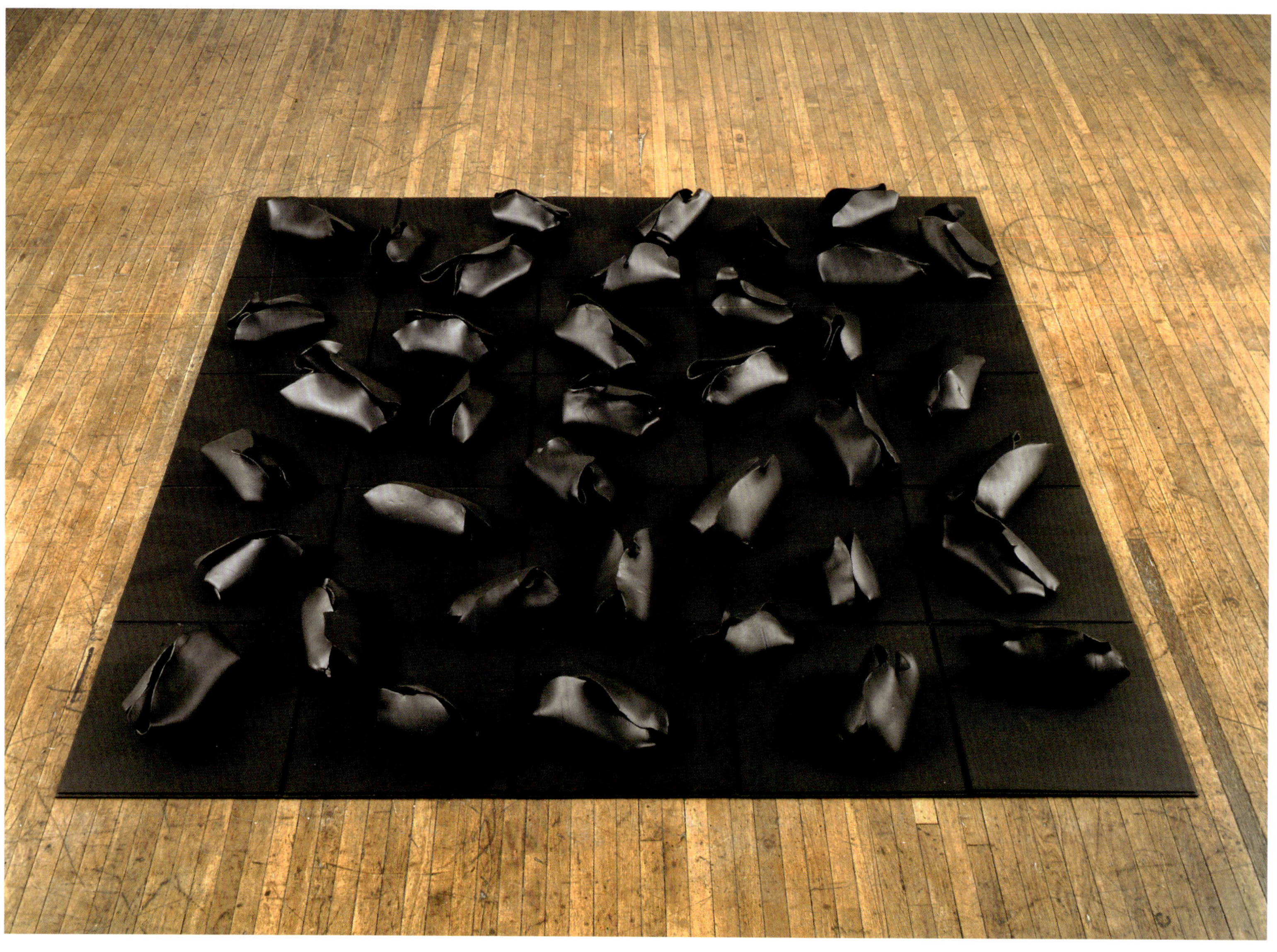

Untitled, 1987–92. Thirty-seven black painted ceramic sculptures on twenty-five painted wood bases, 7 x 98 x 98 in. overall

opposite:
Blue Skies, 1987–92. Nine painted ceramic sculptures on nine painted wood bases; 7 x 58 x 58 in. overall

expression, on the one hand, of an analogy between sneezing and orgasm that it opposes; on the other, with the coldness of the marble, as attested to by the thermometer. Whatever his intended allusion in these two sculptures to eros and its frustrations, they are mooted by Wilke's homages, which are not about sex but about confinement and illness—and about laughing in the face of them. The final ceramic pieces include series of one-fold sculptural groupings in a burnt-looking black; and another, called *Blue Skies*, that is brushed in landscape shades of blue, green, and white (both 1987–92). They seem empty husks of the tender, fleshy pink ceramic cunts with which Wilke launched her career. And, in the latter examples, the sunny, blue-sky surface markings fly in the face of the conditions in which they were forged.

If there is something operatic about the shape of the "Intra-Venus" project, its shake-the-rafters coda is the videotape installation that is its final expression. Shown as a sixteen-monitor installation, it contains over thirty hours of imagery, including serene footage taken on trips out of New York City —to the eastern end of Long Island, where Wilke and Goddard rented houses for two summers, and to the Southwest, to visit Goddard's aging parents—and also passages showing an industrious Wilke working on the "B.C." faces or installing exhibitions. There is also

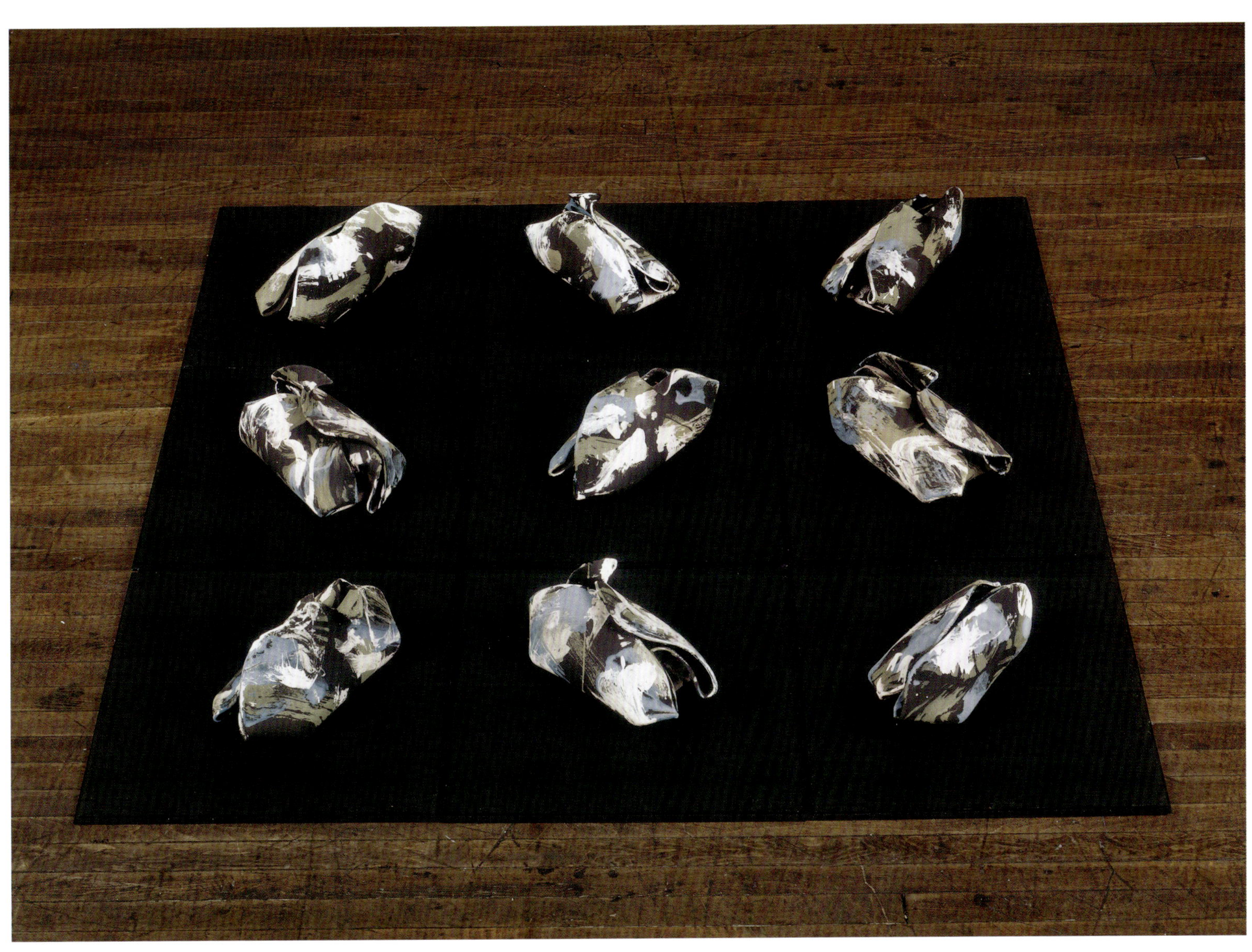

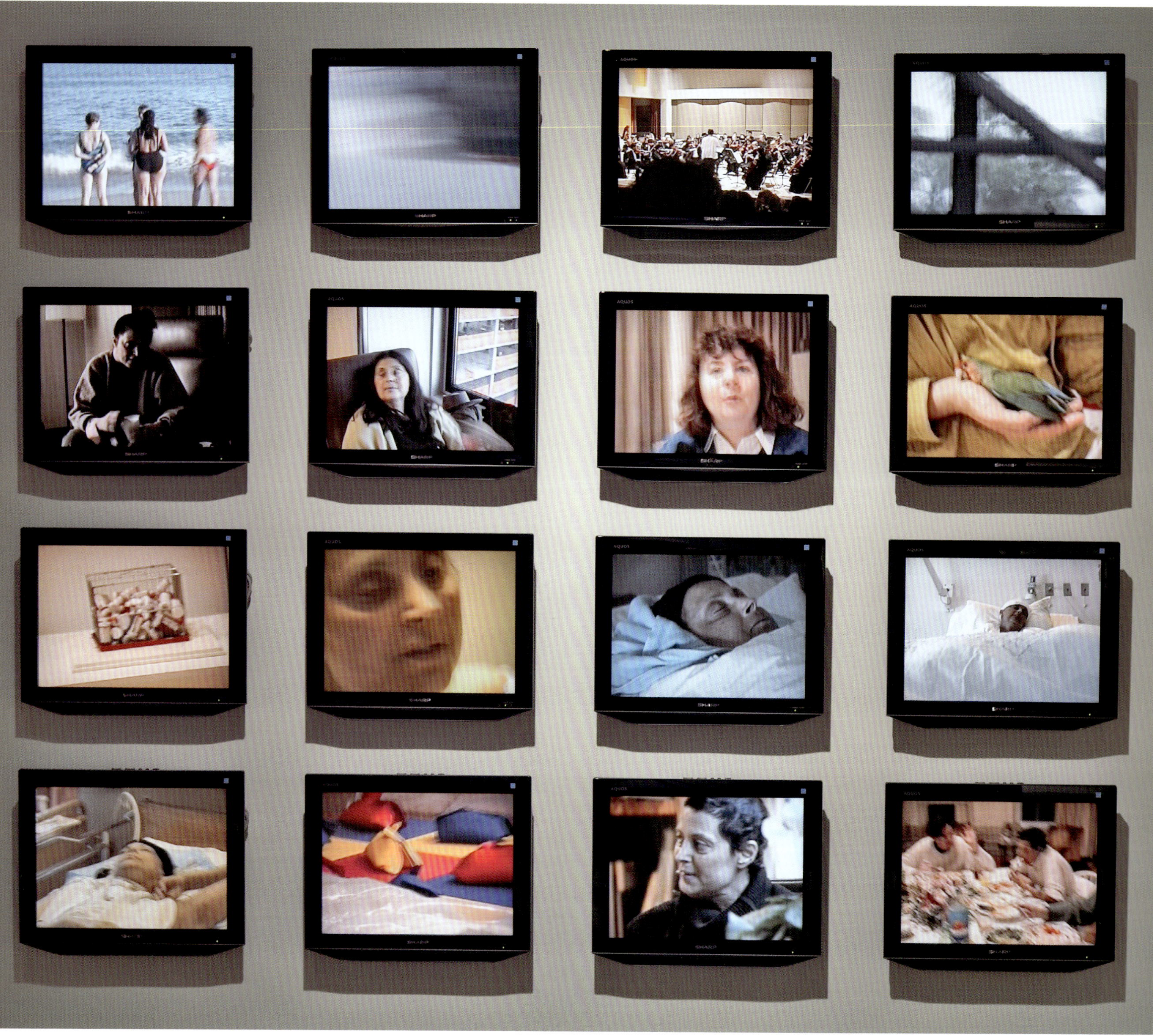

Intra-Venus Tapes, 1990–93. Sixteen-channel video installation, 117 min.

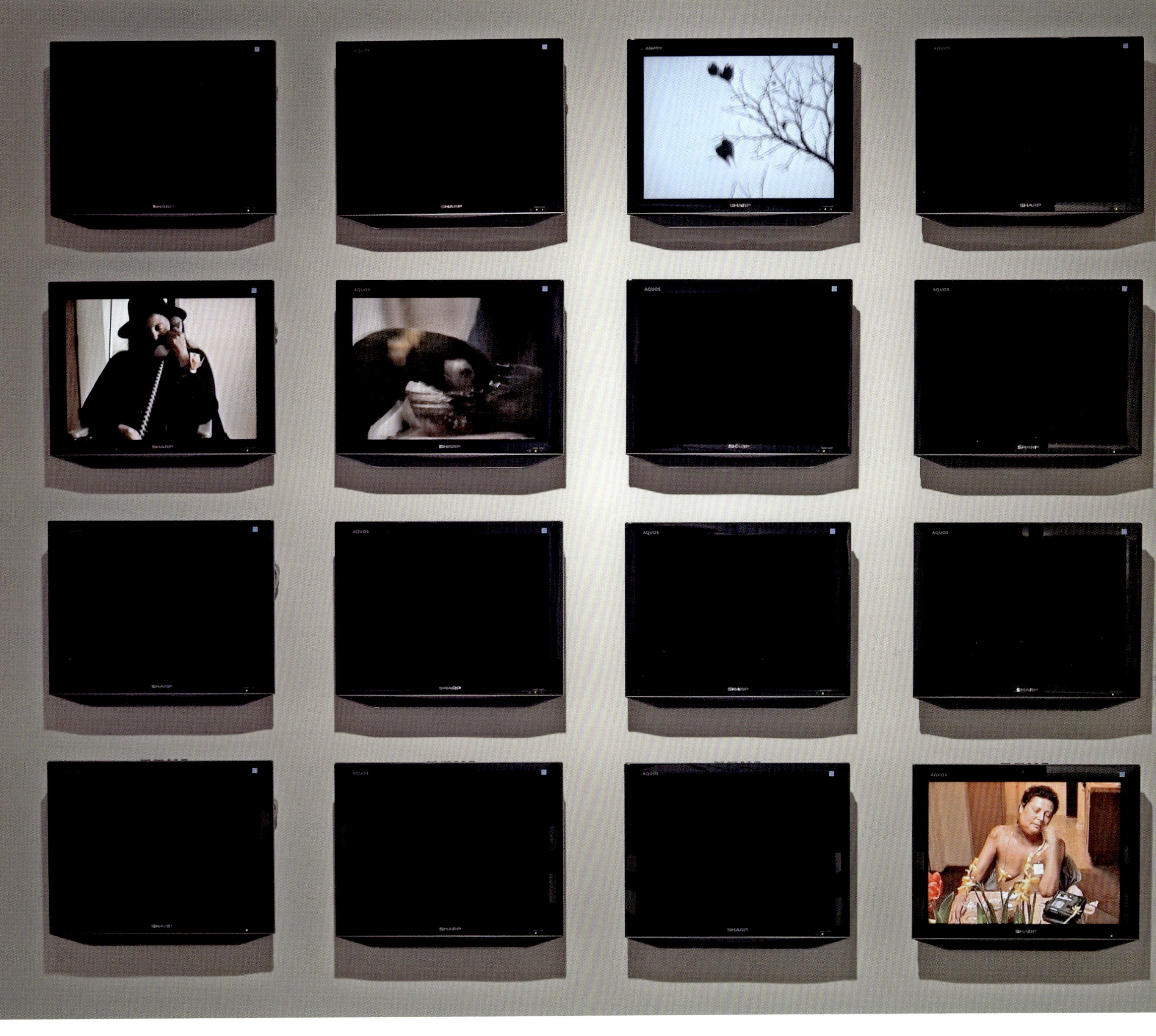

footage of the artist in the hospital brushing her thinning hair, sleeping, throwing up. Three soundtracks are audible at any given time, edited so it is possible to catch snatches of conversation, though calculated so nothing can be absorbed except in a state of distraction. Alternately harrowing, banal, poignant, and funny—and more revealing of her domestic life than anything else she'd done—the tapes are many things at once. Evidence of Wilke's irrepressible life force, her eager interest in everything—from the Pueblo caves of Arizona to Frederic Church's home on the Hudson—even when her face betrayed her desperate medical condition, they are a sometimes rapturous, life-flashing-before-one's-eyes compilation of all that mattered to her: her nearest friends and family, including her sister Marsie, who lived with her during that last year, and her niece and nephews; her art and the art of others, birds and landscapes, simple physical pleasures (swimming, eating), talking. They are also a blinding, raging protest against that enormity's loss, and, in the somehow harmonious orchestration of all of that, testimony to a truly remarkable degree of acceptance. We see her singing "I Feel Pretty" at herself in a mirror, laughing and crying. We also see her wedding (performed by a rabbi) to Goddard; she seems extremely happy, though she is too weak to stand. At one point, talking to Goddard's mother about her own mother's taped voice in "Intercourse With," Wilke says, "The ordinary things sometimes are the most extraordinary. There's honesty in them." Simple enough, and inarguably true. It could be her epitaph.

Depicting fatal illness—her mother's, and her own—did not simply transform the shape of Wilke's career into a tidy narrative arc that goes from beauty to decay, pride to a fall. It also enforced an equation between sex and death. Vulgar, ugly, obscene, unseen: the terms used to denigrate one serve the other just as well; those who are squeamish and prudish are cautioned against exposure to both equally, as if either could be harmful simply on sight. If the *petite mort* of orgasm suggests a nexus of shared sublimity between sexual climax and mortality, the flip side of that transcendence—its fleshly guarantee—is in gross physicality. Wilke chose to represent both, the pink champagne and the weary cunt, the body triumphant and ruinously assailed. The late photos allowed a great many people who had previously been leery of Wilke to embrace her in sympathy, pity and, inevitably, schadenfreude. "To critics who often denigrated her work for being too narcissistic or exhibitionist, Wilke had and deserves the last word," Andrew Perchuk wrote of the "Intra-Venus" series in a 1994 *Artforum* review.[6] Said Richard Vine, in *Art in America*, Wilke's "last gesture, rare in this self-pitying age, demonstrates a better way to handle genuine trauma, without becoming a victim: by facing the truth without blinking, by bearing it."[7] (Given his subject, one assumes Vine welcomed that last clause's pun.) Shocking though they were, the late works, as supporters old and new observed, were of a piece with her early endeavors. The consistency of her concerns and of her means of expressing them were remarked as often as was the terribly sad surprise they represented.

In "Illness as Metaphor" (1977), a protest against the symbolic uses to which cancer is put, Susan Sontag wrote, "My point is that illness is not a metaphor, and that the most truthful way of regarding illness—and the healthiest way of being ill—is one most purified of, most resistant to, metaphoric thinking."[8] Though Sontag's focus was, in part, on esthetics and culture, she was clearly more concerned with injustices done to patients than to language. "Cancer patients are lied to," she wrote, because the disease "is felt to be obscene, in the original meaning of that word: ill-omened, abominable, repugnant to the senses."[9] A substantial part of Sontag's essay angrily examines comparisons between tuberculosis—which was associated with neurotic, gifted people, a disease of wasting bodies, feverish characters, and enhanced sensibility—and cancer, which tends to make its sufferers (as it did Wilke) bloated, blasted, reduced to their bodies and their pain. At the same time, Sontag railed against the trend toward "psychologizing" illness, which offers a false sense of control over disease and thereby undermines its reality. In a secular culture with no consoling notions of an afterlife, she writes, "death is the obscene mystery, the ultimate affront, the thing that cannot be controlled."[10] The terms could well be applied to sex, and it is worth noting that Sontag ended one of her earliest and best-known essays with a similar diatribe against metaphor and psychological interpretation: "In place of a hermeneutics we need an erotics of art" is the final line of her "Against Interpretation" (1964).[11]

Then again, argument against metaphor and interpretation can itself be taken as a rhetorical turn. As T.J. Clark observes parenthetically in *The Sight of Death*, a long meditation on two paintings by Poussin, "making sense of mute things is a *normal* activity of language, and any patter about the special un-translatability of paintings misses that obvious point."[12] Much of Clark's book is concerned with how, in Poussin's *Landscape with a Man Killed by a Snake* (probably 1648), the serenely constructed landscape becomes the grammar that makes the fatality staged within it intelligible. It grants understanding of the mortal incident's consequence by, curiously, establishing a contrast between an implacable, decorously static bucolic setting and the lively, and decidedly sexual, agent of death. "The snake is horrible above all because it has no level, no center of gravity—it is endless obscene motion,"[13] Clark writes. On the other hand, "Death, in the corpse, disappoints us—looks away from us, and no longer has a face of any kind." It is the snake that, strangling its victim, "is the figure of Death itself: the *live-ness* of Death, its patience, its glorying in its power."[14]

Like Sontag, Wilke insisted on exploring and expressing the body's most insistent and powerful conditions, which ultimately refuse to submit unreservedly to language. And, as with Clark's Poussin, she was determined to represent the liveliness of death—along with the equally vivid confrontation with it that may be the definitively human experience.

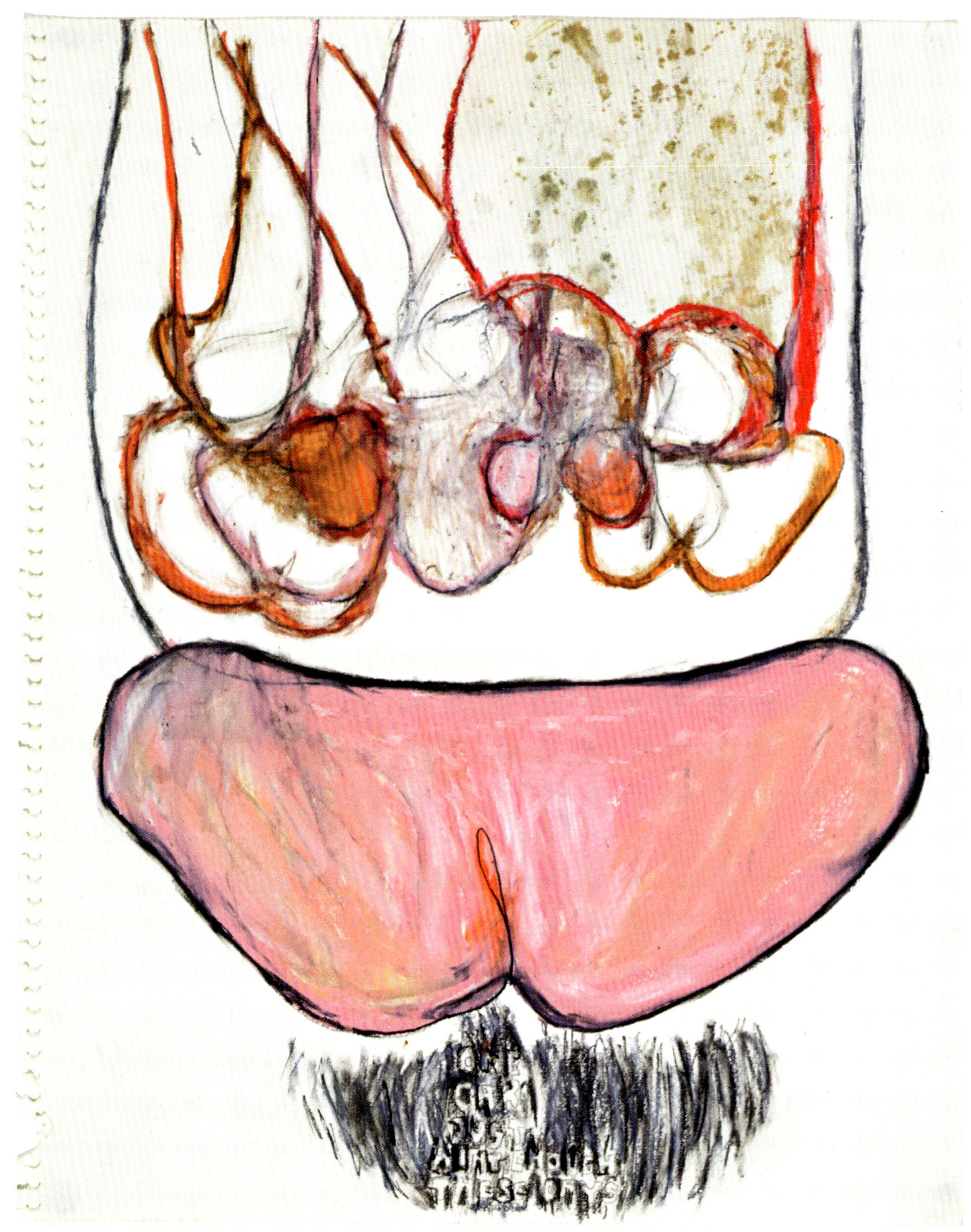

CHAPTER FIVE

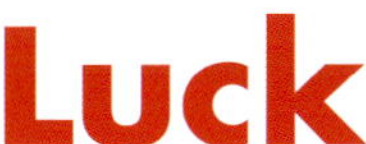

Luck

Wilke's beauty and her premature loss of it are both conditions that could be called fated. The same could be said of her talents as a draftsperson. Just as she made sculpture throughout her career, she also made drawings, even less well known than the three-dimensional works. Those that were executed in the last years of her life have been among the most widely exhibited, and they include some of the rawest images she created. But even in these, as throughout her graphic oeuvre, the issue of beauty is as central as it is in her photographic self-portraits.

By the early 1960s, Wilke was making spirited abstractions in charcoal, pastel and pencil that combine references to the body with allusions to landscape in a manner reminiscent of Arshile Gorky, who was among the artists she most admired (others include Vermeer and Vuillard). In Wilke's early drawings, robust phalluses sprout from thickets of pencil strokes in a manner that is shamelessly appetitive but also unimpeachably elegant. There is something of the illustrational line Warhol developed for his shoe advertisements in Wilke's early drawings as well. Colors are sometimes the bright dissonant shades of the '60s—neon orange, fuschia—but as often are more mute, or suppressed entirely. In the pastel drawing *One Car Just Ain't Enough These Days* (1964), a big pink-tipped penis—it vaguely suggests a butterfly—is headed down toward a pubic-hairy thatch in which the snazzily scribed title is nearly concealed; a cluster of smaller phalluses reinforces the drawing's main instrument. Cocks go every which way in another of the same period, drawn in felt-tip pen. The Museum of Modern Art owns a pastel and charcoal untitled drawing dated 1963–66 in which a trio of phalluses dominate a lush landscape like hallucinogenically monumental mushrooms, one marine blue, another fiery red; an undulating line in the background could be mountains or breasts (p. 126). In an untitled drawing executed in graphite, charcoal, paint, colored pencil, and crayon of 1962–66, a half-pink penis aims boldly upward, a still life of wholesome balls at its base, while wedges of dense black close in from both sides (p. 127). In a particularly cheerful, and Warholesque, drawing of 1964, a bifurcated phallus, its shaft golden and its tip rosy pink, aims straight as cupid's arrow at the gaily curlicued pubic hair between a woman's gracefully delineated spread legs. The profusion of polymorphous genitals, in whole and part, in fertile landscapes from whose fruits they are barely discernible, is especially Gorkyesque.

These early drawings have all the exuberance and more of Wilke's contemporary works in ceramics. By the latter years of the decade she was making more decorous works on paper, which continued to appear in the early 1970s. Lightly constrained by geometry and sometimes containing collaged elements, they are drawn in pencil, both graphite and colored, and often feature horizontal lines, considerable open space and imported illustrations, not infrequently sentimental and sometimes related to the postcards she used for the kneaded-eraser collages. Even more than with the previous works on paper, they reflect an illustrational sensibility. *Stanley Landsman* (1966; p. 128) involves an amorphous swirling form inscribed within a perfect circle and containing within its vaguely organic interior a pair of spectacle-like circles that sit stop a sheet of postage-stamp size photographs of its titular subject

One Car Just Ain't Enough These Days, 1964. Mixed mediums on paper, 14 x 11 in.

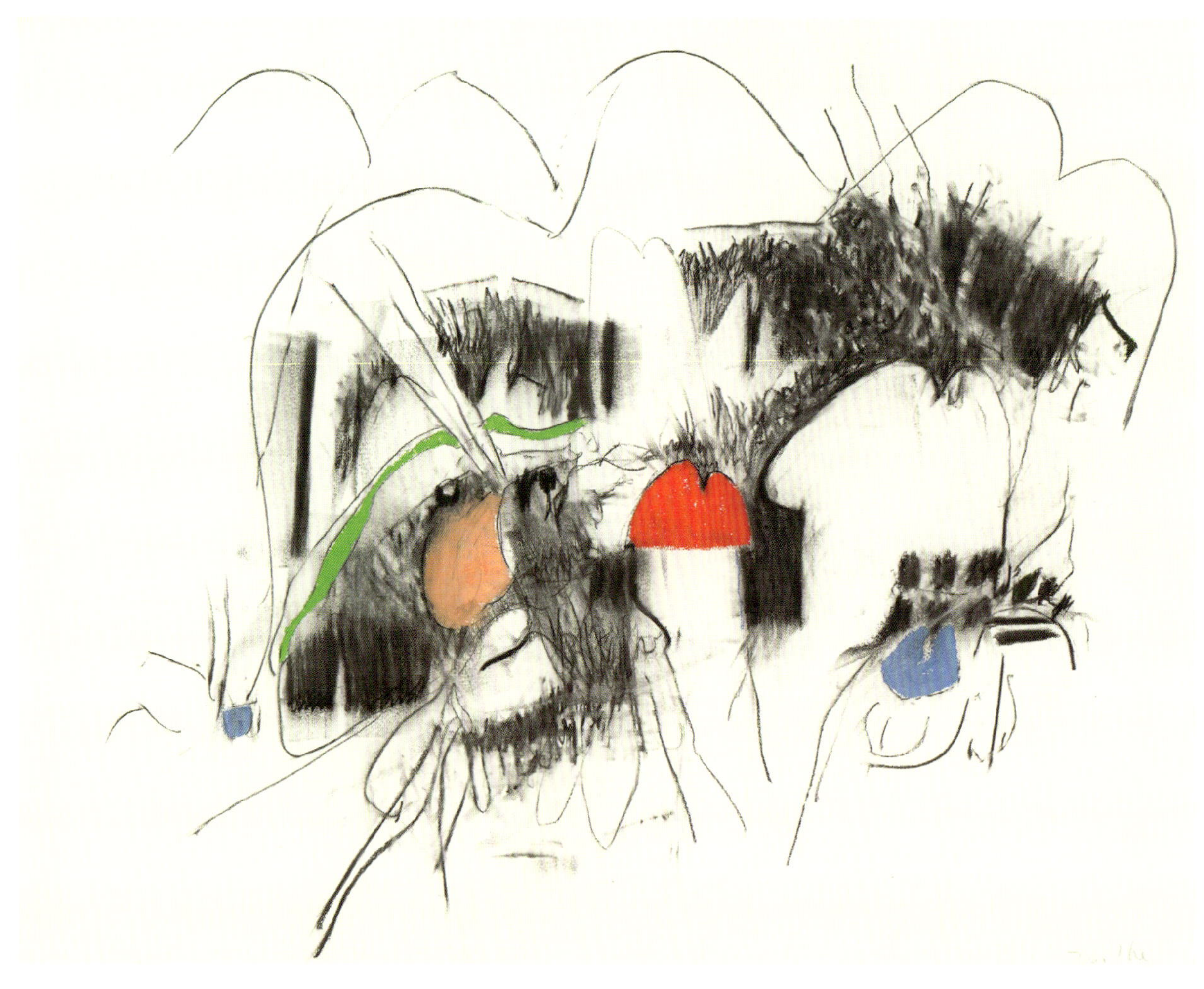

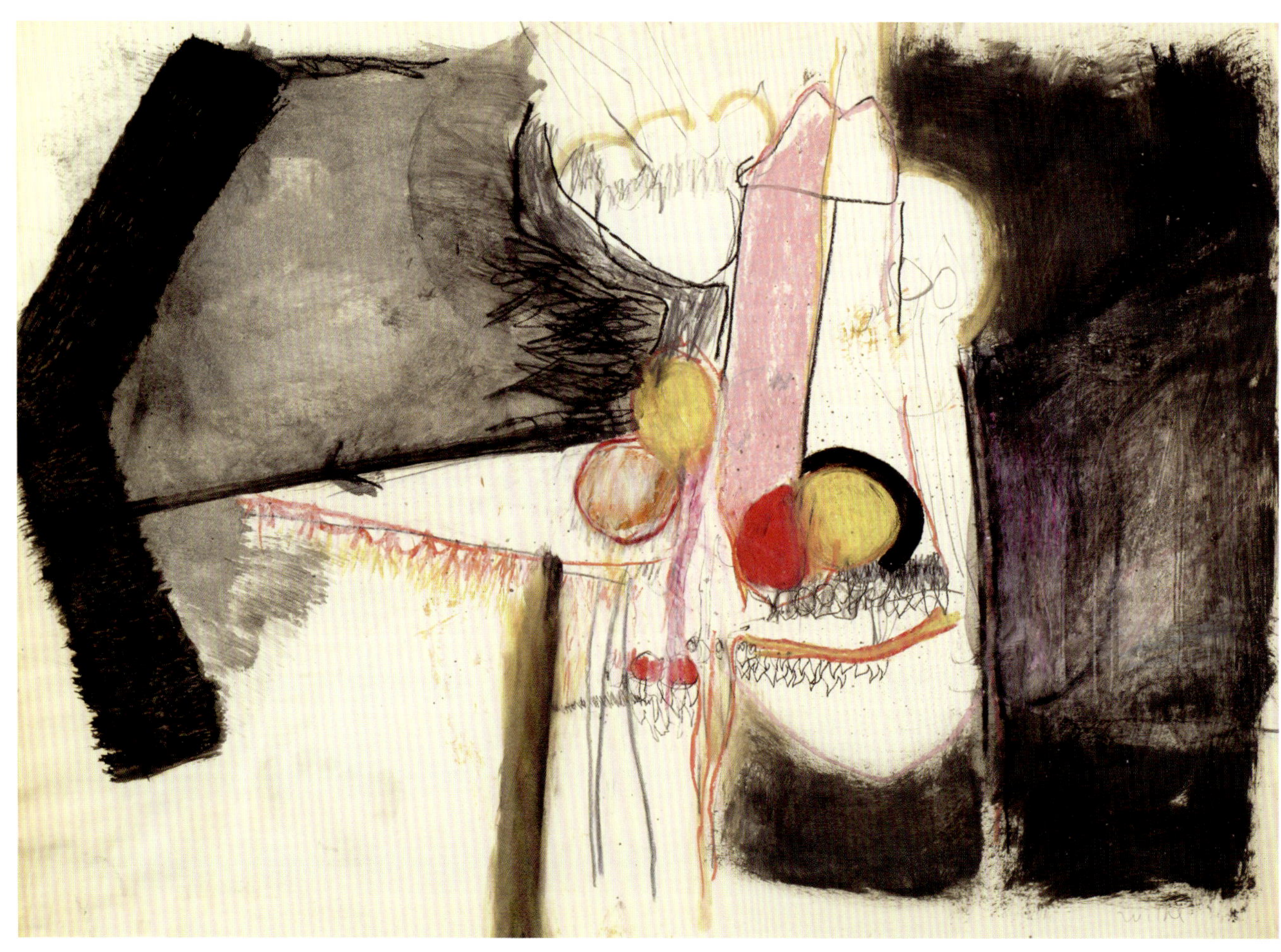

Untitled, 1963–66. Pastel and charcoal on paper, 19½ x 24 in.

Untitled, 1962–66. Graphite, charcoal, paint, crayon, and colored pencil on paper, 22 x 30 in.

(a painter who was Wilke's boyfriend at the time); the whole assumes the air of a slightly comic portrait. In *To Sister* (1973; p. 129), pale bands of pink and blue frame a sentimental greeting card adorned with flowers and addressed "To Sister." *In the Doghouse* (1973; p. 129), 61first a drawing and then a screen-print, is organized by horizontal bands ruled in pencil and filled with pale washes of tan, orange, and green. Set into this abstract composition is a fragment of an illustration that seems to come from a children's book, of a beagle resting its head on the ledge of a rustic doghouse, and dolefully watching two sweet little birds eating from his dish. Some are less overtly woebegone, though more telling. *What'll I Do* (1978) is a collage assembled from the cover of sheet music for a 1923 Irving Berlin song of that name (it was used in Nelson Riddle's Academy-Award winning 1974 score for the movie *The Great Gatsby*); set into an image of a frame on the cover is a photo of Wilke and Oldenburg, she looking dreamy and in love with both the camera and her partner, Oldenburg rather leery of both.

If the early drawings and collages reflected lingering thoughts about pursuing a more conventional artistic career as a maker of objects that could be framed or put on pedestals and considered for the formal problems they explore, Wilke also made, throughout her life, quick contour drawings in ink and pencil of animals and flowers, impelled by an irrepressible and seemingly personal impulse to draw, and an equally strong attraction to her subjects. Donald Goddard worked in the 1980s as senior editor for the Wildlife Conservation Society at the Bronx Zoo, and Wilke often joined him there, sketching the residents. These exceedingly deft, affectionate images capture the vivacity and specificity of animals ranging from sea lions to gorillas, shown in motion and at rest. They are assured and convincing, and immensely appealing. Birds were a particular favorite. Three days after Wilke's mother died, a lovebird flew into Goddard's apartment. She was immediately taken to Wilke's loft and named Seura Chaya. Wilke and Goddard always kept at least one (and up to seven) birds as pets, allowing them to fly freely through her home. The "Intra-Venus" tapes show how much a part of her life, and Goddard's, the birds became; both fed them by hand (and even mouth to mouth), and lavished them with a degree of affection that made some human guests visibly (and amusingly) uncomfortable. The birds found themselves in drawings both as solo subjects and as parts of mixed-medium compositions, including the "Seura Chaya" series. The quality of the line in these drawings of animals could sometimes be called Matissean, an affinity that is even more clearly marked in the many drawings she made of flowers. As with the animal drawings, her observations were acute, bringing to life every particularity of texture and form, blooming health and decay without sacrifice to the delicacy for which flowers are treasured. A group of pen and ink flowers made in the late 1970s feature the most common of blossoms—daisies, daylilies, Queen Anne's lace, roses—disposed casually on the page and depicted with complete assurance.

All of these drawings had personal significance for Wilke. But those that have clearest connections with the photographic performance-based work are the

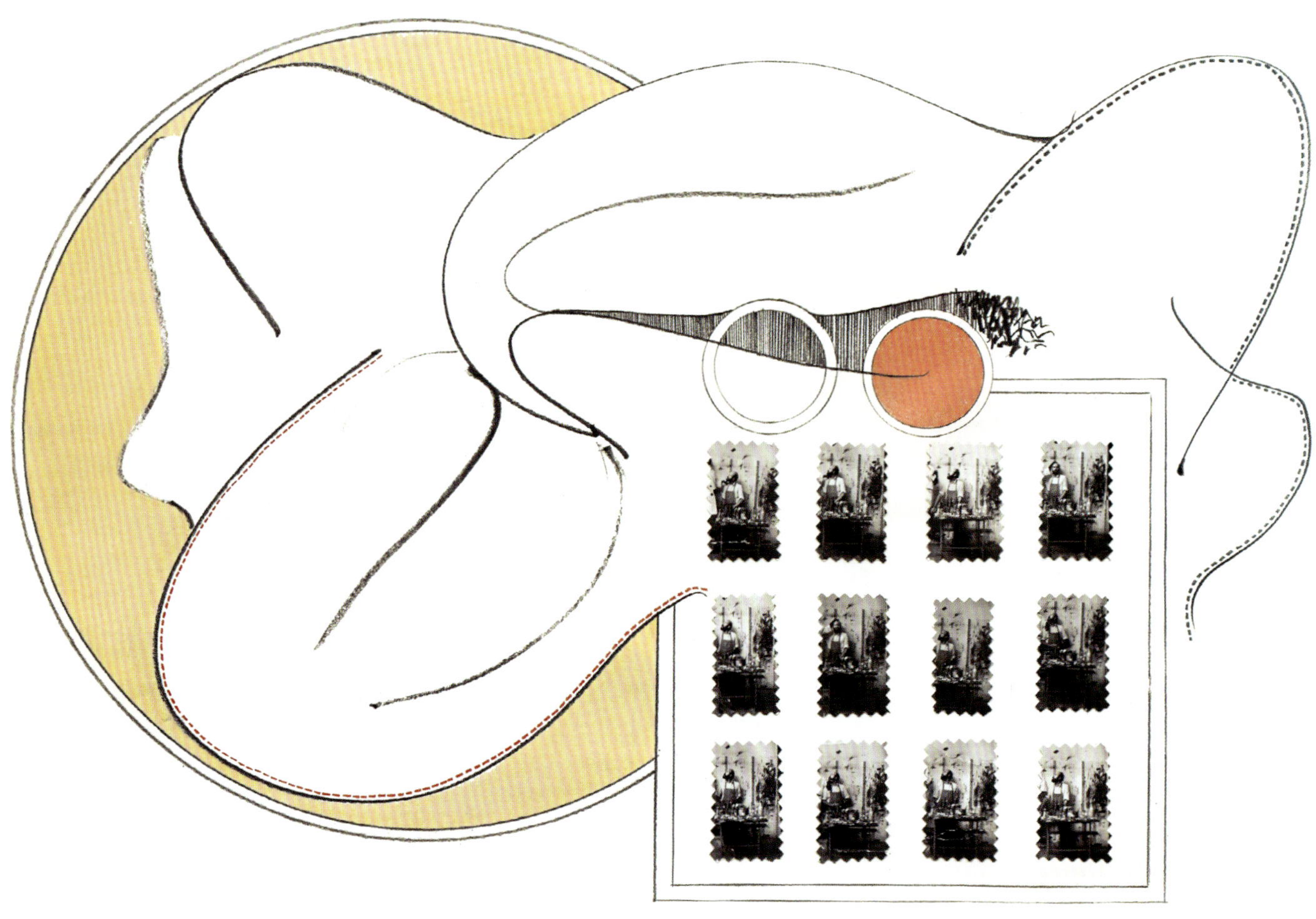

Stanley Landsman, 1966. Pencil, pastel, and photographs on paper, 18 x 24 in.

opposite:
To Sister, 1973. Pastel, pencil, and collage on paper, 18 x 23 in.

In the Doghouse, 1973. Silkscreen, 18 x 24 in.

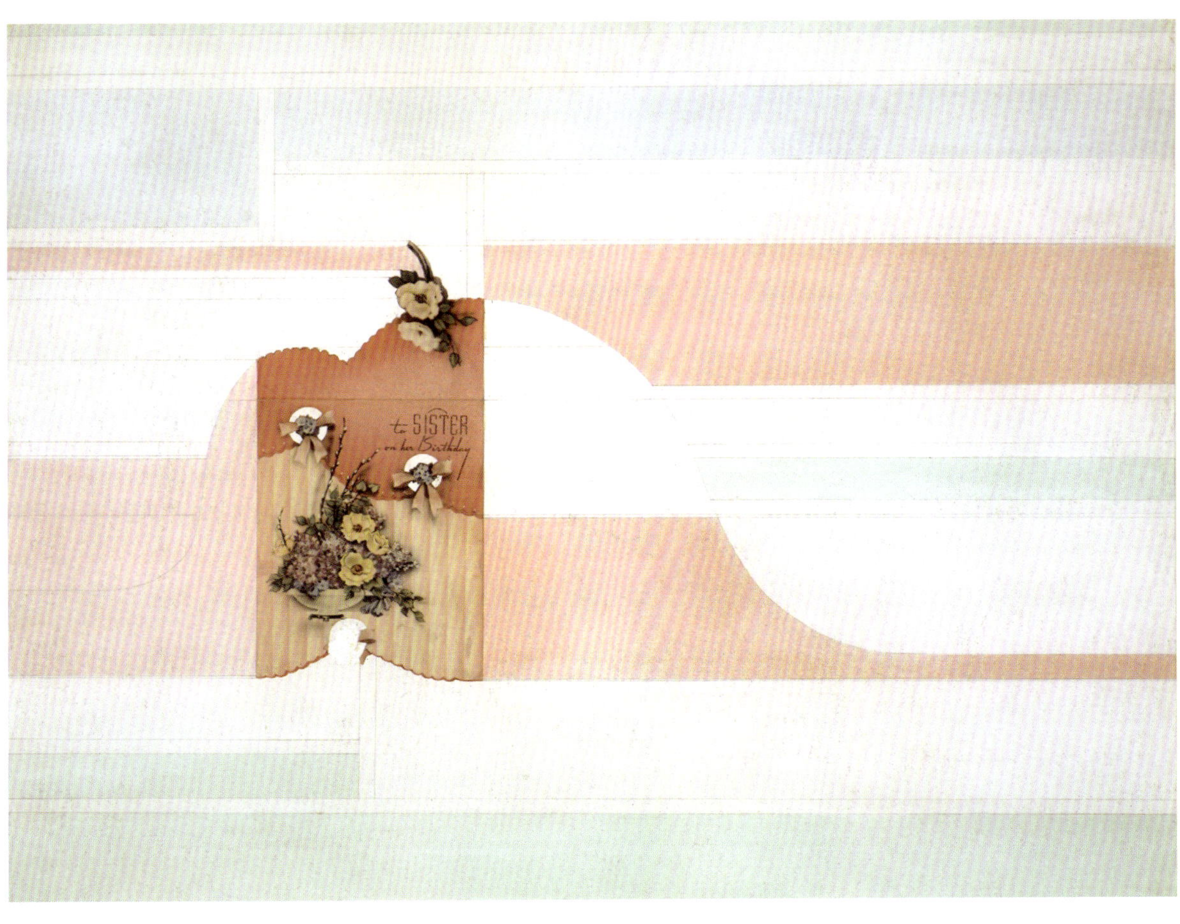
to SISTER
on her Birthday

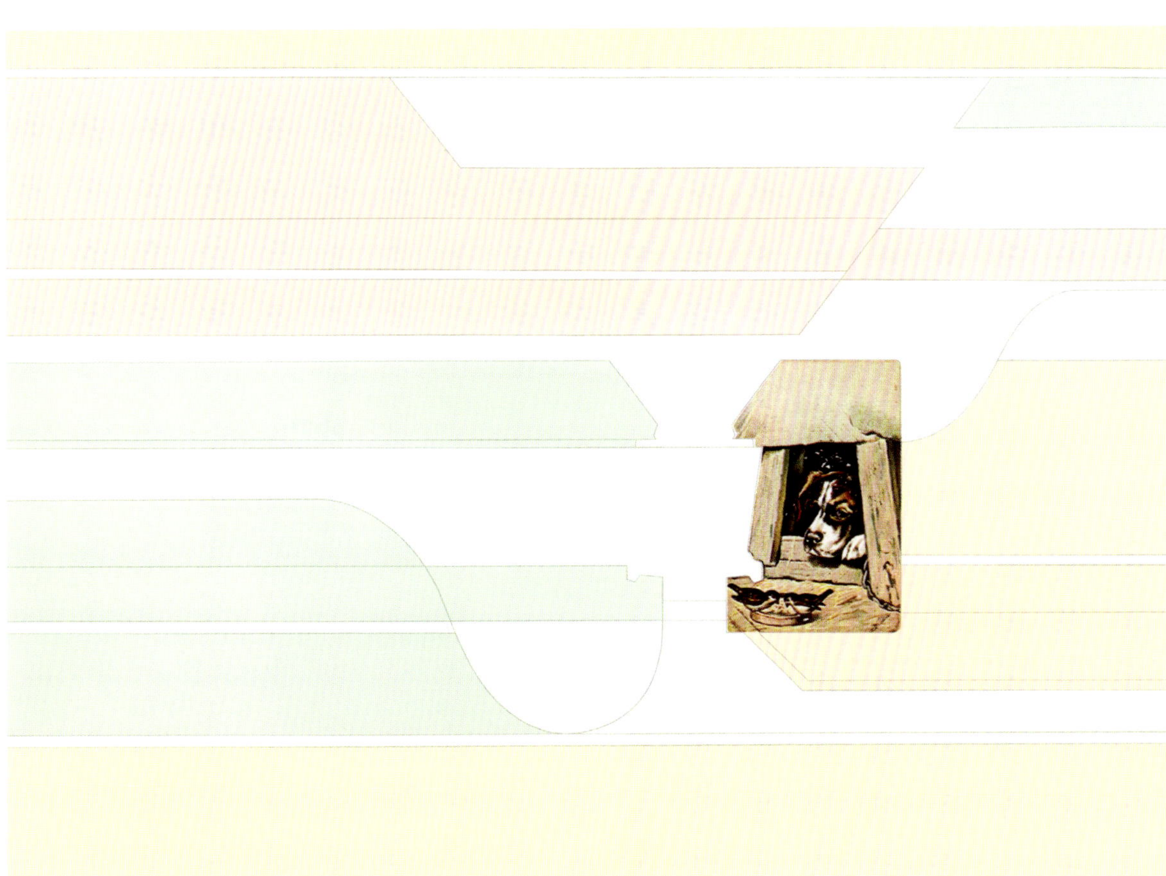

Bees in Easthampton, 1991. One of fifteen drawings; ink wash on paper, 9 x 12 13/16 in.

Gelada Baboon, 1986. Pen on paper, 11 x 8½ in.

Magellanic Penguins and Terns. Pen on paper, 11 x 8½ in.

opposite:
Scarlet Ibis and Chick, 1989. Watercolor on Arches paper, 22½ x 30 in.

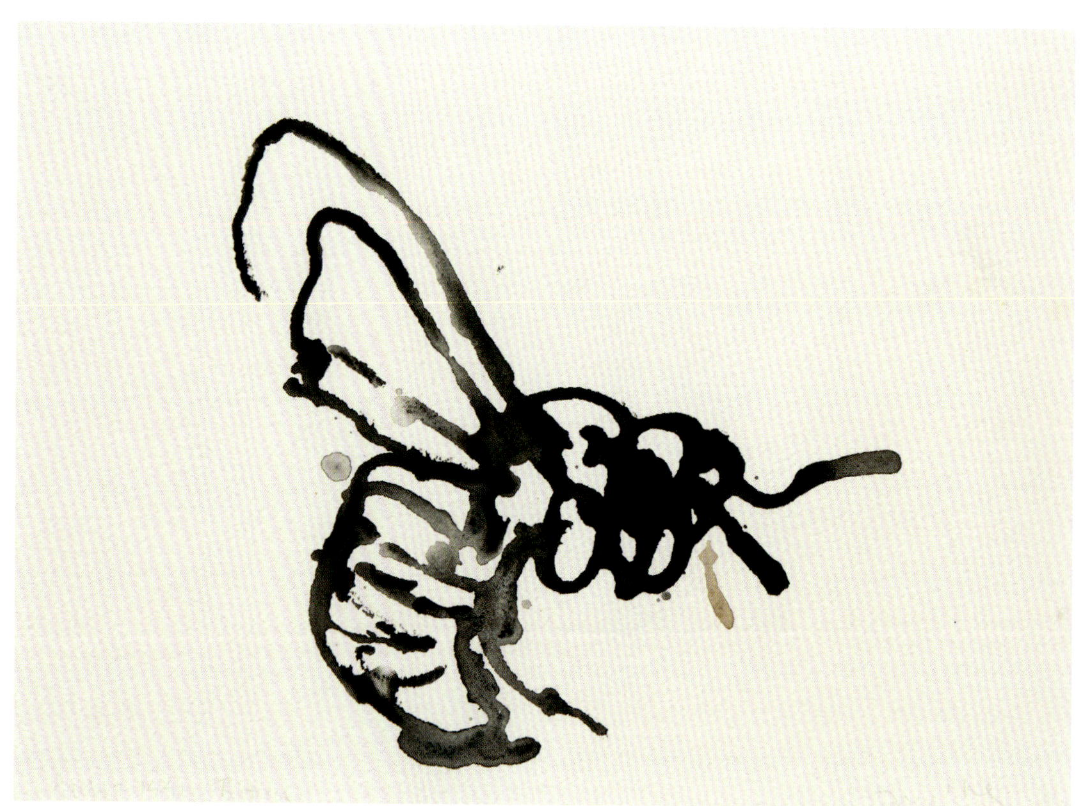

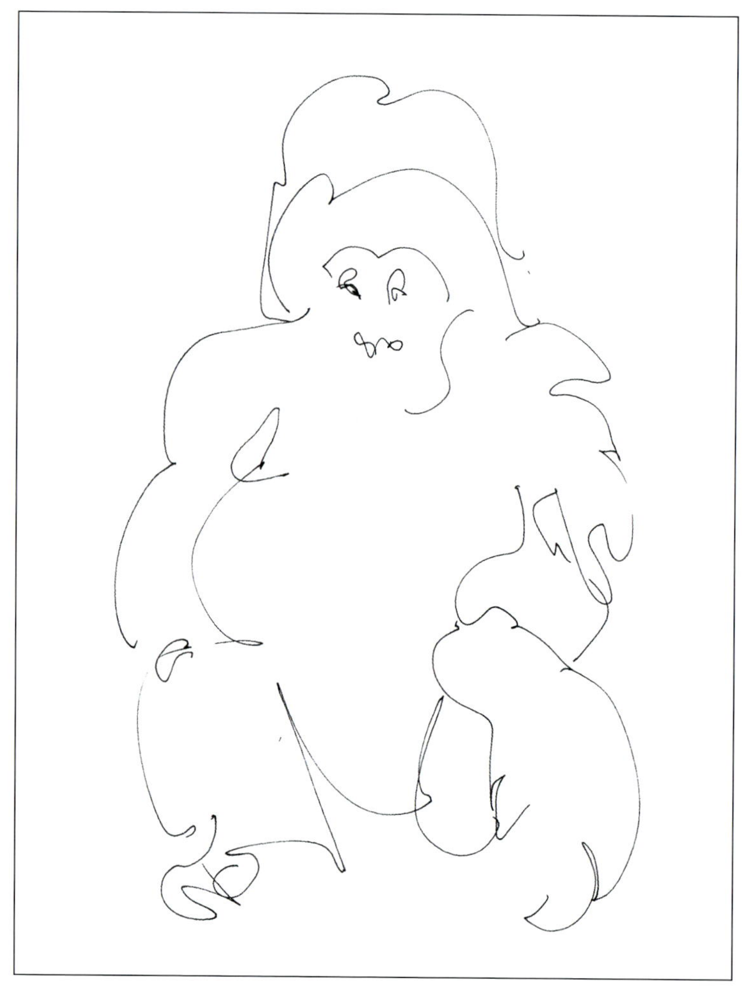

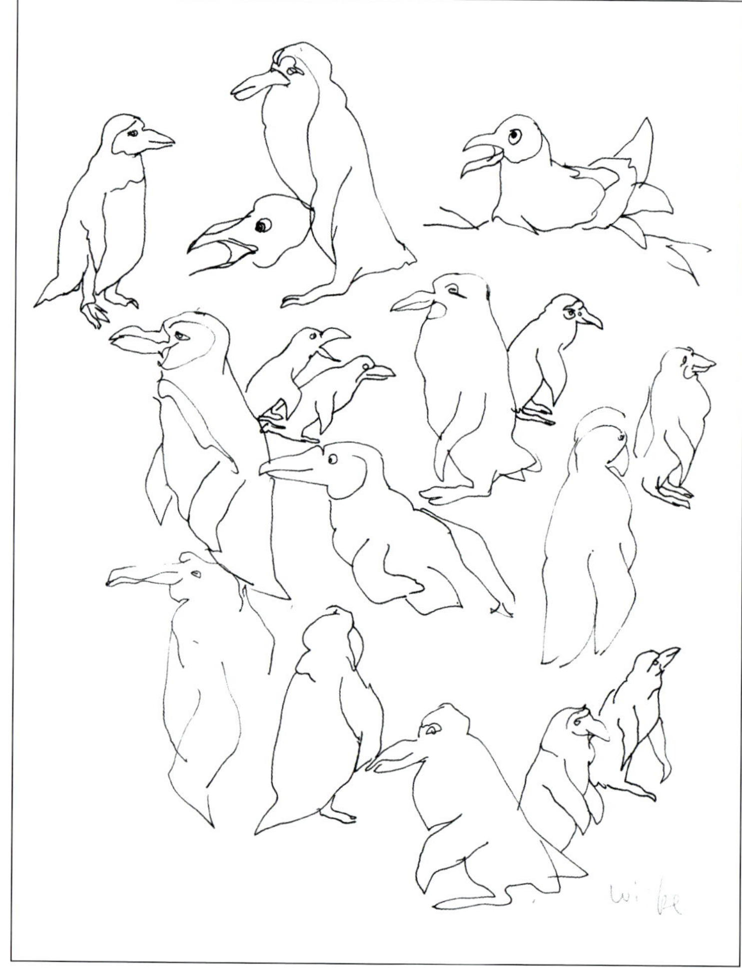

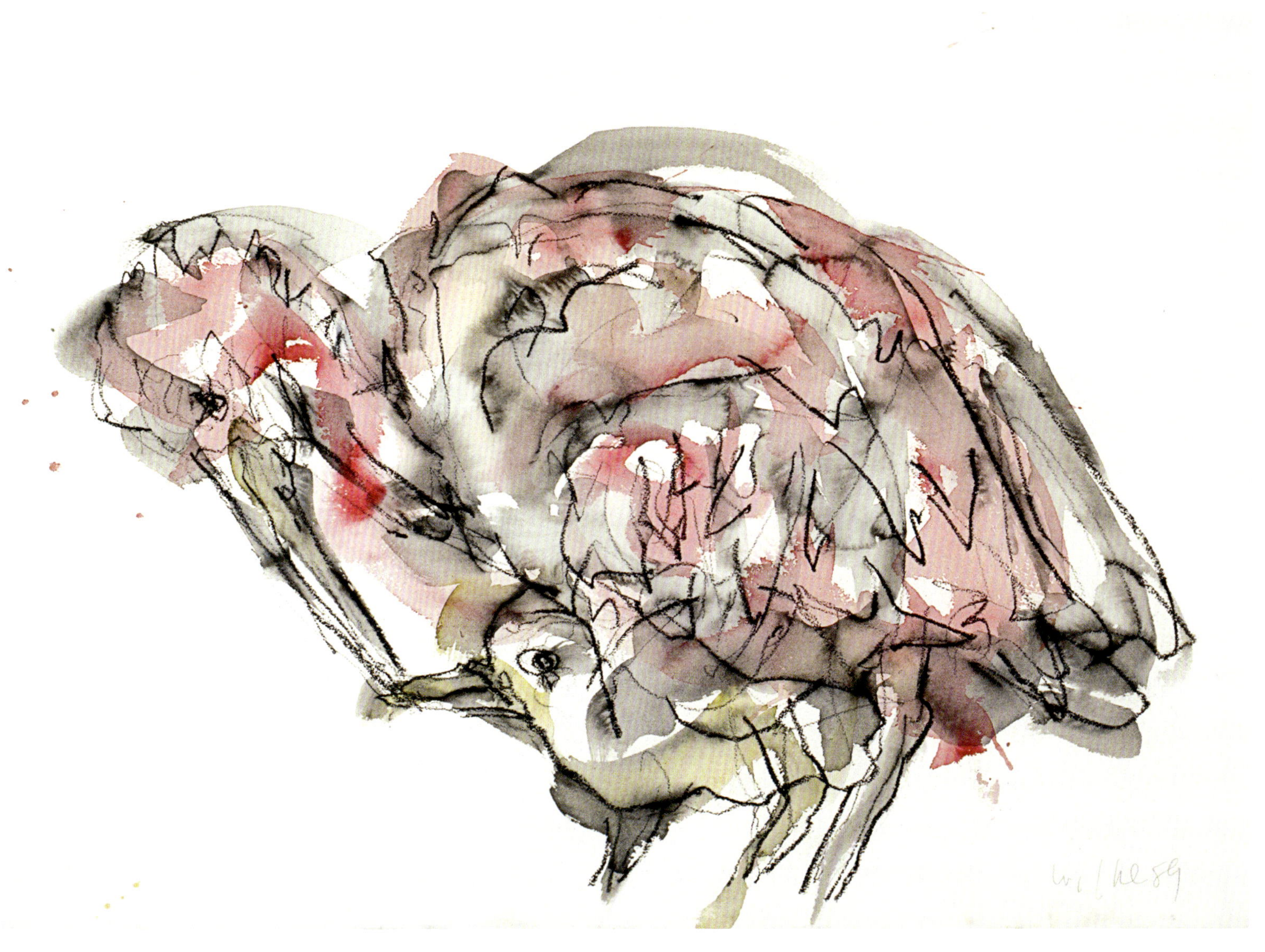

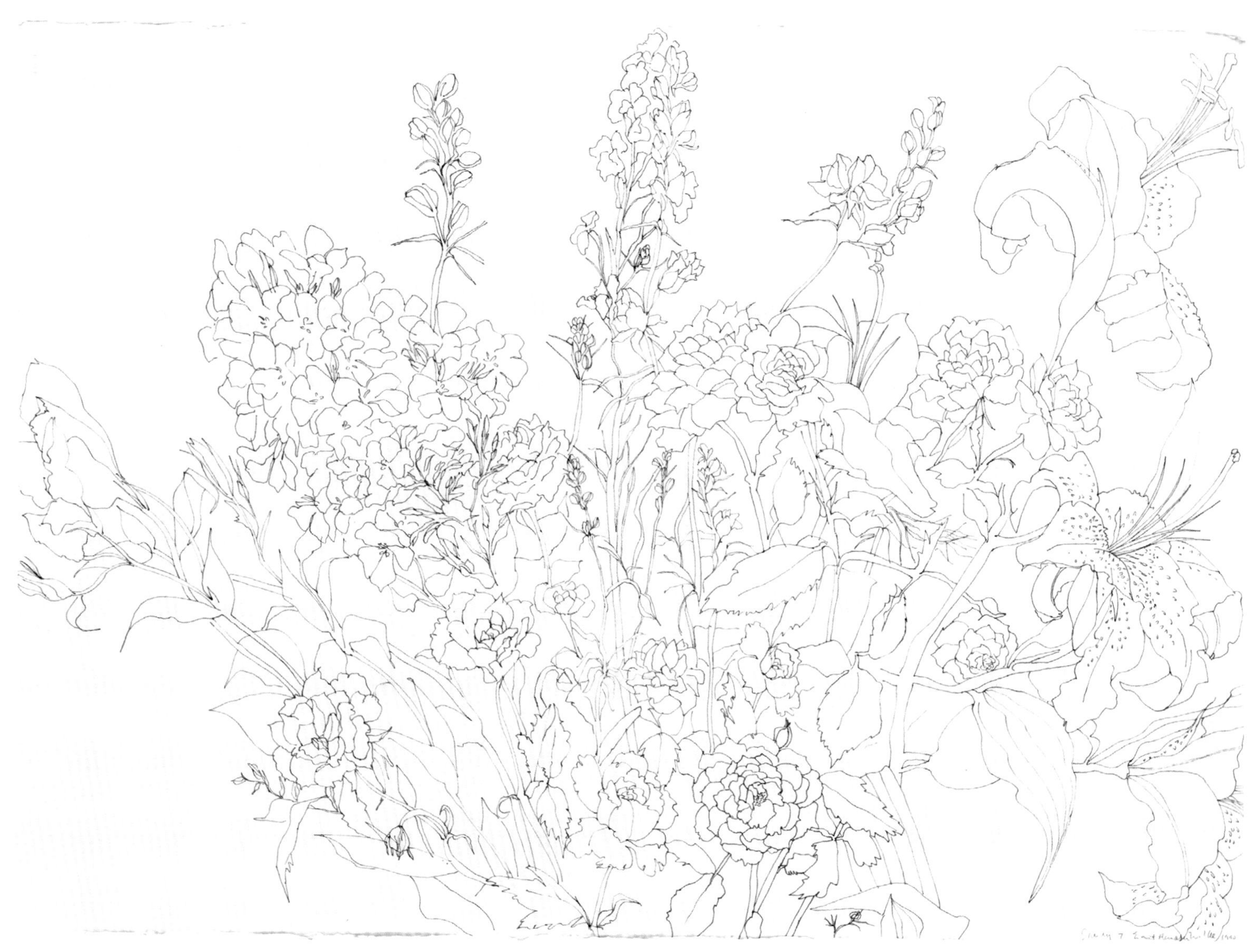

Lilies, 1980. Ink on Arches paper, 22½ x 30 in.

opposite:

Flower Drawing, 1980. Ink on Arches paper, 22½ x 30 in.

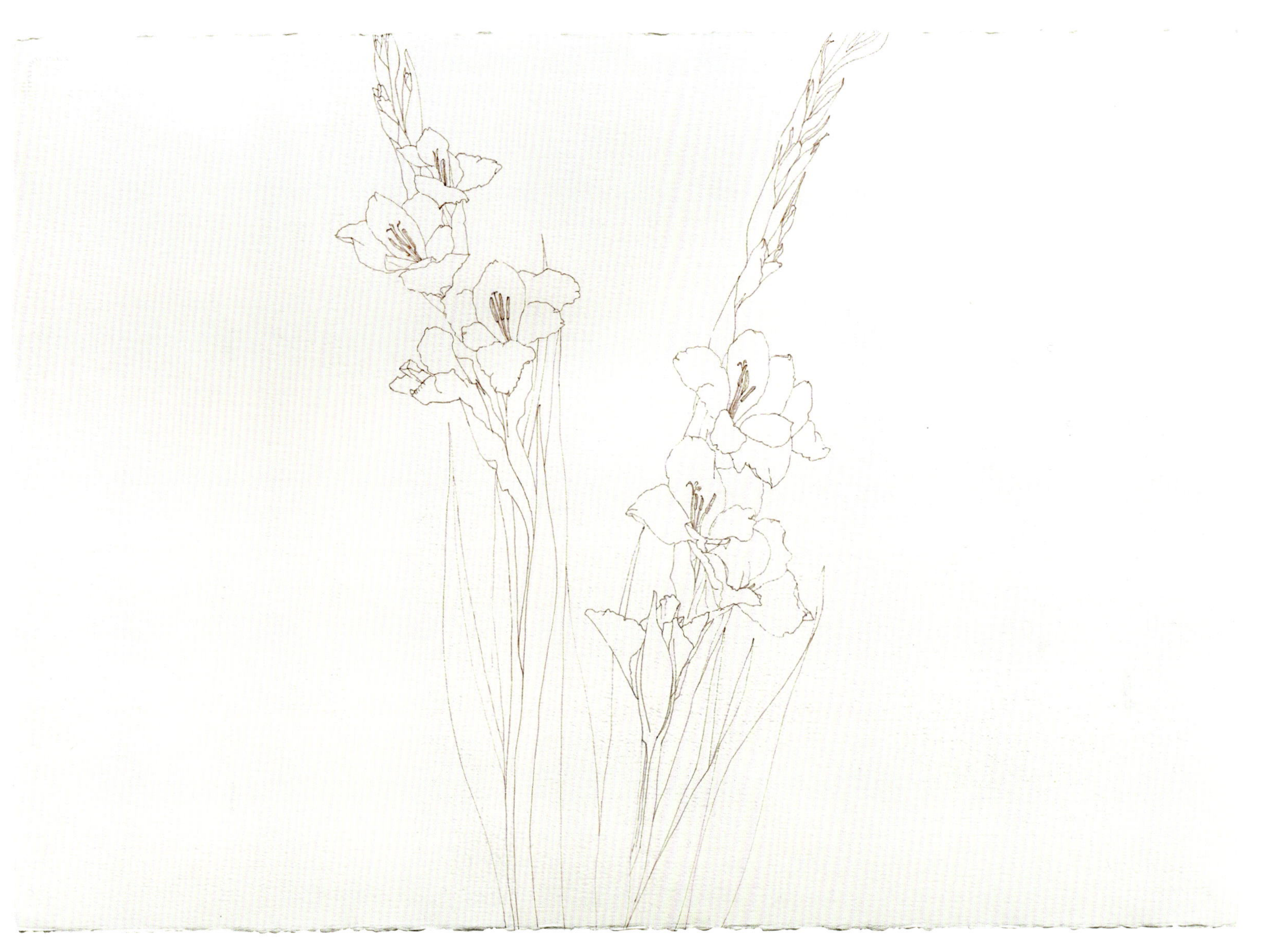

Self-Portrait as Angel with Dürer Wing,
1976. Watercolor and sepia ink on paper, 12 x 15 in.

self-portraits that she executed more or less throughout her career. One that gained relatively wide circulation is a consummately refined rendering in ink of the artist in profile, an extravagantly beautiful wing arching up from her back. Commissioned by the Museum of Modern Art, which used it as a notecard in 1977, this image, chaste and sublime, stands in a kind of inverse relationship to the photographic self-portraits. The lavish wing is drawn from Dürer, the draftsmanship inflected by an Art-Nouveau sinuosity that reflects a period taste (it could easily have graced an album cover of the time). Handwritten in a band that spans the hips of the delicately outlined figure's torso is a dictionary definition of angel: "1. A spiritual being superior to man in power and intelligence . . . 4. A message originating from God in his aspects of truth and love." It is hardly a modest metaphorical garment for the angel Wilke, who is given a softly piled mass of hair and, in profile, a delicately featured face, its eye modestly downcast. The contrast between this Wilke and the one represented in contemporary photo-based works is strong enough to suggest it was conceived with a degree of irony, though one's first impression is of pure delight.

Other versions of this drawing exist, including a 1976 *Self-Portrait as Angel with Dürer Wing* executed in watercolor and ink that has more freedom though no less elegance. But the most substantial group of self-portrait drawings Wilke made is diametrically opposed in character. When she became ill, Wilke made two bodies of watercolor drawings. Staccato strokes denote fragmentary features in the increasingly abbreviated, disembodied faces of the extensive series of watercolor self-portraits Wilke created between 1986 and 1990, during the first years of her illness (pp. 138–39). Alarmingly attenuated, in the manner of de Kooning's last paintings, these drawings—initially called "About Face," and then, after her diagnosis, "B.C." for "Before Cancer"—are largely composed of white space, the details of the face conveyed telegraphically, the manifest speed with which they were executed an eloquent statement of the urgency that impelled them. In their profusion and repetitiveness, they also have an almost ritual feeling, as of an activity undertaken in propitiation. This is true despite the images' manifest liveliness, the way the marks dance across the page: mostly, what they present to the viewer is looming emptiness, and haste. Considered in relationship to the angel Wilke, the "B.C." faces oppose enchanted sublimity with a species of blunt realism, in emotional if not physically descriptive terms.

In that sense, the "Faces" are as expressive as the smaller, more explicitly melancholy "Intra-Venus" drawings of bandaged hands and wrapped heads that followed in 1991 and '92, which are more hesitant in their touch and smaller—seemingly shriveled—in scale (pp. 140–41). The hands (all of the left-handed artist's right hand) seem to tremble, the contours bright but repeatedly interrupted and redoubled. Each hand is wrapped with the tape used to hold an intravenous needle in place. Grimmer by far—in fact, they are, arguably, the only bluntly defeated images Wilke made, though their execution can itself be considered a form of triumph—are the watercolor drawings of heads wrapped in oversize caps. All frontal and, like the hands, small (each twelve and a half by nine and a half inches), they depict an unfamiliar

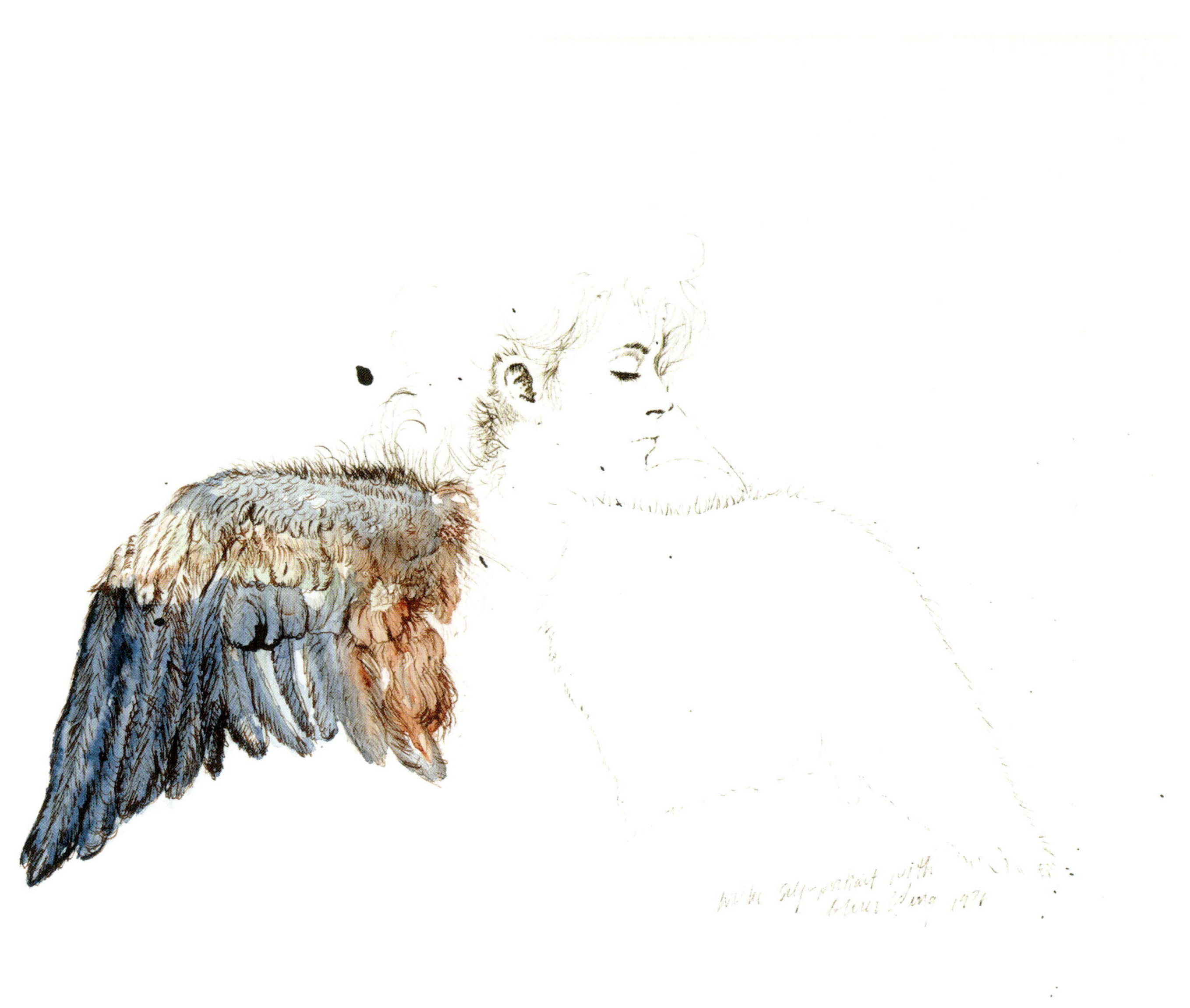

Hannah Wilke working on B.C. Face drawings in her Greene Street studio, 1989.

Wilke. Staring blankly, her eyes are set in deep shadow; wisps of hair escape head-coverings more evocative of war-wounded soldiers than lymphoma patients. In some of the "Intra-Venus" heads, the colors are livid, while others are mostly or entirely rendered in black and gray ink; all are distillations of weariness.

An anomalous project that can be compared with her self-portrait drawings is *Venus Pareve* and the related chocolate *Venus* (both 1982–84; pp. 142, 143). These small (roughly ten inches high) sculptures, modeled in clay and cast in plaster, are half-length likenesses of the artist, cut off at the tops of her thighs. Twenty were created, painted in a spectrum of bright colors including pale yellow, deep acid yellow, salmon pink, deep red, brown, purple, lime green, and turquoise as well as white and black. The facial features are delicate; Wilke's mouth is set, her hair full, her arms, as in a classical bust, terminate just below the shoulders. The skin toward the bottom and at the back is left slightly pebbled, as if to reveal the process by which they were made; elsewhere it is smooth. The chocolate *Venuses*, though headless in several studio photographs, were exhibited intact. No specifications exist about how the series was meant to be shown; installations have included a presentation of figures grouped in a triangle, like racked billiard balls, and in single file, as if on a shelf for retail display. In their size, conventionality, facture, and blatant repetition, they have an unmistakable similarity to tourist souvenirs—and, by extension, to the commodity-critique work being introduced in the early 1980s by such artists as Haim Steinbach (who arrayed various consumer products on Formica shelves) and Jeff Koons (whose luxe tchotchkes were then claiming attention). The chocolate sculptures made by Dieter Roth in the 1960s are also pertinent.

But seen in the light of a photograph that shows Wilke fashioning the original, *Venus Pareve* offers a different reading (p. 144). Standing nude in her studio, her head tilted thoughtfully, she applies a shaping tool to the clay figure. The modeling stand is set atop a stack of books; among the titles legible on their spines are *The Seeing Hand* and *The Artist in His Studio*. Looking like nothing so much as Pygmalion fashioning Galatea, Wilke presents herself in this carefully staged photo as a self-consciously prototypical artist, alone in the studio. Less prototypically, though hardly without precedent, the image she is fashioning is her own. Least conventional of all for the image of a working artist, of course, is her nudity. This picture, of an artist at work wielding the tools of her trade, was one she became increasingly eager to expose; it might be said that it is this activity—the practice of professional craft, of image-shaping—that she chose to withhold from the film *Philly*, when she asked the cameraman not to film her applying makeup. By the time she made the "Intra-Venus" tapes, she had put to rest any doubts about revealing how she created her image or her art. There is as much footage in those late videotapes of Wilke drawing and supervising the installation of her work as there is of her domestic life or hospitalizations. We also see her reading, eating, entertaining friends and family, bathing, traveling, being alone. Though representations of Wilke at work go back to published

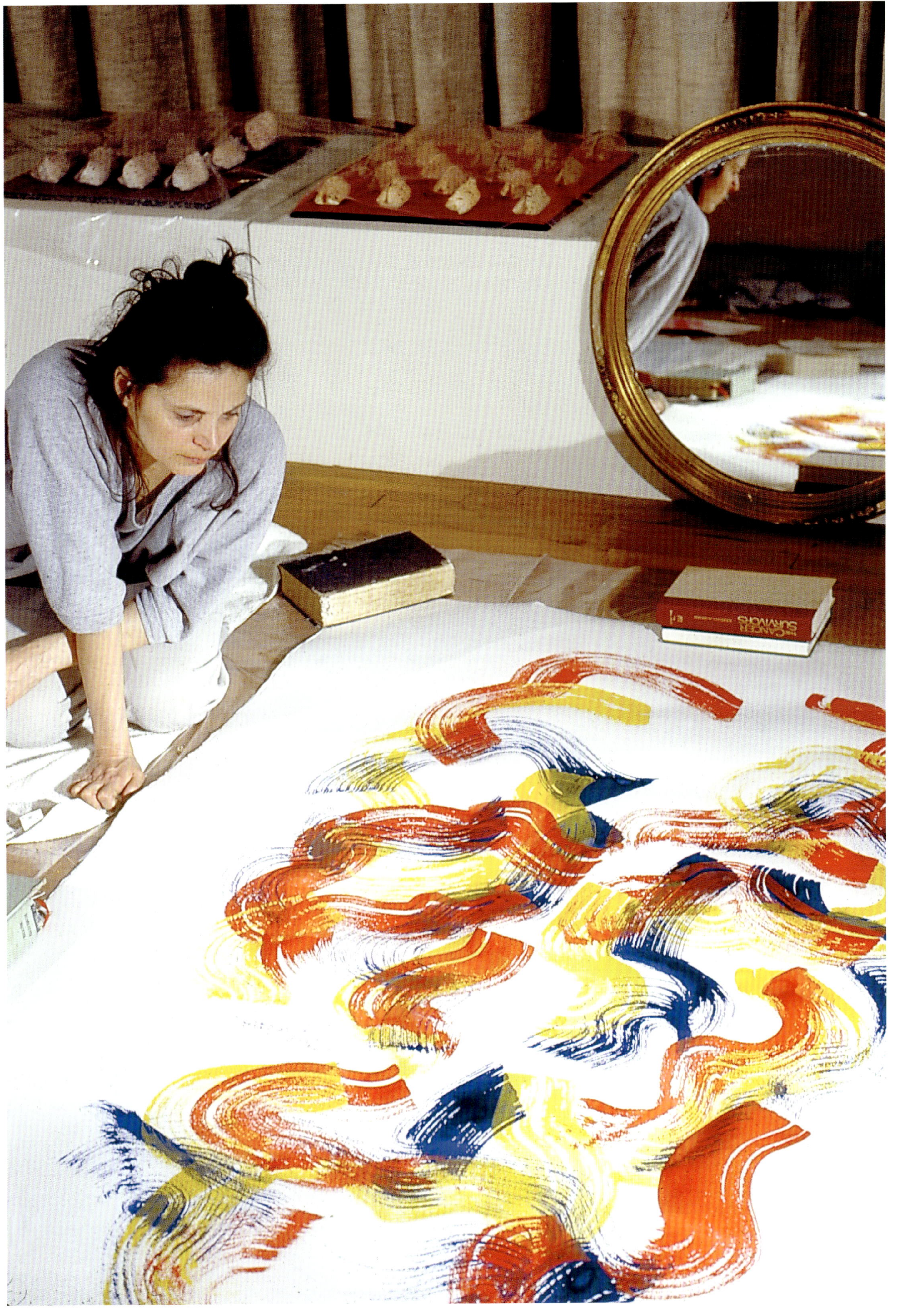
THE CANCER SURVIVORS

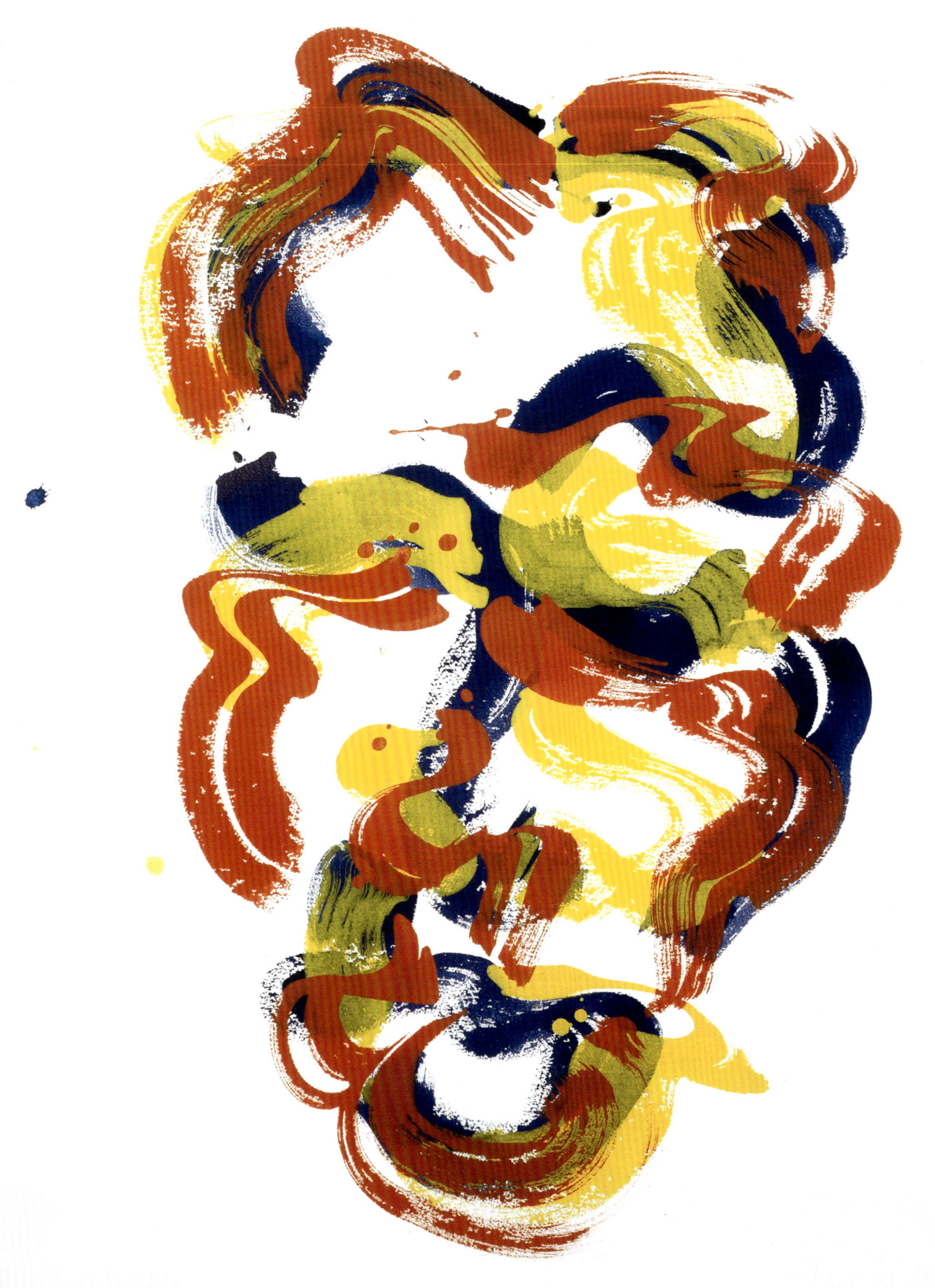

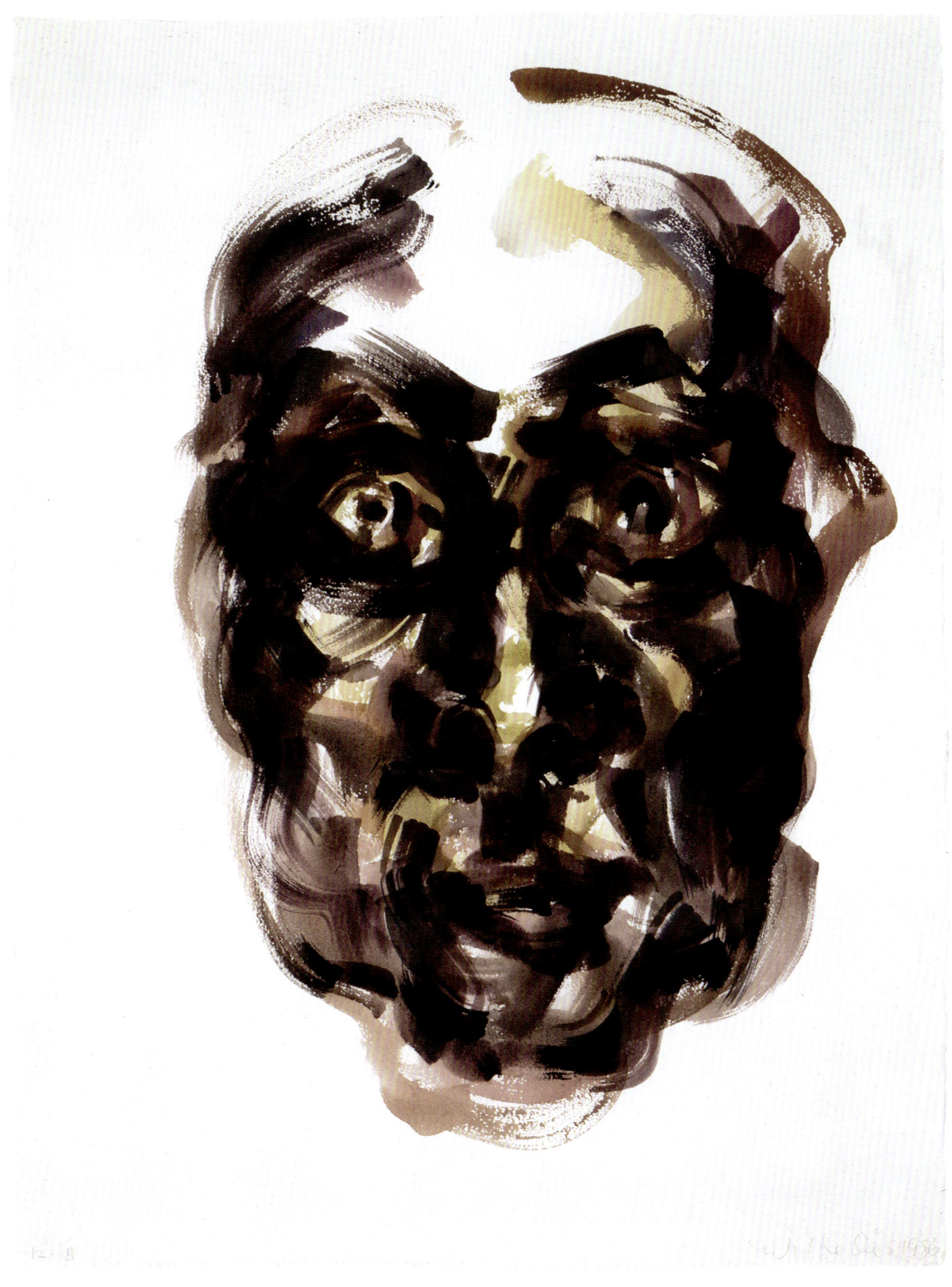

B.C. Series July 26, 1990. Watercolor on paper, 41½ x 19½ in.

B.C. Series, December 15, 1986. Watercolor on paper, 30 x 22 in.

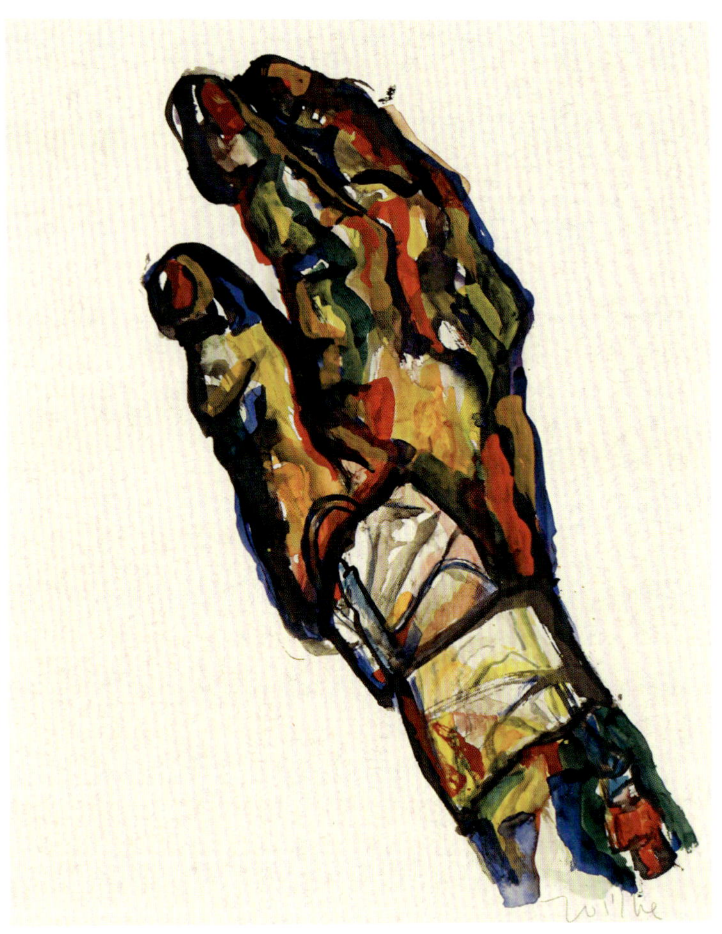

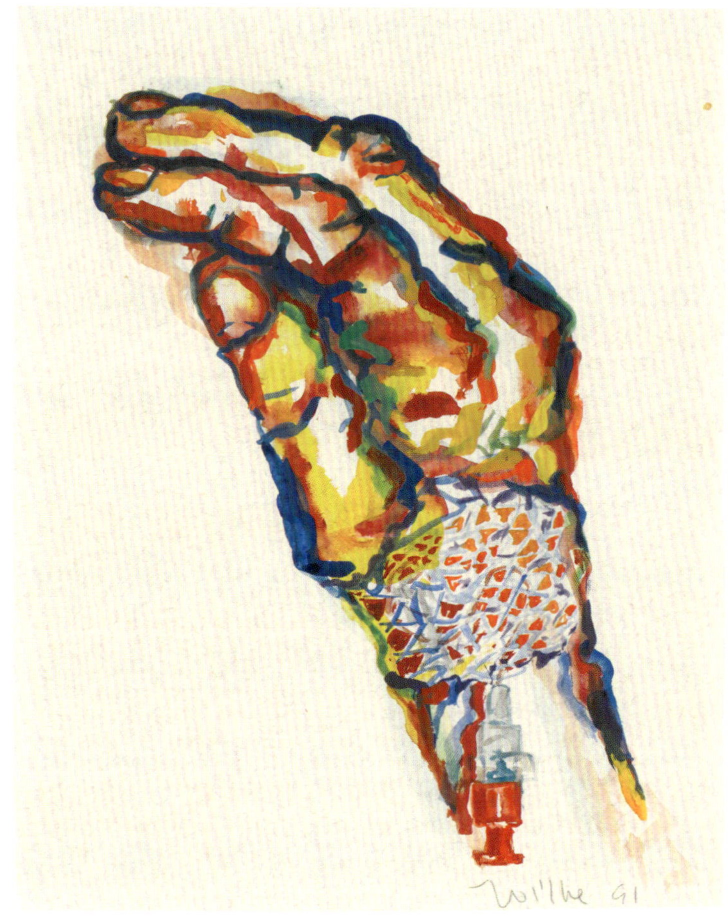

Intra-Venus Hand, 1991. Watercolor on paper, 12½ x 9½ in.

Intra-Venus Hand #9, October, 1991. Gouache and watercolor on paper, 12½ x 9½ in.

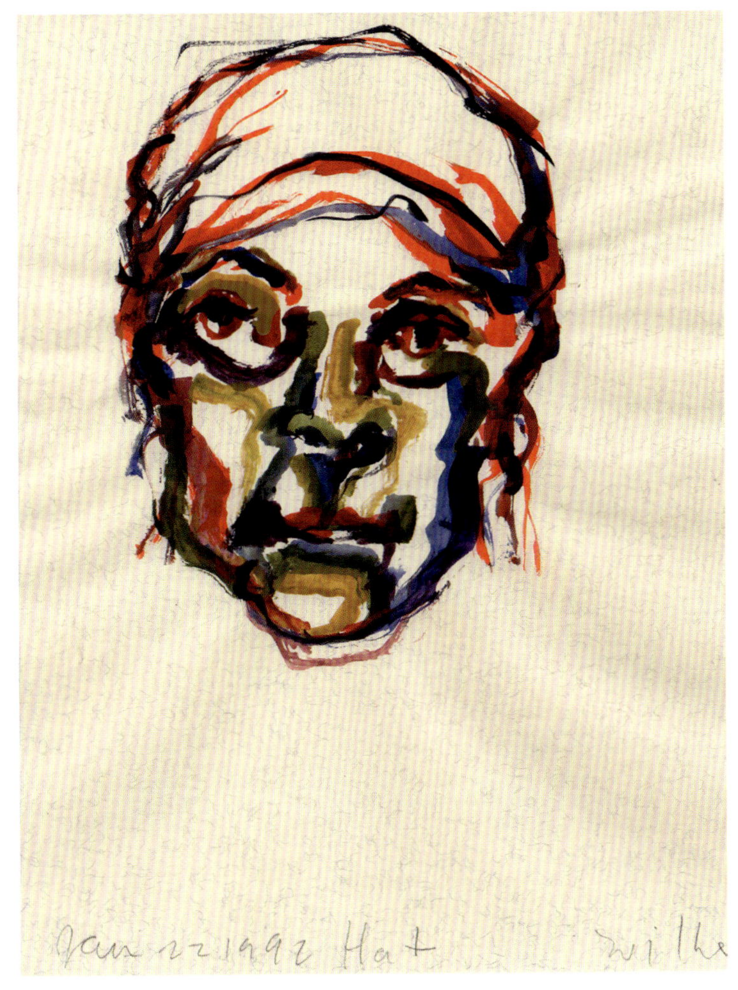

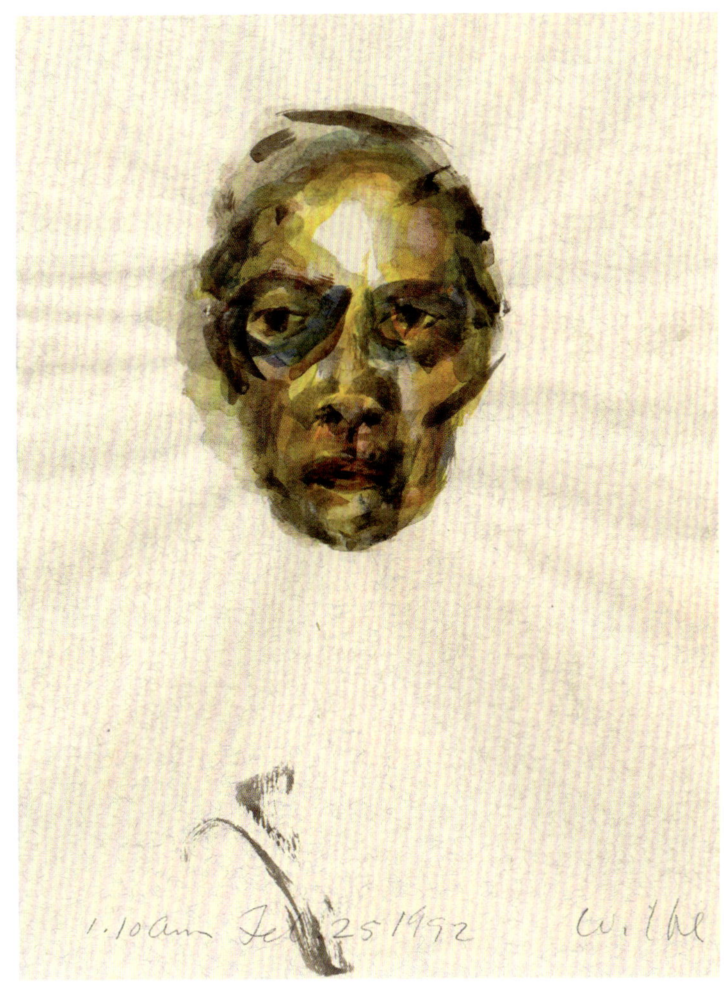

Intra-Venus Face, January 22, 1992.
Watercolor on paper, 12½ x 9½ in.

Intra-Venus Face, February 25, 1992, 10am. Watercolor on paper, 12½ x 9½ in.

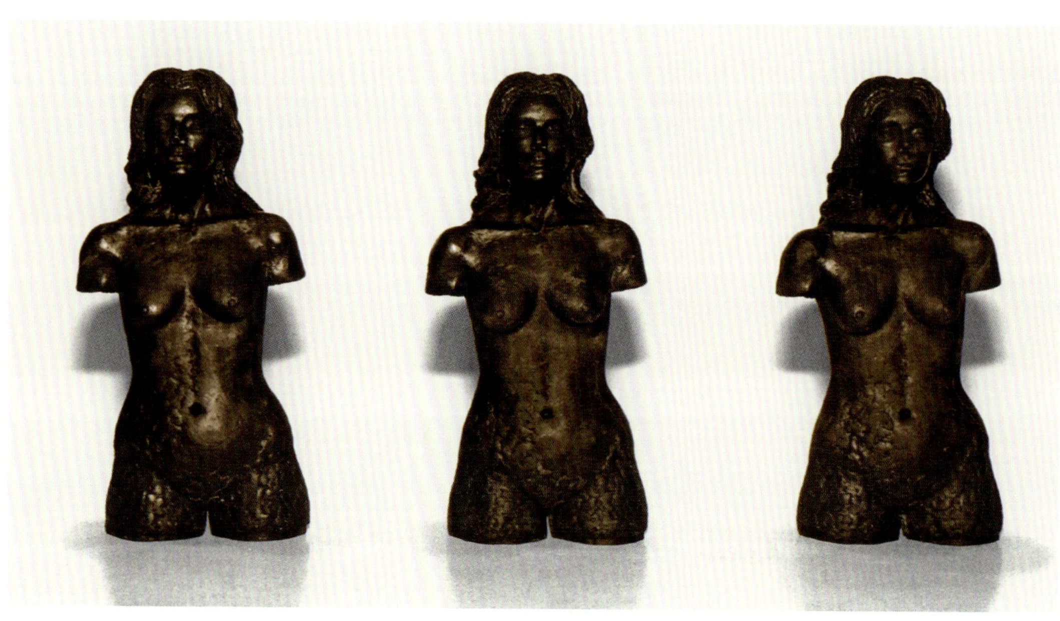

Venus Pareve, 1982–88. Molded chocolate,
10 x 5 x 2 in. each.

opposite:
Venus Pareve, 1982–84. Painted plaster,
10 x 5 x 2 in. each.

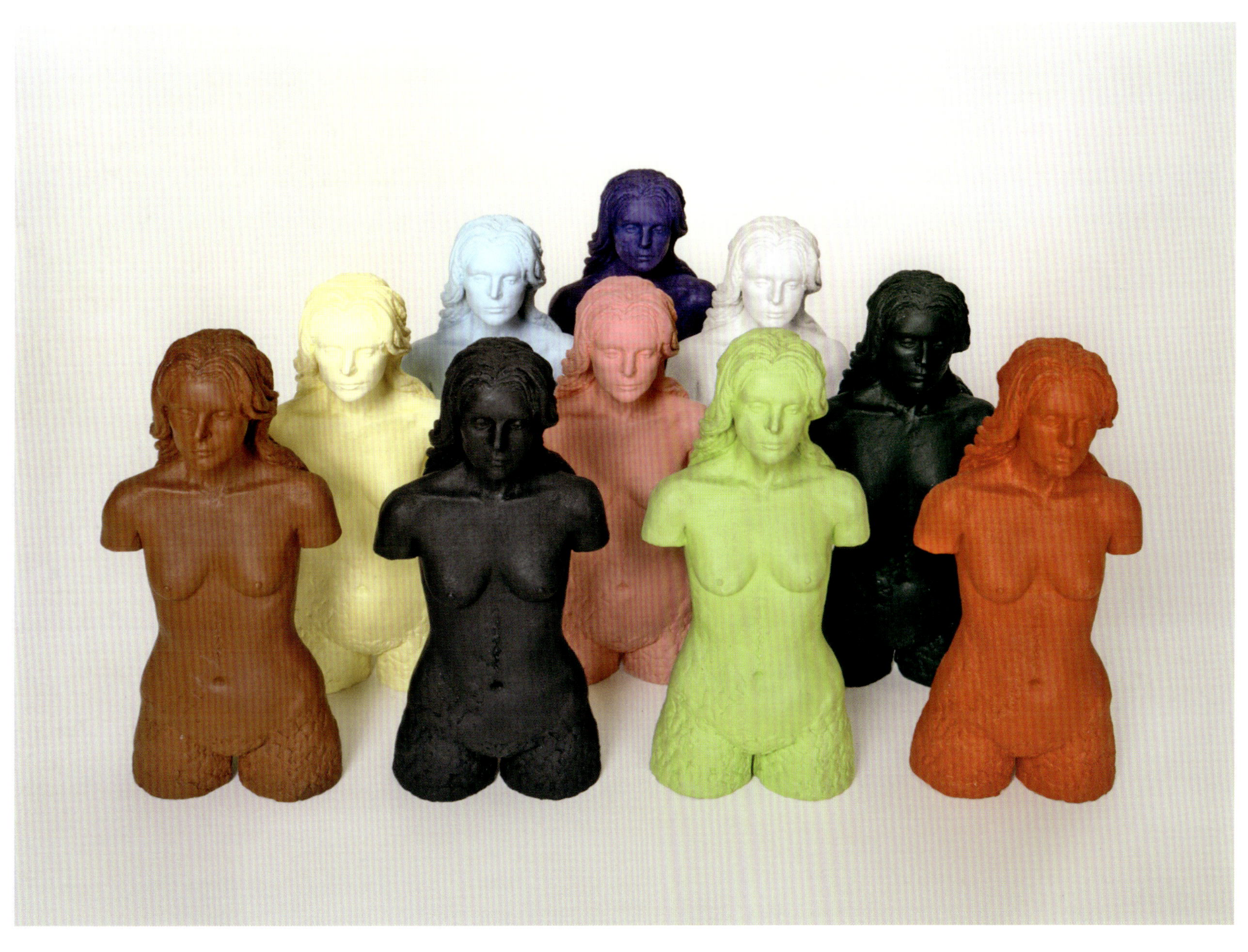

Hannah Wilke carving clay model for **Venus Pareve** sculptures

photographs of her pouring latex, which appeared in the early '70s, it is only in the later photographs and films that we see Wilke shaping an image of herself shaping her self-portraits. This reflexive process became, in a steady progression, her subject, of which fashioning her sexual identity was just a small part. Her work in sum is an epic story of felicity and determination, of drive—the kind of ambition that is particularly suspect in women, and in men is more often simply credited as hard work—and acceptance. This is what it is to be an artist and a woman, her work says: to want to find a place in the world and understand its mechanisms of power, and its immense resources of visual and intellectual pleasure.

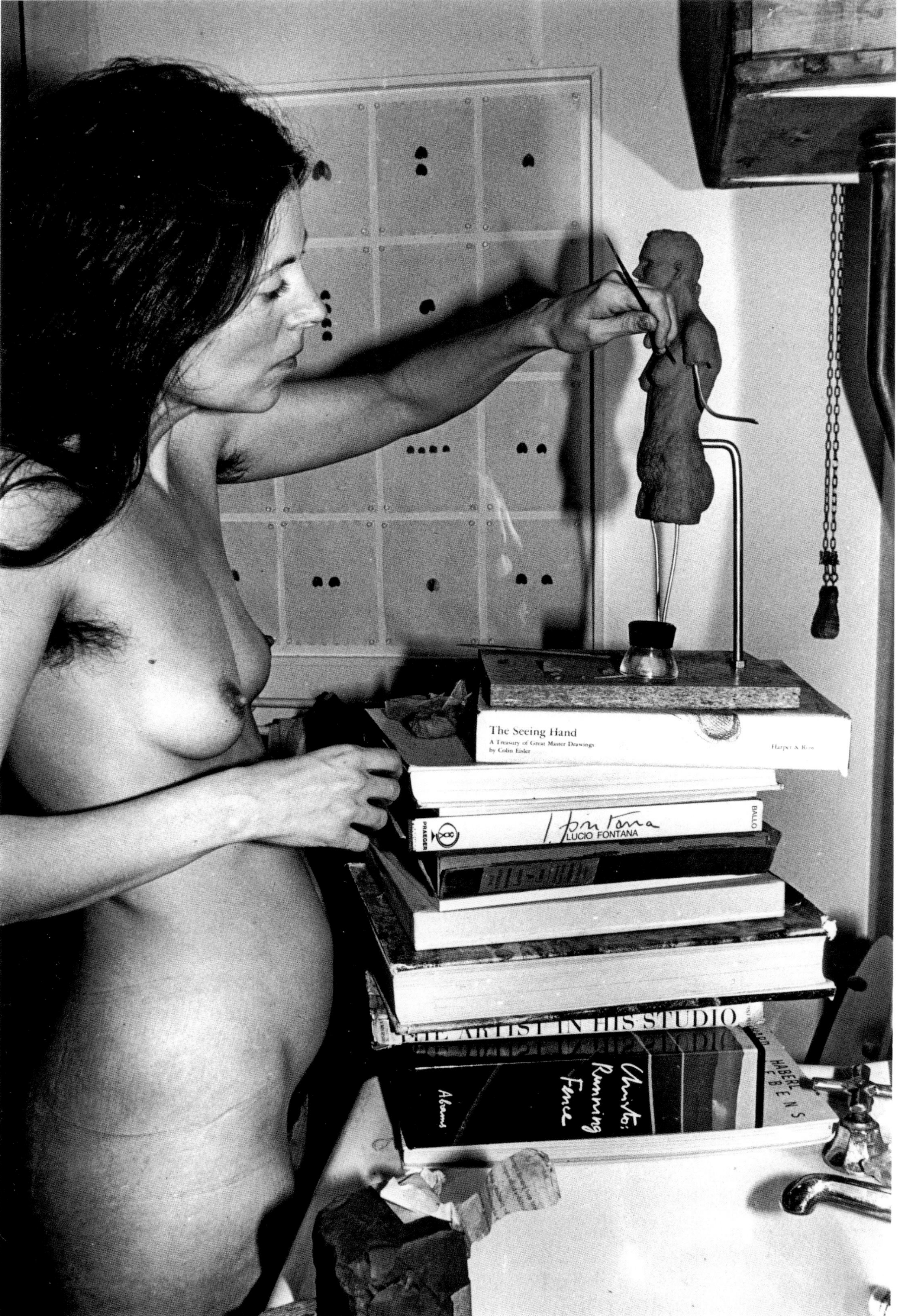
The Seeing Hand
A Treasury of Great Master Drawings
by Colin Eisler
Harper & Row
PRAEGER
LUCIO FONTANA
BALLO
ARTIST IN HIS STUDIO
Christo: Running Fence
Abrams

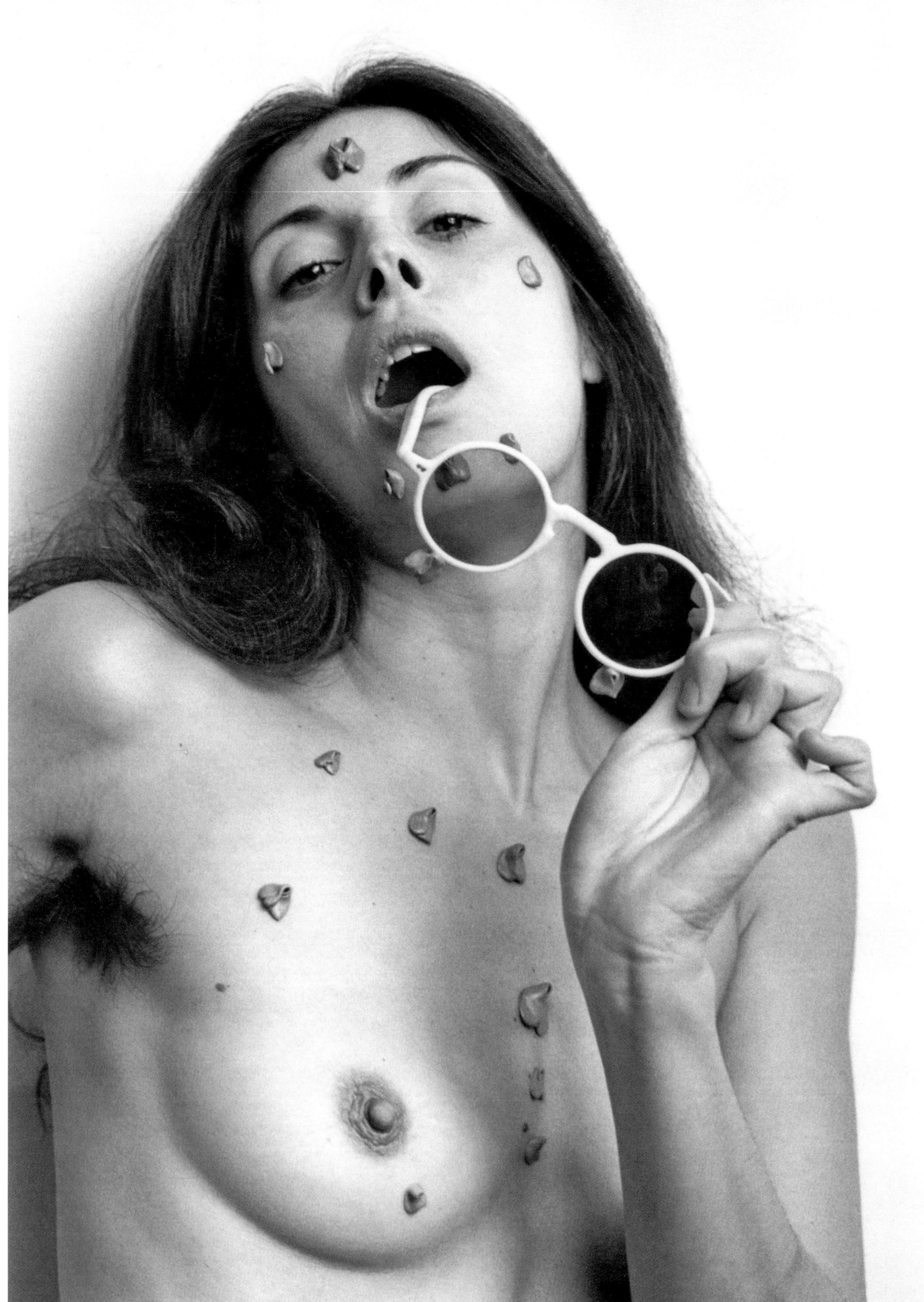

POSTSCRIPT

Carrying On

S.O.S. Starification Object Series [Glasses], 1974. Black-and-white photograph, 11½ x 14 in.

Every important artist is essentially inimitable, but the degree to which Wilke's life and her art were inseparable makes it particularly difficult to trace her effect on the culture. She shared this characteristic and others with Joseph Beuys, whom she admired, and with whom she had a couple of noted confrontations. One was on the occasion of his first visit to New York for a 1974 exhibition at the Ronald Feldman gallery; during his stay, he followed an eagerly anticipated and exceedingly well-attended public dialogue at the New School with a private discussion at the Stanhope Hotel for roughly fifty invited women in the arts. He used the occasion, Elizabeth Baker remembers, to lecture them rather condescendingly; Wilke was among very few to stand up to him, demanding—flirtatiously but vigorously—to know who he thought he was to tell them what to do.[1] Lucy Lippard, who was there as well and vividly recalls Beuys's talk as "patriarchal" and "infuriating," also spoke up; the event was memorable, and came at a time when Beuys's status in the art world was formidable. Wilke's vocal opposition did not come easily to her; Baker found her in tears afterward. But on Beuys's second visit, during which he spoke to another overflow crowd at the Great Hall of the Cooper Union, Wilke again confronted him from the audience.

A charismatic and polarizing figure, Beuys was hard to ignore and even harder to emulate, though his legacy is as broad as it is diffuse. Similarly, the response to Wilke's work has always been colored by the responder's feelings about her as a person (though Lippard has come to publicly embrace her achievements, she still rankles at what she recalls as Wilke's declaration that "nobody in Heresies"—the women's collective Lippard helped found—"was interested in her because she was more beautiful than any of them").[2] As the pungency of her personality has receded, in the years since her death, behind the lasting record of her work, Wilke's influence has become increasingly widespread and broadly, if slowly, acknowledged. That is not to say that in her lifetime she was neglected by critics, scorned by artists, or excluded from the contextualizing exhibitions that draw connections within and across generations and movements or styles, nor to deny the many deep and lasting relationships she had with women artists as well as men. But neither was her contribution always accorded its place. Like most artists, Wilke kept careful score.

When she died, at fifty-two, Wilke had had seventeen solo exhibitions, the great majority at commercial galleries. The most comprehensive survey was at the art museum at the University of Missouri in St. Louis, in 1989. Since then, there have been several museum exhibitions, the most recent organized by the Neuberger Museum at the State University of New York at Purchase (2008); Artium in Vitoria-Gasteiz, Spain (2006); the Neue Gessellschaft für bildende Kunst in Berlin (2000); and the Nikolaj Contemporary Art Center in Copenhagen (1998). The record of group shows in which her work has been included suggests that the many points of connection it offered to younger artists involved with postmodern theory or political activism have not been overlooked. Indeed, the variety of thematic shows represented by her exhibition history demonstrates that Wilke, again like most successful

Hannah Wilke in her Greene Street studio with **Elective Affinities**, 1978. Eighty-six glazed white porcelain sculptures on four painted boards

artists, found herself enlisted in a rather bewildering variety of curatorial gambits. Notably, she was among the artists chosen by Barbara Kruger for a 1981 exhibition at The Kitchen in New York called "Pictures & Promises," described by its press release as "A display of advertising, slogans and interventions." Along with actual ads, it contained work by Richard Prince, Sherrie Levine, Cindy Sherman, Jenny Holzer, Kruger, Dara Birnbaum, Hans Haacke, Joseph Kosuth, Laurie Simmons, and Barbara Ess—precisely those postmodernists who, Wilke believed, and not without justification, were turning their backs on her.

Wilke's work was also included in "Image World: Art and Media Culture" (1989), a landmark show organized by Lisa Phillips and Marvin Heiferman with John Hanhardt which brought the Whitney Museum's imprimatur, and an expanded focus, to the same impulses. Wilke was represented by the poster subtitled "Beware of Fascist Feminism"; it was hung alongside the publicity photo of Robert Morris in spiked collar and chains that had been linked, in 1974, with the infamous Lynda Benglis ad that so riled Wilke. But if the poetic justice of this juxtaposition must have been singularly gratifying for Wilke, the omission of her name from the catalogue's checklist would have been galling in equal measure. Heiferman recalls that the curators were interested from the start in work like Wilke's that focused on "the ways artists were choosing to represent themselves," and does not remember that choosing her work was an afterthought; but her inclusion as an artist of "ephemera"[3] poses questions regarding Wilke's status at the time with respect to the other artists in the show, among them Barbara Bloom, Sherrie Levine, Cindy Sherman, and others who might be considered in some ways her heirs.

Lowery Sims chose Wilke to be in the New Museum's "Art and Ideology" exhibition in 1984; by 1988, she was being celebrated as a post-feminist artist, in "The Decline of Sexual Stereotypes in Post-Feminist Sculpture," at Space One Eleven in Birmingham, Alabama. Two years later, Wilke participated in a panel on "Virgins, Whores, and Martyrs: Sexuality and Religious Art" at the Alternative Museum in New York (other panelists included David Salle, Linda Montano, and Linda Nochlin). Wilke was among the artists represented in a 1993 exhibition at David Zwirner's gallery titled "Coming To Power: 25 Years of Sexually X-Plicit Art by Women." Other group exhibitions highlighted relatively narrow aspects of her art ("Artists' Weapons: A Response to the Arms Buildup," curated by Donald Kuspit and Ted Greenwald for Greenwald's gallery, 1984; "Animals in Art" at the Animal Medical Center, New York, in 1983). Her work was also seen in shows organized around issues of form, material and process (such as "Alternative Supports: Contemporary Sculpture on the Wall," organized by the Bell Gallery at Brown University and the List Art Center at MIT in 1987). Surely among the most surprising invitations she received was to appear at the International Congress of Psychoanalysis at the Plaza Hotel in New York in 1981, where she gave a lecture-cum-performance—during which she removed her shirt—that surely took some clinicians by surprise.

Wilke's work has been acquired by major museums around the world, and

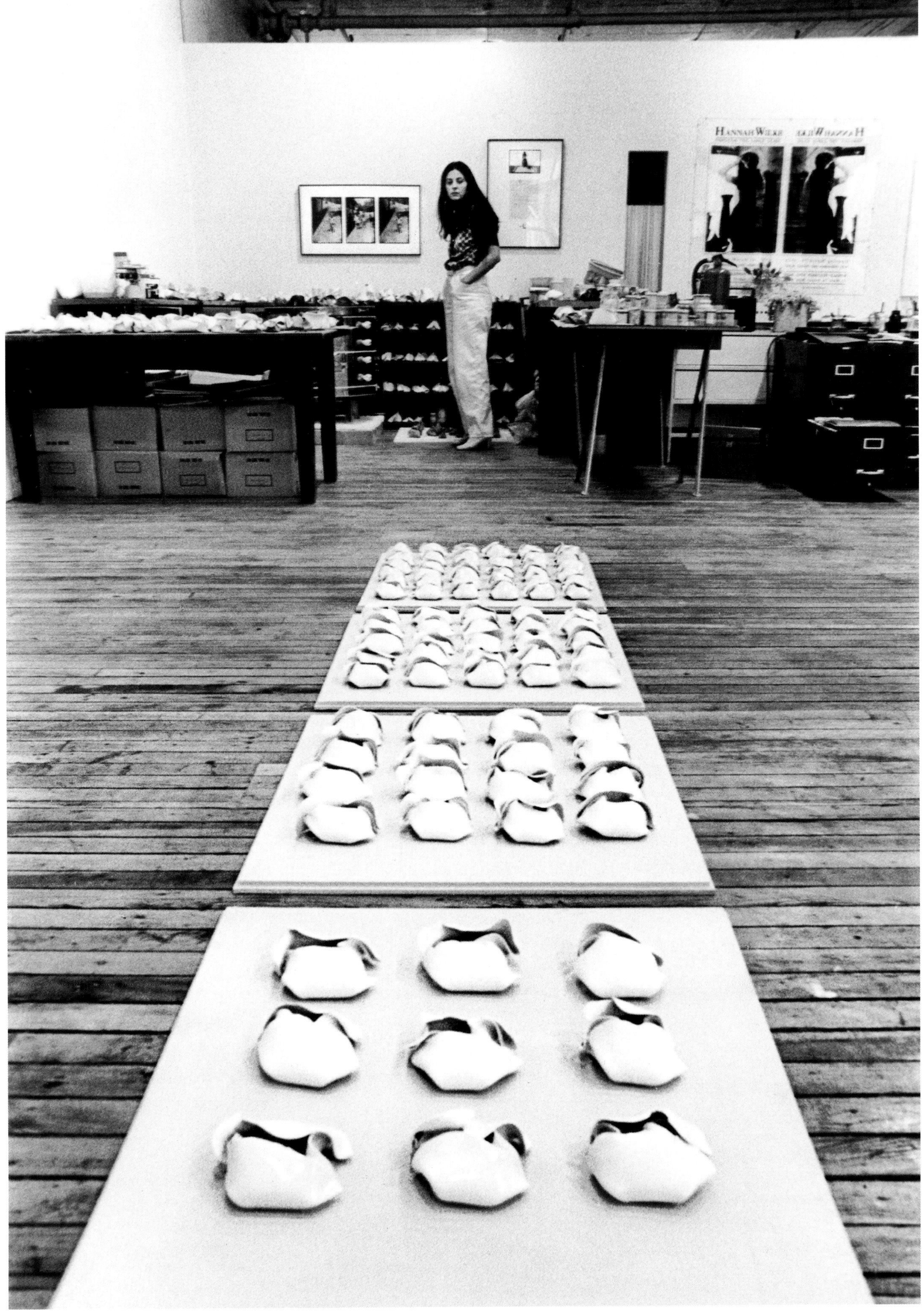
HANNAH WILKE

written about by dozens of important critics and historians. The Centre Pompidou, Paris, acquired Wilke's *S.O.S. Starification Object Series: An Adult Game of Mastication* in 2008, and included it in the 2009 exhibition "Women Artists: elles @ the Centre Pompidou." In a spring 2009 installation of its permanent collection, the Museum of Modern Art in New York presented Wilke's latex sculpture *Ponder-r-Rosa #4, White Plains, Yellow Rocks* (1975) in a gallery that also contained roughly contemporary work by Eva Hesse, Louise Bourgeois, and Bruce Nauman; work by Beuys could be seen in the gallery next door. Wilke would surely have been pleased.

Nonetheless, she could report in late 1989, a little more than three years before she died, "At my show the other night, I couldn't resist saying that you could buy the entire show for the price of one Frank Stella. My entire life's work is worth maybe $750,000."[4] Angry and recklessly forthright, even if the calculation was surely only the roughest guess, her complaint typified the vigilance with which Wilke measured her place in the art world. If she didn't make it the subject of her work (as has, say, David Diao, who has managed to address it while maintaining a sense of humor, no mean feat), Wilke made no secret that she was guarding her reputation, and watching her competitors. Judy Chicago, Lynda Benglis, Cindy Sherman, "Fascist Feminists," Lucy Lippard—the list of the artists and writers against whom she took up her pen was long and subject to change. But she was equally committed to seeing that the work of her peers, as well as her own, would not be minimized or forgotten.

Particularly illuminating is an unpublished letter she wrote to the editor of the *New York Times* "Arts and Leisure" section on October 24, 1983, in response to an article written the day before by Vicki Goldberg about Cindy Sherman. After noting that she had been in Buffalo in 1976 for the Albright-Knox performance and installation, when Sherman was a student there, Wilke says, "I would like to mention the true inventors of the female aesthetic language that preceded Ms. Sherman's retro pictures at Metro Pictures by at least a decade or two. ... A sense of self was explicit in the work of many women artists of the 1970s. My own work includes a 1970 photograph of myself 'sadly waiting by the phone,' which accompanied an audiotape of personal telephone messages ("Lives" exhibition at Artists Space, 1975) [it was also used for "Intercourse With," 1977], the 1976 "C'est la vie rrose," 1973 Glamour Girl photo for the first issue of *Appearances*, a 1974 photographic series of the artist as housewife, maid, woman in purdah, cowgirl, and femme fatale ("Starification Object Series," shown at Ronald Feldman and published widely)." Wilke went on to cite Eleanor Antin, Lynda Benglis (for her notorious publicity shots in particular), Carolee Schneemann, Colette, Adrian Piper, Jacki Apple, Martha Wilson, Annette Messager, Joanne Seltzer, and Alexis Smith as "among the many other women artists who created significant 'personas' during this period." Why, she wonders by way of conclusion, "is there never any mention of those who innovated the women's iconography that is now being imitated?"

She repeated the complaint, and enhanced the wordplay, in a more acid letter (marked "not sent" in the archive) to *Art News* publisher Milton Esterow in 1983:

"Dear Milton," she wrote, "when will we ever stop trying to assimilate? The goisha blonde on the recent cover of *Art News*, who should really be called Ms. Retropictures, is reminiscent of a coming out party at a transvestite bar. . . . How about the innovators instead of the imitators." Earlier angry letters had been addressed to Ingrid Sischy, when she was the editor of *Artforum*, about Ann-Sargent Wooster's article of December 1975; and another in October of 1975 to the editors of the *Village Voice* for its review of "Artists Make Toys." In *Forum*, in 1989, she complained that although she was every bit as much a lightning rod as Robert Mapplethorpe, and had similarly suffered institutional censorship, he had shows at the Whitney and elsewhere, but she hadn't. And, very astutely, she judged her chances of being included in a coming exhibition that featured many women who could be considered her heirs. "I think that because the works are nude, I might not now be in the new media show at the Whitney, which is coming up in a few months. Keeping one's clothes on, we call Post-modernism."[5]

Even more outspoken are the statements she made in *The New Common Good* (1985): "Has Sherry [*sic*] Levine copied a woman artist? No. It wouldn't be advantageous. Would she have gotten anywhere copying all the underrated women artists in America, or elsewhere? The appropriation of journalistic photography which is now in vogue is even less justifiable as many of these journalists often risked and lost their lives reporting the various atrocities of war, famine, and natural disasters. . . . If Barbara Kruger uses a picture of a pretty girl and says this is a stereotype, she's really poking fun at a small element of society . . . . I find Chicago's using large numbers of women making her art—is a form of feudalism."[6] As perceptive in her judgments as she was intemperate, Wilke knew she was burning bridges, an outcome that would be the cause of some remorse, or at least discomfort. In a questionnaire given to artists participating in the "Alternative Supports: Contemporary Sculpture on the Wall" exhibition, Wilke replied to the question, "Are you content living and working when and where you do?" by writing that she'd prefer "a place where women really respected each other more—to achieve a friendship & ties that were not broken by their psycho-sexual needs."[7]

It has become commonplace to observe that women artists of Wilke's generation—those celebrated, for instance, in the exhibition "WACK!," which originated at the Museum of Contemporary Art in Los Angeles, in 2007, and brought together more than 100 women artists who had been active in the late '60s and in the '70s, including Wilke—were, by necessity, an angry and contentious lot. Many feel that their achievements were eclipsed. But a good number have lately come to believe that the tide has turned, and that younger artists recognize the importance of their predecessors' contributions. Janine Antoni is among the most articulate of younger artists who embrace the legacy of Wilke and her peers. Antoni's fourteen *Lick and Lather* self-portrait busts, half of chocolate and the other half of soap (1993–94), are closely related to Wilke's *Venus Pareve*, the chocolate one in particular (though the similarity

Janine Antoni, **Lick and Lather**, 1993. Two self-portrait busts: one chocolate and one soap, two pedestals. Edition of seven plus one full set of fourteen busts, seven of each material, 24 x 16 x 13 in. each

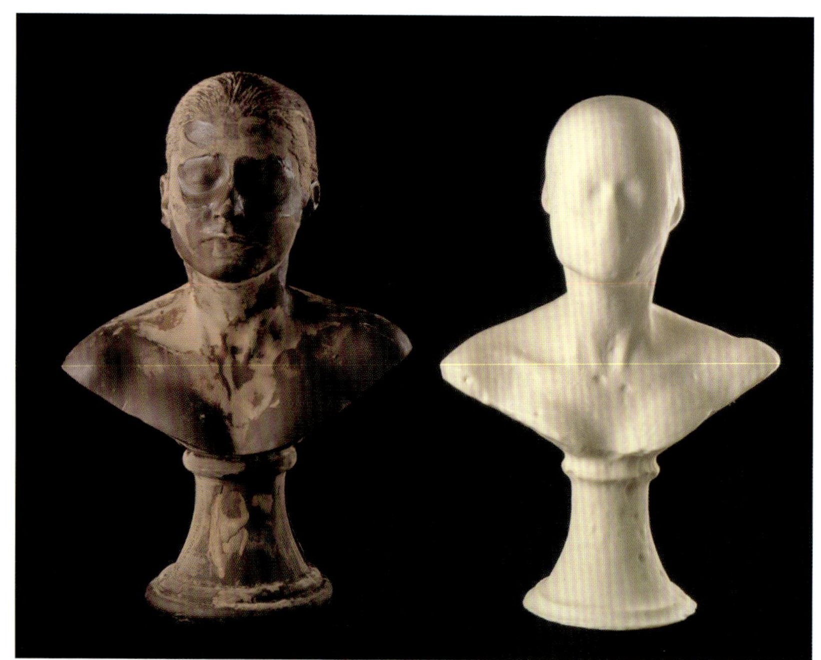

in this example is fortuitous); Antoni's photographic work undertaken with her mother as a joint subject can be compared to Wilke's as well. And Antoni early on expressed her admiration for Wilke's chewing-gum work in particular, and for Wilke's concern with female beauty in general.[8] Like Wilke, Antoni has been told she is simply opportunistic: "I also hear, " she says, "oh, if you weren't pretty you wouldn't put on a Danskin and mop the floor with your hair," as she did in one performance piece; she too feels that a double standard about judging sexual appeal (and its exploitation) operates in the criticism of men and women doing performance work. While she admits to being surprised at finding herself "in the role of feminist flag-bearer," Antoni very generously affirms "the importance of being in a lineage and claiming that as a strength."

On the other hand, some artists of succeeding generations who would seem to owe a debt to Wilke—Vanessa Beecroft, for instance, whose performances starting the early 1990s have marshaled dozens of nude women, all strikingly beautiful and sometimes adopting fashion-model poses—explicitly deny the influence.[9] And though Wilke's sexually provocative work, including especially her proposed availability for rent to players of the "S.O.S." mastication game, seem direct antecedents of such work as Andrea Fraser's controversial 1993 project, in which she videotaped a sexual encounter with a collector who paid to participate in the "performance," Fraser too declines the connection, saying she wasn't aware of Wilke's work at the time she was developing her own.[10] (Sadly, this is credible, though Wilke's perhaps half-jesting proposal to set up a massage parlor in which she would be the client and men would do the work[11] seems to beg for a response from Fraser.)

Not that there is anything like simple equivalence between these women's work and Wilke's. As is true of the masquerades of Cindy Sherman, with whom Wilke had the most active quarrel, the differences are as important as the similarities. Though they set up situations in which they or their proxies submit to full exposure and more, Beecroft and Fraser, like Sherman, present themselves as ciphers; they are abstract, in a sense invisible figures devoted to marking out socially constrained positions within the nexus of popular media, consumer culture, and the fine arts—points of exchange between social and financial forces. Rather than insisting on their foreground status, these women help fill in the coordinates of the grid within which such status is defined.

Other comparisons reveal other distinctions: the self-portrait photography of Catherine Opie, akin to Wilke's in its frankness, differs in the pain it more or less explicitly expresses. The pornographic imagery appropriated in the mid-1980s by such painters as David Salle and Richard Prince can be seen as a rather nasty, cynical retort to Wilke's earnest exploration of sensuality. Marina Abramovic's exercises in endurance and self-exposure have a great deal in common with Wilke's performance work, although Abramovic too is more interested in the testing her strength against expressions of violence and experiences of pain than was Wilke. In a 1998 catalogue essay, Laura Cottingham names, as Wilke's heirs, Rona Pondick (for her early breast and excrement-themed sculptures, argably indebted to Wilke's own early work); Felix Gonzalez-Torres (perhaps because of his use of candy as give-away sculpture, or his performance as a disco dancer); and Matthew Barney (his background as a fashion model?) before going on to say that the "Art that arrives from a similar source of sexualized female self-objectification and deliberate self-spectacularization is being produced in the 1990s by artists such as Vanessa Beecroft, Renee Cox, Tracey Emin, Elke Krystufek, Mariko Mori, Pipilotti Rist, and Kara Walker, among others."[12]

While Wilke certainly made a spectacle, and an object, of herself, that is only half the story, as the double-entendre *I Object* made very clear. As Anna Chave has written, "Lippard was completely justified, of course, in charging that Wilke wanted to have it both ways: she did want to be both agent and object. What often got lost in the ensuing conversation is that, broadly speaking, so do we all, women and men alike."[13] And, still speaking broadly, it was the agency more than the objecthood she wished to explore. In a song recorded for an album produced by Ronald Feldman called "Revolutions per Minute" (1982), Wilke sang, "Stand up when people put you down/ stand up and dance above the ground/ stand up and be your own cliché/ stand up there's no one to betray." The song's final lines are "exposing the truth is like nudity, so stand up, you've got to stand up." Perhaps only Wilke could have written just this anthem. Carrying on her legacy are, really, any artists who flaunt their gifts and flout the proprieties, who provoke and arouse and present irresolvably perplexing challenges to critical protocol—who, in short, carry on.

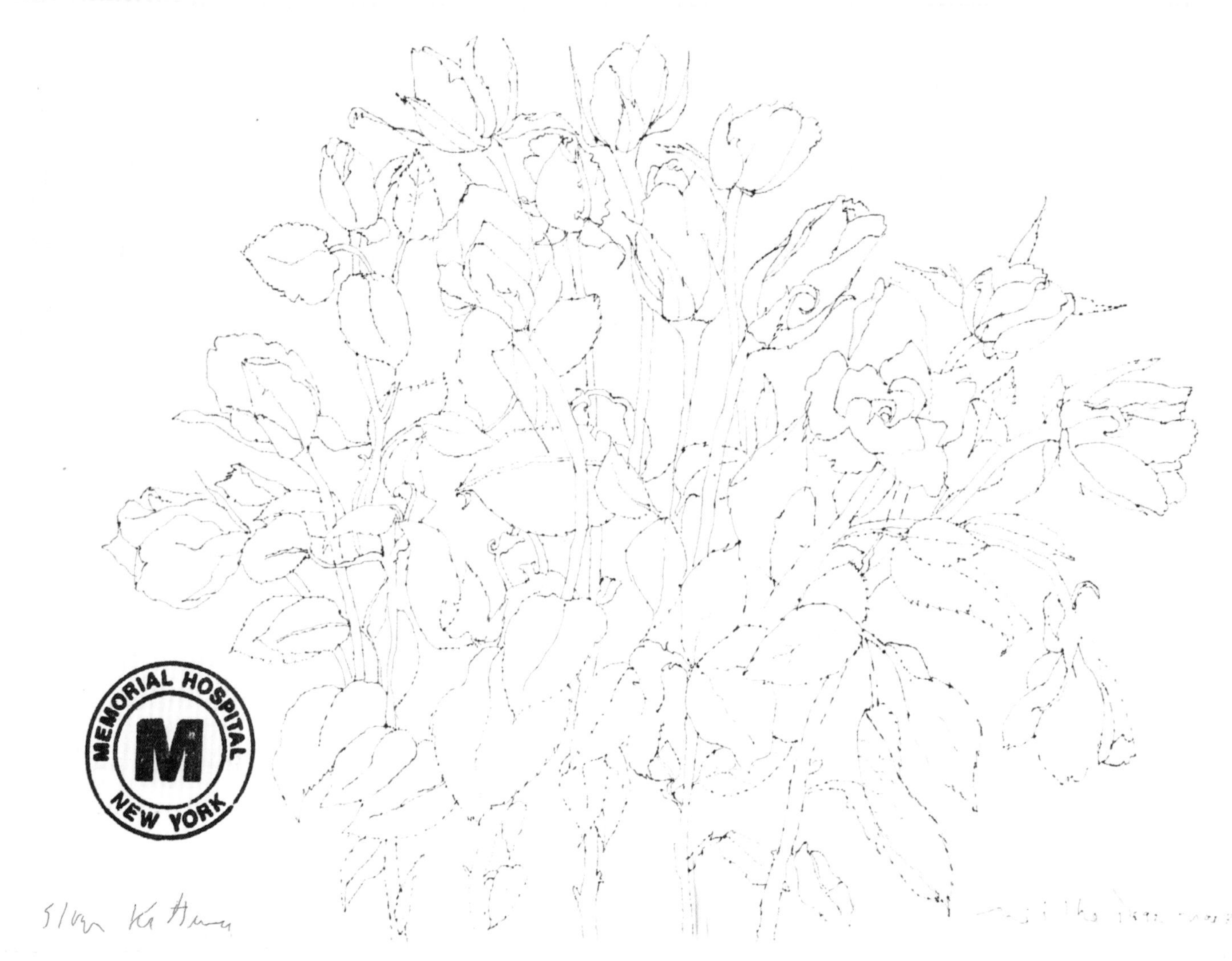

Sloan Kettering, Nov 8, 1992. Ink on pillowcase, 29½ x 19¼ in., 14¾ 19¼ in. folded

Sloan Kettering Memorial Hospital, November 9, 1992. Watercolor on pillowcase, 29½ x 19¼ in.

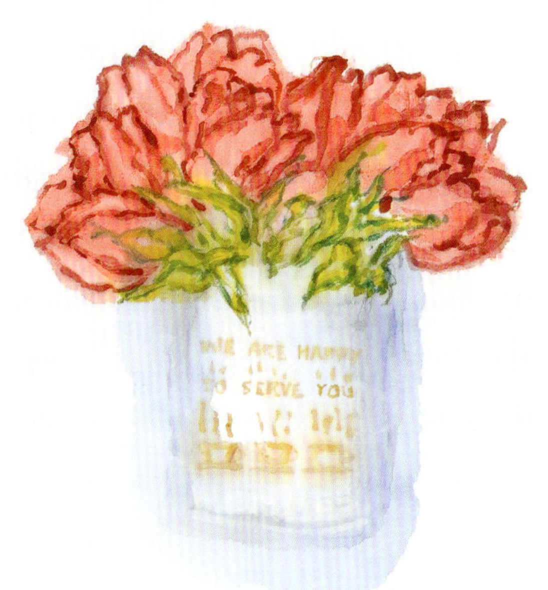

Sloan Kettering M. Hosp

Wilke Nov 9 1992

NOTES

Introduction: Affirmative Actions

1. To Marvin Jones, "Politicizing Art: Hannah Wilke's Art, Politics, Religion and Feminism," *The New Common Good*, May 1985, 10.

2. To Ruth Margolin, in Garry Noland, "Art's Impact Depends On Feminist Content," *Forum* 14, no. 5 (November–December 1989), 9.

3. Conversations with the author, February 23 and 24, 2009.

4. *Forum*, 10.

5. In Cynthia Rose, "O Supernude," *New Musical Express*, March 19, 1983, 12.

6. Conversation with the author, December 20, 2007.

7. *Forum*, 10.

8. In *Hannah Wilke: A Retrospective*, Thomas Kochheiser, ed. [exhibition catalogue; includes writings by Hannah Wilke and an essay by Joanna Frueh] (Columbia: University of Missouri Press, 1989), 68.

9. "Artist Hannah Wilke Talks with Ernst," *Oasis de neon*, 1978, two parts, no pagination.

10. *Oasis de neon*.

11. Frueh, in *Hannah Wilke: A Retrospective*, 44.

12. Amelia Jones, "The Rhetoric of the Pose: Hannah Wilke and the Radical Narcissism of Feminist Body Art," in *Body Art/Performing the Subject* (Minneapolis and London: University of Minnesota Press, 1998), 152.

13. Ibid.,154.

14. Ibid., 166.

15. Ibid., 171.

16. Judith Butler, *Gender Trouble* (New York and London: Routledge, 1990), 42.

17. Ibid., 39.

18. Ibid., 22.

19. Amelia Jones, "The 'Sexual Politics' of The Dinner Party: A Critical Context," in *Sexual Politics: Judy Chicago's Dinner Party in Feminist Art History* (Los Angeles: UCLA and the Armand Hammer Museum of Art and Cultural Center; and Berkeley: University of California Press, 1996), 97.

20. Arlene Raven, "The Eternal Hannah Wilke: Philosophy in Form," in *Hannah Wilke: Selected Work 1960–1992* [exhibition catalogue] (Los Angeles: Hannah Wilke Collection & Archive, Los Angeles, and Solway Jones, 2004), 22.

21. Peggy Phelan, "Survey," in *Art and Feminism*, Helen Reckitt, ed. (London and New York: Phaidon, 2009), 38.

22. Laura Cottingham, "Art You Experienced? Feminism, Art and the Body Politic," in *Seeing through the Seventies: Essays on Feminism and Art* (Amsterdam: G&B Arts International, 2000), 126.

23. Dorothy Seiberling, "The New Sexual Frankness: Good-by to Hearts and Flowers," *New York Magazine*, February 17, 1975, 37.

24. Robin Morgan, Sisterhood is Powerful (1970); cited in Cottingham, "L.A. Womyn," in *Seeing through the Seventies*, 162.

25. Lucy R. Lippard, "Sexual Politics: Art Style," *Art in America*, September 1971, reprinted in *From the Center: Feminist Essays on Women's Art* (New York: Dutton, 1976), 31.

26. Elizabeth C. Baker, "Sexual Art-Politics," in *Art and Sexual Politics*, Elizabeth C. Baker and Thomas B. Hess, eds. (New York and London: Macmillan and Collier Macmillan, 1973), 111, 118.

27. Ibid., 109.

28. Saundra Goldman, "Heresies and History: Hannah Wilke and the American Feminist Art Movement," *Hannah Wilke: Exchange Values* [exhibition catalogue] (Vitoria-Gasteiz, Spain: ARTIUM Centro-Museo Vasco de Arte Contemporaneo, 2006),160.

29. *Womanhouse Is Not a Home*, produced by Lynne Littman for KCET Los Angeles, February, 1972.

30. Photo caption to "Freelancing the Dragon," in Lippard, *From the Center*, 21.

31. Amelia Jones, "The 'Sexual Politics' of The Dinner Party," 97.

32. Ibid., 100.

Chapter One: In Part

1. Lillian Roxen, "H. Wilke Ceramic Erotica," *Comment*, August 1966, 9.

2. Judith Barry and Sandy Flitterman-Lewis, "Textual Strategies: The Politics of Art-Making" [*Screen*, 1980], reprinted in *The Feminism and Visual Culture Reader*, Amelia Jones, ed. (London and New York: Routledge, 2003), 54.

3. Judy Chicago and Miriam Schapiro, "Female Imagery" [*Womanspace Journal*, 1973], reprinted in *The Feminism and Visual Culture Reader*, 40.

4. Anne Wagner, "O'Keeffe's Femininity," in *Three Artists (Three Women): Modernism and the Art of Hesse, Krasner and O'Keeffe* (Berkeley, Los Angeles, and London: University of California Press, 1996), 53.

5. Chicago and Schapiro, "Female Imagery," 42.

6. Lippard, "Prefaces to Catalogues of Women's Exhibitions," in *From the Center*, 49.

7. Quoted in Lippard,"After Consciousness-Raising, What?," *Everywoman* 2, no. 7, May 1971, reprinted in *From the Center*, 73.

8. Quoted in Laura Meyer, "From Finish Fetish to Feminism: Judy Chicago's Dinner Party in California Art History," in *Sexual Politics*, 56.

9. Richard Meyer, "Hard Targets: Feminist Art, Male Nudes, and the Force of Censorship in the 1970s," in *WACK! Art and the Feminist Revolution* [exhibition catalogue], Cornelia Butler, ed. (Los Angeles: Museum of Contemporary Art, 2007), 418–19. Quote is from Schapiro and Wilding, "Cunts/Quilts/Consciousness," *Heresies* 24, 1989, 7.

10. Germaine Greer, *The Female Eunuch* (New York and London: Harper Perennial, 2006), 44–45.

11. Printed in *Re-View, Artists on Art* 1, no. 1, 1978; text for a videotaped performance at the London Art Gallery, London, Ontario, February 17, 1977, 41–42.

12. Andrea Dworkin, "Pornography," in *The Feminism and Visual Culture Reader*, 387.

13. Ruth Iskin, "Hannah Wilke: In Conversation with Rush Iskin," *Visual Dialog* 2, no. 4, 1978, 17.

14. To Bonnie Finnberg, "Body Language: Hannah Wilke Interview," *Cover*, September 1989, 16.

15. Iskin, 18.

16. To Lil Picard, "Hannah Wilke: Sexy Objects," *Andy Warhol's Interview*, January 1973, 44.

17. Iskin, 17.

18. Edit deAk, "Hannah Wilke," *Art in America*, May–June 1974, 110.

19. James Collins, "Hannah Wilke," *Artforum*, June 1974, 72.

20. Barbara Rose, "Vaginal Iconography," *New York Magazine*, May 20, 1974, 58–59.

21. In *Art-Rite*, spring 1974, 7.

22. Saundra Goldman, "Gesture and the Regeneration of the Universe," *Hannah Wilke: A Retrospective* [exhibition catalogue] (Nikolaj: Copenhagen Contemporary Art Center, 1998), 36.

23. David Bourdon, "Hannah Wilke," *The Village Voice*, September 29, 1975, 97–98.

24. Iskin, 18.

25. Ibid.

26. "Hannah Wilke: A Very Female Thing," *New York Magazine*, February 11, 1974, 58.

27. Meredine Merzer, "Scenes: Genital Art," *Penthouse*, September, 1975, 46.

28. Linda Crawford, "Women in the Erotic Arts," *Viva*, January 1974, 82.

29. Barbara Rose, "Present at the Kickoff," *New York Magazine*, October 2, 1972, 68.

30. Robert Hughes, "The Last Salon," *Time*, February 12, 1973, 46.

31. Frueh, 18.

32. Mira Schor, "Patrilineage (1991–92)," *Wet: On Painting, Feminism, and Art Culture* (Durham and London: Duke University Press, 1997), 101.

33. Collins, 71.

34. Lippard, "Eros Presumptive," in *Minimal Art: A Critical Anthology*, Gregory Battcock, ed. (New York: E. P. Dutton, 1968), 210.

35. Ibid., 216.

36. Ibid.

37. E-mail correspondence with the author, October 28, 2009.

38. Conversation with the author, Jan. 23, 2009.

Chapter Two: In Full

1. Iskin, 19.

2. Barbara Schwartz, "Methods and Materials Old and New," *Craft Horizons*, December 1975, 46.

3. Rose Hartman, "Feminists are Talking About," *Feminist Art Journal*, spring 1975, 49.

4. Mark Savitt, "Hannah Wilke: The Pleasure Principle," *Arts Magazine*, September 1975, 7.

5. In Alfred Fischer, *Übrigens sterben immer die Anderen: Marcel Duchamp und die Avantgarde seit 1950* (Cologne: Museum Ludwig Köln, 1988), 266.

6. Hannah Wilke Collection and Archive, Los Angeles.

7. John Rockwell, "'Soup & Tart' at the Kitchen Is a Supper with Avant-Garde," *New York Times*, December 2, 1974.

8. *Oasis de neon*.

9. In Amy Newman, *Challenging Art: Artforum 1962–74* (New York: Solo Press, 2000), 524–25.

10. Ibid., 415.

11. Ibid.

12. Ibid., 419.

13. *Oasis de neon*.

14. Statement written for the catalogue of *American Women Artists*, Saõ Paulo Museum, July 1980, reprinted in *Art and Ideology* [exhibition catalogue] (New York: The New Museum of Contemporary Art, 1984), 69.

15. "Where Are the Great Men Artists?" *Art News*, October 1980, 77.

16. To Bonnie Finnberg, *Cover*, September 1989, 16.

17. Ibid.

18. *Oasis de neon*.

19. Edit deAk, *Art in America*, May–June 1974.

20. Laura Cottingham, "The Damned Beautiful," *New Art Examiner*, April 1994, 27.

21. Marvin Jones, *The New Common Good*, May 1985, 10.

22. Lippard, "The Pains and Pleasures of Rebirth: Women's Body Art," *Art in America*, May–June 1976, 75.

23. Ibid., 75–76 .

24. To Saundra Goldman in "Heresies and History: Hannah Wilke and the American Feminist Art Movement," in *Hannah Wilke: Exchange Values* [exhibition catalogeu] (Vitoria Gasteiz, Spain: Atrium, 2006), 160.

25. Ibid., 162 .

26. Ann-Sargent Wooster, "Hannah Wilke: Whose Image Is It?" *High Performance*, fall 1990, 31.

27. "Hannah Wilke's Bazooka Period," *Oui*, February 1977; "She Ought To Be in Pictures," *Playboy*, April, 1979.

28. Lippard, "The Pains and Pleasures of Rebirth: Women's Body Art," 75.

29. Harriet Senie, *New York Post*, April 1, 1978, 17.

Chapter Three: In Motion

1. Iskin, 20.

2. Goldman, "Gesture and the Regeneration of the Universe," 20.

3. Goldman, "Too Good Lookin' to be Smart: Beauty, Performance, and the Art of Hannah Wilke," doctoral dissertation, University of Texas at Austin, 1999/Ann Arbor, UMI Disseration Services, 102.

4. In Craig Owens, *Beyond Recognition: Representation, Power, and Culture*, Scott Bryson, Barbara Kruger, Lynne Tilllman, and Jane Weinstock, eds. (Berkeley and Los Angeles: University of California Press, 1992),168.

5. Ibid., 180.

6. Ibid., 198.

7. Ibid., 199.

8. Ibid., 214.

9. Ibid., 194.

10. Goldman, "Too Good Lookin' to be Smart," 146.

11. Tim Cone, "Life Over Art: Oldenburg's Privacy, Wilke's Publicity," *Arts Magazine*, September 1989, 25–26.

12. Finnberg, 16.

13. Donald Goddard, previously unpublished statement, Hannah Wilke archive.

14. "I Object: Memoirs of a Sugargiver," in Fischer, *Űbrigens sterben immer die Anderen*, 266–67.

15. Donald Goddard, conversation with the author, Jan. 23, 2009.

16. *Oasis de neon*.

Chapter Four: In Extremis

1. Hannah Wilke, "Seura Chaya," *New Observation*s, June, 1988, reprinted in Frueh, 150–51.

2. Marvin Jones, *The New Common Good*, May 1985, 11.

3. Interview with the author, May 22, 2009.

4. Ronald Feldman provided this information about Wilke's sources.

5. Donald Goddard, "Life Drawings," *Intra-Venus* [exhibition catalogue] (New York: Ronald Feldman Gallery, 1995), 16.

6. Andrew Perchuck, "Hannah Wilke, Ronald Feldman" *Artforum*, April 1994, 94.

7. Richard Vine, "Hannah Wilke at Ronald Feldman," *Art in America*, May 1994, 109.

8. Susan Sontag "Illness as Metaphor," in *Illness as Metaphor and AIDS and Its Metaphors* (New York: Picador, 1990), 3.

9. Ibid., 9.

10. Ibid., 55.

11. Sontag "Against Interpretation," in *Against Interpretation and Other Essay*s (New York: Anchor Books, 1990), 14.

12. T. J. Clark, *The Sight of Death: An Experiment in Art Writin*g (New Haven and London: Yale University Press, 2006), 216.

13. Ibid., 17.

14. Ibid., 228.

Postscript: Carrying On

1. Conversation with the author, July 11, 2009.

2. Telephone conversation with the author, August 20, 2009.

3. E-mail correspondence with the author, August 2009.

4. *Forum*, 11.

5. Ibid., 10.

6. Marvin Jones, 9.

7. Hannah Wilke Collection and Archive, Los Angeles.

8. Laura Cottingham interview, *Flash Art*, summer 1993, 104.

9. E-mail correspondence with the author, June 29, 2009.

10. E-mail correspondence with the author, June 17, 2009.

11. "Hannah Wilke: A Very Female Thing," *New York Magazine*, February 11, 1974, 58.

12. Laura Cottingham, "Hannah Wilke: Some Naked Truths and Her Legacy in the 1990s," *Hannah Wilke: A Retrospective* [exhibition catalogue] (Copenhagen: Nicolaj Contemporary Art Center, 1998), 57.

13. Anna Chave, "I Object: Hannah Wilke's Feminism," *Art in America*, March 2009, 108.

ACKNOWLEDGMENTS

Among the many people on whose very generous help I depended in writing this book, I would like first to acknowledge Marsie Scharlatt and Andrew Scharlatt, who were unstinting in their assistance with innumerable matters large and small. Donald Goddard and, at the Ronald Feldman Gallery, Ronald and Frayda Feldman, Marco Nocella, and Adrienne Lopez, were all instrumental in assembling information and offering recollections of the artist and her work. I am enormously grateful for the crucial support of editor Christopher Lyon, at Prestel Publishing, and for the tireless assistance there of Ryan Newbanks; I am also greatly indebted to Sarah Valdez for her superb editorial help. Others who very kindly shared insights and memories include Saundra Goldman, whose doctoral thesis on Wilke was an extremely useful resource, Janine Antoni, Kathy Goodell, Elizabeth C. Baker, Rochelle Feinstein, Lucy Lippard, David Platzker, Marvin Heiferman, Tracy Fitzpatrick, Elisa Decker, Irving Sandler, and Anna Chave. The groundbreaking writing on Wilke by Joanna Frueh was invaluable in many ways. I'd also like to thank Elizabeth Manzi, at the Jewish Museum, and Kathy Curry and Emily Talbot at the Museum of Modern Art, Michael Blackwood Productions, and the wonderful Electronic Arts Intermix. Last but hardly least, I thank my son Milo, for (among much else) his inspiring commitment to historical fact, and my husband, Joseph LeDoux, for everything.

ILLUSTRATION LIST

"Performalist Self-Portraits" is the term used by Hannah Wilke to give credit to the many people who assisted her in her self-portraits, her performances, and other conceptual works in which she posed and directed herself.

Frontispiece: *Hannah Wilke Super-t-Art*, 1974 (detail). One of twenty black-and-white photographs, 6½ x 4½ in. each, 40¾ x 33 in. framed. Hannah Wilke Collection & Archive, Los Angeles. Performalist Self-Portrait with Christopher Giercke

Page 6: Hannah Wilke in her Broome Street studio, New York, 1973. Archival photo, Hannah Wilke Collection & Archive, Los Angeles

Page 7: *Teasel Cushion*, 1967. Terra cotta, Liquitex, and Astroturf, 9¾ x 7 in. Walker Art Center, Minneapolis

Page 9, left: *First Performalist Self-Portrait*, 1942–79 (detail). Image used for two of three black-and-white photographs in triptych, 19¼ x 35 in. overall. Hannah Wilke Collection & Archive, Los Angeles

Page 9, right: Hannah Wilke (Arlene Butter) in high school dance performance, Great Neck, N.Y., ca. 1955. Archival photo, Hannah Wilke Collection & Archive, Los Angeles

Page 10: *Cover of Appearances and Arlene Hannah Butter*, 1954–77. Diptych of two black-and-white photographs on board, overall dimensions, 24 x 36¾ in. Hannah Wilke Collection & Archive, Los Angeles. Performalist Self-Portraits with Les Wollam (left) and Marsie Butter Scharlatt (right)

Page 17: Susan Frazier, Vicki Hodgetts, and Robin Weltsh, *Nurturant Kitchen* from *Womanhouse*, 1972. Mixed-medium installation

Page 18, left and right: Judy Chicago, *The Dinner Party*, 1974–79. Mixed mediums, 48 x 42 x 3 ft. Brooklyn Museum; gift of the Elizabeth A. Sackler Foundation. Photos: Donald Woodman

Page 19: *It Was a Lovely Day*, 1964. Terra cotta with Liquitex, 3¼ x 3¼ x 4½ in. Private collection

Page 20: Miriam Schapiro, *Ox*, 1969. Acrylic and paper collage on board, 17½ x 22 in. Photo: Max Yawney

Page 23: Early box and six phallic and excremental sculptures, 1960–63. Clockwise from top left: terra cotta, 7 x 4½ x 4¾ in.; terra cotta, 2 x 4¼ x 3¼ in.; brown plaster of Paris, 1¾ x 3 x 2¾ in.; brown plaster of Paris, 2½ x 2¼ x 2 in.; terra cotta, 4½ x 5 x 5½ in.; white plaster of Paris in two parts, 6 x 5 x 6 in.; terra cotta, 7 x 5 x 5 in. Donald and Helen Goddard, New York. Photo: D. James Dee

Page 24: *Scharlatt Rousse*, 1965. Glazed terra cotta, clockwise from top left: 2¼ x 3⅛ x 3⅛ in.; 3½ x 3⅜ x 3$\frac{1}{16}$ in.; 3¼ x 3$\frac{1}{16}$ x 2¾ in.; 2¾ x 2¾ x 3⅛ in. Hannah Wilke Collection & Archive, Los Angeles. Photo: Andrew Scharlatt

Page 25: *That Fills Earth . . .*, 1965. Terra cotta, 9⅝ x 9¼ x 9¼ in. Hannah Wilke Collection & Archive, Los Angeles

Page 27, foreground: *176 One-Fold Gestural Sculptures*, 1973–74. Painted ceramics, 72 x 96 in. overall. Donald and Helen Goddard, New York. Background, left: *Laundry Lint (C.O.'s)*, 1973. Twelve sculptures, double-fold lint, dimensions variable, overall installation 11 x 96 in. Hannah Wilke Collection & Archive, Los Angeles. Background, right: *Fortunate Cookies*, 1974. Fortune cookies, dimensions variable; no longer extant. Photo: eeva-inkeri

Page 28: *Raison d'Etre*, 1980s. Twenty-six glazed metallic folds on white wood base, 48 x 48 in. overall. Donald and Helen Goddard, New York. Photo: Hermann Feldhaus

Page 29: *Sweet Sixteen*, 1979. Sixteen painted ceramic folds on painted wood base, 32 x 32 in. overall. Hannah Wilke Collection & Archive, Los Angeles. Photo: D. James Dee

Page 30: *Hannah Manna*, 1985–86. Seventy-seven painted ceramic sculptures with wall plaque, dimensions variable. "Hannah Wilke Gestures" exhibition installation on Astroturf, Neuberger Museum of Art, Purchase College, State University of New York, Purchase, 2008. Hannah Wilke Collection & Archive, Los Angeles. Photo: Jim Frank

Page 31: *Untitled (Could commodities themselves speak...)*, from the *Sotheby's Series*, 1991. Ink on magazine paper, 16½ x 10$\frac{11}{16}$ in. Hannah Wilke Collection & Archive, Los Angeles. Photo: Jim Frank

Page 33: Hannah Wilke pouring latex in her Broome Street studio, 1974. Archival photo, Hannah Wilke Collection & Archive, Los Angeles

Page 34, top: *Pink Champagne*, 1975. Latex with metal snaps, 18 x 54 x 7 in. Hannah Wilke Collection & Archive, Los Angeles. Photo: D. James Dee

Page 34, bottom: *Rosebud*, 1975. Latex and metal snaps, 24 x 92 x 8 in. Brooklyn Museum; gift of the Elizabeth A. Sackler Foundation. Photo: John Lamka

Page 35: Hannah Wilke in her Broome Street studio with *Centerfold* on the wall, 1973. Archival photo, Hannah Wilke Collection & Archive, Los Angeles

Page 36, left: Eva Hesse, *Repetition Nineteen, III*, 1968. Fiberglass and polyester resin, nineteen units, each 19 to 20¼ (h.) x 11 to 12¾ in. (d.). The Museum of Modern Art, New York; gift of Charles and Anita Blatt

Page 36, right: Lynda Benglis, *Contraband*, 1969. Poured pigmented latex, 116¼ x 398¼ x 3 in. overall (irregular). Whitney Museum of American Art, New York

Page 37: *Vertical Verde for Garcia Lorca*, 1976. Latex, Liquitex, and metal snaps, each 48 x 12 x 8¾ in. Donald and Helen Goddard, New York. Photo: John Lamka

Page 38: Robert Morris, *House of Vetti II*, 1983. Felt and steel brackets, 88 x 142½ x 47 in.

Page 39: *Of Radishes and Flowers*, 1972. Latex; no longer extant. Photo: Hannah Wilke

Page 40: *Laundry Lint (C.O.'s)*, 1971–73. Twelve sculptures, double-fold lint, dimensions variable. Hannah Wilke Collection & Archive, Los Angeles. Photo: Jim Frank

Page 42, above: *New York Public Library*, 1971/73 (detail). Kneaded erasers on postcard on painted wood, 16 x 18 x 2 in. Ronald Feldman Fine Arts, New York. Photo: eeva-inkeri

Page 42, center: *USS Missouri*, 1977 (detail). Kneaded erasers on postcard on painted wood, 16 x 18 x 2 in. Yale University Art Gallery, New Haven, Conn. Photo: John Lamka

Page 42, below: *Atlantic City, New Jersey*, 1975 (detail). Kneaded erasers on postcard on painted wood, 16 x 18 x 2 in. Private collection. Photo: John Lamka

Page 43: *Needed-Erase-Her*, 1974. Kneaded erasers on painted wood, 13½ x 13½ x 2 in. each; four of sixteen. Upper left and lower right: Hannah Wilke Collection and Archive, Los Angeles. Upper right and lower left: Private collection. Photo: Zindman/Fremont

Page 44: Jasper Johns, *Target with Plaster Casts*, 1955. Encaustic and collage on canvas with plaster objects, 51 x 44 x 3½ in.

Page 46: *S.O.S. Starification Object Series (Tie)*, 1974. Black-and-white photograph, 40 x 28 in. Centre Pompidou, Paris; purchase and donation of Centre Pompidou Foundation and gift of Marsie, Emanuelle, Damon, and Andrew Scharlatt, Hannah Wilke Collection & Archive, Los Angeles. Performalist Self-Portrait with Les Wollam. Part of *S.O.S. Starification Object Series: An Adult Game of Mastication*, 1974–75

Page 47, left: *S.O.S. Starification Object Series #1*, 1975. Chewing gum on rice paper in Plexiglas frame, 33 ¾ x 26 in. overall. Donald and Helen Goddard, New York

Page 47, right: *California Series (Gum with grasshopper)*, 1976 (detail). One of six Kodachrome photographs mounted on board, 32½ x 28 in. framed. Hannah Wilke Collection & Archive, Los Angeles

Pages 48–49: *S.O.S. Starification Object Series, An Adult Game of Mastication*, 1974–75. Twenty-eight black-and-white photographs, 7 x 5 in. each, 35¾ x 42¾ in. framed. Centre Pompidou, Paris; purchase and donation of Centre Pompidou Foundation and gift of Marsie, Emanuelle, Damon, and Andrew Scharlatt, Hannah Wilke Collection & Archive, Los Angeles. Performalist Self-Portraits with Les Wollam

Page 49: *S.O.S. Starification Object Series (Curlers)*, 1974. Black-and-white photograph, 40 x 27 in.; two copies. Whitney Museum of American Art, New York; purchase and gift of Marsie, Emanuelle, Damon, and Andrew Scharlatt, Hannah Wilke Collection & Archive, Los Angeles; Collection Helen Kornblum. Performalist Self-Portrait with Les Wollam

Page 50: *S.O.S. Starification Object Series (Guns)*, 1974. Black-and-white photograph, 40 x 28 in. Los Angeles County Museum of Art. Performalist Self-Portrait with Les Wollam

Page 51: *S.O.S. Starification Object Series (Veil)*, 1974. Black-and-white photograph, 40 x 28 in. Hannah Wilke Collection & Archive, Los Angeles. Performalist Self-Portrait with Les Wollam

Page 52: *S.O.S. Starification Object Series: An Adult Game of Mastication*, 1974–75. Game box, 12 x 8½ x 2 in., with photographs, chewing-gum sculptures, playing cards, and chewing gum, dimensions variable. Centre Pompidou, Paris; purchase and donation of Centre Pompidou Foundation and gift of Marsie, Emanuelle, Damon, and Andrew Scharlatt, Hannah Wilke Collection & Archive, Los Angeles

Page 53: Hannah Wilke at *S.O.S.* performance, in the exhibition "5 Américaines à Paris," Galerie Gerald Piltzer, Paris, 1975. Hannah Wilke Collection & Archive, Los Angeles. Photo: Leonard Hessing

Page 54: *My Count-ry 'tis of Thee* performance in the exhibition "Four for the Fourth" at the Albright-Knox Art Gallery in Buffalo, July 4, 1976. Archival photo, Hannah Wilke Collection & Archive, Los Angeles

Page 55: VALIE EXPORT, *Tapp und Tast-kino*, 1968–71. Still from black-and-white film, 2 min.

Page 56: Hannah Wilke performing *Super-t-Art* at the Kitchen, November 1974. Archival photo, Hannah Wilke Collection & Archive, Los Angeles

Page 57: *Hannah Wilke Super-t-Art*, 1974. Twenty black-and-white photographs, 6½ x 4½ in. each. 40¾ x 33 in. framed. Signed "a three-minute performance at the Kitchen, Nov. 1974." Hannah Wilke Collection & Archive, Los Angeles. Performalist Self-Portraits with Christopher Giercke.

Page 59, top: *Hannah Wilke Can*, 1978. Photo reproduction on coin collection can, 6 x 3 in.

Page 59, bottom: *Give: Hannah Wilke Can—A Living Sculpture Needs to Make a Living*, 1978. Photograph from a benefit performance for Public Art Fund for City Walls at Susan Caldwell Gallery, New York, May 22, 1978. Hannah Wilke Collection & Archive, Los Angeles. Photo: Donald Goddard

Page 61: Lynda Benglis, *Artforum* advertisement, November 1974

Page 62: Hannah Wilke in her studio, Chateau Marmont, Los Angeles, August 1970. Black-and-white photograph as used in photowork and advertisement for exhibition at Ronald Feldman Fine Arts, Inc., in *Avalanche*, Summer 1972. Hannah Wilke Collection & Archive, Los Angeles. Performalist Self-Portrait with Claes Oldenburg

Page 63: Hannah Wilke performing in window of Washington Project for the Arts, "Performalist Self-Portraits" exhibition, 1979. Archival photo, Hannah Wilke Collection & Archive, Los Angeles

Page 65: *Marxism and Art: Beware of Fascist Feminism*, 1977. Silkscreen on Plexiglas, 36 x 27½ in. The Museum of Modern Art, New York; purchase and gift of Marsie, Emanuelle, Damon, and Andrew Scharlatt, Hannah Wilke Collection & Archive, Los Angeles

Page 66: Eleanor Antin, *The Last Seven Days from Carving: A Traditional Sculpture*, 1972/1999. Black-and-white photographs and date labels, twenty-eight photos, 7 x 5 in. each; seven date labels. Photo: Hermann Feldhaus

Page 68: *Venus Envy*, 1980. Triptych: three unique Polaroid photographs, 13 x 21 in. overall, framed. Donald and Helen Goddard, New York. Performalist Self-Portrait with Richard Hamilton. Photo: D. James Dee

Page 70: *Gestures*, 1974. Stills from videotaped performance; black and white, sound, 30 min. Hannah Wilke Collection & Archive, Los Angeles

Page 71: Vito Acconci, *Pryings*, 1971. Live performance at Eisner Auditorium, New York University. Black-and-white video, sound, 20 min. Photo: Bernadette Mayer

Page 73: *Hello Boys*, 1975. Still from videotaped live performance, Paris; black and white, sound, 10 min. Hannah Wilke Collection & Archive, Los Angeles

Pages 74, 75: *Hannah Wilke Through the Large Glass*, 1976. Stills from live performance filmed at the Philadelphia Museum of Art. 16mm film, color, silent, 10 min. Hannah Wilke Collection & Archive, Los Angeles

Page 76: *Philly*, 1976–78. Black-and-white photographs with text, 27⅛ x 40 in. framed. Hannah Wilke Collection & Archive, Los Angeles

Page 77: Hannah Wilke and I Sa Lo at the Philadelphia Museum of Art, 1976. Black-and-white photograph used by Hannah Wilke in poster for *C'est La Vie Rrose*, a film directed by Hans-Cristof Stenzel for German television, 1976

Page 78: *I Object: Memoirs of a Sugargiver*, 1977–78. Cibachrome diptych, each photograph 24 x 16 in.; two copies. Hannah Wilke Collection & Archive, Los Angeles; Ronald Feldman Fina Arts, New York. Performalist Self-Portraits with Richard Hamilton

Page 79: Marcel Duchamp, *Étant Donnés: 1° la chute d'eau, 2° le gaz d'éclairage (Given: 1. The Waterfall. 2. The Illuminating Gas . . .)*, 1946–66 (detail). Mixed-medium assemblage, 7 ft. 11½ in. x 70 in. Philadelphia Museum of Art; gift of the Cassandra Foundation, 1969

Page 82, left: Barbara Kruger, *Untitled (Your gaze hits the side of my face)*, 1981. Photograph, 55 x 41 in.

Page 82, right: Cindy Sherman, *Untitled Film Still*, 1977. Black-and-white photograph, 10 x 8 in.

Page 83: *Intercourse with...*, 1973–75 (detail). Black-and-white photograph used on cover of documentation accompanying two-hour audiotape of recorded telephone messages. Hannah Wilke Collection & Archive, Los Angeles. Performalist Self-Portrait with Claes Oldenburg

Page 87: *Intercourse with . . .*, 1977. Stills from video of live performance at London Art Museum and Library, London, Ontario; black and white, sound, 30 min. Hannah Wilke Collection & Archive, Los Angeles

Page 88: *Even-tu-ally*, 1969–91. Cibachrome with silkscreen imprinting of text, 21 x 21 in.

Page 91: *Exchange Values (Marx)* from *So Help Me Hannah*, 1978–84. One of six black-and-white photographs, 60 x 40 in. each. Donald and Helen Goddard, New York. Performalist Self-Portrait with Donald Goddard

Pages 92, 93: *So Help Me Hannah*, 1978–84. Four of forty-eight black-and-white photographs, 14 x 11 in. or 11 x 14 in. each. Donald and Helen Goddard, New York. Performalist Self-Portraits with Donald Goddard

Page 95: *Hername*, 1978–91. Black-and-white etchings on paper, 36 x 26 in. The Museum of Modern Art, New York; gift of Marsie, Emanuelle, Damon, and Andrew Scharlatt, Hannah Wilke Collection & Archive, Los Angeles. Ronald Feldman Fine Arts, New York

Page 98: *Dancing in the Dark*, 1978. Black-and-white photograph, 15½ x 19½ in. Donald and Helen Goddard, New York. Performalist Self-Portrait with Donald Goddard

Page 101: *In Memoriam: Selma Butter (Mommy)*, 1979–83. Photographic triptych with sculpture. Triptych: three groups of six gelatin silver prints, each with press type and art paper, mounted on board, 41 x 61 in. each. Sculpture: three groups of two acrylic-painted ceramics on acrylic-painted Masonite, 13 x 20 x 4 in. each. Hannah Wilke Collection & Archive, Los Angeles. Photo: Jim Frank

Page 102: *Seura Chaya #1*, 1978–89. Black-and-white photograph with watercolors, 59 x 63 in. framed. Jewish Museum, New York

Page 103, top: *Seura Chaya #2*, 1978–89. Black-and-white photograph with watercolors, 59 x 63 in., framed. Donald and Helen Goddard, New York

Page 103, bottom: *Seura Chaya #4*, 1978–89. Black-and-white photograph with watercolors, 59 x 63 in., framed. Hannah Wilke Collection & Archive, Los Angeles

Page 104: *Vein Attempt–Broken Blood Vessels from Heel Kicking Hannah*, 1981. Donald and Helen Goddard, New York. Performalist Self-Portrait with Donald Goddard

Page 105: Nancy Fried, *Self-Portrait*, 1994. Terra cotta, 13½ x 19 x 11 in.

Pages 106–7: *Portrait of the Artist with her Mother, Selma Butter*, 1978–81. Cibachrome diptych, each photograph 40 x 30 in; two copies. Hannah Wilke Collection & Archive, Los Angeles; Donald and Helen Goddard/Ronald Feldman Fine Arts, New York

Page 108: *Intra-Venus Series #5, June 10/May 5, 1992*. Two chromogenic supergloss prints, 71½ x 47½ in. each. Edition of 3. Donald and Helen Goddard, New York; Hannah Wilke Collection & Archive, Los Angeles. Performalist Self-Portraits with Donald Goddard

Page 109, top: *Intra-Venus Series #1, June 15/January 20, 1992*. Two chromogenic supergloss prints, 71½ x 47½ in. each. Edition of 3. Donald and Helen Goddard, New York; Hannah Wilke Collection & Archive, Los Angeles. Performalist Self-Portraits with Donald Goddard

Page 109, bottom: *Intra-Venus Series #4, July 26 and February 19, 1992*. Two chromogenic supergloss prints, 71½ x 47½ in. each. Edition of 3. Helsinki City Art Museum; Tokyo Metropolitan Museum of Photography; Hannah Wilke Collection & Archive, Los Angeles. Performalist Self-Portraits with Donald Goddard

Pages 110–11, top: *Intra-Venus Series Triptych ("Marilyn Monroe")*, 1992–93. Three chromogenic supergloss prints, 26¼ x 39½ in. each. Edition of 3. Donald and Helen Goddard, New York; Hannah Wilke Collection & Archive, Los Angeles. Performalist Self-Portraits with Donald Goddard

Pages 110–11, bottom: *Intra-Venus Series #3, August 17,1992/February 15,1992/August 9,1992*. Three chromogenic supergloss prints, 71½ x 47½ in. each. Edition of 3. Donald and Helen Goddard, New York; Hannah Wilke Collection & Archive, Los Angeles. Performalist Self-Portraits with Donald Goddard

Pages 112–13: *Tree of Life: Red, Yellow and Blue*, 1992. Triptych: three colorized photographs, 14 x 38 in. framed. Donald and Helen Goddard, New York. Performalist Self-Portrait with Donald Goddard

Page 114: *Brushstrokes No. 7, January 19, 1992*. Artist's hair on Arches paper, 30 x 22½ in. The Museum of Modern Art, New York; gift of the Judith Rothschild Foundation

Page 115: *Brushstrokes No. 6, January, 19, 1992*. Artist's hair on Arches paper, 30 x 22½ in., 33 x 25½ in. framed. The Museum of Modern Art, New York; gift of Marsie, Emanuelle, Damon & Andrew Scharlatt, Hannah Wilke Collection & Archive, Los Angeles

Page 116: *Wedges of . . .*, 1992. Two lead alloy radiation blocks, 3 x 6½ x 6 in. each. Donald and Helen Goddard, New York. Photo: Dennis Cowley

Page 117: *Why Not Sneeze . . .*, 1992. Wire bird cage, medicine bottles, and syringes, 7 x 9 x 6⅞ in. Donald and Helen Goddard, New York. Photo: Dennis Cowley

Page 118: *Untitled*, 1987–92. Thirty-seven black painted ceramic sculptures on twenty-five black painted wood bases, 7 x 98 x 98 in. overall. Donald and Helen Goddard, New York. Photo: Dennis Cowley

Page 119: *Blue Skies*, 1987–92. Nine painted ceramic sculptures on nine painted wood bases, 7 x 59 x 59 in. overall. Hannah Wilke Collection & Archive, Los Angeles. Photo: Dennis Cowley

Pages 120, 121: *Intra-Venus Tapes*, 1990–93. Sixteen-channel video installation, 117 min. Donald and Helen Goddard, New York; Hannah Wilke Collection & Archive, Los Angeles

Page 124: *One Car Just Ain't Enough These Days*, 1964. Mixed mediums on paper, 14 x 11 in. Donald and Helen Goddard, New York. Photo: D. James Dee

Page 126, top: Untitled, 1963–66. Pastel and charcoal on paper, 19½ x 24 in. The Museum of Modern Art, New York; gift of the Judith Rothschild Foundation

Page 126, bottom: Untitled, 1962–66. Graphite, charcoal, paint, crayon, and colored pencil on paper, 22 x 30 in. Hannah Wilke Collection & Archive, Los Angeles. Photo: Anthony Cuhña

Page 128: *Stanley Landsman*, 1966. Pastel, pencil, and photographs on paper, 18 x 24 in. Donald and Helen Goddard, New York

Page 129, top: *To Sister*, 1973. Pastel, pencil, and collage on paper, 18 x 23 in. Hannah Wilke Collection & Archive, Los Angeles

Page 129, bottom: *In the Doghouse*, 1973. Silkscreen, 18 x 24 in. The Museum of Modern Art, New York; gift of Marsie, Emanuelle, Damon, and Andrew Scharlatt, Hannah Wilke Collection & Archive, Los Angeles

Page 130, top: *Bees in Easthampton*, 1991. One of fifteen drawings; ink wash on paper, 9 x 12 13/16 in. Donald and Helen Goddard, New York. Photo: D. James Dee

Page 130, bottom left: *Gelada Baboon*, 1986. Pen on paper, 11 x 8½ in. Donald and Helen Goddard, New York

Page 130, bottom right: *Magellanic Penguins and Terns*. Pen on paper, 11 x 8½ in. Donald and Helen Goddard, New York

Page 131: *Scarlet Ibis and Chick*, 1989. Watercolor on Arches paper, 22½ x 30 in. Hannah Wilke Collection & Archive, Los Angeles

Page 132: *Lilies*, 1980. Ink on Arches paper, 22½ x 30 in. Collection Kathlyn Rohrbaugh

Page 133: *Flower Drawing*, 1980. Ink on Arches paper, 22½ x 30 in. Collection Nell Goddard Wilson

Page 135: *Self-Portrait as Angel with Dürer Wing*, 1976. Watercolor and sepia ink on paper, 12 x 15 in. Hannah Wilke Collection & Archive, Los Angeles

Page 137: Hannah Wilke working on B.C. Face drawings in her Greene Street studio, 1989. Archival photo, Hannah Wilke Collection & Archive, Los Angeles. Photo: Donald Goddard

Page 138: *B.C. Series, July 26, 1990*. Watercolor on paper, 41½ x 19½ in. Hannah Wilke Collection & Archive, Los Angeles

Page 139: *B.C. Series, December 15, 1986*. Watercolor on paper, 30 x 22 in. Hannah Wilke Collection & Archive, Los Angeles. Photo: Lisa Kahane

Page 140, left: *Intra-Venus Hand*, 1991. Watercolor on paper, 12½ x 9½ in. Donald and Helen Goddard, New York. Photo: Hermann Feldhaus

Page 140, right: *Intra-Venus Hand #9, October, 1991*. Gouache and watercolor on notebook paper, 12½ x 9½ in. The Museum of Modern Art, New York; gift of the Judith Rothschild Foundation

Page 141, left: *Intra-Venus Face, January 22, 1992*. Watercolor on paper, 12½ x 9½ in. Donald and Helen Goddard, New York

Page 141, right: *Intra-Venus Face, February 25, 1992, 10am*, 1992. Watercolor on paper, 12½ x 9½ in. Donald and Helen Goddard, New York

Page 142: *Venus Pareve*, 1982–88. Molded chocolate, 10 x 5 x 2 in. each; no longer extant. Photo: Hannah Wilke

Page 143: *Venus Pareve*, 1982–84. Painted plaster, 10 x 5 x 2 in. each. Jewish Musuem, New York (eight examples). Photo: Lisa Kahane

Page 145: Hannah Wilke carving clay model for Venus Pareve sculptures. Archival photo, Hannah Wilke Collection & Archive, Los Angeles. Photo: Donald Goddard

Page 146: *S.O.S. Starification Object Series (Glasses)*, 1974. Black-and-white photograph, 14 x 11½ in. Hannah Wilke Collection & Archive, Los Angeles. Performalist Self-Portrait with Les Wollam

Page 149: Hannah Wilke in her Greene Street studio with *Elective Affinities*, 1978. Eighty-six glazed white porcelain sculptures on four painted boards. Hannah Wilke Collection & Archive, Los Angeles. Photo: Hannah Wilke

Page 152: Janine Antoni, *Lick and Lather*, 1993. Two self-portrait busts: one chocolate and one soap, two pedestals. Edition of seven plus one full set of fourteen busts, seven of each material, 24 x 16 x 13 in. each

Page 154: *Sloan Kettering, Nov 8, 1992*. Ink on pillowcase, 29½ x 19 ¼ in., 14¾ x 19¼ in. folded. Hannah Wilke Collection & Archive, Los Angeles. Photo: Yosi A. R-Pozeilov

Page 155: *Sloan Kettering Memorial Hospital, November 9, 1992*. Watercolor on pillowcase, 29½ x 19¼ in. Hannah Wilke Collection & Archive, Los Angeles. Photo: Yosi A. R-Pozeilov

WILKE COPYRIGHTS

Hannah Wilke Art © Marsie, Emanuelle, Damon, and Andrew Scharlatt, Hannah Wilke Collection & Archive, Los Angeles/Licensed by VAGA, New York, N.Y.
Front cover, frontispiece, pp. 6, 9 (left and right), 10, 24, 25, 27 (background, left and right), 29, 30, 31, 33, 34 (top), 35, 39, 40, 43 (upper left and lower right), 46, 47 (right), 48–49, 49 (right), 50, 51, 52, 53, 54, 56, 57, 59 (top and bottom), 62, 63, 65, 70, 73, 74, 75, 76, 77, 78, 83, 87, 88, 95, 101, 102, 103 (top and bottom), 106–7, 114, 115, 119, 126 (top and bottom), 129 (top and bottom), 131, 135, 137, 138, 139, 140 (right), 142, 143, 145, 146, 149, 154, 155. Unless otherwise noted, illustrations provided by Hannah Wilke Collection & Archive, Los Angeles, in association with Alison Jacques Gallery, London, and SolwayJones, Los Angeles.

Hannah Wilke Art © Donald Goddard/Licensed by Ronald Feldman Fine Arts, New York
Back cover, pp. 7, 19, 23, 27 (foreground), 28, 34 (bottom), 37, 42 (above, center, and below), 43 (upper right and lower left), 47 (left), 68, 91, 92 (top and bottom), 93 (left and right), 95, 98, 104, 108, 109 (top and bottom), 110–11 (top and bottom), 112–13, 116, 117, 118, 120, 121, 124, 128, 129 (bottom), 130 (top, bottom left, bottom right), 132, 133, 140 (left), 141 (left and right). Illustrations provided by Ronald Feldman Fine Arts, New York.

ILLUSTRATION CREDITS

p. 71: Acconci Studio; p. 152: Janine Antoni and Luhring Augustine, New York; p. 82 (left): Mary Boone Gallery, New York; p. 17: CalArts, Valencia, Cal.; pp. 36, 61 (right): Cheim & Read, New York; pp. 70, 73, 74, 75, 87: Electronic Arts Intermix, New York; pp. 25, 29, 31, 34, 52, 54, 66, 74, 75, 78, 88, 119, 138, 139: Ronald Feldman Fine Arts, New York; p. 20: Flomenhaft Gallery, New York; p. 105: Nancy Fried; p. 44: Matthew Marks Gallery; p. 36: Digital image © The Museum of Modern Art/Licensed by SCALA/Art Resource, N.Y.; pp. 65, 95, 114, 115, 126 (top), 129 (bottom), 140 (right): The Museum of Modern Art, New York; pp. 30, 31, 40, 101: Neuberger Museum of Art, Purchase College, State University of New York, Purchase; p. 79: Philadelphia Museum of Art; p. 82 (right): Cindy Sherman and Metro Pictures; p. 38: Sonnabend Gallery, New York; p. 18 (left and right): Through the Flower Foundation.

PUBLIC COLLECTIONS

Albright-Knox Art Gallery, Buffalo

Allen Memorial Art Museum, Oberlin, Ohio

Brooklyn Museum, The Elizabeth Sackler Center for Feminist Art

Centre Pompidou, Musée National d'Art Moderne, Paris

Cincinnati Art Museum

Des Moines Art Center

The Edwin A. Ulrich Museum of Art, Wichita State University

Helsinki City Art Museum

The Jewish Museum, New York

List Museum of Art, Brown University, Providence, R.I.

Los Angeles County Museum of Art

The Metropolitan Museum of Art, New York

Museo Nacional Centro de Arte Reina Sofía, Madrid

Museum of Contemporary Art, Los Angeles

The Museum of Modern Art, New York

Neuberger Museum of Art, Purchase College—SUNY, Purchase, N.Y.

Nevada Art Museum, Reno

Pushkin Museum, Moscow

Radford University Galleries, Radford, Va.

Rose Art Museum, Brandeis University, Waltham, Mass.

The Solomon R. Guggenheim Museum, New York

Tate Modern, London

Tokyo Metropolitan Museum of Photography

University of Michigan Museum of Art, Ann Arbor

The Wadsworth Atheneum, Hartford, Conn.

The Walker Art Center, Minneapolis

Whitney Museum of American Art, New York

Yale University Art Gallery, New Haven, Conn.

SELECTED SOLO EXHIBITIONS

"Elective Affinities," Alison Jacques Gallery, London, June 4–August 28, 2010

"Hannah Wilke: Gestures," Neuberger Museum of Art, Purchase College, State University of New York, Purchase, October 3, 2008–January 4, 2009

"Intra-Venus Tapes, 1990–1993," Ronald Feldman Fine Arts, New York, September 8–October 13, 2007

"Hannah Wilke," Alison Jacques Gallery, London, September 5–October 6, 2007

"Exchange Values," ARTIUM Centro-Museo Vasco de Arte Contemporáneo, Vitoria-Gasteiz, Spain, October 4, 2006–January 7, 2007 (catalogue)

"Hannah Wilke: Advertisements for Living," SolwayJones, Los Angeles, April 22–May 21, 2006

"Hannah Wilke," Ronald Feldman Fine Arts at the Armory, New York, March 9–13, 2006

"The Rhetoric of the Pose: Rethinking Hannah Wilke," Mary Porter Sesnon Art Gallery, Santa Cruz, Cal., October 5–December 3, 2005 (catalogue)

"Hannah Wilke: Selected Work 1960–1992," SolwayJones, Los Angeles, January 10–February 21, 2004

"Interrupted Career: Hannah Wilke 1940–1993," Neue Gesellschaft für bildende Kunst, Berlin, September 1–October 8, 2000 (catalogue)

"Hannah Wilke: Sculpture & Other Work," Ronald Feldman Fine Arts, New York, October 1–November 13, 1999

"Hannah Wilke: A Retrospective," Nikolaj Contemporary Art Center, Copenhagen, October 30, 1998–January 24, 1999. Traveled to BildMuseet, Umea, Sweden, March 21–May 16; Helsinki City Art Museum, Helsinki, August 10–October 17 (catalogue)

"Hannah Wilke: Intra-Venus," Woodruff Art Gallery, Atlanta College of Art, Atlanta, October 17–November 30, 1997 (catalogue)

"Hannah Wilke: Performalist Self-Portraits and Video/Film Performances 1976–85," Ronald Feldman Fine Arts, New York, September 21–October 19, 1996

"Hannah Wilke: Works from 1965–1992," Gallery 400, University of Illinois, Chicago, July 29–October 15, 1996

"Hannah Wilke: Intra-Venus," Nikolaj Contemporary Art Center, Copenhagen, June 16–August 6, 1995. Traveled to Yerba Buena Center for the Arts, San Francisco, September 5–October 1; Santa Monica Museum of Art, October 6–November 26; Weatherspoon Art Gallery, Greensboro, N.C., February 8–April 21, 1996; Tokyo Metropolitan Museum of Photography, September 5–October 27 (catalogue)

"Intra-Venus," Ronald Feldman Fine Arts, New York, January 8–February 19, 1994 (catalogue)

"Hannah Wilke, Past and Present," Genovese Graphics Gallery, Boston, October 6–November 1, 1990

"About Face," Ronald Feldman Fine Arts, New York, September 9–October 7, 1989

"Hannah Wilke: A Retrospective," curated by Thomas Kochheiser, Gallery 210, University of Missouri, St. Louis, April 3–28, 1989. Traveled to the University of Missouri, Kansas City, September 1–29, 1989 (catalogue)

"Support Foundation Comfort," Ronald Feldman Fine Arts, New York, December 1–29, 1984

Joseph Gross Gallery, University of Arizona, Tucson, curated by Joanne Frueh, October 29–November 16, 1984

"Hannah Wilke: Performalist Self-Portraits, 1942–79," Washington Project for the Arts, Washington, D.C., 1979

So Help Me Hannah: Snatch Shots with Ray Guns installation, P.S. 1 Institute for Art and Urban Resources, New York, October 1–November 19, 1978

"Through the Large Glass," Ronald Feldman Fine Arts, New York, March 18, 1978 opening

"Hannah Wilke: Sculpture & Drawings," Marianne Deson Gallery, Chicago, October 1977

"Hannah Wilke: Drawings and Sculpture," Margo Leavin Gallery, Los Angeles, March 4–31, 1976

"Hannah Wilke, Scarification Photographs and Videotapes," Fine Arts Gallery, University of California, Irvine, March 2–13, 1976

"Hannah Wilke," Ronald Feldman Fine Arts, New York, September 13–October 11, 1975

"Hannah Wilke," Ronald Feldman Fine Arts, New York, March 16–30, 1974

"Hannah Wilke: Drawings from the Flower Series," Margo Leavin Gallery, Los Angeles, January 24–February 28, 1974

Margo Leavin Gallery, Los Angeles, November 18–December 31, 1972

"Hannah Wilke," Ronald Feldman Fine Arts, New York, September 12–October 13, 1972

SELECTED PERFORMANCES, FILMS, VIDEOTAPES, AND AUDIOTAPES

The Great Ice-Cream Robbery, 1970. Documentary film with Claes Oldenburg introducing Hannah Wilke; 16 mm, color, sound; directed by James Scott. Arts Council of Great Britain.

Hannah Wilke, Super-t-Art, 1974. Performance in "Soup and Tart," curated by Jean Dupuy at the Kitchen, New York.

Gestures, 1974. Videotaped performance; black and white, sound, 30 min. Exhibited at Ronald Feldman Fine Arts, New York, 1974.

White Sheets and Quiet Dots, 1975. Hannah Wilke as Venus in public participation performances by Lil Picard at the Max Hutchinson Gallery, New York.

S.O.S., 1975. Performance in "5 Americaines à Paris" at Galerie Gerald Piltzer, Paris.

Hello Boys, 1975. Videotaped live performance, Paris; black and white, sound, 10 min.

Intercourse with . . ., 1975. Installation of wall work, book documenting calls, and 120 min. audiotape of telephone messages recorded 1973–75. Exhibited at "Lives Show," Fine Arts Building, New York, 1975, and "Hannah Wilke: Scarification Photographs and Videotapes," Fine Arts Gallery, University of California, Irvine, 1976.

I'd Be Rich as Rockefeller/My Count-ry 'tis of Thee, 1976. Protest performance at the Whitney Museum of American Art, New York, in "One Afternoon on a Revolving Stage," curated by Jean Dupuy.

My Count-ry 'tis of Thee, 1976. Photo installation and performance in "Four for the Fourth" at the Albright-Knox Art Gallery, Buffalo

Hannah Wilke Through the Large Glass, 1976. Filmed live performance behind Duchamp's *The Bride Stripped Bare by Her Bachelors, Even*, Philadelphia Museum of Art; 16mm, color, 10 min.

Philly, 1976. Documentary video of the filming of *Hannah Wilke Through the Large Glass* at the Philadelphia Museum of Art; black and white, sound, 30 minutes.

C'est la Vie Rrose, 1976. Hannah Wilke as herself in a film about Marcel Duchamp, directed by Hans-Christof Stenzel for German television; color, 58 min.

Intercourse with..., 1977. Videotaped live performance and lecture, London Art Museum, London, Ontario; black and white, sound, 30 min.

So Help Me Hannah. Audio-video live performance. D.C. Space, Washington, D.C., and Kiplings, New York, 1979; A.I.R. Gallery, New York, 1982; Forest City Gallery, London, Ont. and Windsor Art Gallery, Windsor, Ont., 1985. Ten-monitor installation at Ronald Feldman Fine Arts, New York, 1996.

Intra-Venus Tapes, 1990–93. Sixteen-monitor video installation revealing the last two-and-a-half years of the artist's life. Ronald Feldman Fine Arts, New York, 2007.

SELECTED BIBLIOGRAPHY

Butler, Connie. *Modern Women: Women Artists at The Museum of Modern Art*. New York: Museum of Modern Art, 2010.

Butler, Connie, and Lisa Gabrielle Mark. *WACK! Art and the Feminist Revolution*. Los Angeles: Museum of Contemporary Art; Cambridge, Mass.: MIT Press, 2008.

Delin Hansen, Elisabeth, ed. *Hannah Wilke: A Retrospective*. Copenhagen: Nikolaj Contemporary Art Center, 1998.

Fischer, Alfred M. "Hannah Wilke: Die wirkliche Braut, entkleidet." In *Übrigens sterben immer die anderen: Marcel Duchamp und die Avangarde seit 1950*. Cologne: Museum Ludwig Köln, 1988.

Fitzpatrick, Tracy. *Hannah Wilke: Gestures*. Purchase, N.Y.: Neuberger Museum of Art, 2010.

Frueh, Joanna. "Hannah Wilke." In *Erotic Faculties*. Berkeley: University of California Press, 1996.

Gelin, Cecilia. *Body and Soul: Intra-Venus och Hannah Wilkes kamp för identitet*. Diss., Göteborg University, Sweden, 1996.

Goldman, Saundra Louise. *Too Good Lookin' To Be Smart: Beauty, Performance, and the Art of Hannah Wilke*. Diss., University of Texas at Austin, 1999.

Goldstein, Ann, Rebecca Morse, and Paul Schimmel. *This Is Not To Be Looked At: Highlights from the Permanent Collection of The Museum of Contemporary Art, Los Angeles*. Los Angeles: Museum of Contemporary Art, 2009.

Jones, Amelia. "The Rhetoric of the Pose: Hannah Wilke and the Radical Narcissism of Feminist Body Art." In *Body Art/Performing the Subject*. Minneapolis: University of Minnesota Press, 1998.

———. "Everybody Dies . . . Even the Gorgeous: Resurrecting the Work of Hannah Wilke." In *The Rhetoric of the Pose: Rethinking Hannah Wilke*. Santa Cruz: Mary Porter Sesnon Art Gallery, University of California, 2005.

Jones, Amelia, Robert McKaskell, Donald Goddard, Marsie Scharlatt, and Renny Pritikin. *Intra-Venus: Hannah Wilke*. New York: Ronald Feldman Fine Arts, 1995.

Knafo, Danielle. "Hannah Wilke: The Naked Truth." In *In Her Own Image*. Teaneck, N.J.: Fairleigh Dickinson University Press, 2009.

Kochheiser, Thomas H., ed. *Hannah Wilke: A Retrospective*. Essay by Joanna Frueh. Columbia: University of Missouri Press, 1989.

Marcoci, Roxana. *The Original Copy: Photography of Sculpture, 1839–Today*. New York: The Museum of Modern Art, 2010.

Morineau, Camille. *elles@centrepompidou: Artistes femmes dans la collection du Musée national d'art modern, Centre de création industrielle*. Paris: Centre Pompidou, 2009.

Orgaz, Laura Fernandez. *Hannah Wilke: Exchange Values*. Vitoria-Gasteiz, Spain: ARTIUM Centro-Museo Vasco de Arte Contemporáneo, 2006.

Rattemeyer, Christian. *The Judith Rothschild Foundation Contemporary Drawings Collection: Catalogue Raisonné*. New York: Museum of Modern Art, 2009.

Raven, Arlene, Marsie Scharlatt, and Michael Solway. *Hannah Wilke: Selected Work 1960–1992*. Los Angeles: Hannah Wilke Collection & Archive; Los Angeles, SolwayJones, 2004.

Takemoto, Tina. "Looking through Hannah Wilke's Eyes: Interview with Donald Goddard." *Art Journal* 67, no. 2 (Summer 2008): 126–39.

Taylor, Michael R. "Legacy." In *Marcel Duchamp: Étant Donnés*. Philadelphia: Philadelphia Museum of Art; New Haven, Conn.: Yale University Press, 2009.

Wagner, Frank. *Interrupted Careers: Hannah Wilke 1940–1993*. Berlin: Neue Gessellschaft für bildende Kunst, 2000.